Immigration into Western Societies

IMMIGRATION INTO WESTERN SOCIETIES:
PROBLEMS AND POLICIES

Edited by
Emek M. Uçarer and Donald J. Puchala
for The European Community Studies Association

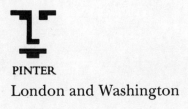

PINTER
London and Washington

PINTER
A Cassell imprint
Wellington House, 125 Strand, London WC2R 0BB
PO Box 605, Herndon, VA 20172

First published in 1997

British Library Cataloguing in Publication Data

A catalogue record for this book is available from the British Library.

ISBN 1 885567 451 3

Library of Congress Cataloging-in-Publication Data

Immigration into Western Societies: problems and policies / edited by Emek M. Uçarer and Donald J.
  Puchala for the European Community Studies Association.
      p. cm.
  Includes bibliographical references and index.
  ISBN 1-85567-451-3
    1. Europe–Emigration and immigration. 2. Europe–Emigration and immigration–Government
policy. 3. European Union countries–Emigration and immigration–Government policy. 4. United
States–Emigration and immigration. 5. United States–Emigration and immigration–Government policy.
I. Uçarer, Emek M. II. Puchala, Donald James, 1939–. III. European Community Studies Association.
JV7590.I457 1997
325'. 1'091821–dc20   96–32673
                                                                                                  CIP

Typeset by York House Typographic Ltd, London
Printed and bound in Great Britain by Biddles Ltd, Guildford and King's Lynn

Contents

Part I: Conceptualizing and analyzing immigration

Part II: Contemporary immigration and Western societies

List of contributors

Nermin Abadan-Unat graduated from Istanbul Law School, and pursued graduate studies as a Fullbright scholar at the University of Minnesota. She taught from 1953 to 1989 at the School of Political Science, Ankara University, where she established the chair of Political Sociology and served twice as Director of the School of Communication. Professor Abandan-Unat taught as guest professor at the University of Munich (1969–70), City University of New York (1973–4), University of Denver (Summer 1984) and UCLA (Spring 1988). Professor Abadan-Unat served as senator in the Turkish Parliament from 1978 to 1980. Her research and writings deal predominantly with the migration of Turks to Europe. Her major books in English are *Turkish Workers in Europe* (1976) and, with R. Keles *et al.*, *Migration and Development* (1976). She currently teaches at Bogazici University, Istanbul, where she has established a Unit for Migration Research.

Chris Bourdouvalis is Assistant Professor of Political Science at Augusta College. He received his PhD in 1990 from Florida State University. Bourdouvalis is an expert on the institutions and policy processes of the European Union. His publications and professional papers include 'Voting behavior of the representatives of the European Parliament,' 'Political leaders of contemporary Europe,' 'The European Union institutions' action on women's employment rights,' 'Educational development in the EC and its effects on European integration,' 'Transnational party coopera- tion and foreign policy issues in the European Parliament,' and 'Elite environmental attitudes and European integration.'

David A. Coleman has been the lecturer in Demography at Oxford University since 1980. From 1970 to 1980 he was at the Anthropology Department, University College London. Between 1985 and 1987 he worked for the British government, as the special adviser first to the Home Secretary, and then to the ministers of housing and of the environment. His research interests include the study of comparative demographic trends in the industrial world and their socio-economic consequences; immigration trends and policies, the demography of ethnic minorities, and housing policy. He has worked as a consultant for the Home Office, for the United Nations, and for private business, and has been the joint editor of the *European Journal of Population* since 1992.

Bimal Ghosh is a Senior Consultant to the International Organization for Migration in Geneva, and he holds a similar appointment with the United Nations on migration and development issues. He is also the Director of the Migration and Refugees Programme at the Centre for Political and Economic Analysis in Geneva and an external consultant on migration matters to the Council of Europe in Strasbourg. He was formely a senior director in the United Nations system, Consultant to the UNDP Administrator, Director of Technical Cooperation and Development in the ILO and Special Adviser to the ILO Director-General. He pioneered the UN/UNHCR program on refugee integration through zonal development. He is Emeritus Professor at the Colombian School of Public Administration and an Honorary Fellow at the School of International Policy and Diplomacy in Bogotá, and is author of numerous technical reports, studies and articles on international political and economics issues.

Hans-Joachim Hoffmann-Nowotny is Professor of Sociology at the University of Zurich, and director of the Sociological Institute. He received his MA from Cologne University (1966) and his PhD from the University of Zurich (1969). His research interests are focused on international migration and minorities and more generally concern the socio-cultural determinants and consequences of socio-demographic developments. Professor Hoffmann-Nowotny has also worked intensively in the field of general sociological theory. His research has resulted in more than 150 publications, among them several books.

James F. Hollifield is a member of the Political Science Department at Southern Methodist University. After receiving his PhD from Duke University in 1985, he served as a member of the faculty of Brandeis University and was an associate at Harvard University's Center for European Studies and Center for International Affairs. In 1992–3, he held a visiting appointment as Associate Director of Research at the CNRS and the Fondation Nationale des Sciences Politiques in Paris. During this period, he was also co-investigator for an NSF project '*Controlling immigration: a global perspective,*' based at the Center for US–Mexican Studies of the University of California, San Diego. Hollifield has published numerous books and the articles in comparative and international politics and political economy. Among his recent publications are *Immigrants, Markets and States* (1992) and *The State and Public Policy* (1996).

Cornelis D. de Jong studied law and economics at the Erasmus University, Rotterdam, the Netherlands. He also obtained a master's degree in political science at the New School for Social Research in New York. His professional career started with the Netherlands Ministry of Foreign Affairs. Subsequently, he has worked for the Netherlands Ministry of Social Affairs and the Department of Justice. Between 1993 and 1996, Mr de Jong worked for the European Commission as an adviser in the field of Justice and Home Affairs. He is currently working at the Permanent Representation of the Netherlands to the EU. He has produced a number of publications in the field of national and European immigration law and policy. He is also writing a thesis entitled 'The freedom of thought, conscience and religion within the framework of the United Nations.'

Rey Koslowki is a lecturer at Rutgers University, Newark. His dissertation is on the consequences of migration for European political integration and international relations. His publications include 'Intra-EU migration, citizenship and political union,' *Journal of Common Market Studies* (1996), 'Understanding change in international politics: the Soviet Empire's demise and the international system,' with Friedrich Kratochwill, *International Organization* (Spring 1994), and 'Market institutions, East European reforms and economic theory,' *Journal of Economic Issues* (September 1992).

Anton Kuijsten is associate professor of demography at the University of Amsterdam, Director of the Netherlands Graduate School of Research in Demography (PDOD) and president of the Netherlands Demographic Society. His main research interests are household and family demography, population projection, international migration, and European population trends. Publications include *Advances in Family Demography* (1986), with Nico Keilman and Ad Vossen (eds), *Modelling Household Formation and Dissolution* (1988), 'The impact of migration streams on the size and structure of the Dutch population' (1996), and 'International Migrations: harmonization of data collection' (1996).

Reinhard Lohrmann studied law and political science at the Universities of Berlin, Saarbrücken and Nice. Between 1970 and 1974 Lohrmann was a research fellow at the German Association for Foreign Policy, Bonn. He is the author of a book analyzing the impact of international labor migration in Europe during the post-war period on international relations between receiving countries and countries of origin. Since 1975, Lohrmann has been working at the International Organization for Migration (IOM), where he is at present Chief of the Division of Research of Forum Activities.

Philip L. Martin has been Professor of Agricultural Economics at the University of California at Davis since 1985. He has previously held positions as a visiting fellow at the Institute for International Economics, Consultant to the International Labor Office project on Turkey's entry into the European Communities, Consultant to the US Department of Labor, and Select Economist with the Select Commission on Immigration and Refugee Policy. His research interests are in farm labor, labor economics, labor relations, and immigration.

Mark J. Miller is Professor of Political Science at the University of Delaware, where he has taught comparative politics since 1978. He has also long served as the assistant editor of the *International Migration Review*. From 1983 to 1988, he served as the US correspondent to SOPEMI, the OECD's committee of international migration specialists. A graduate of the University of Wisconsin, Miller is the co-author, with Stephen Castles, of *The Age of Migration*.

Donald J. Puchala is Charles L. Jacobson Professor of Public Affairs and director of The Richard L. Walker Institute of International Studies at the University of South Carolina. He holds advanced degrees in Political Science and International Relations from Yale University. Dr Puchala is a student of International Organization and European Community Affairs and has served on the executive committees of the Council for European Studies, the European Community Studies Association, and the Academic Council on the United Nations System. His pertinent publications include *Fiscal Harmonization in the European Communities* (1984) and *The Ethics of Globalism* (1995).

Beverly Springer is Professor in the Department of International Studies at the American Graduate School of International Management in Glendale, Arizona. She received her PhD from the University of Colorado in 1974. Her teaching centers on the European Union, labor and management in Western Europe, and the environment for international business in Western Europe. Among her recent publications are *The Social Dimension of 1992* (1992) and 'Changing patterns of employment for women in banks: case studies in the United Kingdom, France and the US,' *International Comparisons in Human Resource Management* (1991). Her recent professional activities include serving as Editor of *International Executive*, as a member of the Executive Board of *The International Journal of Human Resource Management*, and as a member of the Executive Board of the European Community Studies Associations.

Dietrich Thränhardt is Professor of Political Science at the University of Münster. He studied history, literature and social sciences at Munich, Tübingen, Zurich and Erlangen. Thränhardt holds a PhD from Constance on parties and elections in Bavaria. He has published widely on comparative migration in Europe and in Germany and is the author of a history of the

Federal Republic. He has also directed research programs on local government in the Netherlands and Germany, on welfare provision for migrants, and on the social situation of immigrants.

Emek M. Uçarer is a doctoral candidate in the International Studies Graduate Program at the University of South Carolina. She has studied at the Bosphorus University in Istanbul, Turkey, and holds a degree in business administration from West Georgia College and a master's degree in international studies from the University of South Carolina. She is currently working on a dissertation dealing with the processes and implications of policy harmonization on asylum issues in the European Union. Her academic interests center on migration issues, the European Union, German politics, and international organization. She is the author of 'The challenge of migration: the German case,' *Mediterranean Quarterly*, 5, 3 (1994), 95–122.

List of figures

List of tables

List of abbreviations

ACP	Asian, Caribbean, and Pacific
BNA	British Nationality Act
CDU	Christlich-Demokratische Union
CFSP	Common Foreign and Security Policy
CGT	Confédération générale du travail
CIA	Central Intelligence Agency
CIS	Commonwealth of Independent states
COREPER	Commitee of Permanent Representatives (of the EU)
CSCE	Conference on Security and Cooperation in Europe
CSU	Christlich-Soziale Union
DIDF	Federation of Democratic Workers' Associations
DITIB	The Turkish Islamic Union for Religious Affairs
EEA	European Economic Area
EC	European Community
ECSA	European Community Studies Association
EFTA	European Free Trade Area
EU	European Union
FAIR	Federation of American Immigration Reform
FAS	Fonds d'Action Sociales
FIDF	Federation of Workers' Associations
FLN	Front de libération nationale
FN	Front National
GAC	General Affairs Council (of the EU)
GATT	General Agreement on Tariffs and Trade
GDF	Federation of Migrant's Associations
GDP	gross domestic product
GDR	German Democratic Republic
GNP	gross national product
ICCB	The Union of Islamic Associations and Communities
ICPD	International Conference on Population and Development (of the UN)

IGC	Intergovernmental Conference
ILO	International Labor Organization
IMF	International Monetary Fund
IOM	International Organization for Migration
IOT	Turkish Advisory Council
IPS	International Passenger Survey
IRCA	Immigration Reform and Control Act
JHA	Justice and Home Affairs
KOMKAR	Association of Kurdish Workers for Kurdistan
MP	Member of Parliament
NAFTA	North American Free Trade Agreement
NATO	North Atlantic Treaty Organization
NCBS	Netherlands Central Bureau of Statistics
NGO	non-governmental organization
ODA	official development assistance
OECD	Organization for Economic Cooperation and Development
OEEC	Organization for European Economic Cooperation
OFPRA	Office for Protection of Refugees
ONI	Office National d'Immigration
OSCE	Organization for Security and Cooperation in Europe
PAF	Police de l'Air et des Frontiers
PKK	Kurdish Worker's Party
RPR	Rassemblement pour la république
SIS	Schengen Information System
SMA	Swedish Muslim Asssociation
SPD	Sozialdemokratische Partei Deutschlands
TEU	Treaty on European Union
TF	Turkish Federation
TFR	total fertility rate
UDF	Union pour la démocratie française
UN	United Nations
UNCTAD	United Nations Conference on Trade and Development
UNHCR	United Nations High Commissioner for Refugees
WTO	World Trade Organization

Acknowledgments

Many people contributed in many ways to making this book possible. Its conception must be credited to the Executive Committee of the European Community Studies Association, who decided to make immigration one of the central themes of the association's research program. Pierre-Henri Laurent chaired the ECSA Executive Committee at the time that this research project was conceived. The editors of this volume organized the project and assembled the contributors. Contributors did their part by offering astute analyses and meeting deadlines. Financial support was provided by ECSA, by the United States Mission to the European Communities and by the Richard L. Walker Institute of International Studies at the University of South Carolina. Stephen M. Dubrow at the United States Mission was instrumental in arranging funding and following the project through to completion. The project was administered by Sallie Buice. The manuscript was carefully prepared by Rebecca Spyke, and the publication process was most efficiently managed by the editors at Pinter.

Introduction
The coming of an era of human uprootedness: a global challenge

Emek M. Uçarer

The New College German and English Dictionary translates *Völkerwanderung* as 'barbarian invasion.' But cultural historians employ the term more broadly to denote eras of human uprootedness characterized by mass migrations, cultural interpenetrations, social and political disruption, and intercommunal violence. *Völkerwanderungen* have thus often been preludes to civilizational change. Such movements of people have also often led to the enrichment of existing societies and to cross-fertilization of the kind Adda Bozeman speaks of in her insightful *Politics and Culture in International History*.[1]

Current events and interpretations suggest that the world of the late twentieth century may be entering into an era of *Völkerwanderung*.[2] The largest part of the demographic movement today is within and between the developing nations, while South-to-North migration accounts for only two-fifths of total trans-boundary migration flows.[3] But, these movements are trans-cultural, trans-racial, trans-civilizational, and increasingly consequential for receiving societies in the advanced industrial West and for contemporary international relations. Yet, if various waves of migration were indeed the building blocks of civilizations throughout history, how is it that migration today is largely seen as a threat, and why are migrants looked upon as being responsible for many of the social ills of the receiving societies?

In our era of increased human uprootedness, the study of migration has of late received increasing attention from scholars and practitioners of diverse training. The causes and impacts of migration are typically studied by demographers and geographers. But it is becoming increasingly apparent that migration can no longer be regarded as a predominantly demographic issue. In addition to the schools that have traditionally studied migration issues, there is increasing interest in fields such as international relations, legal studies, health sciences, psychology, economics, sociology, and education. Even philosophers have entered the dialogue by asking ethical questions about human movement.

This volume is the product of one recent effort to push forward the dialogue within and among the different disciplines that are taking up migration questions. Our compendium also seeks to maintain a balance between theoretical concerns and policy problems and to highlight their mutual relevance. *Immigration into Western Societies: Problems and Policies* is the product of a 1994 project that involved demographers, economists, sociologists, political scientists, and public officials from nine countries and the European Union. Its aim was to assess the impacts of immigration into Western societies. The project was supported by the European Community Studies Association (ECSA), an academic organization which promotes research into problems affecting the European Union, by the United States Delegation to the European Union, and by the Richard L. Walker Institute of International Studies at the University of South Carolina. In total, 21 papers were commissioned by the project: they respectively addressed the magnitude and composition of immigration flows into Western Europe and North America, the economic, political, and cultural impacts of these flows, current public policy responses to immigration and their consequences, and policy imperatives in decades ahead. Final versions of most of these research papers appear as the respective chapters of this volume.

The prevailing challenges

Before expounding on the challenges that result from the trans-boundary movement of persons, one must begin by cautioning about another set of challenges that vexes research on migration issues. Frustrating the research efforts of many a demographer, economist, sociologist, and political scientist is the difficulty in collecting current, complete, and reliable data with respect to the magnitude and distribution of international migrants. The difficulty is compounded by data that are made available by receiving countries, which have different methods of collecting, categorizing, and publishing. Of course, sending countries also employ varying methods of counting and reporting. Governments may also find reasons for distorting migration data, and, unfortunately, several do. Fully reliable immigration data are therefore non-existent, and conclusions, always based on estimates, are never definitive.

Reflecting the current discourse in the migration field, discussions among researchers on this project evolved ultimately towards evaluating practical matters of immigration policy. But, at the same time, the discussions were underpinned by moral and philosophical concerns. For instance, can liberal societies justifiably close their borders to persons fleeing from tyrannical conditions elsewhere? And what if the asylum seekers number in the tens of thousands? Furthermore, if one is to subscribe to the virtues of liberal economy, where freely flowing goods, services, and capital stimulate flows of labor, as they must under open market conditions, what justification is there for closing labor markets, while other markets are left open? With respect to welcoming asylum seekers and immigrants, as Westerners must do in fidelity to their liberal traditions, at what point does preserving liberal values in openness conflict with preserving liberal values in democracy? To what kinds of civil and political rights are non-citizens entitled? Are all immigrants entitled to citizenship? At what point does keeping societies open to immigrants interfere with maintaining modern welfare states? At what point does keeping societies open to immigrants interfere with keeping them either culturally homogeneous or manageably pluralistic? What ought European and North American industrialized receiving societies to do when any of these crucial points are reached? How is one to appraise the tolerance thresholds of the receiving societies?[4] Is there a carrying capacity with respect to migrants,[5] and if there is, how is public policy to come to grips with this? As we are entering a period in history where liberal democracy has been pronounced with much fanfare to have prevailed over communism,[6] what, if anything, does the end of the Cold War signify for the world's displaced?

Migratory movements traversing state boundaries are bound up with the history of nation states. While migration has always been a feature of human affairs, it became an issue of intensified salience after the nineteenth-century rise of the nation state and the erection of political–territorial borders around ethno-cultural communities. The surveillance of such borders came also to be regarded as one of the indisputable prerogatives of state sovereignty. *What* may legitimately cross political boundaries has been a question of international law since the dawn of the modern state system (indeed, well before that), but *who* may legitimately cross such boundaries, and who belongs within and without, is a particular issue of the era of nationalism. The issue is compounded in our era of industrial capitalism and welfare-statism by the question of who may legitimately share in material abundance and who has a legitimate claim on public treasuries.

Even though the right to leave the territory of one's country is widely accepted as a human right, the corresponding right to enter a foreign territory is not unreservedly recognized, thus leaving the granting of permission to legally enter to the discretion of receiving states.[7] States' abilities to patrol their borders are linked to their geographic locations and to resources available for checking at entry points and otherwise monitoring frontiers. No state, however, intentionally allows for the unlimited and unimpeded crossing of its borders.

In our time, the routine permeation of borders with receiving states' consent has required the elaboration of regulations and the establishment of bureaucracies to control movements. Public policies regulate the influx of immigrants, define the status and residence of aliens, and assign rights and obligations to non-citizens. Selectiveness in the admission of aliens generally occurs at two levels: the first has to do with who may be admitted into receiving states, where those admitted may live, and where and for what length of time they may work. Later, selectiveness comes into play with regard to the integration of aliens into receiving societies and the granting of civil rights and citizenship. Generally speaking, it is invariably the case that only some people are allowed in, and, of those, only some are granted civil and political rights. Historically, there has not necessarily been a linear path from resident alien status to citizenship.[8]

Some countries, such as the United States, Canada, and Australia, have historically regarded themselves as 'immigration countries,' and they have developed their policies to accordingly encourage integration and assimilation. They have concentrated on the 'absorption' of new residents and have extended citizenship and commensurate civil and political rights fairly readily. Absorbing migrants has had two objectives from receiving countries' points of view: immigrant workers were brought in to help economic development, either by taking up jobs or by contributing to population growth to feed labor pools; or immigrants were invited in to fill up underpopulated regions. While these factors played important roles in the development of the traditional immigration countries, they are no longer wholly applicable in these lands. In fact, the world at present has no 'immigration countries' *per se.*

Other countries, departing from the premise that they are not immigration countries, have also set their policies accordingly. In contrast to the immigration countries of North America and Australia, Western European receiving countries have long maintained that they are 'non-immigration' countries, and their policy objectives have been to stabilize inflows, to limit long-term stays, to discourage permanent residence, and to withhold citizenship and its prerogatives. The most notable example of a European non-immigration country is Germany, which continues to adhere to its *kein Einwanderungsland* (not an immigration country) policy.

The problem today is that the policies of the major industrial countries – both the traditional 'immigration countries' that are having second thoughts, and the 'non-immigration countries' that are determined to stay that way – are speaking less and less to the realities of global migration. As Columbia University's John Ruggie aptly puts it, 'Politics is about rule. And the distinctive feature of the modern system of rule is that it has differentiated its subject collectivity into territorially defined, fixed, and mutually exclusive enclaves of legitimate dominion.'[9] In an increasingly interdependent world, this norm of jurisdiction over territory seems to be one of the last holdouts of sovereignty. But, it surely makes an ominous task of efforts to deal in a multilateral manner with transnational issues like migration.[10] In a world still informed by a state-centric paradigm, there is an expanding 'nation of migrants,' who can claim no right to any of the territories walled off by sovereignty. But these people move into and settle and work in foreign lands anyway. They are a reality with which the state-centric paradigm cannot deal, and their existence and needs challenge the very foundations of the paradigm. Therefore, one of the first steps toward coping with the mass movement of poor people today is to begin to look at the world differently and perhaps to reconsider time-honored doctrines like sovereignty and traditional entities like nation states.

There are different types of people on the move today. Sarah Collinson identifies four kinds of migrants based on their motive for moving and on the circumstances under which they leave their countries of origin.[11] First, migration may be mainly economically motivated and the circumstances under which it occurs are voluntary. Such migrants are exemplified by the guestworkers in Europe, Mexican laborers in the United States, and foreign workers in the petroleum-rich Gulf countries. Second, there are migrants with strong political motives who relocate voluntarily. Jews resettling in Israel are examples. When strong political motives combine with involuntary circumstances, the result is a category of migrants best characterized as refugees. Peoples displaced after the Second World War and millions today camped about the Third World are classic examples. Finally, there are economic migrants who involuntarily leave their countries. These are newer types of migrants who move because their economic livelihood is threatened by civil strife, environmental degradation, and other natural disasters in their countries of origin. Contemporary migration figures show that the actual and potential numbers of the first and fourth types of migrants are increasing dramatically.

In a study prepared for the United Nations International Conference on Population and Development (ICPD), held in Cairo in September 1994, the International Organization for Migration (IOM) estimated that there were 120 million people uprooted for various reasons in 1994. This figure is roughly equivalent to 2 percent of the world's population. Excluded from this figure are internal migrants and internally displaced people,[12] which, if included, would, according to the IOM, boost the migration figures tenfold.[13] Considering only international migrants, and using IOM figures for 1990–5, in a matter of five years the ratio of international migrants to the population of the globe increased from 1.7 percent to approximately 2 percent. The trend is clearly upward and apparently accelerating.[14]

This situation presents a challenge to the current norm of exclusive correspondence between nations and sovereign territory, as many political jurisdictions, traditionally perceived as nation states, are rather rapidly becoming multinational states. Furthermore, the IOM's findings indicate that, contrary to current wisdom, humans are *not* as sedentary as conventionally assumed. There is little indication that this state of affairs will reverse; on the contrary, we can expect the migration numbers to go up rather than down. This, naturally, must be a justifiable cause of concern for policy makers in receiving countries.

What induces trans-boundary human uprootedness?

The literature in the migration field suggests that contemporary migration occurs at the nexus of pull factors, attracting migrants to leave their homes in light of more promising conditions elsewhere, and push factors, forcing migrants to leave their homes in light of deteriorating conditions around them.[15] *Demand-pull factors* are those that render Western industrial societies attractive for individuals who have made the decision to seek their fortunes outside their normal place of residence. Among these factors are the level of development and prosperity in target countries, the lenience of immigration legislation, geographic access, the prospect of employment, and sometimes official invitations, as was the case in the late 1950s and early 1960s in Europe. *Supply-push factors* have to do with the circumstances in the countries of origin – poverty, stratification, insecurity, and the like. While historically migration occurred at the equilibrium of the push–pull factors, a unique aspect of contemporary migration is that it seems to be driven largely by the push factors, and it continues to gather momentum even in an era when receiving countries are attempting to eliminate the pull factors.

The reasons behind such supply-driven population movements lie in the contemporary politico-economic conjuncture of the globe. A rapidly increasing global population, disproportionately burgeoning in developing and underdeveloped regions, increasing life expectancies, the inability of struggling economies to create adequate numbers of jobs, the widening of the economic gap between the North and the South, a shift away from labor-intensive to capital-intensive modes of production even in labor-rich countries, and a general shift from manufacturing to services are but a few of the economic underpinnings of the contemporary push factors. Non-economic push factors include wars, ethnic and religious conflicts, ecological deterioration, and natural disasters, all either on the rise in, or more and more dramatically affecting, the poorer countries.

But migration flows are not to be explained only in terms of the over-simplified pull–push/supply–demand calculus. Other factors intervene. *Network groups*, for example, encourage migration by providing valuable information and material and emotional support for the newcomers. These enter the migration equation and influence the direction and the magnitude of the migratory movements.[16] So is it also with the phenomenon of *chain migration*, where spouses and families follow on after first-comers.

Temporary migrants become permanent residents (legally or otherwise). Foreign students do not return to their countries.

All of these factors and the conditions they create ultimately become policy problems, and often contested political issues, for the states involved. But it is becoming increasingly apparent that individual national governments acting by themselves are not able to deal with migration in the world today. Contemporary migration needs to be understood, and addressed, on a broader level, namely as a global phenomenon. Participants in this project were instructed to look into the impacts of migration on *receiving* countries. But, as readers of following chapters will find, attempts to project future migration trends necessarily also involve understanding the social, economic, and political dynamics of the *sending* countries. Effective policies in response to human movements today must include efforts to offset the migratory tendencies in the sending countries, as much as they also include regimes of border control and integration.[17] By the global nature of the problem, the most promising policies must necessarily be arrived at multilaterally.

The access quandary: how much is too much?

On the receiving end of migration, an emotional situation stands out: 'In virtually every capital, the flow of people is regarded with alarm.'[18] The anxiety that the prospect and/or the existence of strong migratory movements creates, mostly in the case of the receiving countries, can be observed in the discourse that surrounds the migration debate. In many minds, migration is pictured as a situation where 'there is no longer a balance between the potential flows and real openings.'[19] Too many migrants are coming, and there simply is not enough economic, political (or physical) space for them. Many of those most deeply concerned about migration tend to attach a normative and often apocalyptical element to the phenomenon.[20] Migration is unwanted; it is an invasion by the poor, who vote with their feet to get out of the economic misery in their home countries, but they perceptibly disrupt the societies which they enter.[21]

Immigration has also been pictured to be a 'serious threat to the freedom of human beings everywhere.'[22] Garrett Hardin, the author of 'The tragedy of the commons,' the environmentalist manifesto of the 1970s,[23] argues that uncontrolled immigration will result in yet another episode of a tragedy of the commons, whereby overpopulated nations will dump their human excess, causing a great strain on the carrying capacity of the environments of the receiving states. Rather than speaking effectively to the deterioration of the earth's carrying capacity, immigration simply moves the problem around, or possibly makes it worse overall. Consequently, Hardin says, the United States, and other industrialized democracies, should 'as rapidly as possible, reduce net immigration ... to zero.'[24] Whatever the merits of Hardin's case, and however tenable his policy prescriptions, for emotional reasons his position finds increasing resonance in North America and Western Europe.

In Western countries, there is increasing apprehension that the economic, social, and cultural fabric of societies is coming unravelled as these societies become ever more multiethnic and multicultural. On the part of people in the receiving societies, this anxiety is expressed in the apprehension that immigrants will dilute national identities and the indigenous population by taking away their jobs, their sons, and their daughters. There is also the concern that aliens pose a threat because they stake a claim on scarce resources, avail themselves of welfare benefits that were initially intended for citizens, and become visible pockets of diversity whose national commitments are ambiguous.

Current policies in the receiving countries are framed almost exclusively in restrictive terms that emphasize controlling migratory inflows. How to control and restrict immigration occupies a very prominent spot on the domestic political agenda of the recipient states,[25] and in some places this is such a highly sensitive issue that it can make or break governments.[26] In some cases, the existence of a non-indigenous population is being used as a political chip that opportunistic politicians have tossed to win favor within troubled electorates that occasionally need scapegoats.[27] The existence of anti-immigrant parties and their successes at the polls are also forcing governing parties to toughen up on immigration in order to avert the prospect of being voted out or having to make even greater concessions to anti-immigrant platforms. Paradoxically, efforts to contain or control immigration have largely failed, thus rendering immigration control as the centerpiece of policy not only practically, but also politically, short-sighted.

Commentaries that compare the migration influx to natural disasters add fuel to political fires, and intense politicization of the migration issue demonstrates little sensitivity to differences among types of migrants, to reasons for the displacement of peoples, and to the general global context. The view shared by many in the receiving states is captured in the comment made by a senior political adviser to the German government, who asserted that 'The numbers are more than we could cope with [and] it is not the job of the German political system to absorb all the migrants of the world and assure them a better life.'[28]

Compassion fatigue is very real in European and North American policy-making circles, and it is echoed in public opinion, which remains divided about immigration, but leans increasingly toward endorsing exclusion. A 1989 Eurobarometer study, conducted among the 12 EC member states, attempted to uncover the attitudes of the public toward immigrants. Attitudes ranged all the way from welcoming immigrants and granting them all the prerogatives of citizenship, to denying rights to newcomers (as well as long-time alien residents), to keeping out immigrants out completely. Revealingly, roughly half of the Eurobarometer's respondents exhibited some degree of intolerance toward immigrants, and proportions increased in those countries most affected by migration. People in countries like the United Kingdom, Germany, and Denmark, with large immigrant populations, and who have been on the receiving end of migration flows for some time, appeared far more reserved in their expressions of tolerance than those in countries like Italy and Spain, who are just now experiencing increasing immigration. Given that there is no end to migration in sight, these findings could be interpreted as being rather ominous.

Receiving countries today are being put to the challenge of reckoning with the cultural, economic, and political effects of growing non-indigenous populations. The scope of this challenge and ways and means of meeting it are what this book is about.

Organization of the book

In this volume, discussion of the impacts of international immigration on Western receiving societies moves from theory to practice to policy. Early chapters by Philip L. Martin, James F. Hollifield, Rey Koslowski and Hans-Joachim Hoffman-Nowotny concern ways of thinking about the immigration phenomenon, and means of identifying and evaluating immigration's impacts. Martin introduces the contemporary migration phenomenon, reflects on its causes and identifies and defines main concepts, such as 'demand-pull' and 'supply-push,' that are used by several other contributors later in the volume. Hollifield employs the notion of 'national model' to categorize, compare, and analyze the ways in which different countries have dealt historically, and are dealing today, with inflows of immigrants. Koslowski dwells on dilemmas facing both liberalism and democracy as today's industrial societies come to look less and less like traditional nation states. Their governments also seem less and less inclined to grant full civil and political rights to newcomers, thus raising questions about the meaning of liberal democracy. Hoffmann-Nowotny contends that there can be no understanding of the massive movement of peoples today unless the situation is conceptualized globally and holistically. He goes on to map conceptual pathways that help us think through the problems. Reflecting the multidisciplinary array of contributors, theoretical eclecticism is much in evidence in our volume.

In the second part of this book, discussion moves to looking directly at the phenomenon of immigration into industrial societies: who is going where, in what numbers, and with what results? Again, the inquiry is multidisciplinary. David A. Coleman opens the second part with a comprehensive analysis of migratory flows into Europe. He cautions readers concerning the inexactness of data, but then responsibly analyzes the figures available and concludes by underlining that recent flows of people into Europe probably cannot continue indefinitely. Bimal Ghosh asks questions similar to Coleman's about the quantity and quality of immigration flows. However, Ghosh's focus is not on Europe but on North America, and his analysis adds an important complement to much of the Europe-focused work in this volume. Dietrich Thränhardt then focuses on the politics of xenophobia stirred by immigration, on efforts to contain it, and on attempts to exploit it. Beverly Springer, in careful comparative analysis, assesses the impacts of immigration on culture in the major Western European receiving states. Anton Kuijsten looks into important economic impacts of immigration, with particular attention to costs and benefits to receiving societies. Then, in a perceptive treatment, Nermin Abadan-Unat discusses the effects of immigration on the immigrants as well as on the countries from which they came.

Policy problems, present and future, are the subjects of the last part of the volume. In an innovative analysis, Mark J. Miller raises questions about the relationships between immigration and national security, and he compares the ways in which related policy problems have been handled on the two sides of the Atlantic. Chris Bourdouvalis surveys the European Union's not-altogether-successful attempts to supranationalize immigration policies within the EU's 'community without internal frontiers.' Keeping the focus on the EU, Emek M. Uçarer examines the issue of granting asylum to individuals fleeing persecution, and she shows how international economic openness within the EU invariably creates imperatives for common immigration policies to control the economic community's common frontiers. Reinhard Lohrmann and Cornelis D. de Jong respectively conclude our volume with two forward looking, though somewhat anxious, essays on future frameworks and requirements for immigration policies. Interestingly, both of these chapters link back to themes developed in the opening theoretical chapters. Future immigration policies are doomed to fail to the extent that they remain unilateral, insensitive to needs and conditions within both sending and receiving societies, and exclusionary. By contrast, there is more promise in multilateral, globalistic, and inclusive policies. But even here there are no panaceas.

The essays included as chapters in this volume are the work of accomplished scholars in migration research. But, at the insistence of the editors, the chapters are written in layman's language and are therefore accessible to a wide readership. In addition to contributing to the existing literature on migration, the volume should prove to be a resource for generalists in international relations because contributors tackle important questions concerning the integrity of modern nation states, the meaning of citizenship and the relevance of sovereignty in an increasingly interdependent world. Contributors to the volume also demonstrate how migration flows relate to larger global problems, such as unequal economic development, population growth, ethnic strife, and environmental degradation. The essays strike a balance between insights gleaned from careful academic research on migration issues and the pragmatic and experiential wisdom of policy makers. Readers will find the studies in this volume, individually and together, to be authoritative and important contributions to the study of an issue that will occupy a prominent position in global affairs well into the new millennium.

Notes

1. Adda Bozeman, *Politics and Culture in International History* (New Brunswick, NJ: Transaction Publishers, 1994).
2. See Karl-Heinz Meier-Braun, 'Vor einer neuen Völkerwanderung? Das weltweite Migrations- und Asylproblem,' in Karl-Heinz Meier-Braun and Martin A. Kilgus (eds), *Einwanderungsland Deutschland* (Stuttgart: SDR-Funkhaus, 1994), pp. 7–25.
3. See the contribution of Bimal Ghosh to this volume.
4. According to Lori Lindburg, 'tolerance thresholds' are 'a point beyond which receptivity towards newcomers is alleged to cease or decline.' Lori Lindburg, 'Thresholds of tolerance: immigration and integration in three industrialized countries,' paper presented at the biennial conference of the European Community Studies Association in Charleston, SC, May 11–14, 1995. See also Donald L. Horowitz, 'Immigration and group relations in France and America,' in Donald L. Horowitz and Gerard Noiriel (eds), *Immigrants in Two Democracies: French and American Experience* (New York: New York University Press, 1992).
5. See Garrett Hardin, 'Cultural carrying capacity,' in Hardin, *The Immigration Dilemma: Avoiding the Tragedy of the Commons* (Washington, DC: FAIR, 1995).
6. See Francis Fukuyama, *The End of History and the Last Man* (New York: Free Press, 1992).
7. Article 13 of the Universal Declaration of Human Rights provides that 'everyone has the right to leave any country, including his own, and return to his country.' The Helsinki Final Act of 1975 also considers the freedom of exit a human right. On the nonexistance of the right to enter a foreign territory, see H. Hull, 'Population and the present world structure,' in William Alonso (ed.), *Population in an Interacting World* (Cambridge, MA: Harvard University Press, 1987), pp. 74–94.
8. See Helga Leitner, 'International migration and the politics of admission and exclusion in postwar Europe,' *Political Geography* 14, 3 (1995), 259–78.
9. John Gerard Ruggie, 'Territoriality and beyond: problematizing modernity in international relations,' *International Organization*, 47, 1 (1993), 151. Ruggie's argument deserves attention by migration scholars. While it is not entirely clear what postmodernity will bring in terms of the territoriality of mankind (which

he argues rather convincingly is a feature of world history beginning in the 1300s), it certainly has direct bearing on an issue area which is intertwined with sovereignty and its exercise over that territory.

10. Migration issues in general are especially prone to such state domination, which partly explains the lack of a global, or even a regional, migration regime. For an interesting discussion about the possible causes of the lack of a migration regime the likes of which can be argued to be present in trade and finance, see James F. Hollifield, 'Migration and international relations: cooperation and control in the European Community,' *International Migration Review*, 26, 2 (1992), 568–95.

11. For an elaboration of this typology see Sarah Collinson, *Europe and International Migration* (London: Pinter, 1993), p. 2.

12. For a discussion of the plight of the internally displaced and the challenges this form of forced migration presents to the state-centric paradigm, see Francis M. Deng, 'Dealing with the displaced: a challenge to the international community,' *Global Governance*, 1, 1 (1994), 45–57.

13. Nino Falchi, *International Migration Pressures: Challenges, Policy Responses and Operational Measures – an Outline of the Main Features* (Geneva: International Organization for Migration, 1995).

14. These figures are cited in Stephen Castles and Mark J. Miller, *The Age of Migration: International Population Movements in the Modern World* (New York: The Guilford Press, 1993).

15. See Philip L. Martin's contribution to this volume.

16. See Philip L. Martin, 'The United States: benign neglect toward immigration,' in Friedrich Heckmann and Wolfgang Bosswick (eds), *Migration Policies: a Comparative Perspective* (Bamberg: Europaeisches Forum für Migrationsstudien, 1994), p. 19.

17. The chronology of the formulation of policies relating to aliens in Germany, and the *ex post facto* manner in which the legislation was conceived is a case in point. Policy formulation has been at best reactive and at worst haphazard, which leads to the current situation of legislation in flux lacking a general immigration policy. For an overview of this process see Emek M. Uçarer, 'The challenge of migration: the German case,' *Mediterranean Quarterly*, 5, 3 (1994), 95–122. For calls to formulate an integrated immigration policy in Germany, see Fritz Franz, 'Plädoyer für ein Einwanderungsgesetz,' *Zeitschrift für Ausländerrecht*, 1 (1989) and Fritz Franz, 'Der Gesetzentwurf der Bundesregierung zur Neuregelung des Ausländerrechts,' *Zeitschrift für Ausländerrecht*, 1 (1990), 3–10.

18. Myron Wiener, *The Global Migration Crisis: Challenge to States and Human Rights* (New York: Harper Collins College Publishers), p. 1.

19. Falchi, *op. cit.*, p. 11.

20. Also see 'Europe, fearful,' *The New York Times*, December 30, 1991, A, 14, 1; 'The pressure on asylum,' *The Wall Street Journal*, June 3, 1993, A, 10, 3; 'The last straw? Refugees occupy Beer's fabled field,' *The New York Times*, March 19, 1992, A, 4, 3; 'Strangers at the gate,' *The New York Times Magazine*, September 15, 1991, 6, 33, 2; and John Rossant, Igor Reichlin and Blanca Riemer, 'The floodgates are bursting: a tidal wave of immigrants could spoil the EC's vision of the future,' *Business Week*, September 9, 1991, 52(A).

21. See Jan Werner, *Die Invasion der Armen: Asylanten und illegale Einwanderer* (Mainz: Hase & Koehler Verlag, 1992).

22. See Charles T. Munger's foreword to Garret Hardin, 'Tragedy of the commons,' in Garrett Hardin, *Exploring New Ethics for Survival: the Voyage of the Spaceship Beagle* (Baltimore: Penguin Books Inc., 1968), pp. 250–64.

23. See Garrett Hardin, 'Tragedy of the Commons,' *op. cit.*, note 22.

24. See Chapter 11 in Hardin entitled, 'Free immigration, the enemy of free enterprise,' *op. cit.*, note 22.

25. Philip L. Martin, 'The United States: benign neglect toward immigration,' *op. cit.*, p. 17.

26. In an interview conducted in July 1995 with a bureaucrat responsible for representing the United Kingdom at the COREPER meetings that dealt with asylum and immigration issues, the government's absolute necessity of appearing in control of the admission of non-nationals into the territory of the UK set the tone of the conversation. Even if the Conservative Party should lose the 1997 elections, the official speculated, the Labourites would not be bold enough to be able to delegate sovereignty to the EU in an effort to forge a common immigration and asylum policy. 'It is that important an issue,' he added in a solemn tone.

27. See Carol Sanger, 'Cash in the asylum dividend,' *Los Angeles Times*, March 9, 1990, B, 7, 1.

28. Quoted in Frank Wright, 'Nation seeks asylum from wave of refugees: open door policy got out of control,' *Star Tribune: Newspaper of the Twin Cities*, December 13, 1993, p. 11A.

PART I

CONCEPTUALIZING AND ANALYZING IMMIGRATION

1 The impacts of immigration on receiving countries

Philip L. Martin

Introduction

The world appears to be on the move. There are about 100 million persons living and often working outside their countries of citizenship, making this 'nation of migrants' equivalent in size to the world's tenth most populous country. This chapter analyzes recent global migration patterns. It then turns to the reasons why people migrate for economic reasons, and lays out twin 'grand bargains' that provide a basis for efforts to reduce unwanted migration in the 1990s.

Three basic migration facts seem important: most people never cross national borders to live or work in another country;[1] at least half of all migrant workers move from one developing country to another, i.e. most of those who cross borders do not enter industrial democracies; and many countries have successfully made the transition from exporting to importing labor, and the migration transition process seems to be speeding up.

Given economic differences between nations, and established networks that could move large numbers of people, the surprise may be how little international migration occurs. One starting point for considering labor migration is demography. The world's population in 1994 was about 5.6 billion, and almost 3.5 billion people are in the 15 to 64 age group from which the world's 2.5 billion workers are drawn. Both the world's population and its potential workforce are increasing by 90 to 95 million persons annually.

Neither people nor income are distributed equally around the globe. The World Bank divides the countries on which it collects data into 22 'high-income' and about 100 middle and low-income countries. High-income countries – the United States and Canada, Western European nations, from

Sweden to Spain, and countries such as Japan, Singapore, and Australia – include 15 percent of the world's population, but they accounted for over three-fourths of the world's US $22 trillion GDP in 1991.[2] The average income in these rich countries was over $21,000 annually in 1991, versus a worldwide average of $4000. These data suggest that an average person from one of the poorer 100 countries could increase his or her income five to six times by moving into one of the 22 richest countries. Young people are responding to the opportunity to 'go abroad,' but most of them travel only a short distance, usually from one developing country to another. Over half of the world's 'nation of migrants' is in developing countries – indicating that there is a great deal of not well studied labor migration between developing countries.

However, there are almost 50 million immigrants, refugees and asylees, and authorized and unauthorized migrant workers in the industrial democracies, and their presence there is an important socio-economic and political issue. Many are unwanted, in the sense that their settlement was not anticipated – as with guestworkers who settled in Western Europe or applicants for asylum whose claims that they would face persecution at home are rejected, but who nonetheless are allowed to stay. The United States may be the world's major recipient of unwanted immigrants. Of the nine million persons who are today considered legal immigrants who arrived since 1982, one-third were previously illegal aliens whose status was regularized; there were, in addition, an estimated three to four million illegal alien residents in 1994. Opinion polls in North America and Europe indicate that a majority of the public wants such unwanted immigration curbed.

Why international migration?

Migration research has identified three major factors that influence economically motivated international migration. These are: demand-pull factors that draw migrants into another country; supply-push factors that encourage migrants to leave their own countries; and networks of friends and relatives already settled in destination countries who serve as sources of information and anchor communities for newcomers.[3] The relative importance of each factor changes over time and in particular migration streams. The most common pattern is that the importance of demand pull factors declines as a migration stream matures.

Demand-pull

Most labor migrations began in the industrial countries, as employers there, with or without explicit government approval, recruited migrant workers. During the early years of such labor migrations, demand-pull factors so dominate that, for example, in Germany during the 1960s, the annual influx of workers could be explained almost entirely by fluctuations in the German unemployment rate, giving governments a false assurance that they really can regulate with precision migrant worker flows.

However, in what has since become a familiar story in industrial democracies, demand-pull, supply-push, and network factors evolved in a manner that justifies the aphorism that there is nothing more permanent than temporary workers. In all of the industrial democracies, migration has seemingly taken on a life of its own, with migrant workers continuing to arrive in Western Europe, the United States, and Japan despite historically high unemployment rates. Migrant workers are often prized for their flexibility: they are willing to accept jobs that offer low wages, unpleasant or seasonal work, or unusual hours. As a result, migrant workers are found in the same industries and occupations in all industrial democracies: construction, agriculture, and service jobs that offer low wages, such as in restaurants and hotels, or night and weekend work, such as nursing. It is sometimes asserted that there would be little unwanted labor immigration if the industrial countries simply opened themselves to products from emigration nations. To paraphrase Mexican President Salinas, if the USA really wanted to keep out Mexican tomato pickers, it should open itself to Mexican tomatoes. There is some truth in this assertion, but careful scrutiny suggests that relatively few migrant workers are employed in industries in which trade in place of migration is a near-term option. Labor-intensive manufacturing industries such as garments and shoemaking are often dependent on migrant workers and protected from developing-nation imports, but freeing up trade in goods would directly affect less than one-fourth of the migrant workers in most industrial countries. Thus, while free trade is desirable as a means to accelerate economic growth, it will not immediately curb the desire to employ migrant construction workers, janitors, and nurses.[4]

Supply-push

The demand-pull of jobs in industrial democracies is matched neatly by the supply-push of low wages and joblessness in the developing countries from which most migrant workers come. About five in six of the world's workers are in the world's poorer nations, and every year another 80 million workers join the two billion strong workforce there. This leads to an enormous job creation challenge. Developing nations from Mexico to Turkey to the Philippines must create 500,000 to one million new jobs annually for the youth who every year enter the workforce. In addition, they need to find jobs for the 20 to 40 percent of the workforce that is currently unemployed or underemployed. On top of these job creation challenges, developing nations must find jobs for ex-farmers and for workers who are not seeking work because there aren't enough jobs. Even though some of these newly industrializing countries have some of the fastest economic growth rates in the world, they have been unable to create enough jobs for new workforce entrants, persons who would like more work, and persons who would look for work if jobs were available. In Mexico, the workforce is about 30 million, but only 10 million workers are in formal employment relationships, meaning that they are enrolled in that country's government-operated health and social security systems. Mexico has been creating only about one-third as many real jobs each year as it needs.

Networks

Demand-pull and supply-push are like battery poles: both are necessary to start the car, but alone, each causes no activity. The demand-pull of jobs in the industrial democracies is linked to the supply-push of low wages and joblessness in emigration countries by migration networks. Migration networks encompass everything that enables people to learn about opportunities abroad and take advantage of them. These networks or linkages have been shaped and strengthened by three of the major revolutions of the past generation: the communications revolution, the transportation revolution, and the rights revolution. The communications revolution refers to the fact that potential migrants know far more about opportunities abroad than did turn of the century migrants from Southern and Eastern Europe who set out for North and South America and Australia. The major source of information is countrymen already settled abroad who can tell the migrants about opportunities in Paris or Los Angeles, and in many cases provide advice and funds to migrate, legally or illegally. The industrial democracies perhaps unwittingly add to their allure by portraying a life of opulence in TV shows such as *Dallas* and *Dynasty*, which are exported even to the remote corners of the globe.

Some migrants have their expectations raised by these portrayals of life in the industrial democracies, and many hope to achieve a better life for themselves by migrating to richer areas. Others are motivated to go abroad by contractors, labor brokers, and other often shadowy middlemen who promise, for a fee equivalent to one-fourth, one-half, or even more of the migrant's first year's earnings abroad, access to the promised land. The transportation revolution is simply the fact that the cost of traveling has dropped enormously, while convenience has increased geometrically. Even the most remote peasant is less than one week away from the bright lights of New York. Once he gets to the capital city of his country, the international network of flights can take him anywhere within a day or two for less than the average monthly earnings of even an unskilled and seasonal worker in an industrial country, $1000 to $2000.

The third revolution that encourages migration is the rights revolution, or the spread of individual rights and entitlements within many nations. All of the industrial democracies have strengthened personal rights *vis-à-vis* government agencies, and most have signed international treaties that, for example, commit them to provide refuge to those fleeing persecution. One effect of this rights revolution is that, once a migrant arrives in an industrial country, he or she can avoid deportation for two, three, or even four years.

While a migrant's case winds its way through the legal system, industrial countries face a Hobson's choice. If they prohibit the migrant from working because his or her legal right to do so is in doubt, then the government must support the migrant. If the migrant is permitted to work, then the humanitarian right to due process becomes a back door guestworker program.

The migration challenge

Demand-pull, supply-push, and network factors are evolving in ways that encourage more migration. In light of these easily understandable forces, the world should be on the move, and it may seem to some that it is: the migrant nation is 100 million strong, and it has in recent years been increasing by between two and four million annually in the industrial democracies.[5] But the surprise to many observers is how few, not how many, migrants move into the industrial democracies. Most people do not move: most people will live and die within a few miles of their birthplace. International migration remains an extraordinary event despite the evolution of demand, supply, and network factors that encourage migration. Furthermore, most of those who migrate internationally move only a short distance. One unlikely country, Iran, includes almost one-fourth of the world's 19 million refugees.

The 50 million migrants in the industrial democracies are significant. But it should be emphasized that most people do not migrate despite ever more incentives to do so. The industrial democracies are not being overrun by a tidal wave of immigrants.[6] The migration challenge remains manageable, and responsible policy makers may not be well served by doomsday scenarios such as those painted in the film *The March*, in which desperate Africans set out for Europe accompanied by news crews while political leaders in Europe debate how to stop them. The logical quick fix for such mass migrations is tight border controls and relief outside the borders of the industrial democracies to avoid rights and settlement, but there are medium-term steps that can be taken to avoid such crises.

Toward international cooperation?

Controlling who crosses a nation's borders is considered one of the most basic aspects of sovereignty. However, unlike defense or economic policies, which are coordinated in an alphabet soup of international organizations that range from NATO to WTO, immigration policy has largely remained country-specific. Indeed, economically motivated migration is probably the major issue facing the industrial democracies that is not being coordinated in an international economic organization, although, as other chapters in this volume show, there are growing pressures for multilateral collaboration concerning immigration.

Still the lack of effective international coordination is evident in the responses of the world's three major industrial areas to today's immigration pressures. In Western Europe, controlling unwanted immigration is a top domestic priority. In Germany, there were more than ten attacks on foreigners every day in 1992 and 1993, including several arson fires that resulted in the deaths of Turkish children born in Germany. France, Europe's traditional immigration country, has announced that its goal is to have no immigration. The European response has been to embark on what has proven to be a contentious process to construct an ever higher external wall around fortress Europe so that there can be freedom of movement within Europe.

The United States and Canada are the world's two major traditional immigration countries: they plan for the acceptance of about one million immigrants annually, or 90 percent of all the immigrants that the industrial democracies plan to accept. Even though they are nations of immigrants, most Americans and Canadians want legal immigration reduced and new efforts launched to curb illegal immigration. This is not a new phenomenon: only once during the past half century, in 1953, did more than 10 percent of Americans favor increasing legal immigration.

The American and Canadian governments have responded to anti-immigrant sentiments by taking what have proven to be largely symbolic efforts to reduce illegal immigration. The United States in 1986 adopted sanctions or fines on employers who knowingly hired illegal immigrants, but this restrictionist symbol spawned a counterfeit document industry that paradoxically made it easier rather than harder for such 'falsely documented workers' to find US jobs. In 1990, the United States approved a cap on legal immigration, but made so many exceptions to the cap that legal immigration is expected to remain at least 30 percent higher than 'planned.' Controlling immigration may be important in North America, but it ranks below creating jobs and controlling health care costs, crime, and welfare costs on the national agenda.

Asian industrial democracies such as Japan and South Korea are becoming, for the first time, destinations for immigrants. Unlike in Europe, where emigration played a large role in nation-building, or the United States, where immigration helped to shape the nation's identity, neither emigration nor immigration has played significant roles in these nations. But these countries are opening side doors for guestworkers to enter, and they have announced their intention to avoid the European mistake of permitting these guestworkers to become immigrants. The migrants living in the industrial countries send remittances to their countries of origin. Worldwide, remittances are at least $75 billion annually, or one and one-half times the level of official development assistance (ODA) provided to developing nations. From Algeria to Yugoslavia, labor is the most important export of many nations, and remittances are the most important source of foreign exchange.

As pressures to enter industrial democracies rise during the 1990s, should the industrial democracies coordinate their migration polices? Logic suggests that they should: if Germany restricts the immigration of persons seeking asylum, some may seek asylum in France, the United States, or Canada. Similarly, as world trade in services grows, migration issues inevitably arise, since many services are delivered in person. The industrial world is at the beginning of a new era of migration. Instead of people moving from Europe to America, the major flow of people will be from South to North. There is as yet little effective coordination or consultation on immigration matters. Perhaps migration issues today are akin to energy in the 1960s. When oil was plentiful and cheap, there seemed to be no need for international coordination. When that fact changed, international organizations were quickly formed, and the industrial nations proved willing to coordinate their efforts in the Gulf War of 1991.

Two grand bargains

Migration is likely to increase rather than to decrease in the 1990s, and there is today only a limited basis for international cooperation to deal with international migration. What should the industrial democracies do about rising immigration pressures? No one knows whether the immigrants arriving in industrial democracies today will be well integrated fellow citizens or an inassimilable underclass tomorrow. Indeed, it is often difficult to engage in a rational discussion about immigration, especially in an immigrant country such as the United States. Past fears that Germans, Italians, or Jews could not assimilate proved to be groundless. Historians and social scientists cannot agree on why the United States was able to achieve *e pluribus unum* – from many, one – and thus they cannot assure a public that today fears that newcomers will be difficult to integrate are groundless, but the fact that past fears of inassimilable newcomers were not borne out places a high hurdle in front of today's proponents of less immigration.

Rather than trying to project the future success of any particular nationality or ethnic group, it is more useful to examine the effects of immigration on the industrial democracies. Throughout human history, most societies have had pyramid shapes: an aristocracy on top, and the poor masses at the bottom. The great achievement of the industrial democracies has been the development of diamond-shaped societies: the number of rich people was limited by taxes, the number of poor people by a social safety net, and the people in the middle class represented the widest band of the diamond.

The immigrants arriving in the industrial democracies have an hourglass shape. According to the US Department of Labor's analysis of Census data, 24 percent of all immigrants aged 25 and older had four or more years of college in 1980, versus 16 percent of the native-born population. Immigrants are also much more likely than natives to have less than a high school education – 41 percent of adult immigrants had less than a high school education in 1980, versus 32 percent of the native born. The hourglass or barbell shape of immigration was accentuated in the 1980s, making immigration another factor probably secondary compared to deregulation, trade patterns, and other economic shifts – that is, increasing inequality in the industrial democracies, a major socio-economic issue of the 1990s.

First-generation immigrants may not mind being at the bottom of the economic ladder. But their second- and third-generation children are likely to have the same aspirations as native children. The challenge for the industrial democracies is to ensure that these children of immigrants have the skills to match their expectations. The studies and speculations about the prospects for the children of immigrants range from very optimistic to very pessimistic. But regardless of expectations, there is almost universal agreement that, to tip the scales more toward success, more should be done to help to integrate immigrants and their children. This raises a dilemma. How can the industrial democracies devote more resources to immigrants and their children when 70 to 80 percent of their people think that immigration should be reduced? The answer is the first so-called grand bargain. Industrial democracies could couple renewed efforts to control immigration with expanded efforts to promote integration. The industrial democracies have often used grand bargains to deal with immigration dilemmas. The United States in 1986 coupled sanctions on employers meant to stop illegal immigration with the world's largest amnesty program. Western Europe in 1974 stopped the recruitment of guestworkers, but permitted families to be unified in France and Germany.

There is also a second dimension to this grand bargain. The remittances sent home by migrants now exceed $75 billion annually, or 1.5 times ODA. If the industrial democracies are able to reduce immigration, they may also reduce the remittances that are the lifeblood of many families, communities, and economies. The industrial democracies are going to have to be prepared to couple trade concessions and aid with new get-tough immigration policies in order to avoid hurting developing nations that depend on international migration.

Using trade to accelerate development produces one of the many paradoxes that bedevil rational discussion of the migration challenge facing the industrial democracies. As industrial countries free up trade with the countries from which migrants come, the trade and investment, which in the long run produce jobs and economic growth, in the short run often lead to an economic restructuring that increases migration pressures. The result is the so-called migration hump: migration pressures first rise, and then fall. In the case of the North American Free Trade Agreement (NAFTA), freeing up trade and investment is expected to increase migration for a decade or more, producing the paradox that the policies which make immigration control less necessary in the long run make it more necessary in the short run.

A migration hump or transition has three important parameters (see Figure 1.1). First, how big is hump A, or how much additional migration is there during the economic takeoff phase of restructuring? Second, when is

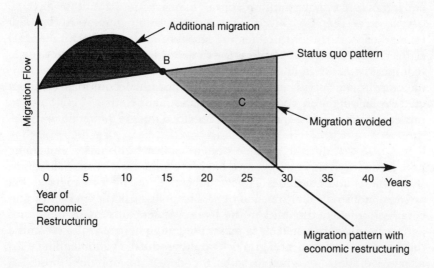

Figure 1.1 The migration hump
Source: Philip Martin, *Trade and Migration: NAFTA and Agriculture* (Washington, DC: Institute for International Economics, 1993).

point B reached, or when does migration return to its pre-take-off levels? Third, how large is C, the migration that did not occur because of stay-at-home development? We could also ask a fourth question: what enables countries such as Italy, Spain, and Korea to get to be net labor importers – within two decades of economic restructuring?

We know very little about parameters such as A, B, and C – neither in already completed migration transitions such as those of Southern Europe or Korea, nor in those under way today, such as Thailand and Malaysia. The Asian tigers may have lessons to teach the world in both economic growth policies and accelerating the migration transition.

The migration hump can serve as an argument for increasing interest in and funding for policies that promote stay-at-home development. Industrial countries today are spending far more on immigration control and integration assistance than on official development assistance,[7] and if there were a more concrete path that could be shown to reduce migration pressures, it may be possible to shift funds toward such policies.

Conclusions

Grand bargains that couple new immigration controls with a redoubling of efforts to integrate the nation of newcomers in the industrial democracies, and renewed efforts to use trade and aid to accelerate development in emigration areas, have intuitive appeal, but they are difficult for any one country to accomplish. Governments are sensitive to employers who want immigrant workers, and neither foreign aid nor rolling back individual rights are politically popular. It is for this reason that the difficult choices that must be made in immigration matters may gravitate toward an international organization, and it may help individual countries to adopt effective immigration controls in the same manner that WTO helps to prevent governments from succumbing to domestic protectionist pressures.

It is true that difficult problems often lead to bad policies. But doing nothing about rising immigration is likely to produce the worst of all worlds. If the status quo continues, large numbers of unskilled immigrants will arrive in industrial countries, and right-wing political parties in Europe and compassion fatigued publics in the United States will support politicians and parties that are not likely to make integrating newcomer immigrants a top priority. Such a political gridlock would produce yet another deficit for later generations to grapple with: the deficit of uplifting those left behind.

Notes

1. There is a considerable amount of internal migration, especially that associated with rural–urban migration.
2. According to the World Bank's *1993 World Development Report*, the 822 million people in the 'high-income countries' that, when ranked by GDP per capita, begin with Ireland and end with Switzerland, are 15.4 percent of the 1991 world population of 5.350 billion (p. 289).
3. Both historically and today middlemen recruiters and transporters have been involved in the migration process. Today, these understudied middlemen – who might be considered as arbitrageurs of differences between international labor markets – play a role in much of the illegal labor migration that occurs, usually extracting a fee from migrant workers or their employers equivalent to 25 to 100 percent of what the migrant will earn in his or her first year abroad.
4. Some industrial countries are engaged in a debate over whether the best way to discourage their employers from preferring to employ unauthorized workers is to step up border and interior enforcement so that such workers are not available, whether it is better to enforce labor laws so that migrant workers are not 'exploited,' or whether both immigration and labor law enforcement is needed. Generally, pro-migrant groups favor placing the emphasis on labor law enforcement, while restrictionist groups favor border and interior immigration enforcement. Over the past five years, a new element has entered the debate over immigration control. In both North America and Western Europe, the argument is that some immigrants come to obtain social welfare program benefits, from education to health care to assistance payments. Such arguments are made most often by those who advocate reducing social welfare programs for citizens and migrants alike.
5. There is a considerable amount of return migration, but the proportion of newcomers who leave is hard to predict and changes as a migration stream matures. In the United States, for example, it is believed that emigrants are equivalent to 20 to 30 percent of immigrants.
6. It is instructive to remember that labor migration often remains region- and village-specific, even after decades of migration. Over two-thirds of Mexico's USA-bound migrants originate in seven of the country's 32 states; they often come from specific villages within these provinces.
7. ODA in 1991 totalled $56 billion.

2 Immigration and integration in Western Europe: a comparative analysis

James F. Hollifield

The current crisis in historical perspective

In the last decades of the twentieth century, international migration has taken on 'crisis' proportions in Western Europe, in terms of both the numbers of migrants involved and their impact on the politics and societies of the receiving countries. In a region with strong national identities, which has been the battleground for competing political and economic ideologies, such as liberalism, communism, and fascism, the surge in immigration in the postwar period has had a profoundly unsettling effect.[1] No state has been able to escape the influx of immigrants and refugees, who are coming increasingly from non-Western European regions. But certain larger states, especially Germany and France, have borne the brunt of postwar population movements, and reaped some of the benefits.[2] It has been difficult for the people and governments of Western Europe to come to grips with the social and cultural realities of immigration, because of a strong sense of ethnic and national identity in states like Germany and France. Moreover, in modern times Western Europe has been a region of emigration, rather than immigration. Nearly 60 million Europeans emigrated to the Americas and other parts of the world, beginning in the sixteenth century.

Today in Germany – which has by far the largest foreign population (about 6.8 million or roughly 8.5 percent of the total population in 1993) of any state in Western Europe – the official doctrine (*Deutschland ist kein Einwanderungsland*) rejects the notion that Germany is an immigration country, and many Germans continue to cling to the hope that unwanted migrants will simply go home.[3] In the 1990s, migration and refugee policies have been driven by the desire to stem the outbreak of racist violence in post-unification Germany and to staunch the massive influx of asylum seekers and other newcomers, which reached one million annually between 1989 and 1992. Despite efforts in the 1980s by various German governments under the Christian Democratic leader Helmut Kohl to address the migration crisis, a new political party, the Republikaner, was founded in Bavaria in 1986 on an anti-immigration platform. The party has had considerable success in local, state (*Landtag*), and European elections, and neo-Nazi/skinhead violence has increased in the years since unification. The breakthrough of extreme right-wing political and social movements has raised the specter of a renewed German nationalism.

In France, which has a longer history of immigration than any other country in Western Europe and the second largest foreign population (about 3.6 million or roughly 6.4 percent of the total population in 1990), pitched ideological battles have been fought between politicians and political parties over immigration and assimilation, or as the French prefer to call it, *intégration*.[4] Elements of the 'republican' left (socialists) and right (Gaullists) have argued for the maintenance of a relatively open society, but with stringent adherence by foreigners to the nationalist and Jacobin ideals of the French Revolution. The French 'republican model' is based on what at first glance would seem to be an oxymoron: a nationalist universalism, which seeks to guarantee the rights of all individuals (as expressed in the Declaration of the Rights of Man *and* the Citizen), but only in the context of the French national state, and under strict conditions of *laïcité* (secularism).[5] The neo-fascist *Front National*, headed by Jean-Marie Le Pen, has pushed for the closing of French borders and the expulsion of the largely Muslim foreign population. The position of the current, right-of-center government, as stated by the neo-Gaullist Minister of the Interior, Charles Pasqua, is to achieve 'zero immigration' as quickly as possible and to make it more difficult for foreigners to settle and acquire citizenship in France. To quote Minister Pasqua, 'France has been a "country of immigration," but it no longer wishes to be one.' In the past decade, immigration stabilized at just over 100,000 legal entries annually, and in 1991 it was estimated to be around 120,000.[6]

Among the larger states in Western Europe, Great Britain stands alone in its apparent capacity to deal with the migration crisis and to control its borders. The foreign population of the United Kingdom was 1.9 million in 1990, or roughly 3.3 percent of the total population. Many explanations for British exceptionalism have been given, from the fact that Britain is an island nation, governed by a strong parliament, to the willingness of government to enact discriminatory legislation, barring entry to certain national and ethnic groups, especially from the New Commonwealth countries of the Caribbean and the Indian subcontinent.[7] But this capacity for controlling immigration – which has been running at about 50,000 to 60,000 annually in the 1980s and 1990s – masks the historical importance of

Ireland as a source of 'immigrant' labor. Moreover, it should be noted that almost 5 percent of the British population is defined as an ethnic (i.e. non-white) minority, a definition which excludes the Irish. Hence assimilation and the problem of race relations have tended to be more important in political and policy debates than the issue of immigration control. Unlike in France or Germany, there seems to be a greater willingness on the part of British politicians and the government to accept the realities of a multi-cultural society, while striving to reduce immigration and refugee flows to an absolute minimum. This 'accommodation' is best reflected in the British Nationality Act (BNA) of 1981, pushed through by the first government of Margaret Thatcher. The BNA set up a kind of gradational citizenship, with different categories of 'Britishness,' thereby codifying the relationship of the UK with British, colonial subjects, and patrials. The decisive steps taken by the first Thatcher government are credited by some with squelching extreme right-wing, anti-immigrant political movements of the 1970s, such as the National Front.

This historical sketch of the migration crisis in Western Europe would not be complete without some reference to the recent transition of the countries of Southern Europe – especially Italy and Spain – from emigration to immigration countries. Italy was the first of the traditional sending countries of the South to experience this role reversal, a process which began in the late 1970s. Yet it was not until 1986 that the first Italian immigration law was passed, primarily in an attempt by the state to gain some measure of control over the labor market and stop the rapidly rising tide of illegal immigration. However, the 1986 law did not set up a visa regime, to determine which nationalities should be required to obtain a visa before entering Italy. The result was a continuing influx of undocumented migrants, primarily from North Africa, leading the Italian authorities to reimpose visa restrictions in 1990, under the so-called Martelli Law. By this time, Italy had an immigrant population of just under one million, including roughly 400,000 non-EC immigrants. Not surprisingly, the focus of policy debates in Italy of late has been on the need to control illegal immigration and on how to integrate the already large clandestine population.[8] As in France and Germany, Italy has witnessed the rise of racial violence, and the founding of an anti-immigrant political party, the *Lega Nord/Lega Lombarda*, which is based in the industrial North and advocates regional autonomy.

The political economy of immigration: a framework for analysis

Few issues have had a greater impact on the politics and society of contemporary Western Europe than immigration. The variety of national responses to the migration crisis would seem to indicate that each state is designing its own policy, and that there is little (apart from European Union initiatives) to link one national experience with another. Moreover, a majority of West European governments and leading political and intellectual elites have rejected any comparisons with the American experience (see below). They argue that the United States is a nation of immigrants, with a much larger territory, and a civic or political culture that is more tolerant of ethnic and cultural differences.[9] Especially since the end of the Cold War, the American 'model' of a multicultural and immigrant society has been derided by many political and intellectual elites in Western Europe as a bad model, which can only lead to greater social and political conflict.[10] The riots in Los Angeles in 1992 provided more grist for the mill of European critics of the so-called American model. Yet it is argued here that the problems of immigration control (and ultimately the assimilation of foreign populations) in Europe are much the same as in the United States, for two reasons.

First, the global economic dynamic which underlies the migration crisis is similar in Western Europe and the United States. The great postwar migrations to Western Europe and the United States began, for the most part, in response to the demand for cheap labor and the pull of high growth economies, which in the 1950s and 1960s literally sucked labor from poorer countries of the periphery, such as Mexico, the Caribbean basin, Southern Europe, North Africa, and Turkey. This international labor migration and *demand-pull* forces were subsequently legitimized by the receiving states through what came to be known as guestworker and *bracero* policies.[11] The economically beneficial movement of labor from South to North was in keeping with the *liberal* spirit of the emerging global economy.[12] Under the Bretton Woods system, international institutions like the IMF, GATT, and the World Bank, as well as the OECD, were set up to encourage and promote international exchange, including trade, foreign investment, and (if necessary to maintain high, non-inflationary rates of economic growth) labor migration.

But what started as an efficient transfer of labor from poorer countries of the South to the North rapidly became a social and political liability in the 1970s, as growth rates in the OECD countries slowed in the aftermath of the first big postwar recession of 1973–4. The recession led to major policy shifts in Western Europe (but not in the United States) to stop immigration, or at least to stop the recruitment of foreign workers.[13] At the same time, however, demand-pull forces were rapidly giving way to *supply-push* forces, as the populations of poorer, peripheral countries began to grow at a rapid pace, and their economies weakened. Informational and kinship networks had been established between immigrants and their home countries (via families and villages). These networks helped to spur immigration, in spite of the increasingly desperate attempts by receiving states in Western Europe to stop all forms of immigration.[14]

Global economic (push–pull) forces provide the *necessary* conditions for the continuation of immigration in Western Europe after the implementation of restrictionist policies in 1973–4. But to understand fully the crisis of immigration control in the 1980s and 1990s, we must look beyond *markets*, to *liberal-republican* political developments in the major receiving states. The struggle to win civil and social *rights* for marginal groups, including ethnic minorities and foreigners, and the institutionalization of these rights in the jurisprudence of liberal-republican states (particularly France and Germany) provide the *sufficient* conditions for continued immigration. Therefore, to get a complete picture of the migration crisis we must look at the degree of institutionalization of civil and social rights in the countries of Western Europe and North America, and at the struggle (between left and right) to redefine citizenship and nationhood in states such as the USA, France, Britain, and Germany. It is the relatively new (i.e. post-1945) liberal-republican dynamic in the politics and laws of the states of Western Europe which has led to a convergence with the North American experience.[15]

The liberal-republican dynamic (of markets and rights) can be depicted as in Figure 2.1. In the twentieth century, we can see the emergence of four ideal types of political economy. First, depicted in cell A, is the international political economy, in which politics and authority relations are largely a function of the power of sovereign nation states, and markets are largely unregulated. In such a situation, which may be more characteristic of a purely Westphalian system, individuals will move in response to market forces (supply and demand); but they are basically at the mercy of sovereign states, and they have no rights. States may choose to accept or not to accept migrants, depending upon the national/state interest. For some time, however, industrial democracies have been moving away from this type of political economy, as nation states have come together to regulate markets

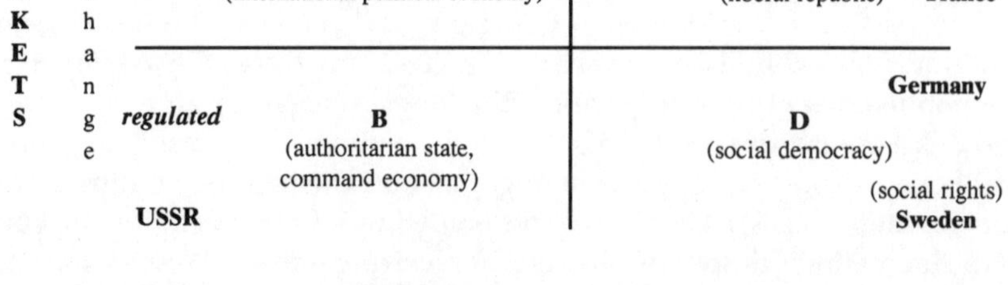

Figure 2.1 Ideal types of political economy

(via treaty arrangements such as GATT, the EU, or NAFTA) and to institutionalize rights for migrants (via international organizations, like the UN or UNHCR, and the ILO).

The second type of political economy, depicted in cell B, is an authoritarian state with a command economy. Here, authority relations are based largely upon the police powers of the state, and the individual has few if any rights. The economy is highly regulated, and borders are closely guarded to prevent unwanted migration. Rule of law is a fiction. The state which came closest to this ideal type was the USSR under Stalin. In the former Soviet state, even internal migration was closely regulated for both political and economic reasons. One could also argue that there are many Third World states which approximate this ideal type, but it is important to note that even very authoritarian states do not completely master their borders; and individuals may find ways of gaining resident status, if not membership or citizenship, in these states. Myron Weiner makes the important point that in the twentieth century many of the largest international population movements have been within the Third World.[16] But such movements (in South Asia or sub-Saharan Africa, for example) have tended to be a direct consequence of decolonization, irredentism, and the aftermath of nation state building, which displaced large numbers of people, especially ethnic or cultural minorities. Such movements are less a function of political economy than of a more purely state/security dynamic. In the oil rich countries of the Middle East, however, we see a situation of market-driven migration in the labor-poor Gulf states – a movement which is closely regulated by the states involved, and in which migrants have very few rights. The case of the Palestinians in Kuwait or the Egyptians in Iraq provides a good example of this type of political economy.

Clearly, however, the bulk of South–North and East–West migrations, since 1945, must be understood in terms of the two cells on the right of Figure 2.1 (C and D). In these situations, the rights dynamic becomes increasingly important, both as a constraint on the actions of states to control their borders and as a potential pull factor, creating legal spaces for foreigners where none existed before. We can place the states of Western Europe and North America on these continua, based on the extent to which rights for ethnic minorities and foreigners have been institutionalized and/ or constitutionalized. Rights, particularly as they pertain to foreigners, can be divided into two categories: civil rights, which are more characteristic of strongly liberal and republican regimes (such as France and the United States); and social rights, which are more evident in the social democracies of Northern Europe, particularly Sweden, Norway, and the Netherlands, but also Germany and Austria. Markets – especially labor markets – are more highly regulated in the latter group of states; whereas in more liberal political economies, like the USA, markets and borders are more permeable. Finally, it is important to note that I have not included political rights in this framework, because they tend to be the last set of rights granted to ethnic or immigrant minorities, usually at the end of the naturalization process. So they are less important for understanding the problems of immigration control, which are more closely linked to the issues of residency, protection from deportation (due process), and basic subsistence (welfare). In the longer term, however, integration and the solidification of the rights of minorities and newcomers are clearly dependent upon voting rights and political participation.[17]

In the comparative historical analysis which follows, we will see that most states in Western Europe have moved closer to the liberal republican type of political economy (cell C). The reasons for this convergence are related to: (a) the victory of the United States and it allies in the Second World War and the settlement which followed, especially the establishment of a liberal republic in West Germany; (b) the creation and institutionalization of a liberal international order, backed in large part by US economic and military power (this new world order helped to disseminate information and encourage trade and the exchange of ideas, in part through new technologies of transportation and communication); (c) the Cold War accentuating the liberal-republican dynamic, by forging political and economic alliances between Western Europe and the United States, and by creating new (rights-oriented) political coalitions, which pushed the USA to live up to what Gunnar Myrdal called its 'liberal creed.'[18] In this sense the history of international migration, since 1945, is closely linked to the civil rights struggles in the United States, which helped to intensify and spread liberal republican ideals. In commenting on the landmark Supreme Court decision in *Brown* v. *Board of Education*, which set in motion the desegregation of American schools and the granting of civil, political, and social rights to African Americans, then Vice President Richard Nixon remarked that the decision was a great victory for the United States in its struggle against communism. In effect, Nixon saw the USA as fulfilling its liberal creed, thereby consolidating its position as the leader of the free world.

The civil rights 'revolution' in America led to a new, more expansive American immigration policy.[19] The dramatic change in domestic politics in the United States had repercussions far beyond American borders, helping to transform relations among states and between states and individuals. To paraphrase John Ruggie, a new liberal republicanism was 'embedded' in international relations, and promoted through the mechanisms of American hegemony.[20] In short, rights became increasingly important in international relations, from the mid-1950s until at least 1989. World politics entered an unprecedented phase of openness (in the West), which had dramatic consequences for the ability of nation states to control their borders.

Partly as a result of this liberal-republican dynamic, the migration tides of the 1950s and 1960s created new and reluctant lands of immigration in

Western Europe, and they brought to the fore questions of citizenship, the rights of minorities, and multiculturalism. The migration crisis also awakened xenophobic sentiments, leading to the creation of new social movements and political parties, which have opposed the extension of rights to non-citizens, ethnic minorities, and asylum seekers.[21] These right-wing movements and parties helped to promote a populist backlash against immigrants, tinged with the fascism and anti-semitism of the past, and opposed to rights-based, liberal republican politics. Yet the migration crisis also demonstrated the extent to which new civil and social rights for foreign and ethnic minorities had become embedded in the jurisprudence, institutions, and political processes of the Western European states since 1945. In effect, the old battleground for competing nationalisms and ideologies in Western Europe was to a large degree transformed by the traumatic experiences of the Second World War and the Cold War. A new sensitivity to the rights of minorities and refugees grew out of these experiences, making it difficult for states simply to expel or deport unwanted migrants, as was done in earlier periods.[22] The West German state could not solve the Turkish problem in the same way that the Kaiserreich had solved the Polish problem earlier in the twentieth century: by mass deportations. In postwar Western Europe as well as the United States, immigration provoked constitutional debates, and it severely tested the capacity of political, judicial, and administrative authorities in liberal-republican states to 'manage' the migration crisis.[23]

Origins of the migration crisis

The origins of the migration crisis in Western Europe can be traced to three historical developments, each of which contributed to the political-economic dynamic described above. First is the crisis of *decolonization*, which led to an unsettled period of mass migrations from roughly 1945 to 1962 or 1963, when national boundaries in Eastern and Central Europe were redrawn and empires in Africa and Asia were dismantled, often through violent processes of rebellion, pogrom, irredentism, and civil war. These developments uprooted entire populations and freed up large supplies of labor in Central and Eastern Europe, and eventually in Africa and the Indian subcontinent. They created new categories of citizens that continue to mark immigration debates in Germany (the *Aussiedler* or ethnic Germans and *Vertriebene* or displaced persons), in France (the *pieds noirs* or French colonists returning from Algeria and the *Harkis*, who fought with the French Army in the Algerian War), and in Britain (the Commonwealth and later New Commonwealth immigrants). The political (in addition to the economic) significance of these movements of populations early in the postwar period should not be underestimated, for it is the aftermath of war and decolonization which created new ethnic cleavages and a new ethnic consciousness in these societies, and thereby laid the groundwork for the rise of extremist, populist, and nativist movements such as the *Front National* (FN)in France, and the *Republikaner* in Germany. It is no accident that Jean-Marie Le Pen, the founder of the FN, is a veteran of the Algerian War, a former *para*, who brags about his role in torturing Algerian prisoners of war. Nor is it sheer coincidence that Franz Schoenhuber, the founder and leader of the *Republikaner*, is a proud veteran of the Waffen SS. By the same token, the influx of people into these old, established societies had many positive effects, especially in Germany, where traditionally Catholic or Protestant regions were transformed virtually overnight. The absorption of displaced persons (*Vertriebene*) in West Germany changed the religious map of many regions, contributing to the formation of new social and political cleavages.

The second wellspring of the migration crisis in Western Europe is the set of public policies known as *guestworker* (*Gastarbeiter*) or rotation policies. These policies for recruiting ostensibly temporary, foreign workers began as early as 1945 in Switzerland, which came to be viewed as the model for guestworker programs in other West European countries, notably in neighboring Germany.[24] The central feature of these policies was the concept of rotation, whereby unmarried male workers could be brought into the labor market for a specified (contractual) period, and sent back at the end of this period. They could be replaced by new workers as needed. This was a rather neat macroeconomic formula for solving what was shaping up to be one of the principal obstacles to continued high rates of non-inflationary growth in the 1950s and 1960s.[25] In fact, it seemed to be working so well in the Swiss case that the newly reorganized Organization for Economic Cooperation and Development (the OECD, which was created from the OEEC) recommended the policy to European states that were experiencing manpower shortages. The Bonn Republic, which had orchestrated the *Wirtschafts-wunder* (economic miracle) in the 1950s under the leadership of Konrad Adenauer and Ludwig Ehrhard, forged a consensus in 1959–60 among business and labor groups to opt for a policy of importing labor, rather than taking industry, capital, and jobs offshore in search of lower labor costs, as was done in the United States. This was the beginning of the largest guestworker program in Western Europe, which would eventually bring millions of young Turks, Yugoslavs, and Greeks to work in German industry. The at first unlimited supply of ethnic German refugees and displaced persons from Eastern and Central Europe, including refugees from the German Democratic Republic (*Übersiedler*), suddenly dried up in 1961, as the last hole in the Iron Curtain was sealed with the construction of the Berlin Wall.

Two fateful turning points in the history of the German guestworker program are of interest. The first came in 1967–8, following the shallow recession of 1966. It was at this point that the Grand Coalition government (1966 to 1969) rotated some Turks and other guestworkers out of the labor market, and back to their countries of origin. This operation was so successful that there was little resistance to bringing the guestworkers back in 1969–70, when the West European economies were heating up again.[26] The second fateful turning point in the history of the *Gastarbeiter* program in Germany came in 1973, when the attempt was made to stop all recruitment of foreign workers (or *ausländische Arbeitnehmer*, as they came to be called in official parlance), repatriate them, and prevent family reunification. At this crucial juncture (see below), the relatively new liberal-republican features of the Bonn regime came fully into play, to prevent the government and administrative authorities from stopping immigration (especially family reunification) and deporting unwanted migrants.[27]

Although France is often mentioned as a European country which pursued guestworker-type policies, this is somewhat misleading. The provisional or tripartite government under General de Gaulle (1945–6), as well as the first governments of the Fourth Republic, put in place policies for recruiting foreign labor (*la main-d'oeuvre étrangère*), which were specified in the various five-year plans, and implemented by a new immigration office, the Office National d'Immigration (ONI). But the new workers were defined from the outset as *travailleurs immigrés ou permanents* (immigrant or permanent workers). It was the policy of Fourth Republic governments to encourage foreign workers to settle permanently, because immigration was part and parcel of population policy, which was itself a reflection of pronatalist sentiments among the policy and political elites. The traditional French preoccupation with depopulation and falling birth rates was a driving feature behind postwar immigration policy. In the 1950s, immigration was viewed as an important asset, especially since most newcomers were from culturally compatible neighboring countries, mainly Italy and Spain. But these admissionist policies of the 1950s, together with the crisis of decolonization and the desire on the part of French authorities not to sever relations with former colonies in North and West Africa, set the stage for the open-door policies of the 1960s.[28]

As the French economy boomed in the 1960s, authorities rapidly lost control of immigration. But instead of sucking more labor from culturally compatible neighboring countries, such as Italy and Spain (which were beginning to develop in their own right), the newly independent states of North Africa (Algeria, Morocco, and Tunisia) became the principal suppliers of foreign/immigrant labor. The major exception was Portugal, which continued to provide large numbers of workers for the French labor market. By the end of the 1960s, however, Algerians were rapidly becoming the most numerous immigrant group. Because of their special post-colonial status (as spelled out in the Evian Agreements, which ended the Algerian War), they had virtual freedom of movement into and out of the former *métropole* of France; and those Algerian nationals born before independence in 1962 were entitled to French citizenship. The result was to create a large undocumented (but not illegal) foreign population in France. The principal 'mode of immigration' during this period was immigration 'from within,' whereby foreigners would enter the country, often having been recruited by business, take a job, and then a request would be made on their behalf by the firm for an adjustment of status (*régularisation*). The ONI, which was created to control immigration, became little more than a clearing house for foreign labor.[29]

By the early 1970s, the rapid increase in North African immigration convinced the Pompidou government that something had to be done to regain control of immigration. The deep recession of 1973–4, which brought an abrupt end to the postwar boom (the *trente glorieuses*, or 30 years of high growth rates), simply confirmed this judgment; and the new government under Valéry Giscard d'Estaing took fairly dramatic steps to close the immigration valve, using heavy-handed statist and administrative measures to try to stop immigration (*l'arrêt de l'immigration*), repatriate immigrants, and deny rights of family reunification.[30] Thus, the French followed much the same logic as the Swiss and the Germans in attempting to use foreign workers as a kind of industrial reserve army or shock absorber (*Konjunkturpuffer*) to solve social and economic problems associated with recession, especially unemployment.[31]

Other labor-importing states in Western Europe followed the same *guest-worker* logic in changing from policies of recruitment to suspension, with a couple of notable exceptions. Britain had never really launched a full-scale guestworker program, because of the availability of New Commonwealth and Irish labor, and because economic growth rates in Britain were never high enough to justify a massive importation of labor. Demand-pull in the British case was very weak.[32] The Swiss, who had been the first to use a guestworker or rotation approach to labor migration, were also the first to try to suspend recruitment of foreign labor (officially in 1970). Enormous xenophobic pressures had built up in Switzerland, because of the sheer size of the foreign population relative to the total population (over 15 percent). But the Swiss economy continued to grow throughout the 1970s (demand-pull remained strong), and unemployment was negligible, thanks in part to the efficacy of foreign worker policies that relied heavily on seasonal and frontier workers. For these reasons, the Swiss returned fairly quickly to their rotation policies, making sure that as few migrants as possible would actually settle and seek naturalization.

As a result, the Swiss were able to ride out the xenophobic backlash against immigration in the 1970s, which coalesced into a national campaign calling for strict limits on the size of the foreign population, the *Nationale Aktion gegen die Überfremdung von Volk und Heimat*. Access to badly needed foreign labor was maintained, and Swiss authorities avoided the trap, into which the French and Germans fell, of freezing the foreign population in place.[33] In effect, by attempting to stop immigration, French and German authorities created a large (and more permanent) foreign population. Workers refused to leave, for fear of being denied re-entry, and they began to bring their families to join them, which led to an upsurge in family immigration. The Swiss writer Max Frisch observed of the guestworker programs: 'we asked for workers, and we got people instead!' Because of the civil rights (especially due process) guaranteed to individuals under the aegis of liberal constitutions, the foreign guests could not simply be sent home (see Figure 2.1 and the discussion above).

The migration crisis in Western Europe in the 1980s and 1990s cannot be fully understood apart from the history of the guestworker programs. These programs created the illusion of temporary migration, leading some states (especially Germany) to avoid or postpone a national debate over immigration and naturalization policy. This problem was compounded by the statist attempts in 1973–4 to stop immigration and repatriate foreigners, which furthered the 'myth of return' and heightened public expectations that governments could simply reverse the migratory process. Also, by taking such a strong, statist stance against further immigration, it became virtually impossible for French and German governments in the 1980s and 1990s even to discuss an 'American-style,' legal immigration policy. Instead, immigration became a highly charged partisan issue, leading to soul-searching debates about national identity and citizenship. The more practical questions – which an American policy maker or politician might ask – of 'how many, from where, and in what status,' simply could not be asked. The result of trying to slam the 'front door' of legal immigration shut led to the opening of side doors and windows (for family members and seasonal workers), and, most important of all, the 'back door' was left wide open (especially in Germany) for refugees and asylum seekers. Not surprisingly, many would-be legal and illegal immigrants (as well as legitimate asylum seekers and others) flooded through the back door in the 1980s and 1990s.[34]

Hence the third historical development in the migration crisis is the influx of *refugees and asylum seekers*, which is causally related to colonialism and to the failed guestworker policies. Large-scale refugee migrations began in Europe in the aftermath of the Second World War, and with the advent of the Cold War. In fact, it was the beginning of the Cold War in the late 1940s which led to the Geneva Convention in 1951 and the creation of UNHCR. These were essentially Cold War institutions, created to handle the flow of refugees from East to West, in a period (the 1950s and 1960s) when there was little doubt as to the meaning of a 'well-founded fear of persecution,' the acid test of political asylum which was incorporated into national and (in many cases) constitutional law.[35] In practice, flight from a communist regime was sufficient grounds for the granting of political asylum in most of the countries of Western Europe. The famous Article 16 of the West German Basic Law, which granted almost an unconditional right to asylum for any individual fleeing persecution, was in fact written with refugees from the East in mind, especially ethnic German refugees (*Aussiedler und Übersiedler*).

Refugee and asylum policies in Western Europe functioned rather well for almost three decades from roughly 1950 to 1980 (during most of the period of the Cold War), but with the closing of front door immigration policies in the 1970s, political asylum became an increasingly attractive mode of entry for unwanted migrants who would come to be labeled 'economic refugees.' These included not only migrants from former colonies (in Africa and Asia), but an increasing number of refugees from the countries of East and Central Europe, especially gypsies. As governments across Western Europe struggled to redefine their immigration and refugee policies in the wake of severe economic recessions and rising unemployment, the pace of refugee migrations picked up: Tamils, Sikhs, and Kurds were coming to Britain and Germany, Zairians and other sub-Saharan African nationals were coming to France at a rate of tens of thousands annually, and Eritreans and Somalis were coming to Italy. The first efforts to address this new movement of populations came at the level of the European Community, where, it was thought, national governments could simultaneously reassert control over refugee movements while avoiding the painful moral and political dilemmas involved in limiting the right to asylum. The Single European Act of 1985 set in motion a new round of European economic integration, which included the goal of 'free movement of goods, persons, services, and capital,' in effect the establishment of a border-free Europe. To achieve this goal, however, it quickly became clear that European states would have to agree upon common visa and asylum policies.[36]

Toward this end, five states (France, Germany, and the Benelux countries) met in the Luxembourg town of Schengen, and in 1985 the Schengen Agreement was unveiled as a prototype for a border-free Europe. The agreement called for the elimination of internal borders, the harmonization of visa and asylum policies, and the coordinated policing of external borders, leading to the construction of a symbolic 'ring fence' around the common territory. Schengen, which was enlarged to include Italy, Spain, and Portugal, was followed in 1990 by the Dublin Convention, which established the principle that refugees must apply for asylum in the first EC member state in which they arrive. But no sooner had the states of Western Europe begun to focus on a common policy for dealing with the refugee and asylum issue, than the entire international system in Europe changed, with the collapse of communist regimes in East and Central Europe, and finally the collapse of the Soviet Union itself.

The first result of the abrupt end of the Cold War was to set off a state of panic among governments and publics in Western Europe that there would be a flood of (economic) refugees from Eastern Europe – sensational headlines such as 'the Russians are coming!' were splashed across Western Europe.[37] These predictions turned out to be exaggerated, at least as far as refugee migration from the Soviet successor states was concerned. But the euphoria associated with the 'triumph of liberalism' over communism did contribute, at least briefly, to a surge of refugee migration. The surge lasted for about four years, from 1989 to 1993, and it placed enormous strains on what were essentially Cold War institutions, namely the Geneva Convention itself and the UNHCR. Governments were forced to reconsider and rewrite sweeping constitutional provisions, which guaranteed the right to asylum, at the same time that new irredentist movements swept the Balkans, Transcaucasia, and other formerly communist territories, leading to civil wars and new refugee migrations. Movements from Africa also increased, placing even more pressure on the entire structure of international refugee law.

How have the states of Western Europe and the European Union responded to the migration crisis? The responses have been at three levels. The first is political, in the sense that politicians, especially on the right, have exploited the migration crisis for political gain. The second is a policy-level response, which has lurched from one extreme to another. Liberal and assimilationist policies of amnesty (for illegals) have been followed by harsh crackdowns on asylum seekers, and attempts to make naturalization more difficult. Finally, emerging from this cauldron of political and policy debates, is a search for national 'models' of immigration and naturalization, which range from a tempered pluralism in Britain to stringent republicanism in France. A *national model* is cultural, historical, legal, and institutional; it links the struggle for control of immigration with the struggle to naturalize and assimilate newcomers. Even though this concept stresses national differences, we have seen a convergence in immigration policies in Western Europe and the United States, because of the political-economic dynamic described above. For some years, the stated objectives of immigration policy in the industrial democracies has been to control/restrict/stop immigration; and to integrate newcomers – what some have called the 'grand bargain.'[38] These struggles to control and integrate are shaped by (the strength or weakness of) the national model, the extent to which it is legitimate in the eyes of the citizenry, and the extent to which it finds expression in the law and public policy.

Political and policy responses: the search for a national model

France

France was the first state in Western Europe to feel the full political force of the migration crisis, in part because of the stunning victory of the left in presidential and parliamentary elections of 1981. The election of François

Mitterrand as President of the Republic and the Socialist Party's triumph in Parliament marked the first truly left government in France since the Popular Front of 1936. This election left the right, which had governed France since the founding of the Fifth Republic in 1958, in a state of disarray. The socialists won the elections in part on a liberal platform, which promised to improve civil rights for immigrants by giving them a firm legal standing. To carry out these promises, the first socialist government of Pierre Mauroy enacted a conditional amnesty, which led to the legalization of well over 100,000 undocumented immigrants. Other measures were taken to limit the arbitrary powers of the police to carry out identity checks, to grant long-term (ten-year) residency permits to foreigners, and to guarantee the rights of association for immigrant groups. These liberal policies, carried out in the wake of the left's electoral breakthrough and with the right in a state of confusion, provided an opening for a little known right wing populist and his neo-fascist party, Jean-Marie Le Pen and the *Front National*. The early 1980s was marked by recession, rising unemployment, and a general sense of insecurity, especially among workers. Le Pen and his group seized the moment and won what seemed to be a small victory (16.7 percent of the vote) in the town of Dreux, near Paris.[39] But this was the beginning of an intense period of immigration politics, as the right struggled to regain power and Le Pen, under the slogan of '*La France aux français*,' garnered more support from an extremely volatile electorate.

The traditional parties of the right, RPR and UDF, under the leadership of Jacques Chirac, Mayor of Paris, began to attack the socialists' handling of the immigration issue. The socialists responded by defending the liberal policies of naturalization and assimilation, holding out the prospect of voting rights for resident aliens in local elections, while promising to enforce labor laws (employer sanctions) in order to crack down on illegal immigration. In the parliamentary elections of 1985, which were fought under new rules of proportional representation, the right, under Chirac, won a narrow victory; and the FN won over 30 seats in the parliament (creating a new parliamentary bloc) and giving Le Pen a forum in which to pursue his anti-immigrant, populist agenda. The Minister of the Interior in the Chirac government of *cohabitation*, Charles Pasqua, launched a series of initiatives and bills, which came to be known as *la loi Pasqua*, intended to give greater power to the police (especially the *Police de l'Air et des Frontières* or PAF) to arrest and deport undocumented migrants, and to deny entry to asylum seekers, who would not be allowed to appeal their cases to the OFPRA, the Office for Protection of Refugees. The Chirac government went one step further in 1986, introducing a bill that would have changed the French nationality code, so that children born in France of foreign parents would no longer be automatically given citizenship at age 18. Instead, they would have been required to apply for citizenship and take an oath. The irony of this bill, which caused a storm of protest from immigrant rights groups, is that it would have in no way altered the citizenship status of second-generation Algerians, whose parents, born in Algeria before independence, were already French nationals.[40] The bill to reform the nationality code was withdrawn by the Chirac government, which suddenly appeared weak and vacillating. Immigrant rights groups, such as SOS-racisme, France Plus, MRAP, and the GISTI, organized protests and legal appeals to stop the reform. Thousands marched in the streets under banners which read *ne touche pas mon pote* (don't touch my buddy), and the French Council of State was called upon to review the legality (and constitutionality) of the government's immigration policy. In the end, a decision was made by the government to appoint a special commission, the Commission des Sages, composed of leading intellectual and political figures, and chaired by Marceau Long, the Vice President of the Council of State. The Commission held public hearings and wrote a long report, concluding that French republican principles of universalism and the right of foreigners born in France to naturalize (*jus soli*) should be upheld. At the same time, the Commission stressed the importance of maintaining the assimilationist, republican principles inherent in French immigration law and practice.[41] The right lost the presidential and parliamentary elections of 1988, essentially failing to capitalize on the immigration issue, while Jean-Marie Le Pen succeeded in gaining 14.5 percent of the vote on the first ballot of the presidential elections. But the FN received only one seat in the new parliament, elected according to the old two-round, single member district rules, which had been used throughout the history of the Fifth Republic until 1985. Le Pen cried foul, arguing that the voices of a significant proportion of the French electorate were not being heard, and opinion polls, which showed that over a third of the voters supported the positions of the FN, seemed to bear him out.

The socialist government of François Mitterrand (as President) and Michel Rocard (as Prime Minister) continued to defend rights of foreigners, but it launched a campaign for tougher enforcement of labor laws and set up a new council for integration (*Haut Conseil à l'Integration*) to study ways of bringing immigrants into the mainstream of French social, economic, and political life.[42] These attempts to take control of the immigration issue were thwarted, at least temporarily, by the so-called *affaire des foulards*, the scarf controversy, when three Moroccan girls wore Islamic garb to a public (secular) high school, thereby violating the republican principles of separation of church and state – *laïcité*. This controversy split the socialist party, between a liberal/pluralist wing (headed by Rocard), which argued for more tolerance of cultural differences, and a republican wing (headed by Jean-Pierre Chevenement), which argued for the maintenance of strict assimilationist policies. The republican argument is that overtly religious behavior is permissible in the privacy of the home or place of worship (church, mosque, or synagogue), but not in a public school. The

Rocard government split the difference by allowing the girls to wear their scarves, as long as they did not proselytize in school. The government received the approbation of the Council of State in this policy.

Immigration in France continued during this period of the 1980s at a rate of about 100,000 annually, and refugee migrations picked up to about 25,000 annually.[43] As the country slipped slowly into recession in 1991–2, the left began to lose its nearly decade-long grip on power. The parliamentary elections of 1993 were fought in part over the issue of immigration control, with the right feeling little compulsion to restrain anti-immigrant, populist sentiments among the public. In fact, the decision was made to try to steal the thunder of Le Pen and the FN by proposing harsh measures for dealing with illegal immigration and asylum seekers. The badly divided socialist party suffered a crushing defeat in March 1993, and the reinvigorated right (RPR–UDF), under the new leadership of Edouard Balladur, wasted little time in implementing draconian measures (by French standards) to stop immigration. Once again, Charles Pasqua was named to head the Interior Ministry, and with the right controlling nearly 80 percent of the seats in the National Assembly, he proposed a series of bills to reform immigration, naturalization, and refugee law (*la loi Pasqua II*). These measures amounted to a broadside attack on the civil and social rights of foreigners. They sought to undermine key aspects of the republican model, as spelled out in the *Ordonnances* of 1945, especially residency requirements for naturalization, the principle of *jus soli*, and the guarantee of due process for asylum seekers.

La loi Pasqua II also included a bill designed to prevent illegal immigrants from benefiting from French social security, particularly health care. This legislation immediately opened a rift in the new French cabinet between the hard line Minister of the Interior, Pasqua, and the more liberal-republican Minister of Social Affairs, Simone Weil, who argued successfully that emergency medical care should not be denied to foreigners. Such disputes over the social rights of immigrants and the public finance dimensions of uncontrolled migration run parallel to debates in the United States, where the governors of California and Florida have brought suits against the federal government to seek compensation for the costs to the states of illegal immigration. The Pasqua initiative also echoes proposition 187 in California. Adopted by referendum in November 1994, proposition 187 promises to roll back social rights for illegal immigrants. *Pasqua II* also limits the civil rights of immigrants and asylum seekers, by increasing the powers of the police and the administration to detain and deport unwanted migrants. Under the new policy, the police are given sweeping powers to check the identity of 'suspicious persons.' Race is not supposed to be sufficient grounds for stopping an individual, but any immigrant (legal or otherwise) who threatens 'public order' can be arrested and deported. Immigrant workers and students are obliged to wait two years, rather than one, before being allowed to bring their families to join them in France, and illegal immigrants cannot be legalized simply by marrying a French citizen. Under this policy, mayors are given the power to nullify a suspicious marriage (*mariage blanc*), and anyone who is deported for whatever reason is automatically denied the right to re-enter the country for a period of one year. Finally, *Pasqua II* resurrected the Chirac government's proposal to reform French nationality law (1986). The children of foreigners born in France are required to file a formal request for naturalization, between the ages of 16 and 21, rather than having French citizenship automatically attributed to them at age 18.

These repressive measures, which were designed specifically to roll back the civil and social rights of foreigners, immigrants, and asylum seekers, immediately drew fire from those institutions of the liberal and republican state that were created to protect the rights of individuals. The Council of State, as it had done several times before (see above), warned the government that it was on shaky legal ground, especially with respect to the 'rights' of family reunification and political asylum. But the rulings of the Council of State are advisory, and no matter how much weight they may carry (morally, politically, and legally), the government can choose to ignore them.[44] The rulings, however, can presage binding decisions of the Constitutional Council, which has limited powers of judicial review. This is precisely what happened in August 1993, as the Constitutional Council found several provisions of the new policy (*Pasqua II*) to be unconstitutional. Specifically, the one-year exclusion from French territory of anyone deported, the new restrictions on family reunification, and tighter controls on marriages between French nationals and foreigners were declared unconstitutional. Key republican principles (universalist and nationalist) as enshrined in the Declaration of the Rights of Man and the Citizen, such as the equality of everyone before the law, were cited in the ruling as grounds for rejecting certain aspects of the government's policy. The ruling also raised questions about asylum policy and about the constitutionality of France's participation in Schengen (see above), since the Preamble of the 1946 Constitution requires French authorities to consider *all* demands for political asylum. This would presumably have prohibited French authorities from summarily refusing to hear asylum cases of individuals who had been refused asylum in another EU country (as both the Schengen and Dublin texts stipulate).[45]

All of this political and legal maneuvering in 1993 led inexorably to a full dress, constitutional debate over immigration and refugee policy in France. The President, François Mitterrand, who had considerable constitutional responsibilities, as well as political and moral authority, stayed for the most part on the political sidelines. The Minister of the Interior, Charles Pasqua, continued doggedly to pursue more restrictionist immigration and naturalization policies, at the levels of both symbolic and electoral politics. Any political victories on this front would seem to come at the expense of the principal rivals of the RPR–UDF, namely the FN on the right and the Socialist Party on the left. Pasqua decided to force the constitutional issue by calling for a constitutional amendment to clarify the legality of France's participation in Schengen; that is, the authority of the government to refuse to hear asylum cases already decided or under consideration in other EC states. An amendment to the constitution was passed in January 1994. Pasqua denounced the interference of the Constitutional Council in the government's immigration policy, calling it 'government by judges' and pointing out that such meddling is an affront to the principle of popular sovereignty and the power of parliament.[46]

These policy and political responses to the migration crisis in France constitute a tacit recognition that there is only so much any state can do to alter push–pull forces, and that a 'roll back' of civil and social rights is the most effective way to control or stop immigration. But in France, as in the USA and Germany, administrative and executive authorities are confronted with a range of constitutional obstacles, associated with the liberal and republican state. The republican model, with its universalist and egalitarian principles, remains essentially intact, despite repeated assaults from the French right. France still has the most expansive naturalization policies of any state in Western Europe (quite similar to the USA), and it has preserved the principles of *jus soli*, as well as due process and equality before the law. Whether the republican model will survive the current assault and whether it can serve as a broader European model remains to be seen.[47]

Germany

Until recently, debates over immigration and refugee policy in Germany were confined to policy and administrative elites, or academic and intellectual circles. But in the late 1980s, and especially since unification, politicians have seized on the immigration and refugee issue. A full blown national debate has erupted, with politicians vying for mass support, and various social movements on the left and the right seeking to influence policy making.[48] Unlike France – where there has been a consensus on the republican model, at least until recently – Germany does not have a ready-made 'national model' around which to organize the immigration/integration debate, despite a long history of absorbing migrants from around Europe: Lutherans from Austria; Huguenots from France; Jews from East and Central Europe.[49] The old *völkisch* (national) models, associated with the first German unification and the Kaiserreich, are unacceptable to the vast majority of the political and policy elite, because of the crimes committed by the Nazis in the name of the *Volks-*

gemeinschaft. This does not mean, however, that debates over immigration, naturalization, and refugee law are devoid of ethno-nationalist or ethno-cultural arguments. The current German nationality law dates from 1913, so there are clear historical and national overtones in the debate.[50] But the experience of the Holocaust and the defeat suffered in the Second World War makes it difficult for German authorities to appeal to the past (or some founding national myth) as a way of coping with immigration.

The particularist approach to issues of citizenship and naturalization, which stresses blood (*jus sanguinis*) rather than territory or birthright citizenship (*jus soli*), and which dates from the 1913 law, was combined under the laws of the Federal Republic with an expansive, universalist, liberal-republican approach to control (via the liberal asylum provision – Article 16 – of the Basic Law). Here we can see a combination of the old *völkisch* traditions with a new liberal and republican political culture, or what Jürgen Habermas and others have called 'constitutional patriotism.'[51] This anomaly put postwar German governments of the left (SPD) and the right (CDU) into the odd situation of letting many foreigners in, but then being unable and unwilling to naturalize and assimilate the newcomers. Problems that arose were finessed by appealing to the only founding myth or quasi-national model available; that is, the model of the *Wirtschaftswunder,* the great economic miracle of the 1950s, which in the eyes of many Germans helped to stabilize the fledgling democracy of the Bonn Republic and which was used to justify the importation of large numbers of guest-workers. This same model was used again by Helmut Kohl and his government to justify a rapid process of unification and absorption of the old German Democratic Republic. But economic symbols or myths (for example, it has been said that the deutschmark is the German national flag) could not be used indefinitely to manage the migration crisis. Until 1989, a consensus existed among political and policy elites simply to avoid debates over immigration, naturalization, and citizenship. Foreigners were granted social and (some) civil rights, but barriers to naturalization remained high (often justified in the liberal or pluralist terms of avoiding 'Germanization' of the foreign population); and the politically explosive issue of reforming the nationality code was avoided by insisting that there was no problem because *Deutschland ist kein Einwanderungsland* (Germany is not an immigration country).[52]

This ostrich-like approach to immigration policy and the elite consensus not to raise the issue simply fell apart under the pressure of events in the 1980s. Decades of repressed nationalism have come bubbling to the surface in contemporary party politics. The first real attempt to address the reality of a large and growing foreign population came in the 1979 Kuhn Memorandum, which was the published report of a special commission created by the SPD government of Helmut Schmidt to study the problem. The Kuhn report argued for a lowering of the barriers to naturalization, in order to facilitate assimilation of second-generation immigrants.[53] But no action was taken, in part because other issues seemed more pressing in the early 1980s, especially the installation of American intermediate range nuclear missiles on German soil and impending recession. This was the period of the rise of social movements, coalescing around peace and environmental issues, and leading to the establishment of the Green Party, which split the German left. The SPD government of Helmut Schmidt fell in 1982, and the immigration issue was used by the right (CDU–CSU) to attack the Social Democrats, especially in state and local elections. Polls, which showed rising opposition to immigration, encouraged politicians to take up the issue. When Helmut Kohl was chosen to head the new government, he introduced a new *Ausländerpolitik*, but in the election campaign of 1982–3 the issue simply disappeared from the national agenda. In effect, policy and political elites decided to return to the earlier consensus of silence. Also during this period of growing economic crisis and rising unemployment, there was another appeal to the founding economic myth of the Federal Republic, the *Wirtschaftswunder*. This national shibboleth suggests that seemingly intractable social, economic, and even political problems can be solved by another German economic miracle. But this economic solution proved insufficient to solve the problems of immigration control and assimilation, especially with rising unemployment rates and severe housing shortages. By the mid to late 1980s, foreigners were increasingly being blamed for taking jobs, housing, and public services away from German citizens.[54]

In the Bavarian *Landtag* elections of 1986, the CSU raised the issue of immigration control, in part to counter the breakaway of a small faction of the party, under the leadership of a former talk show host, Franz Schönhuber. This faction became the *Republikaner* party, and it gained 3 percent of the vote. In the following years the *Republikaner* continued to make inroads at the level of state and local politics. It received 7.5 percent of the vote in the Berlin elections of early 1989, and it won 7.1 percent of the vote in the European elections of 1990. But it could not pass the 5 percent hurdle to gain representation in the Bundestag. With the collapse of the DDR and the unification of Germany in 1989–90, it appeared that the *Republikaner* had lost its appeal. It received only 2.1 percent of the vote in the first all-German federal election in 1990. But its fortunes were to improve in the early 1990s, especially in the *Landtag* elections for Baden-Württemberg in 1992, when it scored almost 12 percent of the vote.[55] Clearly, with the collapse of communism and the end of the Cold War, some of the restraints on overt expressions of German nationalism were removed, and the immigration issue was no longer taboo. A new anti-foreigner slogan, *Ausländer raus*, became the rallying cry of far right, skinhead, and neo-Nazi groups. The massive influx of asylum seekers from 1989 to 1993 contributed to the atmosphere of crisis, placing more pressure on the government to act, and making it easier for politicians (of the right) to use the immigration and asylum issue to get votes.

In 1990, the newly re-elected government of Helmut Kohl faced two problems: (a) how to facilitate the integration and naturalization of the large foreign population, without alienating more of the right-wing electorate; and (b) how to build a consensus for changing Article 16 of the German Constitution to stem the rising tide of asylum seekers, while keeping the front door open to ethnic German refugees from the East. The first task was at least partially accomplished by rushing a bill through parliament to facilitate naturalization (*erleichterte Einbürgerung*) of second-generation immigrants, thereby solidifying the rights of resident aliens, and removing some of the legal ambiguities concerning residency, work permits, and family reunification.[56] This was done quietly in the midst of the social and political euphoria following unification. Another little noticed aspect of the reforms of the early 1990s was the quiet opening of side doors through which over 250,000 new guestworkers (largely Poles) found employment in Germany in 1992 as seasonal and frontier workers, subcontract employees, and apprentices.[57] These changes were made despite record levels of unemployment, which continued to rise as a consequence of unification and recession.

Reform of immigration and refugee policy was given a new urgency in 1992 and 1993 by a series of much publicized racist attacks against foreigners, including a fire bombing by skinheads in the town of Solingen, which resulted in the death of five Turks, who were permanent residents of the Federal Republic. More attacks on foreigners occurred, however, just weeks after the Christian–Liberal government and the Social Democrats agreed in May 1993 to amend Article 16 of the Constitution. Although the language of the new asylum law, which states that 'those politically persecuted enjoy the right to asylum,' is consistent with the Geneva Convention, in practice the new law allows the German government to turn back asylum seekers who arrive through a safe country, while continuing to accept ethnic German refugees from East and Central Europe.[58] Since about 80 percent of non-German refugees enter through Poland and the Czech Republic, an agreement had to be reached with these states to allow for the *refoulement* of asylum seekers. To gain the cooperation of these neighboring states, the German government agreed to pick up the tab (to the tune of tens of millions of dollars) for the shelter and care of these unwanted migrants, and to assist Poland and the Czech Republic in improving border surveillance.[59] Within a matter of months, the official tally of asylum seekers fell from over 30,000 per month in June 1993 to less than 15,000 by September 1993, and it was approximately 8000 per month in the first six months of 1994.[60] It is unclear how many of these *refoulés*, once deported, try to slip back across the German border. But, since the new policy was instituted, the number of migrants apprehended trying to enter the country illegally has sky-rocketed;

and Polish and Czech border guards have shown little enthusiasm for their task of helping German authorities to seal the borders (much like Mexican police along the US–Mexican border). The outbreak of civil war in Bosnia compounded German problems, inasmuch as Germany is a natural destination for many Croatian and Bosnian refugees, who may already have relatives in Germany because of earlier waves of migration from Yugoslavia during the guestworker period. In February 1994, following a meeting of the interior ministers of the *Länder*, expulsion orders for over 100,000 Croatian refugees in Germany were cancelled for legal and humanitarian reasons. Repatriation of Croatians will take place in stages over a long period of time, to avoid a humanitarian crisis.[61]

Despite a great deal of rhetoric following racial violence and fatal attacks on foreigners in 1993 and 1994, the Christian–Liberal government of Helmut Kohl was unable to change German nationality law, which dates from 1913 and rests on the principle of *jus sanguinis* (blood rather than soil or place of birth). The German law also does not allow dual citizenship. Hence, millions of foreign residents have been granted some civil and social rights, but without naturalization. They remain outsiders without full political rights, even though in many cases they have been born, reared, and educated in Germany. Fully two-thirds of the foreign population have lived in Germany for more than ten years, and 80 percent of those under 18 were born in Germany.[62] With the second all-German federal elections approaching at the time of writing, it seems unlikely that the controversial citizenship issue will be addressed, and Germany will remain without an immigration policy, and without a national model for integrating its large foreign population.

Great Britain

Political pressures to reform British immigration policy increased in 1968 following a series of speeches made by the Tory politician, Enoch Powell, who warned of 'rivers of blood' if something was not done to control immigration. The Conservative government, under the leadership of Edward Heath, responded with the passage of the Immigration Act 1971, which dramatically increased the power of the government (especially the Home Secretary) to control immigration. This was the first step in a series of reforms designed to limit coloured or non-white immigration and to back away from the expansive, imperialist concept of citizenship, *Civis Britannicus Sum*. But the 1971 Act did not prevent an influx of 'British Asians' from East Africa in 1972 (the Uganda crisis) and from Malawi in 1976. Support for Powell and the National Front continued to increase in the 1970s, leading the Conservative Party in its election manifesto of 1979 to propose a complete overhaul of British nationality law. Margaret Thatcher was elected leader of the Conservatives in 1975, and she was quite vocal in her support for immigration reform. In 1978 she laid the groundwork for this policy shift by pointing out the 'legitimate fears of our own people that they will be swamped' by too many immigrants.[63]

Once in power, the Conservative government moved to fulfill its campaign promises, by abandoning the feudal and imperial concept of a 'British subject' and replacing it with a kind of gradational citizenship, which would allow for a separate citizenship of the UK, but without completely severing the links between Britain and its former colonies. The British Nationality Act (BNA) of 1981 created three categories of citizenship: British Citizenship, Citizenship of the Dependent Territories, and British Overseas Citizenship.[64] The contrast with French nationality law is quite stark. Because of the strong universalist and republican ideology of citizenship, French authorities were unable and unwilling simply to revoke the citizenship of Franco-Algerians born in Algeria prior to independence in 1962. British authorities felt no legal or ideological compulsion to maintain the citizenship rights of immigrants from the Commonwealth, except for patrials, that is people who were born in Britain, who had a parent or grandparent born in Britain, or who had been resident in Britain for five years. In effect, the BNA codified an ethnic or national origins quota system, whereby millions of Australians, South Africans, New Zealanders, and Canadians (whites) were granted the right of unrestricted entry and settlement in the UK. But nationals from 'New Commonwealth' states of the Caribbean and Indian subcontinent (coloured people or blacks, meaning Asians and Afro-Caribbeans) found their rights of entry and settlement severely restricted. Some exceptions were made for nationals of British Dependent Territories, especially the Hong Kong Chinese. In 1989, the government agreed to grant rights of entry and settlement to 50,000 'key personnel' and their families from Hong Kong.

One of the immediate effects of this shift in British policy was to solidify an emerging pluralist or multicultural model, which recognizes the distinctiveness of ethnic minorities within British society and in the Commonwealth. Riots in 1981, especially in Liverpool and Brixton in London, pushed the issue of race relations to the forefront of the political agenda. The Commission for Racial Equality and special commissions like the Snowden Commission were set up by Parliament to deal with racial prejudice, and to pursue reconciliation between blacks and whites. The Race Relations Act of 1976 makes it illegal to discriminate on the grounds of color or racial origin in employment or recruitment practices.[65] This 'accommodationist' or pluralist approach to race relations constitutes a distinctly British approach (which has some similarities with civil rights policies in the USA) to the problems of assimilation. But neither a willingness to integrate the foreign population nor changes in immigration and naturalization policy (the BNA) have substantially altered the flow of immigrants into Britain, which has remained at about 50,000 to 60,000 annually. As in other West European states, requests for political asylum have been rising, reaching a peak of 56,000 in 1991, comparable to France but much lower than in Germany. Only 3 percent of these unwanted migrants are actually granted asylum, and the vast majority are able to remain illegally in the UK. The current population of illegal immigrants is estimated to be around 100,000.[66] All of these numbers – modest as they are by American and West European standards – led Winston Churchill, an MP and grandson of the former British leader, to speak of the 'relentless flow' of immigrants into Britain.[67] Still, the issue of immigration has not broken on to the agenda of national politics, as it has in France and Germany.

Southern Europe

The countries of Southern Europe – Italy, Spain, Greece, and Portugal – are still far from developing national models for immigration control and assimilation. As the traditional receiving states in Northern Europe tried to close their borders to new immigration in the 1970s and 1980s, more unwanted migrants (especially from Africa) began to enter the European Community via the soft underbelly of Italy, Spain, and Greece. Political change (democratization in Greece, Spain, and Portugal) together with high levels of economic growth contributed to the influx of unwanted migrants. Policy responses have lurched from one extreme to another, in the face of a growing political backlash against foreigners, especially in northern Italy, where the anti-immigrant *Lega Nord/ Lega Lombarda* has been getting about one-fifth of the vote in recent elections. Amnesty was extended to illegal immigrants in Spain (1985) and Italy (1987) in the hope of bringing marginal groups and ethnic minorities into the mainstream of society, offering protection under the rubric of social welfare. But the push to establish a border-free Europe, as a result of the Single European Act (1985), the Schengen Agreement, and finally the Maastricht Treaty, which holds out the prospect in the next century of a kind of European citizenship, has forced the states of Southern Europe to reformulate their immigration and refugee policies. To be a part of a border-free Europe, they must demonstrate a capacity for controlling their borders, and stopping illegal immigration.[68]

Conclusion

The perceived failure of national policies and the lack of a dominant national model for dealing with the migration crisis have led the states of Western Europe, especially Germany, to look for a Europe-wide solution to the problem of immigration control. The hope here is that together the states of the European Union will be able to accomplish what they have been unable to accomplish alone: stop immigration. A common solution could also help these states to avoid or postpone difficult debates (*à l'americain*) over multiculturalism and the rights of ethnic groups.

The weight of the American model

Despite attempts by politicians and policy makers to stop immigration and bury the issue of ethnic politics, the 'American model' is omnipresent in contemporary policy and political debates in Western Europe. How can we define this model *vis-à-vis* the other national models described above? Is it still an exceptional model, as Alexis de Tocqueville, Gunnar Myrdal, Louis Hartz, Robert Dahl, Seymour Martin Lipset, and Lawrence Fuchs, to name but a few, have suggested? What is the importance of this model which many European scholars, intellectuals, and pundits have denounced as a kind of 'multicultural dumping ground,'[69] which promotes the special interests of ethnic and religious minorities, to the detriment of the general interest.[70] What are the connections between the American postwar experience with immigration and ethnicity, and the experiences of other liberal democracies? What is the impact of the American model on the evolution of this global phenomenon (see above) and on the prospects for the development of 'international regimes' for dealing with migration?[71] To offer what will necessarily be a schematic answer to these important questions, we must first recognize – following the diagram and discussion at the beginning of this chapter – that the American *multicultural* model is first and foremost a product of the civil rights movement of the 1950s and 1960s, which led to a break with the older (more racist and ethnocentric) tradition of the melting pot.[72]

The civil rights movement was supposed to resolve the most difficult dilemma of American citizenship, namely the status of black people, or as they are now called (in politically correct parlance), African-Americans. The movement transformed the American political landscape, not only for this specific ethnic minority, but for all marginal/minority groups. It raised political consciousness on the issues of prejudice and discrimination across the board, and thereby contributed heavily to a change in American jurisprudence. This sea change in American politics and law also transformed immigration policy and law.[73] The most important postwar reform of American immigration policy, the Immigration Act of 1965, was passed just after the adoption in Congress of the Civil Rights Act of 1964. The 1965 Act put an end to the invidious national origins quota system, which discriminated against immigrants on the basis of race and ethnicity. But even more importantly from the standpoint of immigration control and integration, the civil rights movement expanded and redefined citizenship in the United States. This change did not stop at American borders; it was felt throughout the international system, because of the influence of American culture, norms, and values, transmitted via institutions, and disseminated by new media and information technologies.

The new American liberal-republicanism went beyond classical contractarian definitions of citizenship (à la John Locke or John Stuart Mill) to embrace a more universalistic, rights-based view of citizenship (to the detriment of privilege and responsibility).[74] The new liberal-republicanism is founded on a jurisprudence which stresses due process and equality before the law (Fourteenth Amendment to the Constitution). This shift in American law places procedure at the heart of the relationship between the individual and the state, and greatly reinforces the power of judges. Although American politics had been slowly moving in this direction since the end of the Civil War, it would be almost a century before the new liberal-republicanism would be institutionalized (in the 1950s and 1960s) at the height of the Cold War. At the same time that the American state and society were grappling with the dilemma of citizenship for blacks, immigration policy was undergoing a profound transformation, which would lead to the fourth great wave of immigration in American history: 2.5 million newcomers in the decade of the 1950s, 3.8 million in the 1960s, 7 million in the 1970s, and over 10 million in the 1980s.[75] The adoption of the 1965 Act led to a dramatic increase in family immigration, especially from Asia and Latin America. Legal immigration increased rapidly, and federal judges began to give very expansive (liberal and republican) interpretations of immigration and refugee law, applying civil rights law to migration issues.[76]

With few exceptions, subsequent reforms of immigration law and policy in the 1980s and 1990s have reflected this new liberal-republican consensus. The first sign of a shift away from this consensus would not come until 1994, with the passage in California of an anti-immigrant ballot initiative, known as proposition 187. The expansive interpretation of the rights of migrants stimulated legal and illegal immigration, while giving greater legitimacy to the political activities of ethnic minorities. African-Americans, Hispanics, and Asians found new means of political expression and were able to shape their own ethnic or group identities, through interaction with the state and political institutions.[77] It is important to recognize the important role of courts in this change, and the rise of a new legal culture in the United States. In effect the courts acted to constrain administrative and executive powers of the state(s). In an important decision, *Plyler* v. *Doe*, the Supreme Court ordered the state of Texas to allow the children of illegal aliens to attend public schools – a decision that has been directly challenged by the passage of proposition 187 in California, which would deny education to the children of illegals living in that state. In writing for the majority in the *Plyler* case, former Justice Harry Blackmun argued that children of illegals (some of whom are actually US citizens because they were born on American soil) should not be held accountable for the crimes of their parents. Peter Schuck argues that this decision concerning the rights of immigrants is equivalent to the famous civil rights ruling, *Brown* v. *Board of Education* in 1954, which marked the beginning of the end of segregation and apartheid in the USA.[78] This is the decision that Vice President Nixon referred to as a great victory in the Cold War struggle against communism (see above), illustrating the very close connection between the struggle to construct American citizenship on a firmer liberal and republican basis and American foreign policy. The bipolar dynamic in international relations from 1950 to 1990 contributed to the strength of the liberal-republican consensus for expanding citizenship.

But what are the attributes of the American model, and how have they influenced immigration policy? Are they *sui generis*? We can see some of the exceptional qualities of the American political and legal system – greater propensity for judicial activism, or as Tocqueville called it, 'government by judges;' but if we look at the outcomes of immigration policy in Western Europe and the United States, they are remarkably similar.[79] Despite efforts to control and restrict immigration, beginning in the 1970s, flows have remained at historically high levels, thereby feeding the migration crisis. From the standpoint of comparative method, even though the American model (or case) may be different from the French, German, or British models (cases), there is an overriding global dynamic (markets and rights) which is driving these population movements (see the model at the beginning of this chapter). It is also possible that the differences between these national models is not as great as we might be led to think by some of the more conventional literature in comparative and international politics. For example, if we examine the specificities of the American model, we can see that some of them are replicated in other national models.

First is the American system of separation of powers, which, through the process of judicial review, gives judges a kind of veto over public policy. This fundamental feature of American politics helps to explain the course of the civil rights movement, and the rise of liberal-republicanism. But we can see much the same institutional dynamic (expanding rights) at work in France and Germany.[80] Both the French and German Republics have some measure of separation of powers, as well as judicial review. Moreover, as citizenship and membership have expanded in each of these republican systems (thanks in part to active judiciaries), so too has the level of associational and political activity among immigrant and minority groups. Tocqueville argued that a propensity to form associations was one of the most exceptional qualities of American democracy.[81]

The second special attribute of the American model was also correctly (and somewhat prophetically) identified by Tocqueville, namely the injustice associated with slavery, which abolitionists like Frederick Douglas equated with original sin. The American Republic was founded on a contradiction: equality before the law (*l'état de droit* or *Rechtsstaat*) for all members of society except blacks. Concerning this peculiarity of American democracy, Tocqueville predicted that 'if ever America undergoes great revolutions, they will be brought about by the presence of the black race . . . that is to say, they will owe their origin, not to the equality, but to the inequality of condition.'[82] This is precisely what happened in the Civil War, and again in the civil rights movement of the 1950s and 1960s. These turning points in the evolution of the American model completely changed attitudes toward citizenship.[83] It is debatable whether other liberal republics have been marked by such a traumatic past, but we can find some similarities with the American experience if we look at the history of racism and violence in France (associated with fascism and Vichy, as well as colonialism and the struggles over decolonization in Algeria) and in Germany (associated with Nazism and the Holocaust). In all three cases, hideous crimes were committed in the name of the nation and the 'people.' These crimes of the French and German past helped to transform the politics of the present and the future, leading in each case to constitutional and institutional reforms. The often violent struggles to achieve these reforms mark a turning point in the history of immigration and refugee policy in France and Germany. French immigration and refugee policy was established in the *Ordonnances* of 1945, in the wake of Vichy and Liberation; whereas the liberal German asylum policy was written into the Basic Law (article 16) with the founding of the Bundesrepublik in 1949, and remained unchanged until 1993 because it was perceived as an atonement for the crimes of the Third Reich. Amending the article was extremely difficult in large part because it was felt among many political actors that this would be reneging on the longstanding commitment of the West German regime to overcome the fascist past. My basic point is that other liberal republics share a checkered history with the United States with respect to civil and human rights; and their histories have intensified debates about the rights of minorities in the contemporary period.

The third attribute of the American model, which is most often cited as a major difference from any of the West European models, arises from what Tocqueville called a 'founding myth' of the republic, namely the fact that the United States is a 'nation of immigrants,' founded on a multicultural and multiethnic basis, and therefore more tolerant of newcomers than the 'older,' more established nation states of Western Europe. Many scholars draw a sharp distinction between nations of immigrants and countries of immigration.[84] The practical import of this myth is that legal immigration has much greater legitimacy in a nation of immigrants than in a non-immigrant society. But as Martin Schain and others have noted, the development and legitimation of this American myth, which is bound up with notions of the melting pot and *e pluribus unum*, were very difficult; and there were periods of American history when American immigration policy was shot through with nativism and racism.[85] Moreover, in the history of polling in the USA on the issue of immigration, never more than 10 percent of the American public have supported an expansive immigration policy.[86] Nevertheless, historically immigration has been viewed as a constitutive element of nation building in the United States (or as a settlement policy for the North American continent), rather than as a destabilizing force in American political and social history.

In the current (1990s) debate over immigration policy, we can see sharply contrasting views over the costs and benefits of immigration to the American society and economy. The libertarian economist, Julian Simon, argues that immigration has been a tremendous boon to the American economy, and therefore governments should not intervene with the basic market mechanisms that determine levels of immigration. Simon uses the long history of the USA as a nation of immigrants in order to justify his argument for relatively open borders.[87] The contrasting view is best represented by a labor economist, George Borjas, who argues that the 'ethnic capital' of today's immigrants is much lower than in previous waves. Therefore, it is incumbent upon the federal government to control the borders, stop illegal immigration (especially from the poorer countries of Latin America), and select more carefully legal immigrants according to strict human or ethnic capital criteria.[88] Borjas is challenging the powerful historical myth of the USA as a nation of immigrants, with a tradition of openness, best symbolized by the inscription on the Statue of Liberty: 'Give me your poor, your tired, your hungry.'[89]

On a more political and historical note, Lawrence Fuchs argues that American society is founded upon the notion of *e pluribus unum*, and immigration has contributed to and reinforced the civic culture, from the moment of the founding to the present. At different times in American history, more stress has been placed on the *unum* or the *pluribus*, but because of the strong republican, civic culture, the country has been able to surmount nativism and racism.[90] How unique is this American tradition of immigration and its accompanying myths? If we look only at France and Germany, we can see that these are societies and nation states which also were heavily shaped by immigration.[91] But unlike in the United States, immigration was not part of a founding myth, because the great periods of immigration came after the formation of the nation and the state. This has made it difficult for France to sustain and legitimate legal immigration policies, although France has a long history of immigration and a strong republican tradition.[92] In Germany, on the other hand, there is a conscious dissociation of immigration from the nation state, beginning in the Second Reich and continuing in the Bundesrepublik (*Deutschland ist kein Einwanderungsland*). Yet there is considerable pressure in contemporary Germany to adopt a legal immigration policy, and to ease restrictions on naturalization.[93] Clearly, in the postwar period immigration has become an integral feature of political, social, and economic development in all three states – the USA, France, and Germany.

Finally, following the arguments of Michael Teitelbaum,[94] we can identify a fourth attribute of the American model: the (until recently) relatively strong consensus between the left and the right on maintaining an expansive legal immigration policy. This consensus, between the republican right, which has been for most of the postwar period strongly attached to the principle of economic liberalism and free trade, and the democratic left, which has been (and still is) strongly committed to political liberalism, civil liberties, and civil rights, has helped to maintain relatively open borders. Furthermore, it is this coalition of 'strange bedfellows' (pro-business, free traders on the right and civil rights activists on the left) which pushed through the 1965 Immigration Act, as well as the 1986 Immigration Reform and Control Act (IRCA), and the 1990 Act reforming legal immigration policy.[95] This coalition of American political and economic liberals reflects very well the dynamic of *markets and rights*, depicted in Figure 2.1; and it is a reflection of what I have called elsewhere the 'paradox of liberalism' or the desire to maintain an open economic system (free trade and free movement of productive factors, capital, and labor) while granting rights to all 'members' of society.[96] The European Union, with its contradictory logics of inclusion and exclusion, clearly has been forced to struggle with this paradox. It is safe to say that in an increasingly interdependent international system, founded on liberal principles of free trade and human rights, few states can escape this paradox. Hence this last attribute of the American model is far from unique. How states respond to this paradox is, of course, very much dependent upon their institutions, as well as their political and legal cultures.

One way in which the advanced industrial democracies have tried to respond to the somewhat contradictory dynamic of markets and rights has been to seek regional solutions, and to construct international regimes to manage increased flows of goods, services, capital, and people. Having set in motion a liberal process of globalization of markets and rights, with the establishment of the United Nations and the Bretton Woods system (including GATT and the IMF) immediately following the Second World War, the United States in effect exported the American model.[97] The creation of the European Community was in part a response to the globalization of markets, and the rise of American (and Soviet) power in the 1950s and 1960s.[98] The European project was to create a common market and gradually eliminate internal borders, to permit the free movement of goods, capital, and people. The first two tasks have been largely accomplished with the ratification of the Single European Act in 1986 and the Maastricht Treaty in 1993; but allowing the free movement of people has been accomplished *de facto*, but not *de jure*. The reasons for this reside in the difficulties of achieving immigration control, which require a common visa and asylum policy.

Conclusion: prospects for a European solution to a global problem

From the Treaty of Rome (1957) to the Maastricht Treaty, which was ratified in 1993 by the UK – the twelfth and final member of the European Community to do so – the logic of European integration has driven the states of Western Europe to cooperate on border control issues. The logic is one of inclusion (free movement of goods, services, capital, *and people*) and exclusion (a common tariff policy, an economic and monetary union, and common visa and asylum policies). The goal of creating a common market for goods and services has been largely accomplished, thanks in part to new life that was breathed into the enterprise of European integration in the mid-1980s by the Single European Act. Likewise, despite recent setbacks with the virtual collapse of the Exchange Rate Mechanism (ERM) in 1992–3, economic and monetary union (EMU) has been kept on track by the final passage of the Maastricht Treaty. But common visa and asylum policies have proved illusive. The prospect of a truly border-free Europe places enormous pressure on member states to cooperate in the policing of external borders.

Control over population and territory are key aspects of national sovereignty, which strike at the heart of notions of citizenship and national identity. Ceding this aspect of sovereignty to a supranational organization such as the European Union is a potentially explosive political issue. For this reason, member states, as well as the European Council and the Commission, have proceeded with great caution. In Dublin in 1990, the European Council established the principle that refugees can apply for political asylum in only one member state. Shortly thereafter, the Schengen Group, which had been enlarged from the original five (France, Germany, and Benelux) to include Italy, Spain, and Portugal, met to sign the Convention that set in motion a process for lifting all border controls among these states. Britain, as an island nation, steadfastly refused to get involved in the Schengen process, for fear of losing its natural advantage in border control.[99] Still the inclusionary and exclusionary logic of Schengen seems to be taking hold in post-Cold War Europe, as other states and regions (particularly the EFTA and Scandinavian states) have scrambled to join the border-free club, creating a larger European Economic Area (EEA). Only Switzerland and Denmark have been reluctant to jump on the border-free bandwagon.

The exclusionary logic is at least as powerful as the inclusionary dynamic. No state wants to be left on the periphery of a border-free Europe, because it will become by definition a 'buffer state' where unwanted migrants will be *refoulés*. With the end of the Cold War, the newly liberated states of Central Europe – Poland, Hungary, and the Czech Republic – have fallen into this trap. Because of the increased labor and refugee migrations across East and Central Europe, these states have become way stations to Western Europe, repositories for unwanted migrants and *refoulés* (especially gypsies), and in some cases they have become the countries of destination. Polish authorities estimate that there are about 200,000 nationals of what was the Soviet Union residing in Poland. The potential for further (supply-push) emigration from the successor states of the USSR – should economic conditions in Russia and the Ukraine continue to deteriorate – is enormous. With over 26 million ethnic Russians living outside of Russia, the chances are high for further displacements and larger population movements from East to West.[100] The disintegration of Yugoslavia is viewed as a harbinger of things to come. This does not mean, however, that East–West movements will be more important than South–North movements. The rise of Islamic fundamentalism and civil disorder in relatively secular societies, such as Egypt and Algeria, which have large and potentially mobile populations, will place increasing pressure on all the states of Western and Central Europe.

How will 'Europe' respond to the global migration crisis? We can learn some things by looking at the recent past, especially the liberal dynamic of *markets* (demand-pull and supply-push) and the liberal-republican dynamic of *rights* (civil, social, and political) described above. We must also compare the European and American experiences, because the European Union and the United States will be the pacesetters in searching for an international solution to the global migration crisis. Will there be an American or European (French, German, British?) model for coping with migration, or will the two models converge? The liberal dynamic and the recent past point to convergence. With the end of the Cold War, all of the OECD states have experienced an upsurge in migration because (happily) people are freer to move, and (sadly) ethnic and nationalist forces have been unleashed, causing a wave of refugee migration. The liberal logic of interdependence and economic integration (European Union, NAFTA, and GATT) has reinforced the propensity of people to move, in search of higher wages and a better standard of living. Supply-push remains strong, but demand-pull is weak. Most of the OECD states are in (or just emerging from) recession. Nevertheless, with slower population growth, especially in Western Europe and Japan, and higher levels of economic growth, as we move closer to the turn of the century demand for immigrant labor is likely to increase. The necessary (economic) conditions for immigration are present and likely to strengthen; hence all of the OECD states will be forced to deal with this reality.[101] But what will political conditions in the receiving states, which are the sufficient conditions for immigration, be like?

At present, it would appear that the politics of xenophobia, nativism, and restrictionism prevail; and that each state is defining immigration and refugee policies in idiosyncratic and nationalist terms. The rights of immigrants and refugees have been restricted and infringed in Europe and the United States, as governments (freed from the bipolar constraints of the Cold War) have sought to roll back some of the liberal-republican political developments (especially in the area of civil rights and civil liberties) of the past forty years. But liberal-republican institutions and laws (often written into the constitutions of OECD states) are quite resilient. It seems unlikely that what have come to be defined as basic human or civil rights (equality before the law, due process, and the like) will simply be suspended for non-citizens. Therefore, the sufficient conditions for immigration, which are closely linked to the institutions and laws of the liberal-republican state, are likely to persist, even if they are weakened by attacks from the extreme right and lack of popular support. It is also unlikely that liberal-republicanism will be abandoned or overridden by supranational institutions, such as the European Union. The same institutional and legal checks found at the level of the nation state are evident at the European level (for example, the Court of Human Rights and the European Court of Justice).

Since immigration is likely to continue, pressure will mount for states to cooperate in controlling and managing the flow. The states of Western Europe have already taken several steps in this direction at the level of the European Union. But no national or regional model for integration of the large and growing foreign populations has emerged. Setting policies for controlling the doors of entry (front, side, and back) will come, barring some unforeseen international catastrophe. Redefining citizenship and nationhood in the older states of Western Europe, however, will be a much longer and more painful process. It remains to be seen which states are best equipped, politically and culturally, to face this challenge.

Notes

1. For a history of nationalism and the various ideologies associated with it in modern Europe, see E.J. Hobsbawm, *Nations and Nationalism since 1780* (Cambridge: Cambridge University Press, 1990).
2. For an overview of the global migration crisis, see Wayne A. Cornelius, Philip L. Martin, and James F. Hollifield, *Controlling Immigration: a Global Perspective* (Stanford: Stanford University Press, 1994), and Myron Weiner, *The Global Migration Crisis* (New York: HarperCollins, 1994).
3. Cf. P.L. Martin, 'Germany: reluctant land of immigration,' in Cornelius *et al.*, *Controlling Immigration*, and Klaus J. Bade, *Vom Auswanderungsland zum Einwanderungsland? Deutschland 1880–1980* (Berlin: Colloquium Verlag, 1983).
4. On the history of immigration in France, see Gerard Noiriel, *Le creuset français: Histoire de l'immigration XIXe–XXe siècles* (Paris: Seuil, 1988) and Yves Lequin (ed.), *La mosaïque France* (Paris: Larousse, 1988).
5. On immigration and republicanism, cf. Patrick Weil, *La France et ses étrangers* (Paris: Calmann-Levy, 1991) and James F. Hollifield, 'Immigration and Republicanism in France: the hidden consensus,' in Cornelius *et al.*, *Controlling Immigration, op. cit.*
6. See J.F. Hollifield, 'Immigration and republicanism in France,' *op. cit.*, and

Andre Lebon, *Immigration et présence étrangere en France 1990/91* (Paris: La documentation Française, 1991).

7. For an overview of the British case, see Zig Layton-Henry, *The Politics of Immigration: Immigration, Race and Race Relations in Post-War Britain* (Oxford: Blackwell, 1992). On British exceptionalism, see Anthony M. Messina, 'Immigration as a political dilemma in Western Europe,' unpublished paper, presented at the European Community Studies Association (ECSA) Workshop, 'Immigration into Western Societies: Implications and Policy Choices,' Charleston, South Carolina, 13–14 May, 1994.

8. G. Cocchi (ed.), *Stranieri in Italia* (Bologna: Misure/Materiali di Ricerca dell' Istituto Cattaneo, 1990). See also Fausto D'Ambrosio, 'Cittadini extracomunitari: regolarizzazione a sanatoria tutela degli interessi e nuovi problemi,' *Codex Convegno de Studio: Applicazione della Legge Martelli*, Florence, June 22, 1991, pp. 35–41.

9. The stark contrast between the 'American model' and various national models in Europe finds its origins in the works of Alexis de Tocqueville, especially *Democracy in America*. This essentially nineteenth-century view finds a wide gap between American and European experiences with immigration. The Tocquevillian perspective has been reinforced in some of the contemporary literature on comparative immigration history. See, for example, William Safran, 'The French state and ethnic minority cultures: policy dimensions and problems,' in J.R. Rudolph and R.J. Thompson (eds), *Ethnoterritorial Politics, Policy, and the Western World* (Boulder, CO: Lynne Rienner, 1989). Also, D.L. Horowitz and G. Noiriel, *Immigrants in Two Democracies: French and American Experience* (New York: New York University Press, 1992), especially the introduction by Horowitz.

10. For a discussion of the French/American debates about immigration and ethnicity, cf. Sophie Body-Gendrot, *Ville et violence: l'irruption de nouveaux acteurs* (Paris: Presses Universitaires de France, 1993), Loic Wacquant, 'The zone,' *Les Actes de la recherche en sciences sociales*, 93, June 1992, and J.F. Hollifield, 'Entre droit et marche,' in Bertrand Badie and Catherine Wihtol de Wenden, *Le défi migratoire: questions de relations internationales* (Paris: Presses de la FNSP, 1994), pp. 59–88.

11. Mark J. Miller and Philip L. Martin, *Administering Foreign-Worker Programs* (Lexington, MA: D.C. Heath, 1982); Kitty Calavita, *Inside the State: the Bracero Program, Immigration, and the INS* (New York: Routledge, 1992); and Johannes-Dieter Steinert, *Westdeutsche Wanderungspolitik, Internationale Wanderungskooperation und Europeäische Integration 1945–1961*, unpublished doctoral dissertation, Universität Osnabrück, April, 1993. On demand-pull migration, see Thomas Straubhaar, 'The causes of international migration – a demand determined approach,' *International Migration Review*, 20 4 (1986).

12. On liberalism and international relations, cf. Robert Gilpin, *The Political Economy of International Relations* (Princeton, NJ: Princeton University Press, 1987), and Robert O. Keohane and Joseph S. Nye, *Power and Interdependence: World Politics in Transition* (Boston: Little, Brown, 1977).

13. For a comparative history of postwar immigration policy in the major receiving countries of Western Europe and the North America, see Cornelius *et al.*, *Controlling Immigration, op. cit.*

14. On supply-push, see Philip L. Martin, *The Unfinished Story: Turkish Labor Migra-*

tion to the Federal Republic of Germany (Geneva: International Labor Office, 1991) and Manuel Garcia y Griego, 'The Mexican labor supply, 1990–2010,' in W.A. Cornelius and J.A. Bustamente, *Mexican Migration to the United States: Origins, Consequences, and Policy Options* (San Diego: Center for US–Mexican Studies, University of California, San Diego, 1989), pp. 49–94.

15. For more on this argument, see James F. Hollifield, *Immigrants, Markets, and States: the Political Economy of Postwar Europe* (Cambridge, MA: Harvard University Press, 1992).

16. See Weiner, *The Global Migration Crisis, op. cit.* See also B. Badie and C. Wihtol de Wenden, *Le défi migratoire*, especially the introductory essay by Bertrand Badie.

17. This discussion of rights closely parallels that of T.H. Marshall, *Class, Citizenship, and Social Development* (Cambridge: Cambridge University Press, 1950). Cf. Bryan S. Turner (ed.), *Citizenship and Social Theory* (London: Sage, 1993). The essays in this volume expand and elaborate upon Marshall's original theoretical framework. On the importance of political rights for immigrants, see Patrick Ireland, *The Policy Challenge of Ethnic Diversity: Immigrant Politics in France and Switzerland* (Cambridge, MA: Harvard University Press, 1994).

18. See Gunnar Myrdal, *An American Dilemma: the Negro Problem and American Democracy* (New York: Harper and Row, 1962). Cf. Robert Dahl, *A Preface to Democratic Theory* (Chicago: University of Chicago Press, 1956), and an excellent essay on American liberalism by Rogers M. Smith, 'Beyond Tocqueville, Myrdal, and Hartz: the multiple traditions in America,' *American Political Science Review*, 87, 3 (September 1993), 549–66.

19. See Peter H. Schuck, 'The transformation of immigration law.' *Columbia Law Review*, 84, (January 1984), 1–90. Also, *idem*, 'The new immigration and the old civil rights,' *The American Prospect* (Fall 1993), 102–11.

20. Cf. John G. Ruggie, 'International regimes, transactions, and change: embedded liberalism in the postwar economic order,' *International Organization*, 36 (Spring 1982), 379–415; and on the concept of hegemony, see Gilpin, *The Political Economy of International Relations, op. cit.*, pp. 65 ff, and Robert O. Keohane, 'The theory of hegemonic stability and changes in international economic relations, 1967–1977,' in Ole Holsti (ed.), *Change in the International System* (Boulder, CO: Westview Press, 1980).

21. Cf. Ireland, *The Policy Challenge of Ethnic Diversity, passim*, Hans-George Betz, 'The new politics of resentment: radical right-wing populist parties in Western Europe,' *Comparative Politics*, 25, 4 (1993), 413–27, and Dietrich Thränhardt, 'Die Ursprünge von Rassismus und Fremdenfeindlichkeit in der Konkurrenzdemokratie,' *Leviathan*, 21, 3 (1993), 336–57.

22. On historical shifts in approaches and attitudes toward migration, cf. Bade, *Vom Auswanderungsland zum Einwanderungsland*, Ulrich Hebert, *A History of Foreign Labor in Germany, 1880–1980: Seasonal Workers – Forced Laborers – Guest Workers* (Ann Arbor, MI: University of Michigan Press, 1991), and Dirk Hoerder, 'People on the move: migration, acculturation, and ethnic interaction in Europe and North America,' Annual Lecture Series, German Historical Institute, Washington, DC, no. 6 (Oxford: Berg Publishers, 1993).

23. On the capacity of states to control immigration, see Cornelius *et al.*, *Controlling Immigration*, especially the introduction, and J.F. Hollifield, 'L'Etat français et l'immigration: problèmes de mise en oeuvre d'une politique publique,' *Revue française de science politique*, 42, 6 (1992), 943–63.

24. See Hans-Joachim Hoffmann-Nowotny and Karl-Otto Hondrich, *Ausländer in der BRD und in der Schweiz* (Frankfurt: Campus Verlag, 1982), and H.-J. Hoffmann-Nowotny, 'Switzerland,' in Tomas Hammar (ed.), *European Immigration Policy* (Cambridge: Cambridge University Press, 1985), pp. 206–36.

25. Thomas Straubhaar, *On the Economics of International Labor Migration* (Bern, Stuttgart: Verlag Paul Haupt, 1988), pp. 53–64. Charles P. Kindleberger, *Europe's Postwar Growth* (Cambridge, MA: Harvard University Press, 1967); and Hollifield, *Immigrants, Markets, and States, op. cit.*, pp. 99–123.

26. On this point, see P.L. Martin, 'Germany: reluctant land of immigration,' in Cornelius *et al.*, *Controlling Immigration, op. cit.*

27. See Knuth Dohse, *Ausländische Arbeiter und bürgerlicher Staat-Genese und Funktion von staatlicher Ausländerpolitik und Ausländerrecht: Kaiserreich bis zur Bundesrepublik Deutschland* (Koenigstein, Taunus: Hain Verlag, 1981) and Peter J. Katzenstein, *Policy and Politics in West Germany* (Philadelphia: Temple University Press, 1987), pp. 209–34.

28. Hollifield, 'Immigration and republicanism in France,' in Cornelius *et al.*, *Controlling Immigration, op. cit.* and Weil, *La France et ses étrangers, op. cit.*

29. J.F. Hollifield, 'Immigration and modernization,' in J.F. Hollifield and G. Ross, *Searching for the New France* (New York: Routledge, 1991), pp. 113–50.

30. On this point see Weil, *La France et ses étrangers, op. cit.*, pp 89–106.

31. The industrial reserve army is a concept taken from Marx, which was widely used in the migration literature of the 1960s and 1970s to explain the demand for immigrant labor in industrial societies. See especially Michael J. Piore, *Birds of Passage: Migrant Labor in Industrial Societies* (Cambridge: Cambridge University Press, 1979), and Stephen Castles and Godula Kosack, *Immigrant Workers and Class Structure in Western Europe* (London: Oxford University Press, 1973), pp. 25 ff. For a critique of this argument, see Hollifield, *Immigrants, Markets, and States, op. cit.*, pp. 22–4, 74 ff.

32. John Salt, 'International migration and the United Kingdom,' SOPEMI report (Paris: OECD, 1991) and Layton-Henry, *The Politics of Immigration, op. cit.*

33. Hoffmann-Nowotny and Hondrich, *Ausländer in der BRD und in der Schweiz, op. cit.*

34. Again, for a comparative analysis of the gap between immigration policy outputs and outcomes, see the various country studies in Cornelius *et al.*, *Controlling Immigration, op. cit.*

35. See Aristide Zolberg *et al.*, *Escape from Violence: Conflict and the Refugee Crisis in the Developing World* (New York: Oxford University Press, 1989).

36. J.J. Bolten, 'From Schengen to Dublin: the new frontiers of refugee law,' in H. Meijers *et al.*, *Schengen: Internationalisation of Central Chapters of the Law on Aliens, Refugees, Privacy, Security and the Police* (Boekerig: Stichting NJCM, 1991), pp. 8–36.

37. This was an actual headline from *The Economist*.

38. See, for example, P.L. Martin, 'The United States: benign neglect toward immigration,' in Cornelius *et al.*, *Controlling Immigration*, pp. 95–8.

39. Nonna Mayer and Pascal Perrineau, *Le Front National a découvert* (Paris: Presses de la FNSP, 1989). Also Martin A. Schain, 'Immigration and change in the French party system,' *European Journal of Political Research*, 16 (1988), 597–621.

40. Weil, *La France et ses étrangers, op. cit.*, pp. 191–6.

41. Marceau Long, *Etre français aujourd'hui et demain, Vols 1–2* (Paris: La Documentation française, 1988).

42. *Haut Conseil a l'intégration, Conditions juridiques et culturelles de l'intégration* (Paris: La Documentation française, March 1992). This report differed little from that of the *Commission des sages*, cited above.

43. Andre Lebon, *Immigration et présence étrangere en France 1990/1991* (Paris: La Documentation française, 1991).

44. Cf. Bernard Stirn, *Le Conseil d'Etat: Son role, sa jurisprudence* (Paris: Hachette, 1991) and Daniele Lochak, *Etrangers: de quels droits?* (Paris: Presses Universitaires de France, 1985).

45. Sources for this review of the 1993 immigration debate in France include *Le Monde* and the *Journal Officiel*, various issues from 1993 and 1994.

46. 'Le Conseil constitutionnel attenue la rigueur de la loi sur l'immigration,' *Le Monde*, 16 August, 1993.

47. For more analysis of the relationship between immigration and republicanism in France, see Hollifield in Cornelius *et al.*, *Controlling Immigration*.

48. Thränhardt, 'Die Ursprünge von Rassismus und Fremdenfeindlichkeit in der Konkurrenzdemokratie,' *op. cit.*

49. Klaus J. Bade (ed.), *Deutsche im Ausland, Fremde in Deutschland: Migration in Geschichte und Gegenwart* (Munich: C.H. Beck Verlag, 1992). For a comparison of the French and German experiences, see Klaus Manfrass, *Türken in der Bundesrepublik, Nordafrikaner in Frankreich: Ausländerproblematik im deutsch-französischen Vergleich* (Bonn: Bouvier Verlag, 1991).

50. On this point, see W.R. Brubaker, *Citizenship and Nationhood in France and Germany* (Cambridge, MA: Harvard University Press, 1992).

51. Jürgen Habermas (ed.), *In Stichworte zur geistigen Situation der Zeit* (Frankfurt: Suhrkamp, 1970), pp. 7 ff. Also Lutz Hoffmann, *Die unvollendete Republik: Zwischen Einwanderungsland und deutschem Nationalstaat* (Koln: PapyRossa Verlag, 1990).

52. Cf. Thomas Faist, 'How to define a foreigner? The symbolic politics of immigration in German partisan discourse, 1978–1993,' *West European Politics*, forthcoming; Rey Koslowski, 'International migration, European political institutions and international relations theory,' unpublished doctoral dissertation, University of Pennsylvania, 1994; and Peter O'Brien, 'German–Polish migration: the elusive search for a German nation-state,' *International Migration Review*, 26, 2 (1992), 373–87.

53. Heinz Kuhn, *Stand und Weiterentwicklung der Integration der ausländischen Arbeitnehmer und ihrer Familien in der Bundesrepublik Deutschland: Memorandum des Beauftragten der Bundesregierung* (Bonn, September, 1979).

54. For an excellent review of the changing terms of debate over immigration,

ethnicity, and citizenship issues, see Thomas Faist, 'Immigration, integration and the ethnicization of politics,' *European Journal of Political Research*, 25 (1994), 439–59.

55. See Michael Mikenberg, 'The New Right in Germany: the transformation of conservatism and the extreme right,' *European Journal of Political Research*, 22 (1992), 55–81.

56. For a review of changes in aliens and refugee policy, see Bundesministerium des Innern, *Aufzeichnung zur Ausländerpolitik und zum Ausländerrecht in der Bundesrepublik Deutschland* (Bonn, July 1993).

57. On the increasing importance of East–West migration, see Heinz Werner, 'Agreements providing for short-term migration for employment and training purposes,' report to the Council of Europe, *Select Committee of Experts on Short-Term Migration* (Strasbourg, 28 March 1994, Council of Europe).

58. See Stephen Kinzer, 'Bonn parliament votes sharp curb on asylum seekers,' *New York Times*, May 27, 1993.

59. Craig R. Whitney, 'Germany to return asylum applicants in pact with Poland,' *New York Times*, May 8, 1993.

60. Reported in *The Economist*, May 14, 1994.

61. See Craig R. Whitney, 'Germany relents on expulsion of 100,000 Croatian refugees,' *New York Times*, February 11, 1994.

62. See Ursula Mehrländer (ed.), *Einwanderungsland Deutschland: Bisherige Ausländer- und Asylpolitik Vergleich mit anderen Europäischen Ländern* (Bonn: Friedrich Ebert Stiftung, 1992).

63. Cf. Anthony M. Messina, *Race and Party Competition in Britain* (Oxford: Oxford University Press, 1992), Gary P. Freeman, *Immigrant Labor and Racial Conflict in Industrial Societies: the French and British Experience, 1945–1975* (Princeton, NJ: Princeton University Press, 1979), and Layton-Henry, *The Politics of Immigration*.

64. For an overview of changes in British policy, see Layton-Henry, 'Britain: the would-be zero-immigration country,' in Cornelius *et al.*, *Controlling Immigration*, *op. cit.*, pp. 273–96.

65. See Donley T. Studlar, 'Ethnic minority groups, agenda setting, and policy borrowing in Britain,' in Paula D. McClain (ed.), *Minority Group Influence: Agenda Setting, Formulation, and Public Policy* (Westport, CT: Greenwood Press, 1993), pp. 15–32.

66. Salt, 'International migration and the United Kingdom,' *op. cit.*

67. William E. Schmidt, 'A Churchill draws fire with remark on race,' *New York Times*, June 1, 1993.

68. See Kitty Calavita, 'Italy and the new immigration,' and Wayne Cornelius, 'Spain: the uneasy transition from labor exporter to labor importer,' both in Cornelius *et al.*, *Controlling Immigration*, *op. cit.*

69. This quote is actually taken from Patrick Buchanan, a leader of the American Republican Party.

70. For a particularly polemical attack on the American model, see Jean-Claude Barreau, *De l'immigration en particulier et de la nation française en général* (Paris: Pre-aux-clercs, 1992). For a more serious critique of multiculturalism, see Arthur Schlesinger Jr, *The Disuniting of America: Reflections on a Multicultural Society* (New York: Norton, 1992).

71. The term international regime has gained wide currency in the international relations literature. For a definition, see Stephen D. Krasner (ed.), 'International regimes,' *International Organization*, 36, 2 (1982). Cf. Badie and Wihtol de Wenden (eds), *Le défi migratoire, op. cit.*

72. For a history of this change and its importance in immigration and naturalization policy, cf. Thomas Archdeacon, *Becoming American* (New York: Free Press, 1983); Schuck, 'The transformation of immigration law,' *op. cit.*; Smith, 'Beyond Tocqueville, Myrdal, and Hartz,' *op. cit.*; and the classic work of Nathan Glazer and Daniel Patrick Moynihan, *Beyond the Melting Pot* (Cambridge, MA: MIT Press, 1963).

73. See, for example, Hollifield, *Immigrants, Markets, and States*, especially chapter 8, *idem*, 'Entre droit et marche,' in Badie and Wihtol de Wenden, *Le défi migratoire*, pp. 59–87; J.F. Hollifield and Yves Charbide (eds), 'L'Immigration aux Etats-Unis,' *Revue Européenne des Migrations Internationales*, 6, 1 (1990). Cf. Daniel J. Tichenor, 'The politics of immigration reform in the United States, 1981–1990,' *Polity*, 26, 3 (1994), 333–62.

74. Probably the best statement of this new vision of citizenship, which stresses social rights and the welfare state, is to be found in John Rawls, *A Theory of Justice* (Cambridge, MA: Harvard University Press, 1971). For other statements of the new American liberalism, see Michael Walzer, *Spheres of Justice: a Defense of Pluralism and Equality* (New York: Basic Books, 1983). Walzer falls back on a more communitarian (and contractarian) position, especially with respect to the status of foreigners, i.e. non-members of a liberal society. Cf. Bruce Ackerman, *Social Justice in the Liberal State* (New Haven, CT: Yale University Press, 1980).

75. See Michael Fix and Jeffrey S. Passel, *Immigration and Immigrants: Setting the Record Straight* (Washington, DC: The Urban Institute, May 1994), p. 20.

76. See Schuck, 'The transformation of immigration law,' and T.A. Aleinikoff and D.A. Martin, *Immigration Process and Policy* (St. Paul, MN: West Publishing, 1985).

77. Ireland, *The Policy Challenge of Ethnic Diversity*, describes a similar dynamic in France and Switzerland. Also, Peter Skerry, *Mexican Americans: the Ambivalent Minority* (New York: The Free Press, 1993), and Alejandro Portes and Ruben G. Rumbaut, *Immigrant America: a Portrait* (Berkeley: University of California Press, 1990).

78. See Schuck, 'The transformation of immigration law,' *op. cit.*

79. For a discussion of American exceptionalism, see Michael S. Teitelbaum, 'Advocacy, ambivalence, ambiguity: immigration policies and prospects in the United States,' *Proceedings of the American Philosophical Society*, 136, 2 (1992), 188–206.

80. Cf., for example, Schuck, 'The transformation of immigration law,' *op. cit.*; D. Lochak, *Etrangers: de quel droit?*, and Kai Hailbronner, *Ausländerrecht* (Heidelberg: C.F. Mueller, 1984).

81. See Alexis de Tocqueville, *Democracy in America* (New York: Vintage Books, 1945), Vol. 2, pp. 114 ff. Patrick Ireland shows how immigrant minorities in France and Switzerland were able to use institutions in these states, especially in republican France, to organize and press their demands on government. See Ireland, *The Policy Challenge of Ethnic Diversity, op. cit.*

82. Tocqueville, *Democracy in America*, p. 270.

83. Cf. David Kettner, *The Development of American Citizenship, 1608–1870* (Chapel Hill, NC: University of North Carolina Press, 1978), Archdeacon, *Becoming American*; and Lawrence Fuchs, *The American Kaleidoscope: Race, Ethnicity, and the Civic Culture* (Hanover, NH: Wesleyan University and the University Press of New England, 1990).

84. See, for example, Gary P. Freeman and James Jupp (eds), *Nations of Immigrants: Australia, the United States, and International Migration* (Melbourne: Oxford University Press, 1992).

85. Cf. Sophie Body-Gendrot and Martin A. Schain, 'National and local politics and the development of immigration policy in the United States and France,' in Horowitz and Noiriel, *Immigrants in Two Democracies*, pp. 411–438; Martin A. Schain, 'The development of the American state and the construction of immigration policy (1880–1924),' unpublished paper delivered at the Annual Meeting of the American Political Science Association, New York, September 1994; and Smith, 'Beyond Tocqueville, Myrdal, and Hartz,' *op. cit.*

86. On this point, cf. Teitelbaum, 'Advocacy, ambivalence, ambiguity,' *op. cit.*; Julian Simon, *The Economic Consequences of Immigration* (Oxford: Basil Blackwell and the Cato Institute, 1989) and Archdeacon, *Becoming American, passim.*

87. Simon, *The Economic Consequences of Immigration.*

88. George J. Borjas, *Friends or Strangers: the Impact of Immigrants on the US Economy* (New York: Basic Books, 1990). See also *idem*, 'Ethnic capital and intergenerational mobility,' *The Quarterly Journal of Economics* (February 1992), 123–150.

89. It is an interesting historical fact that the Statue of Liberty was a gift from one fledgling republic (Third Republic France) to another (the United States) – an act of republican solidarity by France in the wake of the French defeat in the Franco-Prussian War.

90. See Fuchs, *American Kaleidoscope.*

91. See, for example, Noiriel, *Le creuset français* and Bade, *Vom Auswanderungsland zum Einwanderungsland? Deutschland 1880–1980.*

92. Cf. Hollifield, 'Immigration and republicanism in France,' in Cornelius *et al.*, *Controlling Immigration*, and Brubaker, *Citizenship and Nationhood in France and Germany.*

93. See, for example, Ursula Mehrländer and Günther Schultze, *Einwanderungskonzept für die Bundesrepublik – Fakten, Argumente, Vorschlaege* (Bonn: Friedrich Ebert Stiftung, 1992).

94. See Teitelbaum, 'Advocacy, ambivalence, ambiguity,' *op. cit.*

95. For more on these strange bedfellows, as Aristide Zolberg has called them, see Zolberg, 'Reforming the back door: perspectives historiques sur la reforme de la politique americaine d'immigration,' in J. Costa-Lascoux and P. Weil, *Logiques d'Etats et immigration* (Paris: Kime, 1992), Lawrence Fuchs, 'The corpse that would not die: the Immigration Reform and Control Act of 1986,' in Hollifield and Carbide (eds), *L'Immigration aux Etats-Unis*; and Tichenor, 'The politics of immigration reform,' *op. cit.*

96. See the introduction and conclusion of Hollifield, *Immigrants, Markets, and States.* Myron Weiner refers to the same phenomenon as the liberal dilemma. See Weiner, *The Global Migration Crisis.*

97. Again, see Gilpin, *The Political Economy of International Relations*, for a description

of this process. Gilpin is very pessimistic about the ability of the United States to maintain this liberal system. Cf. Keohane, *After Hegemony*.

98. See Stanley Hoffmann and Robert Keohane (eds), *The New European Community: Decisionmaking and Institutional Change* (Boulder, CO: Westview Press, 1991), especially the essay by Andrew Morovascik.

99. Giuseppe Callovi, 'Regulation of immigration in 1993: pieces of the European jig-saw puzzle,' *International Migration Review*, 26 (Summer 1992), 353–72.

100. For an overview of the East–West versus the South–North migration dynamic in Europe, see Heinz Werner, 'Regional economic integration and migration: the European case,' *The Annals of the American Academy of Political and Social Science*, 534 (July 1994), 147–64.

101. For projections of future trends, see OECD, *Trends in International Migration* (Paris: OECD, 1992).

3 Migration and the democratic context of European political institutions

Rey Koslowski

Democracy existed in ancient city states but it was only after the late eighteenth century that democracy and citizenship became organizing principles of large-scale polities functioning within the 'container' of the nation state. Political theories that emerged from reflection on modern European political institutions of the nation state, citizenship, and representative democracy often implicitly assume the continuity of people and place, nation and state, *demos* and the democratic state it rules. These assumptions may have been operable under the demographic circumstances of modern Europe, but the changing demography of European societies leads to practical and theoretical problems that are outside traditional conceptual frameworks.

Declining native population growth, the postwar migration of guestworkers, and the recent influx of asylum seekers has changed European demography by increasing the proportion of resident aliens within Western European populations. Due to their commitment to liberal principles, Western European states demurred from expelling guestworkers once they were no longer needed in the 1970s and allowed migration to continue in the form of family reunification.[1] Nevertheless, most immigrants and a large proportion of their children have been excluded from citizenship because the nationality laws that developed in many European countries are based on ancestral lineage. Commenting on post-war European migration, McNeill notes:

Consequently, polyethnic lamination – the clustering of different groups in particular occupations in a more or less formal hierarchy of dignity and wealth – is again asserting itself ... This change constitutes a reversion to the civilized pattern of the deeper past, when the world's great empires were ruled by small groups – their members often recruited from a multiplicity of ethnic backgrounds – presiding over hierarchies of specialized occupations, each of which tended to be dominated by a particular ethnic group. Such social arrangements do not accord well with liberal theory, which recognizes no significant differences among citizens. When such differences in fact exist, theory gets into difficulty.[2]

This chapter examines how theory gets into difficulty when demographics change. European political institutions and liberal theories that recognize no significant differences among citizens developed in the demographic context of growing populations and emigration of the nineteenth and early twentieth centuries. In Europe's contemporary demographic context of shrinking populations and increasing immigration these political institutions confront practical problems of inclusion. These practical problems, in turn, illuminate theoretical anomalies inherent in modern theories that developed in the previous demographic context.

Migration, polyethnicity, and the nation state

Migratory flows in and out of urban concentrations of humanity were fundamental to the development, maintenance, and expansion of Eurasian civilizations. The concentration of humanity into urban living spaces increased the spread of disease, which routinely killed off high proportions of urban populations. Successive waves of epidemics made it impossible for cities to reproduce themselves, which in turn prompted the immigration of peasants from the rural periphery.[3] In the opposite direction, traders and soldiers, often with missionaries in tow, ventured beyond the frontiers of the civilization in search of scarce resources. If the local peasantry could not fulfil manpower needs, labor became one of those scarce resources. Hence, cities sent armies to conquer peoples from beyond the frontiers of the civilization and bring back captives to enslave. Although not enslaved, ethnic groups from outside of cities were also recruited to particular occupations that dominant urban groups considered undesirable. In this way, a cyclical pattern of migration between the urban centers and peripheries of Eurasian civilizations rendered their societies polyethnic in nature – a norm to which the demography of European societies conformed.[4]

In juxtaposition to European demographic history, modern history, following the tradition of nineteenth-century historiography, is the story of the development of nation states.[5] France and England were the prototypes, albeit quite different in nature. Spain, Portugal, and Sweden have also served as examples of this quintessentially modern political form. Germany and Italy only tenuously conformed to the model, and only at the end of the nineteenth century. The problem with the notion of the nation state is that it did not always conform to the reality of European societies. The populations of what were to become the nation states of Europe were not very

ethnically homogeneous until the dramatic growth of European populations in the eighteenth century.[6] For example, France is generally
considered the archetypical nation state, but the population of what is now
France was formed through successive waves of invasion and intermixing.[7]

In the modern period of European history, social polyethnicity eventually
gave way to greater homogeneity and demographic changes facilitated the
formation of nation states in several ways. First, as religious minorities were
expelled from the kingdoms of early modern Western Europe, the remaining populations reproduced and raised their children in the dominant
religion. In this way, religious homogeneity of Western European societies
increased, provided that new religious minorities did not immigrate. Furthermore, decreasing mortality and increasing fertility rates among
European populations which began in the eighteenth century magnified
the impact of the expulsion of religious minorities and reproduction of the
rest. Not only did the religiously homogeneous indigenous population grow
faster, but this population growth reduced the need for immigration to
replace urban populations. In this way, as will be explained in more detail
below, increasing population growth enabled European societies to break
from the polyethnic norm.

Aristide Zolberg has pointed out that the process of Western European
state formation involved the expulsion of minorities, primarily on religious
grounds, and cumulatively produced approximately one million refugees in
the period spanning the late fifteenth and late seventeenth centuries.[8]
Isabella and Ferdinand expelled Spain's Jews (approximately 200,000) in
1492 and the Moors from Castile in 1502. In 1609, Philip III expelled
Spain's Moriscos (descendants of Moors who converted to Christianity).
The Habsburgs also expelled approximately 115,000 protestants from their
territories in the Low Countries. Puritans and Quakers were driven from
England and over 200,000 Huguenots left France at the time of the
revocation of the Edict of Nantes in 1685. Expulsion of religious minorities
increased the religious homogeneity of some Western European kingdoms,
while increasing the ethnic heterogeneity of many Central and Eastern
European kingdoms. For example, the expulsion of Spain's Jews increased
the polyethnicity of the Polish-Lithuanian Commonwealth, where many
found refuge. Huguenot refugees increased the ethnic diversity of Sweden,
the German states, and Ulster, where they settled and made major contributions to the development of local industries.[9]

Even as some Western European states used expulsion to increase their
religious homogeneity (and in the case of Spain ethnic homogeneity), new
migrations increased the ethnic mix of European societies. During the
sixteenth century, miners from southern Germany were recruited to
develop the tin and copper industry of Cornwall. Workers from Como
migrated to the German states and Moravia, and the Murano glassmakers of
Venice worked all across Europe.[10] As the Dutch developed a commercial

empire during the seventeenth century, Germans also moved west to meet labor demands. 'By the late 1680s, over a quarter of the burghers of Amsterdam were Germans.'[11] The expulsion of Jews increased the religious and ethnic homogeneity of Spain's population, but the demographic effect of expulsions on Spain's population was compounded by severe plague epidemics, celibacy, late marriage, and emigration,[12] that, together, left labor shortages filled by French peasants throughout the sixteenth century.[13] During the seventeenth and eighteenth centuries a circulatory migration pattern developed between the highland region of France and Spanish cities. Young men would go to work in Spain for several years and many stayed. As late as 1797, a French report noted that there were 80,000 French nationals in Spain, many of whom were married to Spanish women.[14]

Although the religious homogeneity of populations fostered national unity, the delineation of a people along religious lines differs from delineation along ethnic or national lines. Indeed, the French revolutionaries proclaimed religious freedom in order to gain the support of all inhabitants of France, regardless of religion, and these revolutionaries forged a new national identity in the process. Similarly, German nationalism was an attempt to overcome the fragmentation of German-speaking peoples into Catholic and protestant states that had been instituted by the Treaty of Westphalia. Although it would be a mistake to confuse the early modern Western European states with nineteenth-century European nation states because political delineation along religious lines differs from delineation along national lines, it is important to recognize that nationalism is older than the nation state.

National identities began to form around urban dialects as early as the sixteenth century. Originating in the Latin *natio*, which the Romans used to characterize the Jews, Greeks, and German tribes,[15] the word 'nation' was first used in reference to a part of the migrating members of the cosmopolitan European elite – denoting groupings of students within medieval universities.[16] It was not until the Reformation and the translation of the Bible into the vernacular, however, that the nation became a delineation around which political identification began to coalesce. Nevertheless, this 'nationalism' was not a mass phenomenon but evident among only a small proportion of the European population – the elites. Nationalism developed particularly among commercial elites, most notably those of England and then the Netherlands.[17] Throughout the sixteenth, seventeenth and eighteenth centuries, nationalism competed with cosmopolitanism in the orientation of the lifestyles, cultural preferences, and political identification of European elites.

Historians and political scientists routinely project back the nation state on to the early modern period, but even the European aristocracies, let alone their subjects, were hardly 'nations' in and of themselves. These aristocracies were polyethnic, not only in the sense of cultural cosmopolitanism, but biologically as well. Due to the longstanding practice of dynastic inter-marriage as a means of forming alliances, expanding and consolidating territory, and providing hostages to secure peace treaties, most rulers of modern European states shared common ancestors and many frequently married 'foreigners.' Pound noted that the political unification of France depended on marriage and inheritance rather than on 'geographically inevitability.'[18] Similarly, the Habsburgs became so politically successful in large measure through territorial agglomeration by marriage.[19]

Given that not only the royal houses but also the other families that composed the various aristocracies migrated and intermarried, state apparatuses were staffed by polyethnic cadres. 'Under the *Ancien régime* any one nation's diplomatic advisers were mixed in nationality.'[20] The armies fielded by the monarchies were often composed of foreign mercenaries, with 'virtually an international officer corps staffing all the national armies.'[21] It has been estimated that at any given time during the seventeenth century between 50,000 and 60,000 Swiss mercenaries were abroad and that over 900,000 Swiss died in the service of foreign countries.[22] In 1798, approximately half of the privates in the Prussian army were foreigners and of the 7000 to 8000 officers in 1806, 1000 were foreigners.[23]

With the English revolutions of 1640 and 1688, nationalism overtook cosmopolitanism within the English political elite, but, as Liah Greenfeld points out, 'Particularistic nationalism, reflecting the dissociation of the meaning of the "nation" as a "people" extolled as the bearer of sovereignty, the central object of collective loyalty, and the basis of political solidarity, from that of an "elite," and its fusion with the geo-political and/or ethnic characteristics of particular populations, did not emerge until the eighteenth century.'[24] As an orientation of political identification, nationalism did not involve majorities of urban populations until the American and French revolutions. Indeed, it was not until the end of the nineteenth century that increasing communication, commerce, and travel between urban and rural populations enabled the spread of a standard national language and its propagation through education and the mass press throughout the entire population of the prototypical nation state of France.[25]

The development of particularistic nationalism and the nation state was based on the demographic shift from polyethnicity to ethnically homogeneous populations fostered by the unprecedented increase in the rate of population growth beginning around 1750.[26] In accordance with the mercantilist view that increasing populations increased wealth, during the seventeenth and eighteenth centuries states facilitated population growth through the introduction of new crops, such as the potato, and through advances in 'disaster management.'[27] State regulations, quarantines, and border controls (*cordon sanitaire*) aimed at limiting the spread of epidemics and epizootics had also become well established in the eighteenth century and contributed to the fact that Western Europe's last major outbreak of the bubonic plague occurred in Marseilles in 1720. While the states' population protection policies helped to increase populations, population growth enabled the development of the ethnically homogeneous societies we have come to call 'nations.' In this way, polyethnic aristocracies facilitated the development of more ethnically homogenous nation states within which representative democracy would develop and replace the *ancien régime.*

As rural populations in Europe began to grow rapidly about 1750, the necessity for immigration from beyond urban hinterlands to maintain urban populations diminished. Rather, great cities could find enough manpower within their immediate environs to sustain their populations and economies. Immigrants from closer to the city were more ethnically and culturally akin to the dominant group of the urban population than those from further away, and found learning the urban language and assimilating to urban ways easier. For example, replenishing urban populations with local recruits enabled the great cities of London and Paris to increase their ethnic and cultural homogeneity. As these migrants adopted London and Parisian dialects as their own and as emigration from the city to the periphery spread the use of these urban dialects, the standardization of language and the development of national cultures around those urban dialects intensified.[28]

As assimilation and identification with the dominant urban ethnic group became a goal shared by rural migrants and urban elites alike, the ideal of equal status of all members of the nation developed as well. This nationalist ideal supplanted the norm of political domination by the dominant ethnic group and a division of labor along ethnic lines for newcomers from the periphery. In the French Revolution, disaffected sections of the middle class mobilized the masses of rural migrants by appealing to national identification against the prevailing hierarchical system based on status determined by birth and a functional division of society. McNeill suggests:

The barbarian ideal of a homogeneous ethnic nation is incompatible with normal population dynamics of civilization. The fact that Europe's achievement of high civilization between the ninth and thirteenth centuries coincided with a swarming of population in northwestern Europe, and that modern Western expansion and nation-building also coincided with population growth of exceptional character, meant that throughout the nineteenth century Europeans were able to combine the barbarian ideal of a single ethos – a nation of blood brothers – with the reality of civilized specialization and urban living. To be sure, the blood-brotherhood of European nations was largely fictitious, but a real cohesion of language and culture was achieved within each nation's boundaries that exceeded civilized norms.[29]

The development of representative democracy in European countries during the nineteenth and early twentieth centuries[30] occurred in the context of unprecedented population growth. This enabled the geographic scope of European democracy to go beyond that of the ancient or Renaissance city state because the potential for identification between rulers and ruled increased as large ethnically homogeneous societies developed.

As the Ottoman and Habsburg empires collapsed and a League of Nations emerged in the wake of the First World War, the nation state had assumed its place as the central organizing principle of European politics. Also about this time, the demography of European societies, somewhat ironically, began to return to the old civilized norm of polyethnicity. Two world wars, increasing use of birth control, and changing social norms led to an aging, and even decline, of the native populations of many of Europe's advanced industrial countries in the postwar period. By 1988, Ireland remained the only EC member state with a fertility rate above the replacement rate of 2.1 children born per woman.[31] Increasing migration from peripheral areas of Europe surrounding its industrialized northwestern core, as well as migration from outside of Europe, provided sufficient manpower to sustain economic growth from the mid-1950s until the early 1970s[32] and compensated for indigenous population decline. The contribution to total population growth by migration between 1980 and 1990 was greater than or equal to the contribution from births in Austria, Germany (West), Italy, Luxembourg, Sweden, and Switzerland. Migration was responsible for all the population increase in Austria and Germany, as births roughly matched deaths in Austria while deaths exceeded births in Germany. By 1989, children born to resident aliens constituted over 10 percent of all births in England and Wales, France, Germany, Luxembourg, Sweden, and Switzerland.[33] Except for a large proportion of those born in England and Wales, these children were not born into citizenship. Essentially, the centuries old trend of net migration leaving Western Europe reversed direction during the 1970s.[34] In sum, the combination of declining fertility rates, increasing migration, and relatively high birth rates among foreigners is returning Europe's demographic makeup to the polyethnic norm while at the same time the political institutions and political theories associated with the ideal of the nation state remain in place.

Migration and the principles of citizenship

The formative nature of migration in the development of political institutions is most clearly evident in the institutions of nationality and citizenship. Representative democracy and citizenship laws emerged coterminously with an unprecedented period of population growth and emigration. Not only was the demographic shift away from polyethnicity critical to the formation of national citizenship in revolutionary France, but the context of migration was critical to the development of nationality and citizenship principles governing ascription and naturalization.

Although citizenship based on ancestral lineage informed the citizenship laws of ancient Greece,[35] and subject status was governed by place of birth in the feudal system[36] and under absolutism,[37] *jus sanguinis* and *jus soli* only became principles of state membership as the classical ideal of city state citizenship became realized in the democratic revolutions of America and France. Laws differentiating the membership of one nation from that of other nations became institutionalized with the innovation of national citizenship in France, giving national citizenship an external as well as an internal dimension. That is, national citizenship not only became constitutive of the nation state but it also became constitutive of the international system, which, in their totality, nation states formed.[38] During the nineteenth century, the inhabitants of the European state system received a 'nationality' when states bounded their membership according to the norms of *Staatsangehörigkeit*, or state membership.[39] With the extension of the European state-system to the rest of the world at the end of the nineteenth century, the norm that everyone belongs to a state, i.e., the elimination of statelessness,[40] helped to establish the world's emerging international system by delineating its parts in terms of population.

In terms of international law, nationality encompasses subjects as well as citizens. At the end of the eighteenth century the terms 'subject,' 'national,' and 'citizen' were used indiscriminately.[41] As popular sovereignty eventually became a norm of state legitimization (at least nominally), a distinction between subject and citizen became clear. In contrast, as polities became more inclusive through the spread of universal suffrage, nationality and citizenship increasingly overlapped. The interrelationship of the terms is expressed in Oppenheim's definition: 'Nationality of an individual is his quality of being subject of a certain State and therefore its citizen.'[42] Weis notes, 'Conceptually and linguistically, the terms 'nationality' and 'citizenship' emphasize two different aspects of the same notion: State membership. 'Nationality' stresses the international, 'citizenship' the national, municipal, aspect.'[43]

Nationality refers to the status of being subject to a state's laws, its taxes, and military conscription, while enjoying the right of protection by the state even when abroad. Citizenship refers to a bundle of civil, political, and social rights possessed by individuals.[44] States have developed a set of shared norms delineating who is subject to which state's laws and many of these norms have been codified in international law. The particular bundle of rights that, together, make up what is understood as citizenship may vary from state to state, and within each state the degree to which nationals possess these different rights may also vary from person to person. Moreover, as Weis notes, 'Every citizen is a national, but not every national is necessarily a citizen of the State concerned.'[45] Citizenship can also mean more than nationality in that it often denotes active political participation[46] and service to the state, such as jury duty or national service,[47] and the willingness to die for the state.[48]

Technically speaking, the principles of *jus soli* and *jus sanguinis* are associated with the acquisition of nationality, or the international aspect of state membership. With respect to the problem of resident aliens for democracy, however, legitimization of the democratic state hinges on the acquisition of state membership in terms of the full political rights of citizenship. In modern representative democracies, that means the rights to vote and stand for election at all levels of the polity – local, regional, and national.

As the number of democratic states grew in the period between 1776 and 1930,[49] they adopted either the *jus sanguinis* or the *jus soli* principle of nationality, delineating which inhabitants of the state could become citizens and therefore be included in the *demos*. Strictly speaking *jus soli* and *jus sanguinis* refer only to ascription of citizenship, whereas *jus domicili* refers to the acquisition of citizenship through naturalization after residence. In practice, however, naturalization is also informed by the distinction between *jus soli* and *jus sanguinis*, in that naturalization of an alien may depend on ancestral lineage, cultural considerations and language skills in addition to residence. In preparation for the 1930 Hague conference organized by the League of Nations to codify customary international law, a study by Harvard Law Research determined that 17 states based nationality solely on *jus sanguinis* (15 of which were European), 25 primarily on *jus sanguinis* (15 of which were European, including Turkey), two on an equal mixture of the two principles and 26 primarily on *jus soli* (three of which were European).[50]

Several reasons have been given for the distinction between the two principles. Armstrong suggests that the principle of *jus sanguinis* originated with nomadic societies that stressed ancestry and kinship to delineate tribal membership, whereas *jus soli* originated with settled agricultural societies.[51] Maxson traces the principle of *jus sanguinis* to rules governing membership in the families, gentes, and tribes of patriarchal societies and rules governing suffrage and rights in ancient cities, whereas *jus soli* emerged from the rules delineating subject status in medieval Europe. According to Maxson and Weis, *jus soli* persisted as part of English common law while *jus sanguinis* became the continental norm with the adoption of Roman law.[52] Brubaker argues that the sequencing of state formation was crucial to the development of the differing principles of citizenship in France and Germany. Whereas in France citizenship developed within the context of a territorially defined nation state, in Germany citizenship developed as a reflection of an ethno-national identity that developed before and outside of a unified nation state.[53]

Armstrong's explanation for the origin of the distinction based on the difference between settled/agricultural and nomadic/pastoral societies does not fit the circumstances in which modern citizenship emerged in the late eighteenth and nineteenth centuries, but it offers an insight as to the role of migration in citizenship development. The common law – Roman law distinction provides an explanation for the differentiation in rules of ascription initially adopted by the American states and France. It does not, however, account for the difference between continental European countries with Roman law traditions that supplemented *jus sanguinis* ascription with the principle of *jus soli* (France) and those that maintained a purer form of *jus sanguinis* (Germany). Brubaker's focus on nation state formation sequencing explains this differentiation between France and Germany but it is not generalizable, particularly to the American states, which pioneered the development of modern citizenship laws. Together, all three conceptualizations contribute to an understanding of how this distinction developed and why states opted for one principle over the other. Principles of citizenship inherited from legal traditions were either strengthened or diluted by differing ideologies of national identity formation and conditioned by the practicalities of the greatest human migration in history.

Rooted in the English feudal law stipulating that those born on the land of a lord were his subjects, *jus soli* became the primary rule for delineating who was or was not a subject of the king of England and, thereby, became an initial qualification necessary for political participation.[54] British subjects in America who renounced their adherence to Great Britain during the American Revolution nevertheless retained the common law principle of *jus soli* for regulating ascription and naturalization into membership of their new states.[55]

Following the Roman law tradition, *jus sanguinis* became the rule for ascription in France[56] and then for the rest of the European continent,[57] but rules governing naturalization differ greatly. In Germany, *jus sanguinis* has strictly governed both ascription at birth and naturalization. In France, ascription of nationality has been based on *jus sanguinis*, but in addition to governing the ascription of children born to foreigners in France, the territorial principle came to inform naturalization as well. The naturalization laws of most other continental countries fall in between these two extremes. As Brubaker points out, *jus soli* came to govern French naturalization because French citizenship developed in the context of a territorially defined state. In accord with its republican ideology and confident in the ability of its schools and army to turn foreigners into Frenchmen, in 1889 France enacted laws that made the French-born children of immigrants into citizens upon reaching the age of majority.[58] German citizenship came to be understood in ethno-cultural terms because it developed in the context of defining a nation prior to a unified state. This non-territorial ethno-cultural understanding of citizenship was codified in the citizenship law of 1913,[59] which maintained restrictions on the naturalization of children and grand-children of immigrants while at the same time enabling German emigrants to keep German citizenship indefinitely and pass it on to their descendants born outside of Germany.[60]

Following Armstrong's line of thought that *jus sanguinis* is associated with nomadic life and *jus soli* with the sedentary, the adoption of *jus sanguinis* by the agricultural societies of continental Europe during modern times must be understood as atavism. European mass migration in the eighteenth and nineteenth centuries did, however, yield a nomadic component to European societies. Whereas American nationality laws developed in the context of immigration, European laws developed in the context of tens of millions of Europeans emigrating to other continents. By the end of the great migration to the New World, in which an estimated 50 million migrants moved between 1820 and 1924, people of European origin who lived outside of Europe constituted one-eleventh of the world's population.[61] Countries formed through immigration, such as the United States, Canada, the Latin American countries and Australia, tended to base nationality primarily on *jus soli* because the principle permits more rapid assimilation of immigrants.[62] Hammar and Brubaker point out that countries experiencing great out-migration, such as Germany, the Scandinavian countries, and Italy, tended to base nationality primarily on *jus sanguinis* because it encourages emigrants to retain their nationality and pass it on to their children so as to facilitate their return and closer ties with their homeland.[63]

For example, Germans who immigrated to the United States routinely returned to Germany, particularly in periods of economic depression. It has been estimated that, in any given year, of the number of Germans who migrated to the United States, between 5 and 50 percent of that number returned.[64] Ironically, these Germans of the nineteenth century were much like Europe's guestworkers of the postwar period. Likewise, Germany attempted to maintain the allegiance of its citizens who emigrated, just as migrant workers' sending states do today.

It is important to note that although the adoption of *jus sanguinis* often coincided with high rates of emigration and *jus soli* with immigration, principles of nationality are not solely dependent on the direction of migration. For instance, British nationality is primarily based on *jus soli* even though Great Britain has consistently maintained a high rate of emigration.[65] Also, Germany based its nationality laws on *jus sanguinis* even though it experienced large-scale immigration, primarily from Poland, starting in the 1880s and continuing up until the 1920s.[66] The issue of the ethnicity of the migrants is also critical to the adoption of *jus sanguinis* or *jus soli*. At the same time that Germany was receiving many Polish immigrants, it was also receiving Germans returning from the United States, as well as their children born abroad. Basing nationality on *jus soli* may have facilitated the assimilation of Polish immigrants, but it would have made it more difficult to integrate ethnic Germans returning from the United States. A preference for ethnic German returnees over Polish immigrants was decisive in the drafting of the 1913 law.[67]

Although the principles of *jus soli* and *jus sanguinis* are associated with common law and Roman law, as well as the sequencing of nation and state building, in practice the distinction between *jus sanguinis* and *jus soli* is, strictly speaking, a function of migration. As Brubaker notes, 'In a zero migration world, they would have identical effects: every person born of citizen parents would also be born in the state's territory, and vice versa.'[68] Once a child is born to a foreigner, or a child is born to a state's national residing abroad, a state must choose whether or not to grant its nationality to that child. This choice sets a precedent for future decisions. When the same choice is repeated, a decision rule develops which becomes codified into law.

As the above noted Harvard Legal Research inventory demonstrated, however, neither principle of nationality is absolute in its application. Ascribing nationality at birth strictly by the principles of *jus soli* or *jus sanguinis* leads to practical difficulties which have prompted some moderation of each principle with certain attributes of the other. Without moderating the principle of *jus soli* by adding a degree of *jus sanguinis* in naturalization, for example, an American tourist's child born in Germany could become neither a US nor a German national. In practice, the United States bestows nationality to such children upon their return through a simple act of registration. Without moderating the principle of *jus sanguinis* in ascription, the American descendants of nineteenth-century German immigrants would continue to be not only US nationals but also German nationals, regardless of whether they had any allegiance to, or even interest in, Germany. The 1913 German citizenship law revoked the nationality of German emigrants who voluntarily took on the nationality of another state or failed to fulfill military obligations, but made it possible for them, or their descendants, to regain it.[69] Inclusive interpretation of article 116, section 1 of the Basic Law[70] has, nevertheless, effectively extended citizenship in the Federal Republic to ethnic Germans from Eastern Europe upon arrival in Germany, even to those descended from the Germans who settled in Hungary and Russia centuries ago.

Legal inheritance and state formation sequencing have been critical to the distinction between *jus soli* and *jus sanguinis*, but one can only understand the development of modern citizenship laws with reference to the demographic context in which they developed. For example, on December 6, 1921 the southern counties of Ireland left the United Kingdom and became a Dominion. The Irish Free State constitution supplemented the common law principle of *jus soli* governing ascription and naturalization that it inherited from the United Kingdom with the *jus sanguinis* rule that anyone whose parent was born in Ireland is entitled to Irish citizenship.[71]

This measure was motivated by the fact that a large proportion of Ireland's population had emigrated during the preceding century.[72] Given that Ireland's citizens continue to emigrate,[73] *jus sanguinis* provisions were strengthened by extending citizenship to anyone with an Irish grandparent.

In sum, international migration forces the issue of whether to grant citizenship to children of foreigners, emigrants, and expatriates. Concern for maintaining ties to emigrants and the preservation of ethnic homogeneity strongly influenced the drafting and revision of citizenship laws in the nineteenth and early twentieth centuries. In this way, the demographic context in which citizenship laws developed played a decisive role in the choice of the *jus sanguinis* or *jus soli* principle.

Principles of citizenship and democratic inclusiveness

The development of democracy in continental Europe during the nineteenth and early twentieth centuries coincided with a great emigration which prompted many of these democratizing states to bound their newly formed citizenries using the rule of *jus sanguinis*. This historical development raises the theoretical question of whether democracy and *jus sanguinis* are compatible. Liberal-democratic European states that based citizenship on *jus sanguinis* may have maintained democratic inclusiveness when their populations were rapidly growing and many of their citizens moved abroad, but in the context of declining populations growth rates and increasing immigration, *jus sanguinis* decreases democratic inclusiveness and thereby undermines the legitimacy of the democracies that abide by this principle.

As political rights were extended in the founding of democratic polities, the *demoi* were often bounded in an exclusive manner by citizenship laws based on ancestral lineage. When in 451 BC pay for the jurors of the popular court made it possible for the poorest citizens to serve, the bulk of Athens's free male adult population became potential participants in Athens's democracy. At the same time Athenian citizenship was restricted to children of Athenian citizens, thereby excluding the resident aliens (*metics*) from the democratic polity that was being constituted, even though *metics* participated in Athens's economy, culture and society.[74] Similarly, as participation in the decision making of early modern towns of Germanic Central Europe and Switzerland expanded, resident aliens were excluded through laws limiting the membership in the polity delineated by ancestral lineage.[75] After the American Revolution the newly formed democratic states maintained the *jus soli* of English common law, but the exclusion of black slaves and Native Americans from citizenship sharply restricted membership in the *demos* constituted, in a manner which had a practical effect similar to that of *jus sanguinis*. French revolutionaries criticized *jus soli* as being too 'feudal' and '*jus sanguinis* was preferred for linking citizens to the state by ties more substantial than those of birthplace.'[76] Practically speaking, it was only beginning in the later half of the nineteenth century that large-scale *demoi* delineated by *jus soli* became operable. This was marked by the passage of the fourteenth amendment to the US Constitution, the establishment of *jus soli* naturalization laws in France, and the development of parliamentary democracy in Canada, New Zealand and Australia.

Even though the territorial principle of *jus soli* has but recently become the principle of bounding the *demos* in several large-scale democracies, political theorists have often assumed that the boundary of the *demos* coincided with the geographical boundaries of the democratic state. Only recently, as guestworkers became permanent resident aliens in established European democracies that base citizenship on *jus sanguinis*, have the inherent theoretical problems posed by resident aliens become evident in political practice.[77] The issues resident aliens raise for justice have been explored by Walzer and Carens.[78] Scholars who study migration in Western Europe in the fields of comparative law and comparative politics, as well as political theorists focusing on migration have begun to explore the problem resident aliens pose for democracy.[79] Recent general works in democratic theory, however, offer hardly a word on the problem of resident aliens.[80] This omission is understandable given that democratic theory usually assumes a bounded group of people who comprise the *demos* that rules.[81] By the end of the Second World War, universal adult suffrage became the generally accepted standard for defining the *demos* in most democracies.[82] Once this happened, debates over which parts of the population should be enfranchised subsided and democratic theorists could focus almost exclusively on the self-government of already constituted *demoi*.

Conceptualizing the *demos* in this way can conflate the geographic boundaries of a state with the boundaries defining membership of that state's *demos*. An individual joins an existing *demos* when he or she becomes a citizen and can exercise full political rights. As the above section amply demonstrates, one can cross the geographic borders of the state and live there for the rest of one's life without ever entering the realm of citizenship and crossing the boundary of the *demos*. Universal adult suffrage may establish an inclusive *demos* generally regarded as legitimate, but when the number of inhabitants who are denied the political rights of citizenship increases as a proportion of a democratic state's population, the legitimacy of the delineation of the *demos* by universal adult suffrage can be questioned.

European democracies that base citizenship on *jus sanguinis*, however, did not experience a significant reduction of democratic inclusiveness as long as their populations grew and more emigrants left than immigrants came. Indeed, when the flow of migration leaves rather than enters a democratic state, and that state's emigrants do not gain citizenship in their host countries, *jus sanguinis* that enables political participation in the migrants' home state can maintain democratic inclusiveness. For example, suppose that during a famine hunger forces a poor citizen of a democratic state to emigrate. Years later when conditions improve, her children wish to move back to their ancestral homeland but since the state's nationality laws are based on *jus soli*, the children are denied citizenship because they were born abroad. In contrast, a richer citizen of the same state had enough wealth to survive the famine and have children in her homeland. Here, access to political rights becomes a function of wealth. Hence, extending citizenship to children born abroad to emigrants could be considered as analogous to extending citizenship to the lower classes. Given the circumstances of mass emigration, the argument could be made that *jus sanguinis* was compatible with liberal democracy in certain nineteenth- and early twentieth-century European states. For example, an annual average of 6.6 per 1000 Norwegians emigrated between 1861 and 1910: 'in some parts of Norway, one adult male in four had spent sometime in the US by the 1920 census.'[83] By 1930 Norway was a democracy that primarily based nationality on *jus sanguinis*. Given the relative preponderance of emigration leaving Norway to immigration entering Norway, the practical effect of its *jus sanguinis* nationality rules was more inclusive than exclusive.

As population growth declined in Western Europe and net migration reversed direction in the 1970s, the number of resident aliens increased as a proportion of the population, the gap between the citizenry and inhabitants grew, and the boundaries between the *demoi* and the states' geographic boundaries diverged. Nationality laws based on ancestral lineage that at one time might have promoted inclusiveness became the basis for excluding resident aliens from the *demos*. In this way, the changing demographics of twentieth-century European societies toward polyethnicity points to an inherent problem in democratic theory.

Along with Whelen, Dahl is one of the few democratic theorists to seriously consider the problems involved in bounding the *demos*. After examining the problem of inclusion, Dahl stipulates as one criterion of the democratic process that 'The *demos* must include all adult members of the association except transients and persons proved to be mentally defective.'[84] Unfortunately, Dahl too casually accepts the rightful exclusion of 'transients.' By focusing on tourists rather than permanent resident aliens, Dahl neglects millions of European guestworkers who share the fate of resident aliens in ancient Athens, a situation which, he himself argues, rendered Athenian democracy exclusionary.[85]

Because resident aliens are foreigners who are, technically speaking, transient, one can argue that they should be excluded from the *demos*. Because they are subject to the laws of a democratic polity, participate in its society and culture, contribute to its economy, and pay taxes, one can also argue that they should be included.

To illustrate the argument for the exclusion of transients, Dahl gives the example of a tourist who happens to be in Paris on election day. Even if the tourist met all the qualifications for voting, she could leave after the election and not bear responsibility for the decisions she made. Therefore the tourist 'ought to be excluded under the assumption that binding decisions should be made only by members.'[86] The problem then becomes one of defining 'transient.' Dahl does confess that 'the definition of adult and transients is a potential source of ambiguity.'[87] He then explores the ambiguity of adulthood, but drops the subject of transience and does not broach the subject of whether or not to include children born to transients.

Dahl's argument for excluding transients from the *demos* does not hold when those transients are temporary workers who become permanent resident aliens, nor does it hold for children of permanent resident aliens. One can argue that many guestworkers' rights to reside in host countries are of a contractual nature and therefore they freely consented to their transient status. Walzer counters that this kind of consent is not sufficient in a democracy: 'Political power is precisely the ability to make decisions over periods of time, to change rules, to cope with emergencies; it can't be exercised democratically without the ongoing consent of its subjects.'[88] Consistently subject to the laws of a democratic polity, permanent resident aliens have resided in their host countries long enough to suffer the consequences of laws they could have participated in making had they been given the political rights to do so. The analogy between resident aliens and tourists only holds for some limited amount of time.

Once resident aliens become permanent, one can make a strong argument that denying them political rights and denying their children citizenship are both unjust.[89] Walzer goes as far as generating his reconceptualization of justice by pointing out the constitutive nature of a community's decision rule regarding new members. 'The idea of distributive justice presupposes a bounded world within which distributions take place. ... The primary good that we distribute to one another is membership in some human community. And what we do with regard to membership structures all our other distributive choices.'[90] While welfare states achieve a high degree of equality for their members, Walzer argues that it is not the members' 'equality but their tyranny that determines the character of the state. ... Democratic citizens, then have a choice: if they want to bring in new workers, they must be prepared to enlarge their own membership; if they are unwilling to accept new members, they must find ways within the limits of the domestic labor market to get socially necessary work done.'[91]

Questions of justice are very salient with respect to resident aliens, but the problem of resident aliens goes beyond issues of distributive justice – the status of resident aliens can be considered a touchstone of democracy in a highly mobile world. Just as decisions that bound a community precede distributive justice, defining a *demos* precedes democracy.[92] The initial boundaries of the geographical units that the established *demoi* of Western Europe now rule are historically given, which often means that they are given by a long history of dynastic marriage, inheritance and war. The geographical boundaries of these states may have bounded their *demoi* well enough at the time of the inception of democracy in each of these states, but these same boundaries cannot adequately delineate the *demos* in the context of extensive migration. If inclusiveness is a fundamental criterion of the democratic process, present decisions on who is allowed to join the *demos* are indicative not only of how just a society is, but also of how democratic a polity is.

Including resident aliens in the polity through rapid naturalization is the solution to the problem they pose to democracy that is most in keeping with liberal principles. Even if a host country added some naturalization laws based on *jus soli* to a set of nationality laws primarily governed by *jus sanguinis,* thereby offering migrants easier naturalization, *jus sanguinis* in migrants' home countries inhibits naturalization. For instance, Italian guestworkers find German nationality difficult to obtain not only because German laws discourage naturalization, but also because Italy's own laws encourage these guest workers to keep their Italian nationality. In addition to basing nationality on *jus sanguinis,* some states consider renunciation of nationality as grounds for losing more than political rights. For example, Turks who renounce their Turkish nationality cannot inherit land in Turkey.

Similarly, some states prohibit the renunciation of nationality by emigrants attempting to naturalize in another state until they pay for the education they received and/or complete required military service.[93] For example, male children of Greek, Turkish, or Iranian parents born in Western European countries may also still be subject to conscription in their parents' home countries if they ever return to visit, even if they have served in the military of the country in which they were born and to which they eventually naturalized. They are then left with the choice of naturalizing to their country of birth and not returning to their parents' home country, naturalizing and serving in the military of both countries, or not naturalizing.[94] Such circumstances, combined with restrictive naturalization rules governed by *jus sanguinis* in many host countries, keep naturalization rates low, as has been the case in Germany. Achieving high rates of naturalization may, therefore, also require a shift in nationality laws from *jus sanguinis* to *jus soli* in immigrants' home countries. However, given the role played by *jus sanguinis* in maintaining ties between emigrants and their home countries, as well as facilitating their return, such changes may not come easily.

The understanding that the functioning of democracy involves more than political rights but also the economic means necessary to realize those rights goes back to the paid juries which enabled the poorer citizens of Athens to fully participate in Athenian democracy. As Marshall pointed out, full citizenship in the modern sense entails social, as well as civil and political, rights. By insuring basic economic security, the European welfare state grants the citizenry the social rights necessary to realize democracy in advanced industrialized societies.[95] Increasing migration illuminates the demographic assumption upon which the theory of the democratic welfare state is based. Specifically, this assumption is exposed by the conflict between liberal principles and fiscal and political constraints that migration raises.

European welfare states are premised on the notion of a closed membership in which citizens are entitled to universal health care, extensive child care benefits, liberal unemployment benefits, state financed higher education, etc.[96] Closed membership could be assumed to encompass most of the inhabitants of the state as long as there was minimal migration and all migrants either did not stay permanently or were easily brought into membership. Once the boundaries of the membership entitled to social rights deviates greatly from the inhabitants of the welfare state, the welfare state's own legitimizing principles are undermined. Effective and legitimate welfare states that are based on closed membership may have been possible in the demographic context of increasing population growth within the established membership, but increasing proportions of resident aliens characteristic of postwar European demography have made sustaining such welfare states increasingly expensive.

Many European states were quicker to extend civil and social rights to resident aliens than to extend political rights. European states were willing to extend social rights to young temporary migrant workers, who, it was assumed, would not remain long enough to collect their pensions and health care benefits in old age. Now, as the number of permanent resident aliens grows, and these resident aliens come to include children and the elderly in addition to young productive workers, the acceptance of the extension of social rights as a fundamental principle runs headlong into fiscal constraints. Practically speaking, if citizenship is offered liberally to immigrants as immigration increases, European policy makers are confronted with a set of unattractive choices: increase taxes to maintain the level of social services for all citizens, regardless of how recent; do not raise taxes, maintain the universality of services, but decrease their quantity and quality; or forsake universality and equality in the delivery of services to all of the country's residents by excluding non-citizens from the benefits of citizenship. The more social services that are provided on a universal basis to the members of a state, however, the more difficult it becomes to not provide similar social services to legal resident aliens.[97] Policy makers are, therefore, caught in a bind between rapidly increasing budgetary outlays for migrants and liberal principles that pre-empt expulsion or denial of social services.

By referring to the extension of civil and social rights to non-nationals, one can question the importance of formal state membership and the distinction between *jus soli* and *jus sanguinis*. The Marshallian differentiation of citizenship's component categories of civil, social, and political rights illuminates different dimensions within which exclusion and inclusion of resident aliens take place and enables one to see how residents may be treated according to the principles of *jus sanguinis* on one dimension while at the same time being treated according to the principles of *jus soli* on another. The issue of political rights incumbent in formal state membership, however, ultimately takes precedence. With respect to the extension of civil and social rights to non-nationals, it must be kept in mind that in a democracy the 'people' giveth and the 'people' can taketh away. Within the bounds of international law, the rights of non-nationals are contingent on the sufferance of the *demos*. If one is not included in the *demos*, opportunities to protect one's civil and social rights by political means are marginal. This dynamic is illustrated by the recent Welfare Reform Bill passed in the US House of Representatives, which would exclude legal resident aliens from various forms of public assistance. In the United States most of the affected resident aliens have the option of naturalization and increasing numbers of resident aliens have taken that option in response to passage of the bill. Were similar legislation to be enacted in certain European states, many resident aliens would be unable to easily attain citizenship due to *jus sanguinis* naturalization provisions.

Inclusion and exclusion on the different dimensions of civil, social, and political rights are interrelated. For example, increasing costs involved in extending social rights prompt political pressure for restrictive redefinition of nationality laws, which in turn limits the extension of political rights to resident aliens and their children. Hence, the question of extending full citizenship, including political rights, has increasingly come to depend on the question of social rights. Given fiscal constraints, policy makers are left with balancing the social rights of present citizens with the political rights of resident aliens. Serious compromise of either can be viewed as a violation of liberal principles.

In sum, the political institutions of European democratic welfare states that bounded their membership using the rule of *jus sanguinis* are now challenged by the changing demographic conditions of native population decline and increasing immigration. This challenge is not just a matter of policy because it reaches down to the assumptions upon which the bounding of the *demos* and the closed membership of the welfare state is based. In turn, these questionable assumptions raise further questions regarding the realization of democracy as well as the legitimization of states by democratic processes.

Conclusions

European societies have been returning to polyethnicity due to declining population growth and immigration. This demographic change conflicts with existing liberal political institutions that developed in the different demographic context of rapidly growing native populations and large-scale emigration. *Jus sanguinis* may have adequately bounded the *demos* in the era when many European democracies developed, but in the context of declining population growth and increasing immigration, *jus sanguinis* decreases democratic inclusiveness, and thereby undermines the legitimacy of the democracies that abide by this principle. The increasing attention given to migration demonstrates that the issue is central to understanding contemporary European politics. The reason migration is so salient goes beyond immediate questions of policy. Rather, policy conundrums generated by conflicts between demography and liberal theories are symptomatic of the reversion of European societies to the premodern norm of polyethnicity. By focusing on these problems raised by migration we can gain insight into the way we have conceptualized politics and constructed our political theories. If recent demographic trends continue in the next century, the question for democratic policy makers becomes, 'How can the demographic transition to the premodern norm of polyethnicity be navigated without a reversion to the hierarchical social and political structures of the past?'

Notes

1. James F. Hollifield, *Immigrants, Markets and States* (Cambridge, MA: Harvard University Press, 1992), pp. 82–96.
2. William H. McNeill, 'Migration in premodern times,' in William Alonso (ed.), *Population in an Interacting World* (Cambridge, MA: Harvard University Press, 1987), p. 35.
3. See William McNeill, *Plagues and Peoples* (Garden City, NY: Anchor Books, 1977).
4. See McNeill, 'Migration in premodern times,' *op. cit.*; William H. McNeill, *Polyethnicity and National Unity in World History* (Toronto: University of Toronto Press, 1986); and John A. Armstrong, *Nations before Nationalism* (Chapel Hill, NC: The University of North Carolina Press, 1982), pp. 122–6.
5. See Ernst Renan, *What Is a Nation?* (1862); Carlton J.H. Hayes, *The Historical Evolution of Nationalism* (New York: R. Smith, 1931); George G. Iggers, *The German Conception of History: the National Tradition of Historical Thought from Herder to the Present* (Middletown, CT: Wesleyan University Press, 1968).
6. See McNeill, *Polyethnicity and National Unity, op. cit.*, pp. 3–29.
7. See generally Fernand Braudel, *Identity of France, Vol. I* (New York: HarperCollins, 1990), pp. 21–167.
8. Aristide R. Zolberg, 'The formation of new states as a refugee-generating

process,' in Elizabeth G. Ferris, *Refugees and World Politics* (New York: Praeger, 1985).

9. E.L. Jones, *The European Miracle* (Cambridge: Cambridge University Press, 1987), p. 120.

10. Fernand Braudel, *The Mediterranean and the Mediterranean World in the Age of Philip II, Vol. I* (New York: Harper & Row, 1972), p. 416.

11. Leslie Page Moch, *Moving Europeans: Migration in Western Europe since 1650* (Bloomington, IN: Indiana University Press, 1992), p. 54.

12. N.J.G. Pounds, *An Historical Geography of Europe* (Cambridge: Cambridge University Press, 1990), pp. 261–2, 265.

13. See Fernand Braudel, *op. cit.*, pp. 417–18.

14. Moch, *Moving Europeans*, p. 85.

15. See F.H. Hinsley, *Nationalism and the International System* (London: Hodder and Stoughton, 1973) p. 20.

16. See Liah Greenfeld, *Nationalism: Five Roads to Modernity* (Cambridge, MA: Harvard University Press, 1992), p. 4.

17. See Greenfeld, *Nationalism*, pp. 29–87.

18. Pound, *An Historical Geography of Europe*, p. 117.

19. Paula S. Fichtner 'Dynastic marriage in sixteenth century Habsburg diplomacy and statecraft: an interdisciplinary approach,' *American Historical Review*, 81 (1976), 243–65.

20. Jones, *The European Miracle*, p. 112.

21. Eugene F. Rice, Jr, *The Foundations of Early Modern Europe, 1460–1559* (New York: W.W. Norton & Co., 1970), p. 115. Also see Anthony Mockler, *Mercenaries* (London: McDonald, 1970).

22. Pound, *An Historical Geography of Europe*, p. 264.

23. See Alfred Vagts, *A History of Militarism, Civilian and Military* (New York: The Free Press, 1959), pp. 66 and 85.

24. Greenfeld, *Nationalism*, p. 14.

25. See Eugen Weber, *Peasants into Frenchmen: the Modernization of Rural France 1870–1914* (Stanford, CA: Stanford University Press, 1976).

26. McNeill, *Polyethnicity and National Unity in World History*, pp. 34–56.

27. See Jones, *The European Miracle*, pp. 134–43.

28. See McNeill, *Polyethnicity*, p. 44.

29. McNeill, 'Migration in premodern times,' p. 35.

30. See Robert A. Dahl, *Democracy and Its Critics* (New Haven, CT: Yale University Press, 1989), p. 239, table 17.1.

31. Source: Central Bureau of Statistics of the Netherlands, reported in Solon Ardittis, 'East–West migration: an overview of trends and issues,' in Solon Ardittis (ed.), *The Politics of East–West Migration* (St Martin's Press, 1994), p. 25.

32. See Charles P. Kindleberger, *Europe's Postwar Growth: the Role of Labor Supply* (Cambridge, MA: Harvard University Press, 1967) and Hollifield, *Immigrants, States, and Markets*, pp. 50–73.

33. See OECD, *SOPEMI: Continuous Reporting System on Migration* (Paris: OECD, 1992), pp. 15, 19.

34. Jonas Widgren, 'International migration and regional stability,' *International Affairs*, 66, 4, 752.

35. See Alan L. Boegehold, 'Perikles' citizenship law of 451/0 BC,' and Adele C. Scafuro,. 'Witnessing and false witnessing: proving citizenship and kin identity in fourth-century Athens,' in Alan L. Boegehold and Adele C. Scafuro, *Athenian Identity and Civic Ideology* (Baltimore, MD: Johns Hopkins University Press, 1994). The restrictive citizenship law of 451 was repealed in 429 BC and then reinstated in 403 BC.

36. Dummett and Nicol, *Subjects, Citizens, Aliens and Others*, pp. 21–38.

37. Rolf Grawert, *Staat und Staatsangehörigkeit, Verfassungsgeschichte Untersuchungen zur Entstehung der Staatsangehörigkeit, Schriften zur Verfassungsgeschichte, Band 17* (Berlin: Duncker and Humbolt, 1973), p. 79.

38. For a discussion of how norms constitute the international system and on the distinction between constitutive and regulative norms, see Friedrich V. Kratochwil, *Rules, Norms and Decisions: on the Conditions of Practical and Legal Reasoning in International Relations and Domestic Affairs* (Cambridge: Cambridge University Press, 1989). For a discussion of norms and system transformation as well as an example of the constitutive role of citizenship, see Rey Koslowski and Friedrich Kratochwil, 'Understanding change in international politics: the Soviet Empire's demise and the international system,' *International Organization,* 48, 2 (Spring 1994).

39. See Grawert, *Staat und Staatsangehörigkeit* and Thomas Hammar, *Democracy and the Nation-State: Aliens, Denizens and Citizens in a World of International Migration* (Aldershot: Avebury, 1990), pp. 41–9.

40. For the codification of this norm see the League of Nations 'Convention on certain questions relating to the Conflict of Nationality Laws, 1930,' 'Protocol Relating to a certain case of statelessness, 1930,' and 'Special protocol concerning statelessness, 1930' in Richard Plender (ed.), *Basic Documents on International Migration Law* (Dordrecht: Martinus Nijhoff Publishers, 1988), pp. 19–35.

41. Richard Plender, *International Migration Law* (Dordrecht: Martinus Nijhoff Publishers, 1988), p. 8.

42. L. Oppenheim, *International Law*, 8th. edn, by H. Lauterpacht (London: Longman, 1955) pp. 642–3.

43. Paul Weis, *Nationality and Statelessness in International Law* (Alpen aan den Rijn: Sijthoff & Noordhoff, 1979), pp. 4–5.

44. See T.H. Marshall, 'Citizenship and social class,' in *Class, Citizenship and Social Development: Essays by T.H. Marshall* (Chicago: The University of Chicago Press, 1964).

45. Weis, *Nationality and Statelessness in International Law*, pp. 5–6.

46. See Derek Heater, *Citizenship: the Civic Ideal in World History, Politics and Education* (New York: Longman, 1990), pp. 96–9, 197–202, 211–24; Benjamin Barber, *Strong Democracy: Participatory Politics for a New Age* (Berkeley, CA: University of California Press, 1984), chapters 8 and 9.

47. See Eric B. Gorham, *National Service, Citizenship, and Political Education* (Albany, NY: State University of New York Press, 1992).

48. See Michael Walzer, 'The obligation to die for the state,' in Walzer, *Obligations: Essays on Disobedience, War, and Citizenship* (Cambridge, MA: Harvard University Press, 1971), pp 77–98.

49. See Dahl, *Democracy and its Critics*, pp. 234–9.

50. See *American Journal of International Law*, 23 (1929) 2nd supplement, p. 29.

51. See Armstrong, *Nations before Nationalism*, pp. 14–53.

52. Charles Hartshorn Maxson, *Citizenship* (New York: Oxford University Press, 1930), pp. 2–5; Weis, *Nationality and Statelessness*, p. 4.

53. Rogers Brubaker, 'Citizenship and nationhood in France and Germany,' PhD dissertation, Columbia University, 1990. The dissertation was published in a shorter version, Rogers Brubaker, *Citizenship and Nationhood in France and Germany* (Cambridge, MA: Harvard University Press, 1992).

54. Dummet and Nicol, *Subjects, Citizens, and Aliens*, p. 24, pp. 231–59.

55. See James H. Kettner, *The Development of American Citizenship, 1608–1870* (Chapel Hill, NC: The University of North Carolina Press, 1978), pp. 173–247.

56. For an extensive of discussion of the initial delineation of French citizenship and combination of the principles of *jus sanguinis* and *jus soli* in that delineation see Brubaker, 'Citizenship and Nationhood' (1990), pp. 100–15, 176–209; and Grawert, *Staat und Staatsangehörigkeit*, pp. 165–70.

57. Portugal is the primary exception to the continental norm of *jus sanguinis* ascription. Spain combines *jus soli* and *jus sanguinis* equally. See Brubaker, 'Citizenship and Nationhood' (1990), p. 167, fn. 16.

58. Brubaker, 'Citizenship and Nationhood' (1992) pp. 1–6, 138–64. The French parliament voted to end automatic extension of citizenship in May 1993.

59. *Reichs-Gesetzblatt* (1913), pp. 583–93. For a translation see Richard W. Flournoy and Manley O. Hudson (eds), *A Collection of Nationality Laws of Various Countries as Contained in Constitutions, Statutes and Treaties* (New York: Oxford University Press, 1929), pp. 306–13.

60. See Brubaker, 'Citizenship and Nationhood' (1990), pp. 264–72. Citizenship in Germany is still based on the 1913 law but it has been modified by the 1990 Foreigners Act which makes naturalization easier for foreigners aged 16–23 who have lived continuously in Germany for eight years. See OECD, *SOPEMI*, 1992, p. 36.

61. See Brinley Thomas, *International Migration and International Development* (Paris: Unesco, 1961), p. 9.

62. See James Brown Scott, 'Nationality: *jus soli* or *jus sanguinis*,' *American Journal of International Law*, 24, 1, 58–64; Hammar, *Democracy and the Nation-State*, pp. 71–2 and Brubaker, 'Citizenship and Nationhood' (1990), pp. 169–72. In the Americas, only Panama and Haiti base citizenship on *jus sanguinis*, *ibid.*, p. 169.

63. See Hammar, *Democracy and the Nation-state*, pp. 71–2; and Brubaker, 'Citizenship and Nationhood' (1990), pp. 169–72.

64. See Guenter Moltmann, 'American–German return migration in the nineteenth and early twentieth centuries,' *Central European History*, 13, 4 (December 1980), 378–92, especially the graph on p. 386.

65. See Thomas, *International Migration and International Development*, p. 9. It is important to point out, however, that the British position on emigrants was 'once born a subject of the crown, always a subject.' Only the children of expatriates born abroad did not gain British citizenship rights.

66. Klaus J. Bade, 'German emigration to the United States and continental immigration to Germany in the late nineteenth and early twentieth centuries,' *Central European History*, 13, 4 (December 1980), 366–75.

67. See Brubaker, 'Citizenship and Nationhood' (1990), pp. 264–304.

68. See William Rogers Brubaker, 'Citizenship and naturalization: policies and

politics,' in William Rogers Brubaker (ed.), *Immigration and the Politics of Citizenship in Europe and America* (Lanham, MD: The German Marshall Fund of the United States and the University Press of America, 1989), p. 102.

69. See Brubaker, *Citizenship and Nationhood* (1992), p. 115.

70. 'Unless otherwise provided by law, a German within the meaning of the Basic Law is a person who possesses German citizenship or who has been admitted to the territory of the German Reich within the frontiers of 31 December 1937 as a refugee of German stock (*Volkszugehörigkeit*) or as the spouse or descendent of such person.' Elmar M. Hucko (ed.), *The Democratic Tradition: Four German Constitutions* (Leamington Spa: Berg, 1987), p. 255.

71. See Dummett and Nicol, *Subjects, Citizens, Aliens and Others*, p. 128.

72. On the history of Irish emigration see, Kerby Miller, *Emigrants and Exiles: Ireland and the Irish Exodus to North America* (New York: Oxford University Press, 1985); and J.A. Jackson, *The Irish in Britain* (London: Routledge and Kegan Paul, 1963).

73. With respect to contemporary migration, 'in 1991, 13.5% of all Irish in the EC do not live in Ireland but in another EC country.' Eurostat, *Rapid Reports, Population and Social Conditions*, 6 (1993), 10.

74. See Simon Hornblower, 'Creation and development of democratic institutions in ancient Greece,' in John Dunn (ed.), *Democracy the Unfinished Journey, 508 BC to AD 1993* (Oxford: Oxford University Press, 1992); Boegehold, 'Perekles' citizenship law of 451/0 BC;' and Scafuro, 'Witnessing and false witnessing.'

75. See Johannes Althusius, *Politica Methodice Digesta*, Frederick S. Carney, trans. and ed. (Boston: Beacon Press, 1964), p. 35; Mack Walker, *German Home Towns: Community, State, and General Estate, 1648–1871* (Ithaca, NY: Cornell University Press, 1971), pp. 108–44; J.K. Bluntschli, *The Theory of the State* (Oxford: Clarendon Press, 1895), pp. 160–8, 211–12; and E. Bonjour, H.S. Offler and G.R. Potter, *A Short History of Switzerland* (Oxford: Clarendon Press, 1952), pp. 103–4.

76. Brubaker, 'Citizenship and Nationhood' (1990), p. 171.

77. See Mark Miller, 'The problem of foreign worker participation and representation in France, Switzerland and the Republic of Germany,' PhD dissertation, University of Wisconsin, 1978; Cheryl Bernard, 'Migrant workers and European democracy,' *Political Science Quarterly*, 93, 2 (Summer 1978); and Martin O. Heisler and Barbara Schmitter Heisler (eds), *From Foreign Workers to Settlers? Transnational Migration and the Emergence of New Minorities. The Annals of the American Academy of Political and Social Science*, no. 485 (Beverly Hills: Sage, 1985).

78. See Michael Walzer, *Spheres of Justice* (New York: Basic Books, 1983) chapter 2; and Joseph H. Carens, 'Membership and morality: admission to citizenship in liberal democratic states,' in William Rogers Brubaker (ed.), *Immigration and the Politics of Citizenship in Europe and North America* (New York: University Press of America, 1989).

79. See Evans, 'Nationality law and European integration'; Gerald L. Neuman, 'We are the people: alien suffrage in German and American perspective,' *Michigan Journal of International Law*, 13 (1992), 259–335; Miller, *The Problem of Foreign Worker Participation and Representation*; William Rogers Brubaker, 'Introduction,' in Brubaker (ed.), *Immigration and the Politics of Citizenship*; Hammar, *Democracy*

and the Nation-state; Hollifield, *Immigrants, States, and Markets*; Shuck and Smith, *Citizenship without Consent*; Carens 'Membership and morality'; and Joseph H. Carens, 'Migration and morality: a liberal egalitarian perspective,' in Brian Barry and Robert E. Goodin (eds), *Free Movement: Ethical Issues in the Transnational Migration of People and of Money* (University Park, PA: The Pennsylvania State University Press, 1992).

80. See, e.g., Anthony Arblaster, *Democracy* (Minneapolis, MN: University of Minnesota Press, 1987); Barber, *Strong Democracy*; Noberto Bobbio, *The Future of Democracy* (Minneapolis, MN: University of Minnesota Press, 1987); William Connolly, *Identity/Difference: Democratic Negotiations of Political Paradox* (Ithaca, NY: Cornell University Press, 1991); Dahl, *Democracy and Its Critics*; David Held, *Models of Democracy* (Stanford, CA: Stanford University Press, 1987); John Keane, *Democracy and Civil Society* (London: Verso, 1988); Arend Lijphart, *Democracies* (New Haven, CT: Yale University Press, 1984); Jane Mansbridge, *Beyond Adversary Democracy* (New York: Basic Books, 1980); William Riker, *Liberalism Against Populism* (San Francisco: W.H. Freeman, 1982); and Giovanni Sartori, *The Theory of Democracy Revisited* (Chatham, NJ: Chatham House, 1987).

81. Frederick G. Whelen, 'Democratic theory and the boundary problem,' in J. Roland Pennock and John W. Chapman (eds), *Liberal Democracy, Nomos XXV* (New York: New York University Press, 1983).

82. See, e.g., Lijphart's delineation in *Democracies*, pp. 37–9 and Dahl's in *Democracy and its Critics*, pp 233–9.

83. Moch, *Moving Europeans*, p. 149. By 1930 Norway was a democracy that primarily based nationality on *jus sanguinis*.

84. Dahl, *Democracy and Its Critics*, p. 129.

85. *Ibid.*, p. 22.

86. *Ibid.*, p. 128, note 11.

87. *Ibid.*, p. 129.

88. Michael Walzer, *Spheres of Justice*, p. 58.

89. See Carens, 'Membership and morality.'

90. Walzer, *Spheres of Justice*, p. 31.

91. *Ibid.*, p. 61.

92. See Whelen, 'Democratic theory and the boundary problem,' pp. 15–16; and Dahl, *Democracy and Its Critics*, pp. 193–209.

93. Hammar, *Democracy and the Nation-state*, pp. 8, 116.

94. *Ibid.*, pp. 116–17.

95. See Marshall, 'Citizenship and social class.'

96. See Gary P. Freeman, 'Migration and the political economy of the welfare state,' in Heisler and Schmitter Heisler (eds), *From Foreign Workers to Settlers?*

97. See Hollifield, *Immigrants, Markets, and States*.

4 World society and the future of international migration: a theoretical perspective

Hans-Joachim Hoffmann-Nowotny

Introduction

The history of mankind is also a history of migration. Even the worldwide, intercontinental migration which forms the subject of this chapter is by no means a new or even exclusively modern phenomenon. If we look at earlier periods of history, to cite but a few examples, we find the first settlement of the Americas by migrants from Asia, the migrations in ancient Europe which culminated in the movements of the peoples (*Völkerwanderung*), and the second colonization of North and South America by Europeans. It would appear that the concept of 'one world,' of the world as a 'world society,' which is to underlie much of the following discussion, has been at least partially applicable to all periods of human history, even if it has never before been so fully appropriate as it is today.

The same is true of the concept of 'mass migration,' as we rightly term the phenomenon of international migration today; considered in relation to the size of the population at the time, even the historical migrations mentioned above may be placed under this heading. In the narrower sense of the term, however, 'mass migration' presupposes those human 'masses' which have resulted from the 'population explosion' of recent times, and is unlikely to come to an end in the foreseeable future.

Demographic aspects of world society

According to United Nations' estimates, the earth's population passed the 5.6 billion mark around the middle of 1993. The same organization predicts that world population will reach 6.4 billion in the year 2000, 8.5 billion in 2025, and 10.0 billion in 2050. So far, longer-term projections suggested that in about 100 years' time, world population would stabilize at around 10.0 billion. Most recent forecasts do not, however, exclude the possibility that world population growth might well not come to an end until the 14.0 billion mark.

With regard to the future migration *potential*, it has to be seen that of today 5.6 billion people inhabiting this world, 1.2 billion live in 'more developed regions' and 4.4 billion in 'less developed regions.' In the year 2025 the corresponding figures will be 1.4 billion in 'more developed regions' and 7.1 billion in 'less developed regions.' The population *explosion* outlined above is practically confined to developing countries (in particular to Africa and South East Asia), while developed countries rather appear to be heading for a population *implosion*. Nowhere is this more clearly the case than in Western European countries like Italy (1.3 children per woman), Germany (1.4), Austria (1.4), and Switzerland (1.5); and with the exception of Iceland (2.2) and Ireland (2.1) all developed European countries are below the reproduction level of 2.1 children per woman.

The obvious question is whether this situation, with an increase in population on the one side and a decrease either already taking place or soon to be expected on the other, is likely to give a further, massive boost to the scale of international migration already taking place today. Assumptions along these lines are voiced again and again, and are clearly based upon some sort of underlying physical model in which the laws of nature dictate that an increase in pressure in one 'vessel' and a reduction in pressure in another will inevitably produce a transfer between the two in order to equalize the pressure throughout the system.

This is, however, not a view that the social scientist will be able to subscribe to as a matter of course, even if the model should lead to a correct empirical description of currents of migration. Rather, his approach must be based upon theoretical considerations, and the scholar will have to ask himself what constellation of socio-*structural* conditions on the one hand and socio-*cultural* factors on the other produce a situation in which, with a certain degree of probability, a potential for migration develops or migration actually takes place. It goes without saying that this theoretical basis should be as general and therefore as widely applicable as possible, so that the phenomenon of 'migration' (which, here, is taken to refer primarily to international migration) can be viewed, described, and explained, not in isolation, but as part of a greater and more complex pattern of events.

A macro-sociological paradigm of international migration

It would be premature to suggest that a fundamental change of paradigm is taking place in sociology, yet it is apparent that individualistic explanatory approaches derived from a variety of backgrounds (rational choice, behavioral theory, theory of action, decision theory, the interpretative paradigm) have gained weight and acceptance in recent times.[1] Contrary to the views of the proponents of such individualistic approaches, whose proponents are the most radical of all in asserting the exclusiveness of their theories, one might equally claim that it is only the level of observation which has shifted. There has been a move away from the level of collective society as the central object of investigation, toward that of the individual who acts and takes decisions. If one sides with the advocates of macro-sociological theories, who are less dogmatic in their view of micro-sociological approaches than is the case the other way round, in regarding society as the object of investigation, then this does not rule out the possibility of regarding micro-sociological and macro-sociological theories as being complementary. Seen from such a viewpoint, the two standpoints would no longer be mutually exclusive. I personally tend toward this view.

Paradigmatic aspects of migration theory

As far as migration theory is concerned, a more fundamental view is put forward by Kubat and Hoffmann-Nowotny.[2] In Kubat's view, all theories attempting to explain the phenomenon of migration are, without exception, based upon the assumption that man is by nature a sedentary being. It then makes no difference whether 'field forces,' 'deprivation,' 'motives' and 'expectations,' 'structural tensions,' or the confrontation with 'systemic problems' are regarded as the determinants of migration. In all cases, a basically sedentary being is prompted to migrate, to become geographically mobile. If all theories now set out to explain why basically sedentary beings decide to move elsewhere, it may or may not be appropriate to speak of their belonging to one basic paradigmatic category. What is certain is that all such theories thus have a fundamental feature in common, which we have chosen to refer to as a 'metaparadigm.' In doing so, however, we leave open the possibility of regarding each different approach to the question of migration – be it macro-sociological, micro-sociological, or whatever – as a paradigm in its own right.

In the article cited above, Kubat and Hoffmann-Nowotny call into question the metaparadigm of man as a sedentary species: 'In inverting the classical migration metaparadigm, we assume that man is mobile by nature.'[3] In addition, we challenge the rationality model which underlies decision theories, and instead postulate 'indeterminate human motivation.' Co-authorship is known to involve compromises, and had I been writing alone, I doubt whether I would have chosen to bear sole responsibility for the socio-biological implications of the proposed metaparadigmatic inversion, even though there is undoubtedly some justification for this standpoint.[4]

I should prefer now to put forward a third variant, one in which man is not regarded as either sedentary or mobile by nature, but – perhaps under the influence of the social anthropology of Arnold Gehlen, who himself takes up the ideas of Max Scheler – as 'receptive to his environment.' Man is a social being whose sociologically significant 'nature' is largely determined by the culture and structure of his society.[5] However, there appears to be no doubt that man has led a mobile existence throughout by far the greater period of human history, and that it was only at the time of the neolithic revolution and the early advanced civilizations that he began to settle down to any real degree.

Questions pertaining to the 'nature' of man from a socio-biological, anthropological, or even ethnological viewpoint are undoubtedly fascinating and worthwhile objects of study. Nevertheless, a sociological analysis need not wait for such research to bear fruit, but should concentrate on the areas and problems which belong to sociology proper, without, of course, ignoring or indeed negating the results achieved in neighboring disciplines. In this case, the real question is not so much whether *man* is mobile or sedentary by *nature*; what we need to ask ourselves as sociologists is when and under what circumstances *societies* are sedentary or mobile, or what factors determine whether their members opt for a sedentary or a mobile existence.

I cannot, here, enumerate the various factors which have caused societies to become sedentary in the past. The fact remains that practically all societies of today have, through a historical process of development, evolved a universally territorial organizational principle in the form of the nation state. Its frontiers are formally laid down and guaranteed by international law, and regarded in principle as inviolable. Thus, it is accurate today to speak of a world of sedentary societies.

An outline of a paradigm of migration

Once societies have established themselves within certain geographical boundaries, or – in cases where this process is not yet complete – aspire to establish themselves on a permanent basis, they depend for their continuing existence upon permanently rendered services on the basis of the division of labor. Given this fact, unchecked geographical mobility is at least partly dysfunctional, not only for society as a whole, but also for the individual, who is ultimately also dependent upon the long-term stability of his or her society, even though this need not be the society to which he or she originally belonged. Thus, the individual undoubtedly has a greater opportunity for mobility than society has. Societies achieve long-term stability through the establishment of norms and institutions, i.e. through cultural systems of symbols which correlate with and are interdependently linked with social structures in which individuals occupy various categories of positions. It is these institutions which actually guarantee the existence of societies, since one of their functions is to ensure a kind of barrier against a massive abandonment of such positions. They are only able to do this, however, as long as positions which become vacant, for whatever reason, are suitably filled again. To take but one obvious example, the drastic measures with which the former German Democratic Republic halted the exodus of its own people clearly demonstrates what can happen when a society, or rather, in this case, the ruling class, finds itself in danger of losing control over the mobility of its members.

The other side of the coin is apparent in the similarly draconic measures which the member states of the European Union (EU) and other European countries began introducing in the early 1970s in an attempt to stop or even reverse the flow of immigration, including repatriation grants for foreigners in France and Germany. Indeed, restrictions have tended to become even more severe in recent times, in response to the rising tide of applicants for political asylum and illegal immigrants.

On the other hand, the continuing pressure of immigration on many societies in Western Europe and elsewhere today shows that societies throughout extensive areas of the world are prepared to remove restrictions on the mobility of their members, even if they would actually prefer to maintain such restrictions, at least on a selective basis, but are no longer able to do so. Norms and institutions, however, serve not only to provide stability, but must also always be seen as a means of selecting the range of potential structures and courses of action available within a given society. From what is in principle an infinite variety, a comparatively small number of possibilities is selected and declared to be desirable and proper, while many others are ruled out. This is an important element in Luhmann's systems theory, for example, in which a 'system' is equated with the maintenance of selective forces.[6] Migration then emerges as one of the possible courses of action which may be either ruled out altogether or permitted on a larger or smaller scale and with greater or lesser limitations imposed upon different categories. A sociological viewpoint of this kind seems to me to be particularly valuable in this context, since it allows migration theory to remain largely uninfluenced by questions of human 'nature,' and in particular the vexed question of whether man is by nature mobile or sedentary.

Nevertheless, Kubat's and Hoffmann-Nowotny's observations are still significant, insofar as they compel migration theorists, who imply that humankind is sedentary by nature, to consider the consequences of this assumption. Let me, however, emphasize once again that a viewpoint rooted in systems theory does not render obsolete the concept of migration as the result of an individual decision-taking process in which, at one end of a continuum of available decisions defined by the society in question, an individual may opt for migration as one of many possibilities open to him or her, while at the other extreme migration may be the only course of action he or she has left, when, for example, driven out of his or her home or faced with the threat of genocide. Sociologists, however, are well advised to address themselves first and foremost to the cultural and structural factors which make migration more or less probable.

To this end, I should like to put forward a macro-sociological paradigm, based upon the 'theory of structural and anomic tensions'[7] which preceded the 'structure-culture paradigm.'[8] This theory is extended here to embrace aspects of classical approaches as proposed by Simmel, Weber, and Durkheim, including, in the later version, the views of society taken by Hobbes, Freud, Elias, and Luhmann.[9]

Since the above-mentioned theory has its roots in systems theory, it seems logical, ultimately, to contemplate an analysis of world society both in its parts and as a whole. Thus, *an analysis of migration will not simply examine tensions in individual societies, but will regard these in their turn as interrelated subsystems within the world system.* Consequently, migration does not primarily depend upon the tensions within any given society, but rather upon the distribution of tensions throughout the system as a whole; it is not tensions as such, but the uneven distribution of tensions, which leads to migration. Thus, to return to an earlier example, the former German Democratic Republic could permit unrestricted emigration to the former USSR without fear of any significant population drain, whereas it would have been rather inadvisable for the USSR to adopt a similar policy even toward the German Democratic Republic.

In addition to the systems-theory related aspects outlined above (the system as a selective force, which, from the *dynamic* point of view, implies socio-cultural change while at the same time securing stability), we now need to consider a theory of the control mechanisms. That is to say, societies must not only select and limit the possible courses of action open to their members, but must also enforce this selection to ensure that those courses of action not selected by the system remain unavailable.

Seen in this context, the anomic tensions produced by structural tensions imply a relaxation of the control mechanisms limiting the range of individual action, which also includes the possibility of migration. It is important to remember, however, that these control mechanisms are not limited solely to the various means by which the state keeps a watch on its citizens, even though this is certainly a very significant factor in modern societies. This supervisory function rather permeates every level of our socially institutionalized existence. It may safely be assumed, however, that social systems which are based upon 'organic solidarity' (Durkheim) or which can be termed 'society' or *Gesellschaft* (Tönnies) can rely much less upon family, neighborly, or other 'ties' to limit the mobility of their members than is the case with social systems of the 'community' or *Gemeinschaft* type (Tönnies), which owe their cohesion to 'mechanical solidarity' (Durkheim). Thus, it is possible to postulate an intensification of state supervision as a means of compensating for the weakening of the constraints imposed by social ties. This hypothesis is supported by the assumption that, compared with socialization in 'communities,' the process of socialization in complex modern societies is deficient in internalized control mechanisms, even though this has a positive function with regard to development and change. Thus, when taken together with the internal and external distribution of tensions, it is these various 'control mechanisms' which finally determine which categories of persons may or may not emerge as potential or actual migrants, and in what order.

Given a certain configuration of interdependent tensions spanning all levels from that of world society, through various societal strata down to that of the individual, further central factors determining migration take the form of specific control mechanisms operating in each case – or, to be precise, the severity or leniency with which they are applied. On the individual level, there are additional, internalized social constraints to be considered, apart from those imposed from outside. Finally, it also has to be borne in mind that certain constraints, such as those which limit or suppress the social mobility of particular categories of persons, may tend to reinforce structural tensions and contribute to their translation into anomic tensions. Then, the relaxation of constraints designed to maintain a sedentary society may be instrumental in enabling the individual to break free, not only of these constraints, but also of others. In this sense, 'town air' can be just as liberating (*Stadtluft macht frei*) as 'pilgrimage'. The same viewpoint, however, also covers the case of young people leaving home; once they reach the age of majority, they are able to decide for themselves where to live, and in so doing are also able to break free of other parental controls. The fact that these two apparently quite disparate phenomena can be interpreted in the same terms once again illustrates the advantages of adopting a comprehensive theoretical viewpoint.

This view of society as a systemically organized set of selection and control mechanisms raises the question of whether migration, the expression of less strictly enforced constraints, may be taken as marking a certain degree of freedom granted to the individual by a given society. If this is the case at all, it is undoubtedly true only to a limited extent and for a limited time. Experience, both contemporary and historical, has shown that migration may initially go through an anomic phase in which it is subject to few constraints, but that it quickly tends to be institutionalized and supervised in its turn. This has been the case throughout history, beginning with the migration of the peoples (*Völkerwanderung*), the pilgrimages of the Middle Ages, the migration of journeymen, right up to modern large-scale emigration, and finally even mass tourism, which may legitimately be regarded as temporary migration. Even this form of migration represents a transfer of tensions between societies, as we see, for example, if we consider the passions aroused by the question of its effects on Third World countries in the context of development policy.

To put this in somewhat different terms, we might say that if societies either cannot actually prevent migration or choose not to do so – for example, because migration provides an outlet for tensions and thus helps to sustain the status quo – then at least they try, as far as possible, to keep the process under control. At the opposite end of the scale, the same is true, of course, of potential immigration societies, which seek to safeguard themselves against an unwelcome transfer of tensions by establishing complicated systems of immigration laws and regulations designed to keep the migration process fully under control. Here again, there are numerous historical and contemporary examples which could be cited.

It is irrelevant from the theoretical point of view whether the accumulated tensions within a society find release in tribal migration, in pilgrimage, in juvenile uprisings (*Saubannerzüge*), in mercenary service abroad, in modern labor migration, or in the present rising tide of asylum seekers, refugees, and illegal immigrants. Any such development should, however, be anticipated on the theoretical basis of specific preconditions and circumstantial factors, including the specific historical situation, and demonstrated by means of systematic, empirical evidence.

Finally, if migration becomes institutionalized, as we see it has been again and again throughout history, it may acquire a cultural and structural momentum which sustains it quite independently of the configuration which originally gave rise to it. For particular categories of persons, specific forms of migration may then develop into a cultural norm (e.g. temporary or permanent labor migration from certain countries and regions), or even into a prescribed element in the standard life-course (e.g. the Muslim's pilgrimage to Mecca), dispensation from which may only be granted under certain clearly defined conditions. Having begun by viewing migration as an anomic phenomenon defying established social controls, we have finally come to see the individual's active participation in it, not merely as one culturally-selected and standardized possibility open to him or her, but as a positive duty which he or she is under a religious obligation to fulfill.

World society and international migration: a macro-sociological approach

Based on the theoretical approach developed in the foregoing section, modern mass migration (or at least the potential for mass migration which is present within the international system) has to be seen against the background of the concept of 'one world', or the world as a *world society*, which is becoming more and more of a reality.[10]

From a *sociological* point of view, a theoretical treatment of intra-European migrations, as well as of worldwide international migrations, or, with a view to the future, the international migration *potential*, must thus initially proceed from the fact of (a) the rise of a 'world society.' But, as far as the rise of a 'world society' is concerned, a further and *demographic* fact has to be taken into account, namely (b) the explosive growth in world population.

It seems obvious that with this, an immense worldwide migration *potential* is given; however, it is not self-understood that this potential would actually result in migrations. Rather, this depends on certain structural and cultural characteristics of world society. The most important among these characteristics which finally determine the migration potential are: (a) *developmental disparities* between national units of the world society as a *structural* factor; and (b) *value integration* of this society, which produces and legitimizes the demand for social mobility, as a *cultural* factor.

Developmental disparities mean that the *structure* of world society is characterized by a form of inequality which allows it to be termed a 'stratified' or 'class society.' Thus, it is possible to speak, for example, of an international lower class, an international middle class, and an international upper class.[11] The concept of social strata implies a society which is in principle 'open;' that is, a society which permits social mobility, which in turn is often linked with geographical mobility. Social mobility may, in principle, be realized on two levels: that of *individual* and that of *collective* mobility. In the first case, the individual seeks to improve his personal situation by his own efforts, as it were, for example by emigrating. In the second case, the situation of the individual is improved by changes in the collective to which he belongs, for example as the result of successful development policy in a particular region or country.

International migration can then be seen as one of the means to achieve upward social mobility. It is a 'functional equivalent' to either internal individual social mobility or contextual mobility. If we consider migration from less developed areas of Europe and from developing countries, it is clear that millions upon millions of people are no longer prepared to wait for collective efforts to bear fruit, but are seeking to improve their individual situation in life by emigrating.[12]

Developmental disparities may be regarded simply as quantifiable structural distances between nations, which we can measure objectively by reference to economic, social, and demographic indicators. Seen in these terms, however, they are not sufficient in themselves to account for international migration and the international potential for migration. Indeed, the very concept of 'development' would be meaningless if the world as one society did not share the common conceptions of affluence, welfare, social justice, mobility, etc. that appear to be universally accepted as desirable goals.[13] In other words, the second important precondition and determinant is the homogenization of values, or cultural integration, throughout the world. Without this, the stratification of the international system and the inequality this implies cannot enter the individual consciousness. As a result of the diffusion of values, this process has been largely completed by now, a fact which owes a lot in turn to the liberal doctrine on the cultural level and the economic interests associated with it on the structural level, as well as to the structural expansion of Western societies.

As we know, this doctrine, upon which capitalist society is based, postulates the free circulation of goods, capital, and labor throughout the world market. The guardians of this doctrine never tire of denouncing what they regard as protectionist measures on the part of individual countries and portraying them as violations of the 'pure spirit,' for which, it is claimed, the perpetrators will receive their just punishment in the form of an inevitable decline in their overall prosperity.[14]

In the political sphere, both national and international, this doctrine is extended to become the ideology of the liberal, constitutionally governed state, upholding such ideals as 'democracy', 'equality,' 'social justice', etc., and of a liberal order throughout the world. It then embraces, for example, the free choice of domicile, the unrestricted exchange of information,[15] the right of free speech, and so forth.

Yet if we really take the liberal doctrine seriously and accept its full implications, it is hard to see why the concept of free interchange should only apply to goods and capital (in the economic sphere) and to information (in the cultural sphere), but not to labor (i.e. workers) or indeed to people as such. As we know, however, all countries in the developed world are closing their doors ever more tightly, and with ever more determination, to the influx of unwanted immigrants, thus committing a massive violation of the liberal doctrine both as an economic and as a political ideology.[16] This policy makes a potential mockery of the right of asylum, which among others may be derived from the right of free speech, since protection must be given to anyone who exercises this latter right and faces persecution as a result.[17] At the same time, as we have said, such countries never fail to protest against any hint of protectionism in the movement of goods and capital, and link both development aid in general and applications for credit in particular to an 'opening' of the markets concerned. There is, undeniably, something rather schizophrenic in all this, and it would be intelligible only if those who are not merely urged to espouse the liberal doctrine but who all too often have it thrust upon them began to ask why the doctrine as a whole is not promoted.

Given that life is full of contradictions we have to learn to live with, we might choose to do likewise in this case and simply accept the fact that governments implement one set of rules, but find it convenient to ignore others which the 'unadulterated liberal doctrine' would deem to be equally right and proper. All the same, in the context of our theme such a stance would seem to be highly questionable, if not cynical. Even if we choose to ignore any ethical misgivings we may feel toward the inconsistency described above, the causal analysis implicit in the scientific method obliges us to acknowledge the significance of our social and economic system and the doctrine upon which it is based – as well as its worldwide diffusion – in the context of international migration.

Both in the past and in the present, this process of diffusion has not only been allowed to take place, but has been actively encouraged and, where necessary, even imposed willy-nilly, for example by the IMF on the *structural* side and UNESCO in the *cultural* sphere. In this case, it is easy to imagine why the process of diffusion of Western values fails to obey those selectivity criteria which the nations of the West would like to see at work, and that the model as a *whole* gains ground. This means that the 'rest of the world' is also beginning to see the unrestricted movement of persons as a possible individual development strategy.

'World society' has so far become an *institutionalized* reality only in part. It is to be expected, however, that the process of the institutionalization of world society will continue, and that within the respective international organizations, the free movement not only of capital, goods, and services but also of persons will become an ever more important issue.

As far as an *institutionalized* growing together is concerned, the countries forming the European Union have gone much further in this respect than is the case on the world level. Barriers against completely free movement of capital, goods, services, *and* persons *within* these countries have disappeared. Since – due to low birth rates – there is no actual 'population pressure,' and *value integration* has already taken place, we are, as far as *intra-European migration* is concerned, left with the determinant *developmental disparities*. Since structural disparities within the EU are diminishing, the question is not so much whether there will be an increase in intra-European migration of *nationals* of the EU countries, but whether the right of free movement should, and will, be extended to immigrants from outside the EU living in the EU countries.

Two more institutional processes will (or already do) influence intra-

European migration. First, the former Soviet satellites will officially demand membership in the EU. If full membership were granted unconditionally, this would lead to East–West migration streams very probably comparable in size to those from Europe's South to the North, which had their peak in the 1960s and early 1970s. Already by now there is not only migration from the East of Europe to its West, but also in the opposite direction, first of all migration of entrepreneurs and of many members of the professional class. In addition, the former socialist countries have already themselves become a destination to Third World migrants, to applicants for asylum, to migrants from countries of the former Soviet Union.

Second, there are the specific problems created by the process of German unification (internal migration from Germany's East to its West), and the agreements between the Federal Republic of Germany and Poland (visa-free entrance of Poles into Germany and vice versa) and between Germany and Poland, the Czech Republic, and Romania regarding their obligation to take back illegal immigrants. Of continuing importance are the agreements between Germany on the one side and Poland, Romania, and Russia on the other regarding the repatriation of citizens of these countries of German descent.

It would be unrealistic to claim that we can derive concrete numbers of future immigrants into and within Europe or worldwide from the theoretical frame sketched above. I do believe, however, that rather marked tendencies have been demonstrated which come out clearly enough to serve, for example, as a basis for migration policies and policy measures, although this was not the main purpose of my analysis.

Specific preconditions and circumstantial factors governing international migration

International migration is generally preceded by an initial phase of *internal* migration toward the urban centers of the home country, and internal migration of this kind may be said to be governed by the same factors which are responsible for international migration. Statistics available clearly reveal the scale of this population drift, and the extent to which many Third World cities have grown as a result in recent decades, and are likely to continue doing so in the future.[18]

It is in this rapidly increasing urbanization of the Third World that the migration potential of the nations concerned is most visibly manifested. For all the squalor and poverty actually encountered in these urban centers, to those who have chosen to live there they still symbolize the hope for a better life, and moving to the city represents the first step toward a developed world. In the cities, 'our' structures become tangible and visible, and the adoption of 'our' values continues, but at the same time newcomers also experience the gulf which exists between themselves and the lifestyle to which they aspire. Yet it is not only newcomers who find themselves in this situation; from a subjective point of view, the discrepancy is perhaps felt even more acutely by that class of city-dwellers who have had access to various levels of the educational system, modeled, as far as possible, on that of the developed world, with obvious consequences for the process of socialization, but who then find themselves unemployed, under-employed or, at any rate (again seen from a subjective point of view), underpaid by comparison with wages paid in the developed world. Thus, if we examine both immigration from the Third World and migration from the less developed to the more developed regions of the world over the past 25 to 30 years, we may expect to find that, at least in the early stages, migration of this type constitutes a kind of 'brain drain.' There is ample empirical evidence to confirm that this is the case. It is only later that this first group of migrants is followed by those who have, in a sense, been 'pre-socialized' for migration by a process of 'step-by-step migration' in the cities of the developing world. In Third World urban centers, potential emigrants have access to migration-oriented information, and they also have access to the transport systems – again, either modeled on or operated by 'our' world – without which international migration from one continent to another would remain technically impossible.

In Ferdinand Tönnies's terminology,[19] the 'development' or 'modernization' of the Third World implies the transition from 'community' to 'society;' in that of Emile Durkheim, it involves the progressive replacement of a type of social system that is bound together by 'mechanical solidarity' by one which depends for its cohesion upon 'organic solidarity;' that is, upon the functional dependency resulting from the division of labor.[20] As Durkheim demonstrates, this type of society is characterized by a weakening of individual and social ties, and by a reduction in social controls. This, of course, is a situation with which we are more than familiar today.[21] The loosening of ties and the weakening of social controls are further important preconditions of geographical mobility. They impair or disrupt the transmission of static structures and their associated values and norms, which in turn fosters the urge to migrate. As Durkheim noted, this tends most of all to happen when individuals migrate to the cities, in which, he says, 'man is much freer of the collective yoke.'[22]

Other factors governing currents of migration have their origins in the history of the nations concerned. The specific composition of the immigrant populations of Great Britain, France or the Netherlands, for example, can be traced to these countries' colonial past; or, in more general terms, such cases imply an interplay of structural and cultural elements the effects of which were not only felt during the colonial period itself, but have continued to affect the post-colonial era, too, and to influence patterns of migration up to the present. Yet, even if there are no such special circumstances, once a flow of migrants has been established in a particular direction, it tends, for whatever reason, to continue. One major factor in such cases is the relative geographical proximity of the migrant's country of origin and his or her new home. Within Europe, for example, there is a strong tradition of Italian migration into Switzerland, while we are currently witnessing a massive increase in migration from Mexico into the United States, partly due to the fact that in this particular case a Third World country and a Western industrialized nation share a common border. Finally, it is worth bearing in mind that substantial migration apparently also takes place between underdeveloped countries at different stages in their development.[23]

Ultimately, of course, the potential for migration cannot be translated into large-scale migratory movements, unless those who wish to emigrate are given reasonable freedom to do so. Actual migration presupposes that the countries of origin do not match the restrictive immigration policies of the developed nations with restrictive emigration policies of their own. In fact, it was only in the so-called 'socialist world' that we found obstacles to emigration perfected to any real degree.

Although their importance is sometimes overstated, the immigration policies of countries of destination are a significant factor in determining both the extent of international migration and the composition of migrant groups. Looking back over history, we find policies ranging from total bans on immigration at one end of the scale, through every imaginable form of quota system, to more-or-less completely unrestricted entry at the other. By contrast, immigration regulations in force throughout the developed world today are only variations on the first two themes, and the overall pattern must be seen as highly restrictive. The fact that immigration policy is generally so restrictive may be interpreted as a clear indication that the potential for *emigration* is many times greater than the level of *immigration* which developed countries are prepared to accept. This major discrepancy is manifested, on the one hand, in the various and often desperate ploys to which would-be immigrants resort in their attempts to slip through the net of immigration controls, and, on the other, in the often hopeless efforts made by developed countries to keep immigrants out. Thus, the drastic methods employed to prevent immigrants from crossing the border between Mexico and the United States of America offer one extreme example of a country endeavoring to enforce existing restrictions on immigration.

At the same time, the almost constant updating of legislation relating to political asylum by European nations makes it equally clear how difficult it is in practice for a country to close every loophole in its immigration laws. It would be overstating the case to claim that restrictive immigration policies and controls are therefore wholly ineffective, but there is ample evidence to suggest that measures taken by the state to control immigration are by no means the complete answer. There are, for instance, several million 'undocumented aliens' in the USA, while in Europe there are several hundred thousand illegal workers and a similar number of applicants for political asylum, many of whom it would also be reasonable to regard as migrant workers. This indicates that governmental restrictions against immigration proved to be relatively ineffective. For obvious reasons, whether or not Third World countries might wish to adopt similarly restrictive emigration policies themselves, they do not have access to such powerful instruments as an 'iron curtain' to prevent emigration. Admittedly, Third World countries repeatedly complain that they are losing their best brains, and they occasionally demand compensation for the cost of the education that such emigrants have received. All the same, we must bear in mind that the attitude of Third World rulers toward emigration is, to say the least, ambivalent.[24] One may say that emigrants represent a loss of development potential for their countries of origin. But at the same time taxes and other levies paid, in particular by temporary emigrants, often account for a substantial portion of their home country's foreign currency earnings.[25] Emigrants also represent a section of the population that can be seen as a potential threat to the political status quo, which the ruling class would generally prefer to maintain, and the higher the proportion of people who opt for individual in preference to collective mobility the smaller the threat to the status quo. There are, without doubt, a number of Third World country potentates who would sleep more soundly in their beds if the advocates of collective change could be persuaded to emigrate, and we may safely assume that they would even be happy to follow the example of immigration countries in offering financial incentives to those willing to do so.

To summarize, it is clear that certain preconditions and circumstantial factors can influence the direction, scale, and composition of migration *streams*; they do not, however, significantly affect the actual migration *potential* which has been theoretically postulated as a consequence of the progressive development of the world into one society, and of its increasing structural and cultural penetration by the Western model. On the other hand, this potential is also a function of the growing populations of those countries in which the situation is conducive to emigration. This latter point must be particularly emphasized, since population growth in itself by no means automatically leads to an increased potential for migration, or to an increase in actual migration.

Conceptions and policies with regard to future immigration

It seems that there are differing *conceptions* regarding future immigration in Europe. Left-wing and 'green' groups plead for 'liberal' regulations and practices. In contrast, right-wing groups adhere to a more or less total closure of the borders and, in addition, to repatriation of many of the immigrants, and especially of asylum seekers. Overtly xenophobic political parties are rather successful in gaining electoral support, while parties opposing such a tendency are losing voters.

In contrast to the diversity of *conceptions* still expressed in public debate, governments, irrespective of their ideological orientation, seem to increasingly arrive at rather similar *policies* regarding future immigration. Policy *divergence* has obviously come to an end; instead, there is now a trend toward policy *convergence*. The most striking aspect of this trend is that today all EU countries impose fairly strong restrictions on immigration from outside the EU countries, but an equally restrictive policy is also to be found in European non-EU countries. There is a clear trend toward even stronger restrictions and this is true whatever the differences between the countries mentioned may be.

There is also convergence with regard to the fact that the governments of all countries have repeatedly declared that they are *not* immigration countries. There are, moreover, clear indications that there is an especially strong trend toward more restrictive policies and procedures concerning the granting of *asylum*, and regarding stricter border controls against all forms of *illegal immigration*.

In the meantime, migration experts in many European countries have come to the conclusion that instead of applying the asylum procedure to people who in their vast majority are not refugees but simply migrants seeking to escape the social and economic misery of their home countries, the immigration countries should formulate a 'new' immigration policy setting quotas for the number of such immigrants they are willing to accept each year. This and similar proposals are currently being discussed, but have not yet led to legislative decisions.

All European governments officially declare that the legal status and social situation of immigrants should be improved, that integration should be furthered, and that discrimination should be avoided and outruled. It seems, however, that there are still differences with regard to the extent that such declarations have led to government actions, and, in addition, to the effectiveness of such actions. This is especially the case with regard to *illegal* immigrants.

Governments who effectively improve the status of immigrants, be they legal or illegal, find themselves rather soon in an ambivalent situation: there is ample evidence to assume that measures leading to an improvement of the situation of immigrants can have a boomerang effect in that they stimulate further immigration, and might thus increase the problems they were meant to solve. All in all, it is not surprising that all European countries expect further immigration despite restrictive immigration policies and deterring measures, and despite the fact that by now none of them views itself as an immigration country in the stricter sense of this term.

The future of international migration

If we begin by assuming that the population forecasts quoted at the beginning of this chapter are broadly correct and that all other factors remain constant, then it seems likely, simply in view of the huge anticipated growth in the population, that we will witness a vast and growing *potential* for migration in the less developed regions of the world.

However, if we apply the theoretical macro-sociological model outlined earlier, it is possible to make some rather more specific predictions. These may be derived from Figure 4.1, which represents certain assumptions about likely trends in what we have identified as the two central parameters of world society relevant to migration, namely the 'development differentials' or structural distance on the one hand, and 'value integration' or cultural distance on the other.

As we see, migration potential is regarded as a function of changing cultural and structural distances throughout world society. Thus, Figure 4.1 takes no account of the predicted growth of the population, though of course this has to be taken into consideration to the extent outlined above. It is immediately apparent that four of the nine possible combinations of factors are assumed to lead to a decrease in migration potential, four others to an increase, and one to a continuation of the status quo.

This last variant applies if the present distances remain unchanged. If we accept that world population will in fact continue to rise, we may take it that this combination, too, will lead to an increase in migration potential. We may additionally assume that changes in cultural distance have a greater influence on migration potential than changes in structural distance. An increase in cultural distance, incidentally, corresponds to a decrease in the

| | | Structural distance | | |
		Increasing	Constant	Decreasing
Cultural distance	Increasing	– – –	– –	–
	Constant	+ +	=	–
	Decreasing	+ + +	+ +	+

Migration potential: +, increasing; =, constant; –, decreasing.

Figure 4.1 Migration potential as a function of structural and cultural distance.

integration of values, which in turn implies the rejection of a development ideology based upon the Western model and the concept of 'modernization.' This process may be seen at work under the growing influence of Islamic fundamentalism and until recently the same was also true of China. There are, furthermore, repeated calls for a similar rejection of 'Western' values in both Latin America and Africa.[26] If cultural distance as we have defined it increases, then migration potential will always decrease, the sharpest decrease taking place when there is a sharp increase in structural distance. If structural distance increases, but at the same time there is a further decrease in cultural distance, then the potential for migration may be expected to rise dramatically. Given a decrease in cultural distance, then the more sharply the structural distance decreases, the more pronounced the decrease in migration potential is likely to be. Ultimately, it would shrink to a negligible value at the point where the development differentials cease to exist and the integration of values is complete.

Figure 4.1, of course, only gives a general summary of the *logical* range of potential trends in the two independent variables (structural and cultural distance), and their resultant effects upon the dependent variable, migration potential. In order to predict which course this potential itself is likely to take, we ought now to assess what degree of empirical probability we may ascribe to each of the various combinations of those independent variables. It goes without saying, of course, that any such assessment implies a considerable risk of error.

If we begin by considering concrete examples, then it would appear that what we might term the 'lone course' is extremely difficult, if not ultimately impossible, to maintain. Even if a country barricades itself off completely, as China once tried to, for example, it seems that the cultural 'colonization' of the less developed nations and regions of the world will continue its inexorable course and create a restless potential which craves for mobility. Either this potential must be channeled into collective progress, or it will prove very difficult to deny it the chance of individual mobility through emigration. It would be wishful thinking to suggest that the present discrepancy between developed and underdeveloped nations is likely to diminish significantly in the foreseeable future. On the contrary, the gulf is, if anything, likely to widen still further and *we are therefore likely to witness a continuing, and probably even steeper, rise in migration potential in the future.*

Once again, this sweeping assertion needs to be qualified from case to case. There is a real chance that other countries may follow the example of Iran, and we certainly cannot rule out the possibility of similar developments taking place elsewhere in the Islamic world (e.g. in Algeria, Egypt, or Turkey). If this were to be the case, the blame would ultimately rest upon the failure of the Western development paradigm and a resulting return to traditional concepts of the individual, the state, the economy, and society. All the same, it seems doubtful whether such attempts to stop and even turn back the cultural clock will gain more than a limited geographical hold or be able to achieve long-term durability. Instead, these are rather to be seen as temporary setbacks in a process which cannot ultimately be reversed, but which will always bear the stamp of the historical and present circumstances of the specific context in which it takes place.

Thus, the extent to which a growing migration potential is translated into actual migration, and the particular direction it takes, will be governed by the stance adopted by the potential migrants' home countries; that is, do they seek to impede or to encourage emigration?[27] On the other hand, the scale of migration which can actually take place appears to be dictated also by the immigration policies of the potential countries of destination, and more specifically by the extent to which they are able to develop and effectively deploy suitable means of keeping potential migrants at bay. We may take it for granted that attempts to do so will become more and more commonplace. At the same time, both the scale of illegal immigration and the number of would-be migrants applying for political asylum are on the increase, so that it would be naive to overestimate the effectiveness of measures designed to limit migration. There remains the question of whether a number of nations whose populations are expected to decrease might not be willing to permit a level of immigration which would at least maintain a state of equilibrium.

The size of future immigration into Europe

Estimates of the size of the immigrant populations in European countries and their share in the total population vary considerably. Some countries foresee a further increase (e.g. the Netherlands, Great Britain, Germany), some assume a decrease (France). Switzerland maintains that it can and will keep the number of aliens and their share in the total population constant.

But are there good reasons to assume that these projections will come close to the figures we shall observe in the years to come? Or, alternatively, is it realistic to expect that governments will be able to control their borders and refuse potential immigrants to the extent necessary to keep immigration at the levels mentioned above? A glance at today's migration scene evokes a great deal of skepticism with regard to a positive answer to these questions.

Applicants for asylum have become one of the central issues in recent debates on immigration into European countries. It seems that during the 1980s and even more so in the 1990s immigration via application for asylum has increasingly become a substitute for 'regular' immigration. Meanwhile, asylum seekers are outnumbering regular immigrants. The data on the number of applications prove, however, that not all countries are equally attractive for asylum seekers, and a glance at the countries from which asylum seekers arrive shows that if receiving countries are former colonial powers, this is reflected in the national composition of the applicants for asylum.

The forthcoming harmonization of procedures regarding asylum within the EU aims at a more effective control of asylum migration and a reduction in the number of asylum seekers. These aims could so far not be reached to the extent wanted. It can be shown that the number of asylum seekers has been reduced to some extent by more rigorous asylum procedures. However, it cannot be excluded that the stricter asylum regimes will simply increase the obviously already considerable number of illegal immigrants. A large number of illegal immigrants very definitely exist in all European countries, and this is seemingly true especially for the traditional European emigration countries of Italy, Spain, and Greece.[28] There is little doubt that this type of immigration will continue.

Conclusion

Both in view of the anticipated growth in the earth's population and in view of apparent trends in the relevant cultural and structural parameters, there are good theoretical grounds for predicting that worldwide potential for migration is very likely to increase. Against this, there are equally good grounds for assuming that potential immigration countries will do everything in their power to prevent this potential from being realized in terms of actual migration. Considering the likely scale of potential worldwide migration, it certainly seems strange to imagine that lifting restrictions on immigration might lead to a state of *socially acceptable* equilibrium – however this might be defined – in population levels. Migration is the manifestation of the inability of the international system to solve the problem of underdevelopment and the developmental disparities at its source. It cannot make this inability any easier to accept, nor is it any substitute for development itself, no matter how substantially migration may improve the individual immigrant's prospects in life. At the same time, it is unlikely that defensive strategies will prove to be very effective.

The macro-sociological paradigm presented in this chapter cannot claim to account for every aspect of the phenomenon of 'migration,' nor can it be considered in any way definitive or final. Nevertheless, it is a valid and promising approach which might prove fruitful for both the theorist and the empiricist in helping each to avoid the twin excesses of theoretical eclecticism on the one hand, and empirical research totally divorced from theory on the other.

Notes

1. See Thomas S. Kuhn, *Die Entstehung des Neuen: Studien zur Struktur der Wissenschaftsgeschichte* (Frankfurt/Main: Suhrkamp, 1978).
2. Daniel Kubat and Hans-Joachim Hoffmann-Nowotny, 'Migration: towards a new paradigm,' *International Social Science Journal*, 33, 2 (1981), 307–29.
3. *Ibid.*, p. 312.
4. *Ibid.*, pp. 320ff.
5. Arnold Gehlen, *Die Seele im technischen Zeitalter, Sozial-psychologische Probleme in der industriellen Gesellschaft* (Reineck bei Hamburg: Rowohlt, 1957).
6. Niklas Luhmann, *Soziale Systeme: Grundriss einer allgemeinen Theorie* (Frankfurt/Main: Suhrkamp, 1984).
7. See Hans-Joachim Hoffmann-Nowotny, *Migration: ein Beitrag zu einer soziologischen Erklärung* (Stuttgart: Ferd. Enke Verlag, 1970) and Hans-Joachim Hoffmann-Nowotny, *Soziologie des Fremdarbeiterproblems: eine theoretische und empirische Analyse am Beispiel der Schweiz* (Stuttgart: Ferd. Enke Verlag, 1973).
8. Hans-Joachim Hoffmann-Nowotny, 'Social integration and cultural pluralism: structural and cultural problems of immigration in European industrial countries,' in William Alonso (ed.), *Population in an Interacting World* (Cambridge, MA: Harvard University Press, 1987), pp. 149–72.
9. Hans-Joachim Hoffmann-Nowotny, 'Weltbevölkerungswachstum und internationale Migration,' *Österreichische Zeitschrift für Soziologie*, 13, 3 (1988), 4–15.
10. Peter Heintz, *Die Weltgesellschaft im Spiegel von Ereignissen* (Diessenhofen: Rügger, 1982). This is the result of a 'colonization' of the world by the Western nations or, in terms that do not imply so much of a value-judgment, the diffusion of the structural and cultural model which, according to Max Weber (1905/1981), we owe to the 'protestant ethic' that gave birth to the 'spirit of capitalism'. 'Colonization' in this case is, of course, not to be interpreted only literally; the historical phenomenon may well have accelerated the process of diffusion mentioned above, but this process itself would no doubt have taken place even if there had been no physical occupation. Even today the mentioned diffusion has by no means come to an end, despite the fact that some parts of the world are experiencing a 'fundamentalist' backlash involving a broad rejection of the Western model.
11. Heintz, *op. cit.*, pp. 17–18; Hedley Bull, 'Population and the present world structure,' in William Alonso (ed.), *Population in an Interacting World* (Cambridge, MA: Harvard University Press, 1987), pp. 74–94.
12. Hans-Joachim Hoffmann-Nowotny, 'European migration after World War II,' in William H. McNeill and Ruth S. Adams (eds), *Human Migration – Patterns and Policies* (Bloomington, IN: Indiana University Press, 1978), pp. 85–105; Heinz Werner, 'Post-war labour migration in Western Europe – An Overview,' *International Migration*, 24, 3 (1986), 543–57.
13. Francis Fukuyama, 'The end of history?,' *The National Interest*, 16 (1989), 3–19; Francis Fukuyama, *The End of History and the Last Man* (New York: Free Press, 1992); Perry Anderson, *Zum Ende der Geschichte* (Berlin: Rotbuch, 1993).
14. If we speak here of *capitalist* systems and, explicitly or implicitly, assume that certain injustices were simply inherent in the nature of capitalism, then we can also ask ourselves whether these same injustices were unknown in *socialist*

countries. This is not a question of seeking to defend a particular ideology, but is simply an attempt, from the scientific point of view, to establish whether certain phenomena are of a universal or of a system-specific nature. As far as the free movement of persons is concerned, the answer is that socialist countries were vastly more radical in their exclusion of immigrants and would-be refugees than capitalist nations (though since socialist countries were relatively unattractive to begin with, it was not so difficult for them to enforce highly restrictive immigration policies). At the same time, it has to be borne in mind that socialist countries did not claim to advocate the free exchange of goods, capital and information in the first place, and so at least they cannot be accused of having violated their own ideology if they also failed to apply this principle to people.

15. Cf. the debates that have taken place in UNESCO about a 'new approach to the worldwide exchange of information.'

16. The outstanding example here is, of course, Japan, which makes full use of the liberal economic order to flood the world's markets with its own products, yet at the same time not only effectively bans immigration, but also refuses to grant asylum to persons whose refugee status is beyond question.

17. It goes without saying that, in the present situation, restrictive immigration policies are bound to lead to abuses of the right of asylum, but this is another matter.

18. Whereas, in 1950, a worldwide total of some 600 million people lived in cities, this figure had risen to 2000 million in 1986, and to 2400 million in 1990. According to what strike me as rather conservative estimates, the urban population is likely to reach 3620 million (or more than half the total world population of 7000 million) by the year 2010. Official UN projections suggest that, by the year 2000, Mexico City is likely to have 26.3 million inhabitants, São Paulo 24 million, Bombay 16 million, Delhi 13.3 million, Cairo 13.2 million, Djakarta 12.8 million, Lagos 8.3 million, Nairobi 5.3 million, and so on. In this context, it should be remembered that, according to World Health Organization estimates, almost 1000 million people currently live in inadequate accommodation, again primarily in developing countries; 90 percent of the inhabitants of Addis-Ababa, for instance, 'live' in slums, while the corresponding figures are nearly 60 percent for Mexico City, around 50 percent for Lusaka, and more than 30 percent for Manila.

19. Ferdinand Tönnies, *Gemeinschaft und Gesellschaft: Grundbegriffe der reinen Soziologie* (Darmstadt: Wissenschaftliche Buchgesellschaft, 1887, 1979).

20. Emile Durkheim, *De la division du travail social. Über die Teilung der sozialen Arbeit* (Frankfurt/Main: Suhrkamp, 1892, tr. 1977).

21. Hoffmann-Nowotny, 'The future of the family,' *op. cit.*

22. Durkheim, *op. cit.*, p. 339.

23. A report on the situation in Bangladesh concludes as follows: 'Faced with poverty and the imminent threat of starvation, many, in desperation, migrate, either into the highlands or across the border into the relatively sparsely-populated provinces of north-east India. In both cases, there have recently been tensions as a result; the first group have become embroiled in bloody conflicts with the native highland tribesmen, who fear for their own livelihood, while the second group have run foul of the Indian government, which is facing growing

pressure in the north-east to repatriate even those Bengalis who entered the country from Bangladesh a considerable time ago. If all else fails, the Indian authorities have threatened to erect barbed-wire barricades on their side of the border or even, as a last resort, to shoot anyone trying to cross the border illegally.'

24. Reginald Appleyard, 'The impact of international migration on Third World development,' *International Migration*, 23, 2 (1985), 177–210.

25. Myron Weiner, 'International emigration and the Third World,' in William Alonso (ed.), *Population in an Interacting World* (Cambridge, MA: Harvard University Press, 1987), pp. 190ff; Allan M. Findlay, *The Role of International Labour Migration in the Transformation of an Economy: the Case of the Yemen Arab Republic* (Geneva, ILO: International Migration for Employment-Working Paper, 1987), pp. 24ff.

26. Peter Waltner, 'Migration und soziokultureller Wandel in einer nordma-rokkanischen Provinz – Strukturelle und kulturelle Aspekte der Aus- und Rückwanderung marokkanischer Arbeitskräfte vor dem Hintergrund von Unterentwicklung und wiedererwachtem islamischen Selbstbewußtsein: Eine empirische Untersuchung,' PhD dissertation, University of Zurich, 1988; Marie-Louise Kauz, 'Der islamische Fundamentalismus: Darstellung eines rückwärts gerichteten Geselleschaftsmodells,' MA thesis, University of Zurich, 1991.

27. Imagine what might happen if, for example, China, India and other populous Third World countries sought to moderate the growth of their own populations by *actively encouraging* emigration; or if demands for a 'new approach to worldwide migration' were placed before bodies such as the UN; etc.

28. Umberto Melotti *et al.*, *La nuova immigrazione a Milano* (Milano: Mazzotta, 1985). Umberto Melotti *et al.*, *Dal Terzo Mondo in Italia* (Pavia: Dipartamento di Studi Politici e Sociali dell'Università degli Studi di Pavia, 1988).

PART II

CONTEMPORARY IMMIGRATION AND WESTERN SOCIETIES

5   Europe under migration pressure: some facts on immigration

David A. Coleman

Europe – a continent of immigration?

No Western European country regards itself as a 'country of immigration.' However, almost all appear to be becoming *de facto* countries of immigration. Much of the increase in migration to Europe is caused by asylum claimants or ethnic migrants, particularly to Germany, or by illegal immigrants from the East and from the South. At the same time, migration streams – such as labor migration or family reunion – which, in the early 1980s, had been thought to be under control or declining, have revived. Family formation migration of fiancé(e)s and spouses from the Third World has increased. Almost all countries in Europe except Ireland and Portugal have experienced these changes, even the Mediterranean countries which until the 1980s were emigration countries. Central and Eastern European countries have come under immigration pressure for the first time, from the European republics of the former Soviet Union and from immigrants from the South using Eastern Europe as a back door into the West. In its turn, the Russian Federation became Europe's foremost immigration country in 1994, with 1.14 million immigrants. Almost all of these were Russians leaving, or being driven from, former Soviet republics. Germany has taken the lion's share of asylum claimants as her generous asylum laws and powerful economy have proved irresistible for those seeking entry to Europe. These processes and domestic responses to them have come to the top of the political agenda of many Western countries in the 1990s, and have proven salient in electoral politics.[1]

Since the late 1980s, Western Europe has received a gross annual inflow of up to two million immigrants, of whom up to 600,000 were asylum seekers in 1991, 1992, and 1993. This and previous migrations had produced a legally resident foreign population in Western Europe in 1994 of over 18 million, about 4.5 percent of the European Union (EU 12) total of 345 million. Several million more foreign immigrants have become naturalized. Of the foreigners legally resident in the European Communities (EC) in 1991, 5.1 million were citizens of other EC member states, another 1.7 million were from other European countries, and 6.5 million were citizens of non-European countries, mostly from the Third World. Thirty-six percent of the total number of foreign residents and more than half of the non-EC nationals come from the Maghreb, Turkey, and Yugoslavia. The pattern of migration with respect to Eastern Europe and the former Soviet Union is less well known, and aggregate totals are even more difficult to compute, especially as such movement is irregular and a higher proportion of the foreign population in some Central and Eastern European countries is either undocumented or resident illegally. In these areas, large-scale migration is a post-1989 novelty and the systems for controlling and measuring it are still being developed.

Migration data – a health warning

It is necessary to begin with a health warning about migration data. The volume of data on migration may seem impressive but the quality is often poor. Comparable figures are in short supply. The scale of international travel makes it difficult to measure that small fraction of movement which should be considered as 'international migration.' Thus, while the United Kingdom experienced about 48 million international arrivals and departures in 1992, almost the same number as the total population of England and Wales, only about 200,000 of these in each direction could be described as 'international migration.' People move between countries for variable lengths of stay and for many different purposes, and may do so several times a year. The United Nations definition of an international migrant is a person who enters another country for at least 12 months having been absent from it for at least 12 months. In all of Europe only the UK provides data which match that criterion, and those only from a sample survey of passengers (the International Passenger Survey or IPS) which suffers serious problems (see below). Immigration statistics are not produced for the convenience of demographers but are a by-product of the process of control. Different national systems, recording movement defined by their own unique immigration laws, often produce partial or incompatible statistics.[2] For example, it should be possible to test the adequacy of statistics by comparing the number of people noted as leaving country A for country B with the figures for arrivals in country B from country A. Of 132 possible pairs of such data from the 12 countries of the EC, only six of the possible comparisons yielded similar numbers of migrants.[3]

The inflows of foreign workers to Great Britain in 1991, estimated from various sources, vary by a factor of three. Some of these discrepancies, but not all, can be explained by differences in definition (work permits do not apply to EU workers, IPS data do not include migration from Ireland). In Western Europe, 415,000 labor migrants are known to have entered in 1991 through various work-permit arrangements.[4] Most of the increase since the 208,000 in 1989 was due to new policies in Germany described below. These figures, however, come from just the six European countries which publish figures (only four of which are members of the EU). In respect of the latter four, labor migrants from other EU countries do not require work permits, although some of them nonetheless appear in the figures. No comparable data are available either on the return of these labor migrants or on the departures of 'native' labor migrants with work permits to other countries.

The data on aggregate international migration published for most Western European countries in the Organization for Economic Cooperation and Development's (OECD) annual SOPEMI Report[5] are in fact derived from new registrations in the national registration system of residents, rather than control through the ports or grants of entitlement to settle. Some countries, such as Austria, publish no data on the aggregate level of migration into the country from all migratory processes, though data are made available for flows through specific channels such as work permits or asylum claims. Many others, including France, collect and publish no data on emigration. Yet others, such as Bulgaria, publish only data on emigration, and that probably only a fraction of the total flow. Aggregating data from different countries can be like adding apples and pears.

All migration streams produce return migration but in democracies which do not control exit emigration data tend to be less reliable than immigration data. Controls are substantially evaded by illegal immigrants, and national control systems are poorly funded, with particular neglect of modern information technology systems. No European country yet links arrivals and departures electronically as Australia does.

Data on stocks of population of foreign origin are also unsatisfactory. In most continental European countries, the essential criterion is citizenship. Few people from abroad who lack a close personal connection with the receiving country arrive with its citizenship. Populations of foreign citizenship (i.e. nationality) are known from census counts and also on a continuous basis from the population registration systems operated by most continental countries. Problems of comparison arise with those countries where citizenship is, or has been in the past, ill-defined. For example, citizens of independent countries within the British Commonwealth continue to enjoy the status of British subject or Commonwealth citizen. Until 1962, such status conferred an unqualified right of entry and of indefinite residence in the UK. The right to vote in all UK elections is still enjoyed by such persons and by citizens of the Republic of Ireland. Until 1981, British citizenship was defined as 'Citizen of the UK and Colonies.' The concept of citizenship was accordingly so weakened and confused that no question was asked concerning it since the census of 1961, despite reform in 1981. Questions on citizenship have been asked successfully in the Labour Force Survey since 1981, however.

In the UK context, therefore, birthplace is more useful than citizenship. Use of the 'ethnic minority' concept, including persons born in the UK as well as immigrants, is widespread in the UK. About half of the ethnic minority population is immigrant, though most are British citizens. In Europe, formal ethnic minority categories are used only in the Netherlands, and the categories are different from those in the UK. Other countries, notably France, reject the ethnic minority concept, believing it to be divisive. These countries emphasize instead the importance of an equal shared citizenship. In Eastern Europe and in Southern Europe, citizenship law on the status of resident foreigners is only now being established and data are even less comparable. Almost all countries ask questions on nationality (citizenship) and birthplace in their censuses. These provide detailed information about the foreign and immigrant population, albeit at approximately ten-yearly intervals.[6] Although many European countries (all in Central or Eastern Europe) ask census questions relating to ethnic origin, these are directed at indigenous European minorities, with the unique exception of Great Britain, which asked a question on ethnic group membership directed at non-European populations of recent immigrant origin for the first time in its 1991 census.

The ease of naturalization has an important bearing upon figures for the stock of foreign population. In Germany and Switzerland, for example, the acquisition of citizenship has typically been slow and difficult, the culmination of a process of integration and assimilation. Not only are most immigrants foreign nationals, but also children of foreigners born in Germany will not automatically acquire the citizenship of their country of birth. France and Sweden, on the other hand, pursue vigorous naturalization policies (Table 5.1). In France the pace of naturalization has been greater than that of net immigration – despite a decade of net immigration, the 1990 census revealed fewer foreigners than in 1982. Consequently there are many more immigrants than there are foreigners in France, and even more persons of foreign origin. To complicate things further, the rules on acquiring citizenship, and therefore the rate of loss of resident foreigners by conversion into citizens, often change. Belgium and Germany have moved to make the process easier; France is ending the near-automatic acquisition of citizenship by the French-born children of foreigners at age 18; the Netherlands changed its rules in both directions in the 1980s.

Table 5.1   *Naturalization: selected countries 1990, 1991*

Country	Foreign naturalizations		Population 'at risk' (0000s)		Percent 'at risk' naturalized	
	1990	1991	1990	1991	1990	1991
Austria	9199	11,394	413.4	512.2	2.2	2.2
Belgium	2049	1409	904.5	922.5	0.2	0.2
France	54,366	72,213	3607.6	3607.6	1.5	2.0
Germany	101,377	141,630	5241.8	5882.3	1.9	2.4
Netherlands	12,790	29,110	692.4	732.9	1.8	4.0
Norway	4757	5055	143.3	147.8	3.3	3.4
Spain	7049	3752	398.1	360.7	1.8	1.0
Sweden	16,770	25,907	483.7	493.8	3.5	5.2
Switzerland	8658	8757	1100.3	1163.2	0.8	0.8
UK	57,271	58,642	1875.5	1791.0	3.1	3.3
Total	274,286	357,869	14,860.6	15,614.0	2.3	2.3

Notes: In France children of foreign parents acquire nationality following parents' naturalization, and acquire nationality automatically in their own right at age 18. Inclusion of these categories would increase the totals to 88,500 in 1990 and 95,500 in 1991. Denominator for both years in France is the 1990 total, the only one available. Total percentages naturalized exclude Belgium, France, Germany.

Sources: SOPEMI, 1991, Tables A2, F1–F10; SOPEMI, 1992, Table I.4, Annex Table 1; OECD, 1994, Tables 1.6, A1.

Flows of migrants into Europe

Each year since the late 1980s, between 1.5 and 2 million immigrants, including asylum seekers, have entered Western European countries, which is equivalent to approximately 5 immigrants per 1000 population per year. These figures include labor migrants, the dependents or spouses of previous immigrants entering for family reunification, who comprise the largest number of regular migrants, and the exceptional inflow of German 'ethnic migrants' or *Aussiedler* to Germany from Eastern Europe (397,000 in 1990).

Excluding the majority of asylum seekers, the total gross 'regular' movement into Western Europe in 1990 was 1.41 million and in 1992 (excluding data from Greece, Italy, or Spain where most immigrants are illegal or irregular) it had risen to a peak of 1.8 million (Table 5.2). In 1993, however, these figures fell back to about 1.5 million. Total migration is increased to about 2 million each year by the large numbers of asylum seekers, most of whom remain in Europe even though the asylum claims are usually rejected. People also leave; net legal immigration is half the gross figure. Net migration totals differ somewhat according to source. The incomplete data on net migration given in Table 5.2[7] include departures, but not arrivals, of

Table 5.2 *Gross inflows of population into Western Europe 1980–1993*
(thousands, asylum seekers not included, except where indicated)

Country	1980	1981	1982	1983	1984	1985	1986	1987	1988	1989	1990	1991	1992	1993	Total 1980–93
Belgium	46.8	41.3	36.2	34.3	37.2	37.5	39.3	40.1	38.2	43.5	50.5	54.1	55.1	53.0	607.1
Denmark[a]			13.0	11.6	17.9	24.6	26.6	23.8	22.2	24.4	26.2	29.2	29.1		248.6
France[b]	59.4	75.0	144.4	64.2	51.4	43.4	38.3	39.0	44.0	53.2	102.4	109.9	116.6	99.2	1040.4
Germany[f]	523.6	451.7	275.5	273.2	331.1	398.2	478.3	473.3	648.6	770.8	842.0	920.5	1207.5	986.9	8581.2
Greece										25.0	13.4			38.4	
Ireland[d]								17.2	19.2	26.7	33.3	33.3	40.9	35.0	205.6
Italy									81.2	96.7				177.9	
Luxemburg	7.4	6.9	6.4	6.2	6.0	6.6	7.4	7.2	8.2	8.4	9.3	10.0	9.8	10.1	109.9
Netherlands[e]	78.5	49.6	39.7	36.4	37.3	46.2	52.8	60.9	58.3	65.4	81.3	84.3	83.0	87.6	861.3
Norway[f]	11.8	13.1	14.0	13.1	12.8	15.0	16.8	23.8	23.2	18.5	15.7	16.1	17.2	22.3	233.4
Spain					6.2	4.3	5.3	9.7	14.4	13.7				53.6	
Sweden[g]				22.3	26.1	27.9	34.0	37.1	44.5	58.9	53.2	43.9	39.5	54.8	442.2
Switzerland[f]	70.5	80.3	74.7	58.3	58.6	59.4	66.8	71.5	76.1	80.4	101.4	109.8	112.1	104.0	1123.9
UK[h]	69.8	59.1	53.9	53.5	51.0	55.4	47.8	46.0	49.3	49.7	52.4	53.9	52.6	55.5	749.6
Total	867.8	777.0	657.8	573.1	629.4	720.4	812.4	845.2	1041.5	1295.4	1503.1	1478.4	1763.5	1508.4	14473.0
Total – G,I,S,S[i]	867.8	777.0	657.8	550.8	603.3	686.3	774.1	785.6	968.1	1114.2	1281.2	1387.8	1683.1	1418.6	13555.3
Germany %	60.3	58.1	41.9	47.7	52.6	55.3	58.9	56.0	62.3	59.5	56.0	62.3	68.5	65.4	804.8

Notes: Data generally from population registers except for France and the UK.

Data from annual SOPEMI reports can differ substantially from data given in earlier reports (e.g. Norway, Sweden).

[a] Entries of foreigners staying in Denmark for more than one year. Asylum seekers and refugees with provisional permit not included.

[b] Up to 1989, includes entries of new foreign workers with permanent and provisional work permits, and family reunification. After 1990, provisional work permits not included, but spouses of French nationals, parents of French children, refugees and those eligible for a residence permit are included.

[c] Data include reunited Germany after 1990.

[d] Mostly returning Irish citizens. Net migration negative in all years but 1992. Source: Sexton (1994), t.5.

[e] Register data include asylum seekers with provisional stay permits, recognized refugees, those admitted on humanitarian grounds. Asylum seekers in reception centres excluded.

[f] Foreigners intending to spend more than 6 months in Norway.

[g] Residence notification entries for less than one year are not included (mostly citizens of other Nordic countries).

[h] Foreigners with annual residence permits and permanent permits returning to Switzerland. 92, 93 Clerc 94, p. 8 after a temporary stay abroad. Includes (up to December 31, 1992) holders of permits of less than 12 months' duration. Seasonal and frontier workers excluded. Data from Home Office Control of Immigration Statistics; 'accepted for settlement' only. Most persons 'accepted' will have actually entered the UK in previous years. Asylum seekers not included except for the small number recognized and accepted for settlement. No gross inflow data available for Austria for all reasons (only net, and labor)

[i] Total minus Greece, Italy, Spain, and Sweden

Other sources: Greece, Italy, Spain, Salt (1994), table 7.5. Otherwise OECD, SOPEMI, Table A.2

asylum seekers from Germany and exclude ethnic migrants. The data in Table 5.3 refer to the European Economic Area (EEA) which embraces the 12 (now 15) EU countries and the countries of the European Free Trade Area (EFTA), except Switzerland. The demographic consequences are complex.[8] To begin with, as fertility has fallen, migration has increased, so that while net migration accounted for about 23 percent of Western Europe's population increase in 1975, by 1991 it accounted for 68 percent. As a result, population increase (which was falling up to the mid-1980s) is comparable to the levels of around 1970 in some countries.

Mass migration to Europe is particularly a German phenomenon, even excluding asylum seekers. Over the past decade, 'regular' migration to Germany has accounted for between 42 and 69 percent of the Western European total, and asylum claimants up to 65 percent. Both the *Aussiedler* migration and the high proportion of asylum claimants going to Germany are consequences of the German Basic Law. Both *Aussiedler* immigration and asylum claimants to Germany fell slightly following the legal and policy changes of 1993. Substantial inflows have also been received by other North, Western, and Central European countries, notably Switzerland, Belgium, and the Netherlands. Data on inflows are not even recorded for earlier years for the former 'emigration' countries of Southern Europe. These data are likewise very difficult to compare between countries. For some countries data on emigration are also available on the same basis, so, for example, the gross inflow into the UK in 1991 of 150,000 turns into a net gain of 48,000 once departures are accounted for. France, however, provides no data on departures. Net migration figures can, however, be inferred by comparing the data from population registers for successive years.

All these categories of migrants into Western Europe – legal, asylum and illegal – have been increasing since the mid-1980s. By contrast. migration within Western Europe has been declining. Many of the workers from the Southern European countries, especially from Italy and Greece, have returned home. Labor migration between EU states has been relatively static or even declining, despite the persistence of considerable disparities in employment rates, wage levels, and labor demand. Evidently, even without formal barriers to movement, the costs of migration to individuals, and frictional forces such as shortages of housing, are sufficient to impede net shifts of population which might be expected to persist between low-wage and high-wage areas.[9]

Legal migration into Eastern countries remains on a smaller scale, according to the limited data available. Until 1989, immigration and emigration into Eastern European countries for any purpose was strictly controlled. Limited labor migration on a 'guestworker' basis was arranged between member states of Comecon, which included Cuba, North Korea, and Vietnam. Official inflows for residence were between 1000 and 2000 per year in three countries for which data were available until the collapse of

Table 5.3 *Net inflows of population into selected Western countries 1980–1993 (thousands, asylum seekers not included, except where indicated)*

Country	1980	1981	1982	1983	1984	1985	1986	1987	1988	1989	1990	1991	1992	1993	Total 1980–93
Belgium	5.5	1.4	-4.2	-5.9	1.3	4.0	6.6	5.3	5.9	16.0	24.3	35.2	27.0	21.8	144.2
Denmark			2.7	2.6	5.1	11.1	13.2	10.0	7.7	9.7	11.1	11.6	11.7		96.5
Germany	137.8	36.2	-157.8	-171.4	-249.3	-42.3	30.9	80.9	186.3	211.2	376.4	423.0	582.9	276.7	1721.5
Netherlands	54.9	23.8	11.0	6.4	7.7	16.4	23.4	26.6	29.4	29.9	39.5	41.4	60.3	65.4	436.1
Norway[a]	4.5	5.9	6.8	5.1	5.2	7.4	8.1	6.6	7.1	3.4	1.9	3.1	9.1	11.8	86.0
Sweden[b]				0.9	-0.5	-0.5	4.0	7.4	13.1	15.8	7.7	12.4	26.3	40.0	126.6
Switzerland[c]	6.8	16.3	12.1	-3.4	3.0	5.1	14.0	17.7	20.3	22.9	41.8	43.4	31.7	32.8	264.5
UK[d]	28.0	29.0	32.0	45.0	45.0	56.0	49.0	33.0	33.0	63.0	65.0	48.0			526.0
Total	237.5	112.6	-97.4	-120.7	-182.5	57.2	149.2	187.5	302.8	371.9	567.7	618.1	749.0	448.5	3401.4
Total – G,I,S,S	237.5	112.6	-97.4	-121.6	-182.0	57.7	145.2	180.1	289.7	356.1	560.0	605.7			2143.6

Most of these data are from population registers, not from immigration/emigration statistics.

[a] Foreigners intending to spend more than 6 months in Norway.

[b] Some short duration entries are not counted (mostly citizens of other Nordic countries).

[c] Foreigners with annual residence permits and permanent permits who return to Switzerland after a temporary stay abroad. Includes (up to December 31, 1992) holders of permits of less than 12 months' duration. Seasonal and frontier workers excluded.

[d] Data from International Passenger Survey; UN immigration criterion.

Source: Salt (1994), Table 7.7 (up to 1991); OECD (1995), Tables A.2, A.4 1992, 1993 (and Germany 1990–3).

communist regimes in 1989. Since 1989, the international migration scene in those regions has been transformed, with much more movement both in and out than hitherto, although not yet on the scale forecast in the early 1990s. Most recent official data considerably underestimate actual entries; there is considerable illegal or undocumented movement from further east (Romania and the former Soviet Union) and from the South into Eastern Europe, representing people in search of work or transit to the West. The whole administrative and legal system of control, statistics gathering, and citizenship has had to be reconstructed, including the creation of policies toward asylum claimants, in response to new domestic realities and novel pressures from abroad. Some Central and Eastern European countries, such as Poland and Hungary, now contribute to the OECD migration reporting system SOPEMI.

To a considerable extent the countries of Eastern Europe were more concerned with keeping people in than keeping them out. The most notable example of control was the Wall erected in 1962 between East and West Berlin to stem the hemorrhage of population loss to the West, the renewal of which, with Hungarian connivance, proved terminal to the GDR in 1989. Elsewhere, most outflows were numerically trivial except for movement from Poland and Romania and the substantial guestworker migration from former Yugoslavia (mostly Croatia). Most of this earlier, legal emigration consisted of people of German origin going to Germany or Jews to Israel. However, there was also a substantial emigration of Poles in the 1980s, especially of those with 'temporary' exit permits.

Stock of foreign population in Europe

As a result of this growing influx, the Western European countries have a bigger and more diverse immigrant or foreign origin population than ever. Table 5.4 shows detailed data for selected countries. In 1994, foreign population ranged from 19 percent of the total population in Switzerland, to 11 percent in Belgium, 9 percent in Germany, and 6 percent in France. In Spain and Italy only between 1 and 2 percent of (legal) residents are foreign. However, most recent immigration to those countries has been illegal. The Swiss percentage foreign is about the same as the proportion of population born abroad in Canada (15.6 percent in 1986) and Australia (22.7 percent in 1991). In the USA, the overseas-born population looks quite modest (19.8 million, 7.9 percent in 1990) compared with some European countries.

The legacy of past immigration from poorer European countries is still apparent in North and West Europe. Despite considerable return migration, Italians still form the single largest minority in Belgium, and the Irish in Britain remain prominent even in comparison with West Indian and

Table 5.4 *Foreign population in selected European countries by country of origin 1994*

(a) Distribution of foreign population, thousands

Country of origin	Country of residence										
	Belgium 1994	France 1990	Germany 1994	Italy 1993[a]	Netherlands 1994	Norway 1994	Spain 1993[a]	Sweden 1994	Switzerland 1994	UK 1994[b]	Total
France	97.1	–	94.2	19.8	10.4	1.9	25.5	3.2	53.4	55.0	360.5
Germany	30.2	51.5	–	39.9	52.3	4.5	34.1	12.9	88.2	46.0	359.5
Greece	20.7	6.7	352.0	16.5	5.8	0.2		5.2	7.9	19.0	434.0
Ireland	2.8	3.3	14.7	1.2	4.5	0.4		0.8	1.2	473.0	501.9
Italy	216.0	253.7	563.0	–	17.5	0.8	15.9	4.0	370.7	78.0	1519.6
Portugal	15.1	645.6	105.6	–	9.6	0.5	32.3	1.4	122.1	32.0	964.1
Spain	49.4	216.0	133.2	17.0	16.9	0.9	–	3.0	106.9	41.0	584.1
UK	25.4	50.1	111.7	29.1	44.8	11.4	58.2	10.9	19.2	–	360.9
Other EC	86.8	82.0	161.3	29.5	26.1	21.1	26.1	23.5	12.7	48.0	517.0
Finland	0.8	1.6	13.0			3.2		108.9	2.0		129.6
fr. Czechoslovakia		2.0	52.0			0.0		1.6	5.5		61.1
Hungary	0.7	2.9	62.2		1.2	0.2		3.4	4.4		75.1
Poland	4.8	46.3	260.5	21.1	21.1	2.8		16.1	5.3		378.0
fr. Yugoslavia	7.4	51.7	1239.0	72.4	24.7	13.6		32.4	244.4		1685.6
fr. USSR		4.3	63.6			0.5		1.5	4.0		73.9
Algeria	10.2	619.9	23.1								653.2
Morocco	145.4	584.7	82.8	97.6	164.6	1.9					1077.0
Tunisia	6.0	207.5	28.1	44.5	2.4		61.3				349.8
Turkey	88.3	201.5	1918.4		203.1	5.4		23.6	75.6	44.0	2559.9
Iran			101.5			7.0		36.1			144.6
India		2.5		14.3		3.0	5.7			125.0	150.5
Pakistan						10.4				89.0	99.4

Table 5.4 *continued*

	Belgium	France	Germany	Italy	Netherlands	Norway	Spain	Sweden	Switzerland	UK	All selected countries
Total above	679.8	2982.3	5285.5	343.2	542.2	83.3	199.5	272.3	981.9	949.0	12,319.3
All EC (SOPEMI)	543.5	1308.9	1535.6	153.0	187.7	41.7	192.1		782.2	792.0	5536.7
Foreign January 1, 1994 (CoE)	1078.7	3596.6	7054.6	987.4	778.8	162.3	430.4	507.5	1291.8	1946.0	17,834.1
Population January 1, 1994	10,100.6	57,803.6	81,338.1	57,138.5	15,341.6	4324.8	39,117.0	8745.1	6968.6	60,037.0	340,914.9
% foreign	10.7	6.2	8.7	1.7	5.1	3.8	1.1	5.8	18.5	3.2	5.2

(b) Percent of total foreign population from each country of origin

Country of origin	Country of residence										All selected countries
	Belgium	France	Germany	Italy	Netherlands	Norway	Spain	Sweden	Switzerland	UK	
France	9.0	–	1.3	2.0	1.3	1.2	5.9	0.6	4.1	2.8	2.0
Germany	2.8	1.4	–	4.0	6.7	2.8	7.9	2.5	6.8	2.4	2.0
Greece	1.9	0.2	5.0	1.7	0.7	0.1	0.0	1.0	0.6	1.0	2.4
Ireland	0.3	0.1	0.2	0.1	0.6	0.2	0.0	0.2	0.1	24.3	2.8
Italy	20.0	7.1	8.0	–	2.3	0.5	3.7	0.8	28.7	4.0	8.5
Portugal	1.4	17.9	1.5	0.0	1.2	0.3	7.5	0.3	9.4	1.6	5.4
Spain	4.6	6.0	1.9	1.7	2.2	0.5	–	0.6	8.3	2.1	3.3
UK	2.4	1.4	1.6	2.9	5.7	7.0	13.5	2.2	1.5	–	2.0
Other EC	8.0	2.3	2.3	3.0	3.3	13.0	6.1	4.6	1.0	2.5	2.9
Finland	0.1		0.2			2.0		21.5	0.2		0.7
fr. Czechoslovakia		0.1	0.7					0.3	0.4		0.3
Hungary	0.1	0.1	0.9		0.2	0.1		0.7	0.3		0.4

Table 5.4 *continued*

Poland	0.4	1.3	3.7	2.1	2.7	1.7		3.2	0.4	2.1
fr. Yugoslavia	0.7	1.4	17.6	7.3	3.2	8.4		6.4	18.9	9.5
fr. USSR		0.1	0.9		0.3			0.3	0.3	0.4
Algeria	0.9	17.2	0.3							3.7
Morocco	13.5	16.3	1.2	9.9	21.1	1.2				6.0
Tunisia	0.6	5.8	0.4	4.5	0.3		14.2			2.0
Turkey	8.2	5.6	27.2	0.0	26.1	3.3		4.7	5.9	14.4
Iran						4.3		7.1		0.8
India		0.1	1.4	1.4		1.8	1.3		6.4	0.8
Pakistan							6.4		4.6	0.6
Total above	63.0	82.9	74.9	34.8	69.6	51.3	46.4	53.7	76.0	69.1
All EC	50.4	36.4	21.8	15.5	24.1	25.7	44.6	0.0	60.6	31.0
All countries	100.0	100.0	100.0	100.0	100.0	100.0	100.0	100.0	100.0	100.0

Notes: Blank indicates no data. 0.0 indicates less than 0.05 percent.

[a] Italy, Spain data actually December 31, 1993 (source OECD SOPEMI)

[b] UK data from Labour Force Survey 1994 (taken throughout the year). The LFS cannot accurately record populations of less than 10,000.

Most foreign population data relate to December 31. France (census) February 1990.

Council of Europe data relate to foreign population at January 1 of year stated (here usually 1994). OECD data relate to December 31 of year stated (here usually 1993). CoE data are preferred. The totals may differ considerably, and also the former Yugoslav total.

Sources: OECD (1995), T A.1. T B.1, Council of Europe (1995), Table T1.1, 6, Salt (1995), Table 4.1

Asian immigrant populations, as do the Finns in Sweden. In France in 1990, the Portuguese still slightly outnumbered Algerian citizens. The largest legally resident immigrant group in Spain in 1993 were the British, retirement settlers on the 'costa geriatrica', joined by a substantial number of Germans. Undoubtedly, both are outnumbered by illegal immigrants of North African origin. In Germany Turks now comprise by far the largest group, as they also do in the Netherlands. So far, Eastern Europeans except for Poles (in Germany) and persons from former Yugoslavia, are present in relatively small numbers. Many of those from Eastern Europe in Germany are of German ethnic origin.

Components of growth

Immigrant populations continue to grow, at between 1 and 6 percent per year, through a combination of continued immigration and high natural increase. Naturalization, on the other hand, tends to reduce the numbers of foreign nationals. Accordingly, while population growth of foreigners continues rapidly where naturalization is difficult (Austria), elsewhere, rapid rates of naturalization neutralize the statistical effects of continued immigration and the high levels of natural increase among immigrants. But population of foreign origin continues to increase. In Great Britain, for example, ethnic minority population, irrespective of nationality or birthplace, increases at about 5 percent per year through the combined effects of immigration and high fertility, compared with about 0.3 percent for the population as a whole. As rates of immigration and fertility are comparable, similar rates of increase probably prevail among the (statistically invisible) 'ethnic origin' populations of European countries.

Although immigration increases and the origins of immigrant populations become more diverse, the fertility of foreign populations in Europe is generally declining. Among some populations, such as Indians in the UK and people of Caribbean origin in the Netherlands and the UK, fertility is about the same as the national average, although thanks to a young age-structure the number of births still increases. In other cases, especially Turks and some other Muslim populations, fertility, although lower than originally, remains equivalent to about three children or more.[10]

The proportion of all births to foreign mothers ranges from 7 percent in the Netherlands, 10 percent in Sweden, 11 percent in France and Germany, to 12 percent in the UK (immigrant mothers). These percentages have not shown much upward trend in the past decade or more. The process of naturalization removes mothers of immigrant origin from observation. Whether these children will themselves be 'foreigners' depends on the citizenship laws of each country.

An interesting consequence of immigration is the increasing proportion of marriages and informal unions between people of different citizenships, birthplaces, and ethnic or racial origin. Statistics on such unions are often regarded as an indicator of social integration or assimilation of immigrant groups.[11] Figures on marriages based upon citizenship suffer the same drawbacks as those faced by data on fertility; even so, the number of such marriages is increasing. In France, Belgium, and the Netherlands in 1990 mixed marriages, defined by nationality, comprised about 10.5 percent of all marriages, in Germany 9.6 percent, and in Switzerland 8.1 percent. Where data are available according to the birthplace[12] or ethnicity of the populations concerned, irrespective of citizenship, the prevalence and rate of increase of these unions is greater. For example, about 20 percent of the unions of males of West Indian immigrant origin, and 40 percent of the unions of West Indian males born in the UK, appear to be with white females. The proportion of marriages of Italian immigrant men with French women approached 80 percent in the late 1980s.[13] Other groups show markedly lower levels of inter-ethnic marriage; for example, Muslim Bangladeshis in the UK and Turks in the Netherlands.[14] As a result of these inter-ethnic unions, large numbers of children of mixed ethnic and racial ancestry are born in European countries.

Major sources of migration to Europe

Several streams of migration contribute to the overall movement into Europe. Legal labor migration has been a constant feature of migration in Europe for centuries. It proceeds free of restrictions among the countries of the EU and, since 1993, additionally among the countries of the European Economic Area. Otherwise, it is usually regulated by work permit systems. The inheritance of past obligations or promises continues to bring in substantial flows of dependents of former guestworkers and other migrants, including more recent labor migrants and asylum claimants who have been accepted, mostly from the South, and ethnic migrants guaranteed entry to Germany from the East. To these substantial streams have been added new labor migrants, new marriage partners, and fiancé(e)s for the immigrant populations; most of the latter come from Third World countries. Two new geographical features are apparent. First, many of the workers from the countries of Southern Europe who migrated to the growing economies of North West Europe have returned home. These countries have now turned for the first time into *de facto* immigration countries with the arrival of new populations from North Africa, most of them illegal or (where immigration law is underdeveloped) undocumented. Either way, the movement is mostly unwanted, although some are recruited, or at least welcome, for clandestine employment under ill-paid conditions. For the first time since the Second

World War, the collapse of communist regimes in Eastern Europe and in the former Soviet Union has opened up the possibility of large-scale movements from the East to the West.

Labor migration

Mass immigration to Western Europe started in the 1960s (earlier in a few countries). Much of it was organized as 'guestworker' programs by bilateral agreement between companies and governments.[15] Since the 1960s, however, industrial structures have changed. Mass demand for low-skill metalworking and assembly work is now over. Much of the official labor migration within and into Europe at present is high-level manpower of persons with managerial or professional qualifications. Much of it involves transfers of personnel between components of the same large organization ('inter-company' transfers).[16] Most future growth in labor demand is expected to be in occupations requiring higher qualifications.[17] Until the mid-1980s, labor migration in Europe in general had been at a low ebb for some years. It is not true that migration within or between European countries (for labor or other purposes) always tends to increase in what has been described as a 'world on the move'. It is movement into Europe from outside which keeps on rising.

The total of recorded labor inflow covered by statistics into European countries in 1989 was 211,000. In 1990, it increased sharply to 350,000, in part following a temporary surge in the German economy provoked by reunification. By 1992, the number had increased again to 589,600 although it fell back somewhat to 456,800 in 1993. Most of this increase was caused by a change in the inflow into Germany. Other countries, such as Austria and Switzerland, have restricted the numbers of work permits in response to public concern about the growth of foreign population. Since 1975, Norway has issued very few permits to citizens of non-Nordic countries, and Greece and Ireland take very limited numbers. As citizens of EU countries can enter other EU countries for work initially without bureaucratic difficulty, it can be argued that the real entry figure is considerably higher, though it is not possible to estimate it accurately. It is not clear why general labor immigration should increase up to 1992 in countries such as France and the UK, given unfavorable labor market conditions in Europe. By mid-1991 the EC had 12 million unemployed, of whom least 1.5 million were themselves immigrants, and the total is forecast to rise to 20 million by 2000.

Most of the recent increase in Germany follows from three new trainee and recruitment schemes involving temporary workers from Eastern Europe. Despite the tightening of the immigration controls and growing unemployment in Western countries, a number of Eastern European countries (Hungary, Poland, Romania, Russia) have proposed that Western countries take temporary workers, trainees, and apprentices on a contract or short-term basis. Only Germany has responded, and this despite the problems of unemployment in the former East Germany after unification in 1990. Four categories of workers are defined in the new bilateral agreements. Up to the end of 1994, work contracts (*Werkverträge*) operated through subcontractors were limited by national quotas to an average of 41,000 per month for a maximum of two years, mostly in construction. Other categories are guest employees (*Arbeitnehmer*), with up to 5529 placements for one year, mostly in construction; seasonal workers (up to three months), with no limit on numbers; and cross-border commuters, without limit of number or employment.[18] The work contracts are most popular, especially in construction and near the border, although not without controversy. Amid accusations of unfair competition from trade unions and employers, the quotas have been cut and agreements not extended. Consequently, the numbers involved halved from 1992 to 1994.

The rise in inflows may not be associated with a commensurate increase in the total labor force (except in Germany), but rather with a higher turnover. Statistics on stocks of foreign workers have wider coverage than those on inflows, although the former will be affected by the naturalization process. The stocks of foreign workers in most of the countries of Western Europe, including Germany and France, are scarcely higher in 1991 than in 1981. These totals, unlike most of the inflow figures, will include EC nationals in other EC countries.

Family reunification and family formation migration

Family reunification followed the male-dominated labor migration of the 1960s and 1970s. It was never intended to happen in the countries which organized guestworker programs, but pressures for family reunification are difficult to resist in liberal democracies. Until the rise of asylum seeking, it was the single most important component of recent immigration into Europe and it remains the dominant 'regular' stream. In France, such migration has comprised about 70 percent of legal immigration in recent years.[19] In the UK, almost all the net immigration of approximately 30,000 persons per year from the Third World countries of the New Commonwealth arises from continued family reunification or from the immigration of new spouses.[20] A growing proportion of the spouses, however, are men. In theory, this commitment was expected to be finite and declining. The practice has proven otherwise. The obligation to keep families together has been extended to spouses and dependents of more recent work permit holders and asylum claimants granted leave to settle, and to former illegal immigrants whose position has been regularized by amnesties in various countries. Additionally, there are further migration streams created by marriages with foreigners, particularly from cultures where arranged marriage is normal. Such 'family formation' migration has overtaken family reunification among Turks and Moroccans in the Netherlands,[21] and is responsible for much of the increased immigration to the UK from the New Commonwealth since 1987.[22] These instances lend credibility to the observation that immigration networks, once established between liberal welfare states and Third World countries with high fertility rates, extended household systems, and traditions of arranged or in-group marriage, are difficult to end.

Asylum seeking

Between 1980 and 1993, almost four million applications for asylum were registered in Western European countries. Most of the claimants appear still to be in these countries. In most countries, demand for asylum was relatively infrequent in the 1970s. Germany was an exception, with large numbers claiming asylum from Eastern European countries in some years. During this time, countries could maintain generous asylum policies without suffering adverse consequences. Since the 1980s, this pattern has come to an end. Western Europe received 426,000 applications for asylum in 1990, 544,000 in 1991, and 680,000 in the peak year of 1992 (two-thirds of the last to Germany). At the time of writing, asylum claims had fallen substantially to an estimated 284,000 in 1995. This decline follows radical revision of asylum provisions in the German constitution in 1993, and further measures to deter false claims and speed up the investigation process in most other European countries.[23] Much of the increase from 1991 to 1992 was due to flows of people fleeing conflict in former Yugoslavia. An additional 270,000 were given temporary protection status in European countries outside the formal asylum system. Mass asylum claiming is regarded by some as a form of betterment migration, albeit often from politically unstable countries, and in some cases as the continuation of illegal immigration or of overstaying by other means. Well under 10 percent of applications in recent years have been accepted as refugees under the 1951 Geneva Convention in most Western European countries. But some claimants, although refused asylum as Convention refugees, are allowed to remain on humanitarian grounds. Some claimants originally gain entry ostensibly for short-stay visits, others arrive or overstay illegally. A high proportion (over 60 percent in the case of the UK) apply for asylum only after having been resident in the country for some time. Multiple applications in several countries were common before various Europe-wide agreements inhibited such practices. Many take care to destroy their documents and appear to be well informed about the mechanisms of asylum and welfare in European countries. Organizations to arrange transport and provide false documents are active in African and Eastern European countries. Organized trafficking in asylum claimants and illegal immigrants is now attracting serious attention from governments and their police forces and international organizations such as the Intergovernmental Consultations and the International Organization for Migration.[24] Although most of those refused asylum have no legal entitlement to remain, few are known to leave Europe and few are removed.

Up to the early 1980s, most of the then much smaller numbers of asylum seekers came from the communist countries of Eastern Europe (then, as now, particularly to Germany) and most applications were accepted. In the 1990s, streams from such countries as Hungary, Czechoslovakia, and Poland were greatly reduced as political circumstances changed. As most Eastern European countries are now designated as 'safe countries,' applications received from these countries are mostly rejected. This applies particularly to the continued inflows from Romania and Bulgaria, where the motives for applying for asylum are regarded as being primarily of an economic nature. The civil war in Yugoslavia provided the majority of claimants from Eastern Europe: 245,000 out of a total of 596,000 claimants in 1991, and 421,000 out of 680,000 in 1992. Meanwhile, the numbers of claimants from Third World countries continue to increase. Claimants now come from almost all countries of the Third World. While applications originally tended to be made to countries which had some historical connection with the sending countries (Sri Lankans, Nigerians and Ghanaians to the UK), applications are now made much more widely according to where access is believed to be easiest.

Illegal immigrants

It is difficult to assess the scale of illegal immigration. Some estimates come from the response to past 'regularization' programs and amnesties, for example in France, Italy, and Spain. Other minimal indications come from apprehensions and deportations. In the UK, for example, in 1992, 6000 persons were dealt with as illegal immigrants, about six times the number in 1980. In 1991, there were estimated to be almost two million illegal immigrants in Western Europe, plus 500,000 persons refused asylum and having no legal right to remain.[25] Many of the illegals are concentrated on Western Europe's boundaries: in the East (Austria and Germany) and the South (Italy, Spain, Portugal, and Greece). Of the 2.7 million foreign population of the latter countries, about half are believed to be illegal immigrants, the largest number being in Italy. Most of the immigrants in the latter group are from the Maghreb. Estimates of illegal inflows into Western Europe made by informed international sources range from 350,000 per year[26] to 500,000.

Elsewhere, illegal immigrants from most Eastern European countries, and from the western parts of the former Soviet Union, can be found in most Western European countries, especially in Germany, Austria, and Switzerland. Central and Eastern European countries are also acquiring illegal immigrant populations, many in transit from further east, or from the South, to intended destinations in Western Europe. No estimates of numbers are available, but flows appear to be substantial: for example, in 1993 about 700,000 persons were apprehended at the border in Hungary. Central and Eastern European countries have been obliged to develop new legislation on immigration and on the status of foreign residents and asylum claimants.[27]

The return of the European ethnic diaspora

Many Italians and Spaniards who left to work in richer Northern European countries in the 1960s have returned as the economies of their own countries have developed. Beyond that, return migration back to the home country has been encouraged by policies which give automatic citizenship to those with an ancestral connection with the host country. Such provisions in Germany's Basic Law have encouraged the return of the *Aussiedler* to Germany. From 1950 to 1986, the annual inflow except from East Germany was under 50,000. Movement from East Germany (*Übersiedler*) averaged over 200,000 per year until the building of the Berlin Wall in 1962.

The resumption of this demographic hemorrhage via Hungary in 1989 provoked the final collapse of the GDR. Some 79,000 *Aussiedler* returned to Germany in 1987, rapidly increasing to 377,000 in 1989, and 397,000 in 1990, mostly from the former Soviet Union, Poland, and Romania. In 1991, however, numbers declined to 222,000. The ethnic migrants, many of whom no longer speak German, had found it difficult to reintegrate into a modern urban society. Since the Ethnic Germans Readmission Act, German policy now concentrates upon assistance given to the German populations in place, to encourage them to stay where they are. Annual *Aussiedler* inflows are now limited to about 225,000 people. Greece welcomes the return of people of Greek origin (Pontic Greeks), from populations settled in the Crimea (14,000 in 1990) after their expulsion from their ancestral homelands in Northern Anatolia (Pontus) in 1922. Until 1989, most emigration from Eastern Europe and the Soviet Union, including that of Jews to Israel, was of this ethnic kind, and its volume tended to vary with the temperature of the Cold War.[28]

New ethnic migration has followed the collapse of the Soviet Union in 1991. In Soviet times there was much outward movement of the Russian population to all parts of the Soviet Union, following earlier expansion of the Russian Empire. Forced movement of individuals and whole peoples also changed demographic distributions. By the time of the last Soviet census of 1989, about 25 million persons of Russian 'nationality' lived in the Soviet Union outside the Russian Federation. In Soviet times some of this movement followed a policy of Russification, which was intense in the Baltic states, where it has resulted in almost numerical parity between Russians and Latvians by 1989. The independent governments of the Baltic states are keen to secure the peaceful removal of Russians who do not wish to embrace local citizenship. They also encourage the return of persons of Baltic origin or of those who are entitled to local citizenship; over 200,000 were deported to other parts of the Union in Soviet times. The return of Russians to the Russian Federation from former Soviet republics, especially in Central Asia, comprises almost all the legal immigration to that country and has reached very large proportions (1.14 million in 1994). About a quarter of these immigrants have been forced out, and the present and likely future size of these flows is creating a severe additional problem for Russian reconstruction. Also for the future, perhaps 800,000 of the white population of South Africa could claim UK patrial immigration status by virtue of having at least one UK-born grandparent, and therefore the right of abode in the UK, should they decide to exercise that right.

East–West migration

The expected mass migration to the West from the East, following the events of 1989, is still to happen. Legal and regular migration has not been substantial beyond ethnic return migration. Most legal migrants are still *Aussiedler* going to Germany. Poles have been especially mobile as legal and illegal labor, border migrants and tourists, some of whom overstay. In Germany in 1990 there were believed to be 241,000 Poles. In that year Germany agreed to an annual quota of 35,000 Polish workers for two years, with up to 50,000 seasonal workers. Since then Germany has negotiated new guestworker agreements with Poland and other Central European countries. Germany has received substantial numbers of Romanian illegal immigrants and asylum claimants, but has managed to return some of them. Immigrants for the former Soviet Union have reached most Western countries, many as illegal immigrants, some as students and scientists. In 1990, Western newspapers spoke of 6, 15, or even 20 million Russians poised to move. But the prospects of large-scale legal immigration are slight: labor demand is not great or the supply is inappropriate,[29] and there is no pretext for family reunion.

In the context of East–West migration, the justification for most asylum claims disappeared after 1989. Mass illegal immigration will not be easy;

transport and language are serious barriers. There are few existing nucleus Eastern European or Russian populations already in the West to act as bridgeheads for chain migration, or in which illegal immigrants could hide.[30] The Eastern European countries which lie between the West and the former Soviet Union are also improving their own immigration controls, as they have become a favored avenue for illegal migration and asylum seeking to the West from the South as well as the East.

Many Eastern European countries are now preoccupied with the novel rise of immigration (mostly illegal) into their territories from other Eastern countries (CIS and Romania) and asylum seeking. Like the Mediterranean Western European countries, they are becoming receiving countries as well as sending countries. Eastern European countries are naturally in the front line. The weak Eastern European economies are still attractive to residents of the former USSR. For example, in the early 1990s, there were startling increases in the number of tourists entering Poland; over 8 million from the former USSR in 1991 compared with 3 million in 1989; at least 25,000 are thought to have become overstayers. Romanian tourism to Poland increased from 19,000 in 1989 to 325,000 in 1990. The real push, however, could follow political collapse in Russia or other CIS countries, which might generate a flood of refugees with great social and security complications for Eastern Europe and then for the West.

Another novelty for the East is the rise of South–East Third World migrants in search of entry to Western European countries, illegally, as asylum claimants, or in any other way, for whom the East, like Southern Europe, is an easier point of entry. These include Iraqis, Indians, Pakistanis, Lebanese and many others. Eastern European countries are establishing new controls on movements from the CIS and the poorer areas of Eastern Europe (Bulgaria and Romania) and on Third World asylum seekers and illegal immigrants. In October 1991, for example, regulations requiring all foreigners entering Hungary to carry hard currency led to 46,000 being refused entry in three days, and in 1992 and 1993 about 700,000 foreigners were refused entry. Most illegal immigrants to Hungary appear to come from Sri Lanka, Bangladesh, China, and Vietnam, many entering from Romania on their way to Germany. The Czech Republic has similar problems: in 1993, 43,300 people were apprehended crossing the border illegally, 35 percent more than in 1992. Most were from former Yugoslavia, Bulgaria, Romania, Vietnam, and China.[31] Irregular and illegal immigrants have tended to accumulate in Central European countries since the improvement of measures against asylum claiming in Western countries and the development of agreements to return rejected claimants to 'safe third countries' and various bilateral agreements. The Russian Federation also has a problem of illegal immigrants or transit migrants from the South seeking an easy way to the West. Large numbers of illegal immigrants from China are reported to be living in Eastern areas of the Russian Federation;

about 150,000 in the Russian Federation as a whole in 1994. It is impossible to be precise about numbers, but the mobilization of the Chinese population has already led to about 500,000 Chinese migrants in the 1990s making their presence felt in many Western countries, including the United States and Canada, as well as in Russia and Eastern Europe. That migration, so far almost entirely illegal, it is likely to become one of the dominant features of twenty-first century migration streams.

Conclusions

Despite the weakness of data, it is clear that a substantial increase in gross and net migration flows has occurred in Western Europe since the mid-1980s, even though most European countries do not want more migrants and do not regard themselves as countries of immigration. Net immigration is now more important than natural population increase in Europe. The increase in asylum claiming has been most substantial, compounded by the crisis in former Yugoslavia. This appears to have peaked in 1992 and numbers of applicants are declining in most Western European countries. However, it may be that, as little has changed to counteract migration pressures, numbers of illegal immigrants, already substantial, may increase correspondingly.[32] Regular migrants have also increased: the inflows of dependents for family reunification continue to be a substantial part of the legal flows, reinforced or overtaken in some countries by increased migration for purposes of marriage. The apparent increase in labor migrants is more difficult to understand, although a good part of the increase is due to new arrangements in Germany which are peculiar to Germany's situation.

Germany is the focus of immigration to Western Europe, receiving about half the legal migrants and over half the asylum claimants, partly as a consequence of German law and policy, both of which have recently changed. Most European countries have changed their laws on asylum and entry in recent years to try to moderate migration flows. In many cases the reforms of legislation in the late 1980s or early 1990s have proved inadequate and further changes are in progress. Meanwhile, populations of foreign origin continue to grow through their own natural increase through births, as well as from the additions of immigration, and have created often visibly distinct populations comprising between 2 and 16 percent of legal residents of European countries.

All this poses a number of important questions. At home, the integration of the majority of those immigrants who choose to remain in Europe still presents major economic, social, and political problems. New cultural diversity challenges previous perceptions of national coherence. Different European countries have adopted a variety of responses to meet this challenge, such as multicultural policies, the encouragement of assimilation or return, and *laissez-faire* policies. The political structure of Western democracies, and the influence of focused pressure groups, can make it particularly difficult for policy makers and enforcers to control migration pressures effectively. Abroad, continued population growth, economic weakness, and political instability in the Third World, and the latter two factors in Eastern Europe, sustain immigration pressures. But the recent increases in migration and asylum applications (and recent reductions) are not easy to understand in terms of these underlying factors, which have not changed commensurately in the past few years.

Migrants have become easier to mobilize, and asylum claiming more attractive, as immigrant bridgeheads grow in size and become more numerous, as information becomes more widely available, and as European internal borders become weaker. Information on whether and how potential migrants respond to amnesties, multicultural policies or other initiatives, and changes in rules might be the key to moderating flows. But little is known about these phenomena. In the short run, foreign aid and development programs and free trade arrangements may increase immigration pressures, even if they serve to moderate them in the longer run.[33] The economic and demographic disparities cannot abate substantially for some decades; true convergence in socio-economic conditions with the West is unlikely to occur in the foreseeable future in some sending areas, such as tropical Africa, much of South America, and parts of South Asia.

Some level of immigration is a natural part of the economic and social exchanges between countries. No system would want to stop it. However, the important question is whether immigration over and above the current legal level, beyond that arranged through work permit systems, is desirable on economic or demographic grounds. Some have argued that free migration of labor would benefit the host economy, by preventing wage inflation and ensuring that enterprises are not constrained by shortage of labor. The contrary view is that an immigration free-for-all reduces wages or wage growth of natives, produces higher unemployment, traps economies into low-wage low-productivity strategies, and incurs all the costs of multicultural societies, while being unable to solve the problem of aging.[34] To resolve this debate is beyond the scope of this chapter. The only unequivocal benefits of migration, however, appear to accrue to the migrant.

International migration is one of the most important long-term issues in European domestic and foreign politics. It may not be beyond the powers of European governments to resolve or at least to moderate inflows substantially and to integrate successfully the large new foreign populations which they have acquired since the 1950s. But to do so requires a recognition of this priority, open discussion of the issues, policies based firmly on facts, and the willingness of domestic electorates to make sacrifices in terms of expenditure and possibly convenience in the search for more order in domestic and international affairs.

Notes

1. Philip L. Martin, 'The migration issue,' in Russell King (ed.), *The New Geography of European Migrations* (London: Belhaven, 1993), pp. 1–16.
2. John Salt, A. Singleton and J. Hogarth, *Europe's International Migrants: Data Sources, Patterns and Trends* (London: HMSO, 1994).
3. M. Poulain, 'Confrontation des statistiques de migrations intra Européennes: vers plus d'harmonisation?,' *European Journal of Population*, 9, 4 (1993), 353–81.
4. OECD, *Trends in International Migration: SOPEMI Annual Report 1994* (Paris: OECD, 1995), table A.7
5. *Ibid.*
6. Y. Courbage, *Results of the Survey on Statistical Information Sources Concerning National Minorities in Europe* (Strasbourg: Council of Europe, 1995).
7. John Salt, A. Singleton and J. Hogarth, *Europe's International Migrants: Data Sources, Patterns and Trends* (London: HMSO, 1994); and OECD, *Trends in International Migration: SOPEMI Annual Report 1994* (Paris: OECD, 1995).
8. See S. Voets, J. Schoorl and B. de Bruijn (eds), *The Demographic Consequences of International Migration* (The Hague: Netherlands Interdisciplinary Demographic Institute, 1995).
9. EC Commission, *Employment in Europe 1991* (Luxembourg: EC Commission, 1991).
10. David A. Coleman, 'Trends in fertility and intermarriage among immigrant populations in Western Europe as measures of integration,' *Journal of Biosocial Science* 26, 1 (1994), 107–36.
11. David A. Coleman, 'Ethnic intermarriage,' in A.H. and D.F. Roberts Bittles (eds), *Minority Populations: Genetics, Demography and Health: Proceedings of the Twenty-seventh Annual Symposium of the Galton Institute* (London: Macmillan, 1992), pp. 208–40.
12. F. Muñoz-Perez and M. Tribalat, 'Mariages d'étrangers et mariages mixtes en France: évolution depuis la Première Guerre Mondiale,' *Population*, 39, 3 (1984), 427–62.
13. M. Tribalat *et al., Cent ans d'Immigration: Etrangers d'hier, Français d'aujourd'hui* (Paris: Presses Universitaires de France, 1991), p. 13.
14. P. Muus, *Migration, Minorities and Policy in the Netherlands: Recent Trends and Developments* (Amsterdam: Department of Human Geography, University of Amsterdam, 1991).
15. See W.R. Böhning, *The Migration of Workers in the United Kingdom and the European Community* (Oxford: Oxford University Press for the Institute of Race Relations, 1972); and John Salt and H. Clout (eds), *Migration in Postwar Europe* (Oxford: Oxford University Press, 1976).
16. John Salt, 'Migration processes among the highly skilled in Europe,' *International Migration Review*, 26, 2 (1992), 484–505.
17. EC Commission, *op. cit.*
18. H. Rudolph and F. Hillmann, 'Labor migration between Eastern and Western Europe,' *Employment Observatory East Germany*, March 14, 1995, 3–7. The second category, which demands training and accommodation, has not flourished. These projects, which are claimed to be genuinely short term, appear to be at

least in part more concerned with foreign aid and strengthening diplomatic links rather than meeting any unmet needs in the German economy, which is itself in recession and has acute problems of unemployment in the former East zone.

19. C.V. Maire, 'L'Immigration en France dans les années 90: nouvelle donnée et nouveaux enjeux,' in R. Cagiano de Azevedo *et al.* (eds), *Immigrants Integration Policies in Seven European Countries* (Rome: Università degli Studi di Roma, 1994), pp. 61–88.

20. See Home Office, *Control of Immigration: Statistics United Kingdom 1994* (London: HMSO, 1995).

21. P. Muss and H. Cruijsen, *International Migration in the European Community* (Luxembourg: EUROSTAT, 1991).

22. David A. Coleman, 'Immigration to the UK: a changing balance?,' in Reinhard Münz and Rainer Fassmann Münz (eds), *Mass Migration to Europe* (Vienna: Edward Elgar, 1994).

23. Jonas Widgren, *The Key to Europe: a Comparative Analysis of Entry and Asylum Policies in Western Countries* (Stockholm: Fritzes, 1994).

24. Intergovernmental Consultations, *Illegal Aliens: a Preliminary Study* (Geneva: Intergovernmental Consultations, 1995); International Organization for Migration, *Trafficking Migrants* (Geneva: IOM, 1994).

25. Böhning, *op. cit.*

26. Widgren, *op. cit.*

27. *Ibid.*

28. J.C. Chesnais, 'Migration from Eastern to Western Europe, past (1946–1989) and future (1990–2000),' in Council of Europe (ed.), *Second Meeting of Senior Officials Entrusted with Preparing the Conference of Ministers on the Movement of Persons Coming from Central and Eastern European Countries* (Strasbourg: Council of Europe, 1990); J.C. Chesnais, 'The USSR emigration: past, present and future,' in OECD (ed.), *International Conference on Migration* (Paris: OECD, 1991).

29. David A. Coleman, 'Contrasting age-structure differences of Western Europe and of Eastern Europe and the former Soviet Union: demographic curiosity or labor resource,' *Population and Development Review*, 19, 3 (1993), 523–56.

30. Coleman, 1993, *op. cit.*

31. OECD, 1995, *op. cit.*

32. Intergovernmental Consultations, *op. cit.*

33. Philip L. Martin, 'Foreign direct investment and migration; the case of Mexican maquiladoras,' in IOM (ed.), *Tenth IOM Seminar on Migration: Migration and Development* (Geneva: International Organization for Migration, 1992).

34. David A. Coleman, 'Does Europe need immigrants? Population and workforce projections,' *International Migration Review*, 26, 2 (1992), 413–61.

6 Magnitude, trends, and dynamics of immigration into North America. The need for a global perspective: the contextual framework

Bimal Ghosh

This chapter briefly deals with the magnitude, trends, and dynamics of immigration into Canada and the United States and raises some of the issues associated with them. It does not seek to explore the full range of interrelationships between these movements and the global migration system. A global perspective, however, is essential to fully understand these specific immigration flows and especially to design a sound framework for policy responses to the issues involved.

There are several important reasons for this. First, contemporary trans-boundary migration flows have become closely interrelated, so that changes in one could and often do have repercussions on several others, often at both ends of the flow. These linkages stem largely from globalization of the migratory process. Just as countries are now involved in migration, a growing number of them are becoming engaged in both sending and receiving migrants. The widening of the geographical scope of migratory movements has opened up new destinations and an unprecedented diversity in the countries of origin, leading to the formation of a dynamic and constantly evolving network of global migration.

A second reason, related to the first, is that despite the significant rise in immigration into North America and especially Western Europe in recent years, these movements cover only a part of the migration landscape. By far the larger part of the trans-boundary movements continues to take place between developing countries. Of the world's stock of 100 to 110 million migrants, 60 to 70 million are to be found in developing regions, with North America and Western Europe taken together accounting for less than two-fifths of the total (Table 6.1). Should even a part of the movements that have hitherto been primarily confined within the developing regions be diverted

Table 6.1   *World's migrant population: distribution of stocks by major regions (in millions)*

Africa	21–25
(refugees)	(5.3)
Middle East, South and East Asia	19–23
(refugees)	(7.2)
North America	25–27
(refugees)	(1.0)
Europe (excl. former USSR)	24–25
(refugees)	(4.3)
Central and South America	8–13
(refugees)	(0.8)
Overall total	97–111

Sources: United Nations (1989), ILO (1994) UNHCR (1993), and author's own calculations.

in future to North America or Western Europe, the configuration of the latter flows could dramatically change; the effect would be felt not only on the scale or magnitude of immigration but also on its composition, in terms, for example, of the skills, ethnicity, and social and cultural traits of the immigrants.

There is yet another, and equally compelling, reason why immigration into Western Europe and North America and the issues it entails need to be addressed from a global perspective. Major migration hardly ever takes place in a vacuum. Each movement is influenced by an interplay of several factors – some rooted in history and tradition, including established social and cultural ties across countries, with geography frequently playing a part. But many others are constantly new, reflecting changes in sending or receiving societies and in the outer world.

As migration becomes globalized, it tends to be more profoundly influenced than in the past by the transformation of the world economic and political order. Such transformation results from changing patterns of trade and capital flows and of interstate relations and security arrangements. It is the product of the increasing interpenetration of the communication and media system, and such diverse, even conflicting, trends as the growing interdependence of nations and integration of the world economy, alongside regional cooperation, economic protectionism, and the involuntary marginalization of weaker economies. At the same time migration itself has emerged as a powerful factor for economic and political change at the national and international levels, and thus for the shaping of the global order. Migration as a global process is now inextricably intertwined with the changing world economic and political system, in which the former often acts as what some analysts would call a subsystem. An important conclusion follows: in order to be meaningful as a policy-making tool, any analysis of the magnitude and trends of specific immigration flows must be placed within a wider, global framework.

This chapter does not examine in detail various immigration streams and their specific characteristics, although several of them would normally merit special attention in the context of the general theme. The focus here is on immigration into the United States and Canada, and the discussion takes into account both temporary and permanent migration. Although in traditional receiving countries temporary categories are considered non-immigrant, they deserve mention not just because of the weight of their numbers or their considerable impact on the labor market and the economy, but also because many of them subsequently change their status. With a few exceptions, temporary immigrants who are not visitors (about 4 million out of a total of 18 million in 1991) are routinely allowed by the USA to stay for up to five years. As in Canada, significant proportions of them become permanent immigrants. In the case of the USA, irregular immigration assumes additional importance because of a recent large-scale legalization program.

Immigration into North America: tracing the historical evolution

Until the 1880s immigration into the USA was practically unregulated, except that US employers actively encouraged, and a multitude of agencies and shipping companies systematically helped to organize, migratory movements across the Atlantic. Between 1800 and 1930, coinciding with the opening up of the US economy with its vast potential resources, some 40 million people from Europe – Irish and German nationals, followed by Italians, Greeks, and Eastern Europeans – moved to the New World. The prevailing general (though not universal) mood in the country was beautifully captured in Emma Lazarus's emotional poem, 'The New Colossus,' inscribed on the pedestal of the Statue of Liberty:

> Give me your tired, your poor
> Your huddled masses yearning to breathe free
> The wretched refuse of your teeming shore
> Send these, the homeless, tempest tossed, to me
> I lift my lamp beside the golden door ...

In 1883, when Lazarus wrote the poem, the French meaning of the statue, as Marvin Trachtenberg reminds us, was already lost, and a new significance had emerged. The beacon of liberty seen across the sea was not intended to serve France or any other nation, but rather to guide those Europeans eager for a new life away from Europe to 'the golden door' of America, where an uplifted torch became symbolic of welcome.[1]

But immigration into the USA has not always been a smooth or easy process, and associated conditions were not always happy. Western Europeans, at the turn of the twentieth century, were migrating to the USA in search of a new and better life. But another large migratory movement to America took place between 1700 and 1850. Before slavery was officially ended in the southern states of the USA in 1865 (the Atlantic traffic was abolished by the Great Powers in 1815), some 15 million (the estimates range between 10 and 20 million) slaves were transported from Africa to work in the USA and other parts of the Americas.[2]

Even after the Civil War, when the USA was experiencing industrial takeoff, helped by the immigrants from Western Europe, the use of nominally liberated Afro-Americans continued for years to meet the labor needs of cotton and other plantations, which were providing vital supplies for the emerging US industrial economy, including its external trade. By 1910, cotton, produced with black immigrant labor, accounted for half or more of all US exports[3] and was of particular importance to the expanding British textile industry. Later events have shown how the involuntary movement of such large numbers of Africans to the USA, their employment as slaves, and their subsequent liberation profoundly influenced, and still continue to influence, US economy and society, including its migration policy.

During the long and eventful history of US immigration, there have been several periods of strong anti-immigration feeling. Even in the 1840s and 1850s, as the waves of immigrants from Europe were rising, the anti-immigrant sentiment, of which the Know-Nothing Party was a beneficiary, influenced American politics. In the 1880s, campaigns against Chinese and other Asian immigrants led to the adoption of laws barring Chinese labor immigration in 1882 and restricting Japanese immigration in 1907. In the 1920s and 1930s, the anti-immigrant feeling was a significant political force in many states. The 1924 National Origins Act, which was the first comprehensive immigration law, consolidated the increasing number of restrictions and controls that had been established over a period of time, leading to a substantial reduction in the annual immigration flows in subsequent years. This restrictive attitude, reflecting the fear of the 'wild' entry of foreign masses into the United States, has found a lucid expression in the poem of Bailey Aldrich:[4]

> Wide open stand our gates
> And through them passes a wild motley throng
> O Liberty, white Goddess! Is it well
> To leave the gates unguarded?

In the decade 1931 to 1940 the gates were almost closed and immigration fell to the level of 500,000, the lowest in the recent history of US immigration. It rose to one million between 1941 and 1950 and 2.5 million between 1951 and 1960. Since then legal immigration into the United States has been rising steadily, reaching the level of 7.3 million in the decade 1981 to 1990.

The 1965 amendments to the Immigration and Nationality Act marked a watershed. Although designed as part of the civil rights legislation and originally intended to remove the discrimination that had been embedded in the United States' national-origins quota arrangements, the amendments in effect created a system of worldwide immigration. Immigrants from the developing regions, notably Latin America and Asia, took full advantage of the new provision, and a significant shift in the ethnic and geographical composition of the flows began to appear. In 1965, when the new legislation was enacted, the ratio of European to non-European immigrants was nine to one. By the mid-1980s the ratio had been reversed. The trend has continued in more recent years.

The enactment of the Immigration Reform and Control Act of 1986 was another important development in the history of US immigration. Although its primary purpose was to improve control over irregular immigration, the implications of the new initiative were much wider, as were underlying motivations. The specification of several categories of erstwhile irregular migrants, as envisaged in the enactment, had social and fiscal implications, and it modified to some extent the future pattern of immigration into the country; for example, by opening opportunities for chain immigration based on family reunification. The result was to multiply flows from particular source countries.

In a way, this also distorted the statistical picture of immigration by listing as permanent settlers those successful irregular alien applicants who in fact had already been residing within the US territory. To illustrate, in 1991 the registered permanent settlement entries for Mexicans rose to 946,200, of which only 52,900 were new arrivals, and the rest resulted from new definitions and allowances created in the 1986 legalization. The increase in the number of permanent immigrants consequent to legalization has also implied a decline in the relative shares of other categories in the total inflow. Thus, in 1983 family immigration accounted for nearly 70 percent of all inflows of permanent immigrants, but the share fell to 25 percent in 1991 as large numbers of legalized Mexicans were registered as permanent residents. The share of refugee inflows fell to 18.3 percent in 1991.[5]

The most recent phase in US immigration was marked by the passing of the Immigration Act of 1990. The new legislation maintains the basic principles of non-discrimination with regard to ethnicity and national origins of immigrants to the USA and reaffirms family reunification and formation as a centerpiece of US immigration policy. At the same time, it provides a clearer recognition of the role of immigration in enhancing US economic growth and competitiveness, by significantly increasing the number of employment-based immigration visas and by seeking to meet employers' needs for additional skilled labor while protecting the interests of US workers.

The full effect of the changes under the new legislation which came into operation in October 1991 has not yet filtered through into the migration statistics, but the broad thrust is clear.[6] Despite the growing concern in the industrial world over immigration and tendencies toward restrictive policies, the determination of the USA to maintain a high level of immigration has been reaffirmed by the new legislation. Leaving aside the effects of legalization under the 1986 Act, the US annual intake of permanent settlers hovered between 550,000 and 650,000 in the 1980s; it is projected that, as of 1995, when the transition period would be over, the level could rise to as high as 750,000 a year.[7]

Meanwhile, immigration to the USA, including entries resulting from legalization, reached record-breaking levels in 1990 and 1991, in both years surpassing the previous record set in 1907. In 1991, total US immigration was at an all-time high at 1.82 million, of which 1.1 million (or 61.5 percent) were legalized aliens and 139,000 refugees and asylees. Legal permanent immigration into the USA stood at the level of 7.3 million for the decade of the 1980s, second only to the highest immigration decade, 1901 to 1910 (Tables 6.2 and 6.3).

The intriguing question is whether the trends will continue to sustain such magnitudes of immigration. Or will there be a backlash against flows of immigration into the USA in the future? To put the question somewhat differently: will the USA increasingly align itself with, and thus reinforce, the restrictive policies of most industrial receiving countries, especially those in Western Europe? Or will it be exploring, jointly with other nations, an alternative approach to meet the new migration challenge?

Canada as a traditional receiving country

Immigration into Canada has followed a pattern broadly similar to that in the USA. In the late eighteenth century Canada had its share of the large trans-Atlantic immigration flow – from Britain, France, Germany, and other North West European countries. After the American Revolution, many loyalists of British origin moved to Canada; and to escape slavery thousands of Afro-Americans moved from the USA, with the result that by 1860 there were 40,000 black people in Canada.[8] The gold rushes and opening up of the vast prairie areas (with grants of 160 acres of free land to develop their agricultural potential and to help assert Canada's sovereignty over those areas) fueled further immigration from Europe in the nineteenth century.

There was a large influx from Southern and Eastern Europe between 1895 and 1914, and the Asian inflows from China, India, and Japan, which started in the late nineteenth century, continued. Between 1871 and 1931 Canada's population increased from 3.6 million to 10.3 million.[9]

Beginning as early as 1886, a series of measures were introduced to restrict Asian immigration into Canada. It was prohibited between 1923 and 1947. Canada remained keen on encouraging British immigration and, in 1931, it designated four preferred categories of immigrants, including US citizens.[10] The suppression of the national origins quota system in 1962, three years before the USA took similar action, prompted a large increase in the number of immigrants from developing countries, alongside a relative decline in immigration from Europe. This intake sharply increased between 1985 and 1990. In 1990 Canada introduced a five-year immigration plan, which maintained the importance of family connections and support for refugees and increased entries based on skills- and employment-based criteria. The plan aimed at raising the level of total entries to 220,000 in

Table 6.2 *Shares of US decennial population growth attributable to immigration, 1820–1990 (population in thousands)*

Year	Total US population	Population increase in the decade	Immigrants to the USA	Immigrants as % share of the increase
1820	9638			
1830	12,866	3228	143	4
1840	17,069	4203	599	14
1850	23,192	6123	1713	28
1860	31,443	8251	2598	31
1870	38,558	7115	2315	33
1880	50,189	11,631	2812	24
1890	62,721	12,532	5247	42
1990	76,747	14,026	3688	26
1910	92,198	15,451	8795	57
1920	106,005	13,807	5736	42
1930	123,197	17,192	4107	24
1940	132,184	8987	528	6
1950	151,291	19,107	1035	5
1960	179,420	28,129	2515	9
1970	203,302	23,882	3322	14
1980	226,546	23,244	4493	19
1990	248,710	22,164	7338	33

Source: US Bureau of the Census and Immigration and Naturalization Service 1990 Yearbook.

Table 6.3 *United States, inflows of permanent settlers by entry class[a]*
(thousands, fiscal years)

	1981	1982	1983	1984	1985	1986	1987	1988	1989	1990	1991
Immediate relatives[b]	152.4	168.4	177.8	183.2	204.4	223.5	218.6	219.3	217.5	231.7	237.1
Relative preference[c]	226.6	206.1	213.5	212.3	213.3	212.9	211.8	200.8	211.1	214.6	216.1
Worker preference[d]	44.3	51.2	55.5	49.5	50.9	53.6	53.9	53.6	52.8	53.7	54.9
Western hemisphere[e]	58.4	2.3	–	–	–	–	–	–	–	–	–
IRCA legalization[f]	–	–	–	–	–	–	–	–	478.8	880.4	1123.2
Non-preference[g]	–	–	–	–	–	–	3.0	6.0	7.1	20.4	12.3
Refugees[h]	107.6	156.6	102.7	92.1	95.0	104.4	96.5	110.7	84.3	97.4	139.1
Others	7.4	9.6	10.3	6.7	6.4	7.3	17.7	52.6	33.4	38.4	44.5
Total	596.6	594.1	559.8	543.9	570.0	601.7	601.5	643.0	1090.9	1536.5	1827.2

[a]With the exception of immediate relatives of US citizens, immigrants in a class of admission include principal beneficiaries, i.e. those aliens who directly qualify for the class of admission under US immigration laws, and derivative beneficiaries, i.e. the spouses and unmarried children of principal immigrants.

[b]Numerically unrestricted immigrants comprising spouses, unmarried minor children, and orphans adopted by US citizens as well as parents of adult US citizens.

[c]Numerically restricted relatives comprise the following four preference classes: first, unmarried adult sons and daughters of US citizens; second, spouses and unmarried sons and daughters of US permanent resident aliens; fourth, married sons and daughters of US citizens; fifth, brothers and sisters of adult US citizens.

[d]Numerically restricted workers comprise the following two preference classes: third, members of the professions or persons of exceptional ability in the sciences and arts; sixth, skilled and unskilled workers in short supply.

[e]For the period 1968–77, immigrants from independent Western hemisphere countries were not included under the preference system; however, they were subject to a 120,000 cap. Although the Western hemisphere category of admission was eliminated in 1977 through the extension of the preference system to that hemisphere, a number of Western hemisphere immigrants were admitted after 1977 as a result of lawsuits.

[f]Under the 1986 Immigration Reform and Control Act, foreigners who had been accorded temporary legal status could apply, between December 1988 and December 1990, for a permanent residence permit.

[g]If preference classes are undersubscribed, the unused numbers become available to non-preference immigrants (who have established that their admission will not have an adverse effect on the US labor force). Although non-preference slots have been unavailable since 1978, recent lawsuits have resulted in the admission of a small number of non-preference immigrants. Under the 1986 Immigration Reform and Control Act, immigrants from certain countries determined to have been adversely affected by the 1965 immigration reform were admitted under a special 'non-preference' category.

[h]Refugees were admitted under various laws. The Refugee Act of 1980 now governs all refugee admissions.

Source: SOPEMI, 1993.

1991, and to 250,000 per year during 1992 to 1995. Total admissions increased from 89,000 in 1983 to 192,000 in 1989, and to 230,000 in 1991, an increase of about 7.2 percent in 1990. Family class entries increased by 17.1 percent in 1990–1; investors were the fastest growing business category, up 23.8 percent (Table 6.4).

Despite some divergence,[11] immigration into the USA and Canada shares many common features and a high degree of convergence is also discernible in the recent policy trends in the two countries. Under their most recent legislation, for example, both have shown determination to increase rather than decrease the number of immigrants; at the same time both have indicated the increased importance of education and skills in selecting

Table 6.4   *Canada, inflows of permanent settlers by entry class (thousands)*

	1981	1982	1983	1984	1985	1986	1987	1988	1989	1990	1991
Social											
Family Class[a]	51.0	50.0	48.7	43.8	38.5	42.2	53.6	51.3	60.8	73.5	86.0
Humanitarian											
Convention refugees[b]	0.8	1.8	4.1	5.6	6.1	6.5	7.5	8.7	10.2	11.4	18.3
Designated class[c]	14.2	15.1	9.9	9.7	10.7	12.7	14.1	18.1	26.8	28.3	34.8
Economic											
Assisted relatives[d]	17.6	11.9	5.0	8.2	7.4	5.9	12.3	15.6	21.5	25.4	22.2
Retirees	2.1	2.3	2.1	2.3	2.1	1.8	2.7	3.2	3.6	3.5	4.2
Entrepreneurs[e]	0.9	1.5	1.9	3.6	5.0	5.9	8.4	11.4	13.0	12.3	9.9
Self-employed[f]	5.1	4.9	4.4	2.7	1.5	1.6	2.3	2.7	2.3	2.0	2.0
Investors[g]							0.3	1.0	2.3	4.2	5.2
Independents[h]	36.9	33.7	13.2	12.3	13.1	22.6	50.9	49.9	51.6	53.7	47.3
Total	128.6	121.1	89.2	88.2	84.3	99.2	152.1	161.9	192.0	214.2	229.7

[a] Immigrants sponsored by Canadian residents (spouses, dependent children, parents and persons in their charge).
[b] Persons meeting the conditions established by the United Nations Convention on Refugees.
[c] Persons who do not strictly meet the conditions established by the UN Convention on Refugees.
[d] Family members in the broad sense (primarily siblings of Canadian residents and independent children).
[e] Heads of firms employing a certain minimum number of Canadian citizens or permanent residents.
[f] Immigrants in a position to create employment for him/herself.
[g] Immigrants who are willing and able to invest specified sums of money in risk ventures in Canada.
[h] Independent immigrants able to pass a selection test based on economic criteria.

Source: SOPEMI, 1993

future immigrants, without prejudice to family-based admissions. The difference has mainly been one of degree; for example, over the years emphasis on skilled immigration has featured rather more prominently in Canada's immigration system. Currently, again in common with the USA, Canada faces a complex, unanswered question: what should be the nature and magnitude of future migratory inflows into the country?

Measuring levels and assessing significance of immigration

Immigration can be seen in different contexts of the receiving society, just as it can be measured in many different ways. Much of the controversy surrounding immigration is in fact linked to the selection of the contexts in which it is seen and the manner in which it is assessed. The perception of the level of immigration itself could be influenced by the specific criterion or criteria used for measuring it.

One common way of measuring immigration concerns the stocks of immigrants in the host society. But a definitional problem immediately arises: in the USA, as in Canada, available data reveal the number of foreign-born persons, which is a different and much broader concept than the notion of foreigners used in Western European countries. In Europe, relevant data are collected on the basis of foreign passports rather than on foreign births. The implication of this difference could be quite important: if holding a foreign passport were the main criterion, it would reduce the number of immigrants of traditional receiving countries by half, on the assumption of a 50 percent rate of naturalization among foreign-born persons, an approach followed in a most recent International Labor Organization (ILO) estimate of 'global economic migration.'[12]

Immigration, demographic targets, and societal models

The foreign-born population in the USA rose from 14.1 million in 1980 to 19.8 million in 1990, representing nearly 8 percent of the US population (Table 6.5). The proportion was 4.7 percent in 1970 and 6.2 percent in 1980, and since then it has been rising. Viewed in a historical perspective, however, the current ratio is far from the highest: in 1900, for example, it was 12 percent and in 1910 as high as 14.6 percent. The total US population for the selected years was 76 million and 92 million respectively.

As shown in Table 6.5, the share of foreign-born population has traditionally been much higher in Canada: it was 15.6 in 1986, almost unchanged from 1971 when the ratio was 15.3, although there was a slight rise in 1981 (16.1 percent). For Western Europe the proportion of those counted as foreign residents varies widely among countries (Table 6.6). In 1991 the proportion for the European Community countries as a whole was 4

Table 6.5   *Trends in the foreign-born population as a proportion of the total population and labor force in selected OECD non-European countries*

Country	Year	Total population (thousands)	Total labor force (thousands)	Share of foreign born persons in	
				total population (%)	total labor force (%)
Australia	1971	12,756	5707	20.0	24.5
	1981	14,576	6823	20.6	25.7
	1986	15,602	7629	20.8	25.4
	1991	17,336	8412	22.7	25.8
Canada	1971	21,568	8727	15.3	20.2
	1981	24,343	11,973	16.1	20.1
	1986	25,353	12,823	15.6	21.9
United States	1970	205,052	84,889	4.7	5.3
	1980	227,757	106,085	6.2	6.7
	1990	248,710	125,182	7.9	9.3

Source: Censuses and Labor Force Surveys.

percent. But straight comparisons between North American and Western European countries are questionable because of the definitional discrepancies involved.

Another way of measuring immigration is to look at the *gross flow* of immigrants as a *proportion to the yearly resident population*.[13] When proportions of emigrants to immigrants are high, *net* immigration could be low, or even negative, as was the case, for example, in the USA during the 1930s. The gross immigration data could give a wrong impression of the scale of permanent immigrants, and are particularly misleading for estimating demographic or labor force growth in the receiving country. On the other hand, the level of gross yearly immigration could be meaningful in assessing the intensity of the flow and the absorption capacity of the receiving society at a given point in time. In the USA the current annual intake (including new irregular entries) represents 0.40 percent of the population; in Canada it was much higher, around 0.92 percent. The US immigrants arriving in the decade 1901 to 1910 constituted 9.6 percent of the population at the end of the decade; the arrivals in 1960 to 1971 and 1971 to 1980 represented 1.6 and 2.0 percent. In 1981 to 1990, the ratio of gross immigration (including immigrants legalized under the 1986 Act, but not new irregular entries) was 7.3 percent, lower than in the 1901 to 1910 decade.

Immigration can also be seen as a ratio of total population growth. In the 1820s immigration accounted for 4 percent of the total increase in US population (Table 6.2). It reached the highest point, 57 percent, in the

Table 6.6 *Stocks of foreign population in selected OECD countries[a]*
(thousands)

	1981	1982	1983	1984	1985	1986	1987	1988	1989	1990	1991
Austria	299.2	302.9	275.0	268.8	271.7	275.7	283.0	298.7	322.6	413.4	512.2
% total population	3.9	4.0	3.6	3.6	3.6	3.6	3.7	3.9	4.2	5.3	6.6
Belgium[b]	885.7	891.2	890.9	897.6	846.5	853.2	862.5	868.8	880.8	904.5	922.5
% total population	9.0	9.0	9.0	9.1	8.6	8.6	8.7	8.8	8.9	9.1	9.2
Denmark	101.9	103.1	104.1	107.7	117.0	128.3	136.2	142.0	150.6	160.6	169.5
% total population	2.0	2.0	2.0	2.1	2.3	2.5	2.7	2.8	2.9	3.1	3.3
Finland	13.7	14.3	15.7	16.8	17.0	17.3	17.7	18.7	21.2	26.3	35.8
% total population	0.3	0.3	0.3	0.3	0.3	0.4	0.4	0.4	0.4	0.5	0.7
France[c]		3714.2								3596.6	
% total population		6.8								6.3	
Germany[d]	4629.8	4666.9	4534.9	4363.7	4378.9	4512.7	4630.2	4489.1	4845.9	5241.8	5882.3
% total population	7.5	7.6	7.4	7.1	7.2	7.4	7.6	7.3	7.7	8.2	7.3
Italy[e]	331.7	358.9	381.3	403.9	423.0	450.2	572.1	645.4	490.4	781.1	896.8
% total population	0.6	0.6	0.7	0.7	0.7	0.8	1.0	1.1	0.9	1.4	1.5
Luxembourg	95.4	95.6	96.2	96.8	97.9	96.7	99.0	101.8	104.9	109.1	
% total population	26.1	26.2	26.3	26.5	26.7	26.2	26.6	27.1	27.7	28.4	
Netherlands	537.6	546.5	552.4	558.7	552.5	568.0	591.8	623.7	641.9	692.4	732.9
% total population	3.8	3.8	3.8	3.9	3.8	3.9	4.0	4.2	4.3	4.6	4.8
Norway[f]	86.5	90.6	94.7	97.8	101.5	109.3	123.7	135.9	140.3	143.3	147.8
% total population	2.1	2.2	2.3	2.4	2.4	2.6	2.9	3.2	3.3	3.4	3.5
Spain[g]	198.0	200.2	210.4	226.5	242.0	293.2	334.9	360.0	249.6	278.7	360.7
% total population	0.5	0.5	0.5	0.6	0.6	0.8	0.9	0.9	0.6	0.7	0.9
Sweden[h]	414.0	405.5	397.1	390.6	388.6	390.8	401.0	421.0	456.0	483.7	493.8
% total population	5.0	4.9	4.8	4.7	4.6	4.7	4.8	5.0	5.3	5.6	5.7
Switzerland[i]	909.9	925.8	925.6	932.4	939.7	956.0	978.7	1006.5	1040.3	1100.3	1163.2
% total population	14.3	14.4	14.4	14.4	14.5	14.7	14.9	15.2	15.6	16.3	17.1
United Kingdom[j]				1601.0	1731.0	1820.0	1839.0	1821.0	1812.0	1723.0	1750.0
% total population				2.8	3.1	3.2	3.2	3.2	3.2	3.2	3.1

[a] Data as of December 31 of year indicated extracted, except for France and United Kingdom, from population registers. Stocks of foreign population by nationality are given in Tables Bl.
[b] In 1985, as a consequence of a modification of the nationality code, some persons who formerly would have been counted as foreigners were included as nationals. This led to a marked decrease in the foreign population.
[c] Population censuses on March 4, 1982 and March 6, 1990.
[d] Data as of September 30 up to 1984 and in 1990 and as of 31st December from 1985 to 1989 and in 1991. Refers to western Germany up to 1990. As from 1991, data cover Germany as a whole.
[e] Data are adjusted to take account of the regularizations which occurred in 1987–8 and 1990. The fall in numbers for 1989 results from a review of the foreigners' registers (removing duplicate registrations and accounting for returns).
[f] From 1987, asylum seekers whose requests are being processed are included. Numbers for earlier years were fairly small.
[g] Numbers of foreigners holding a residence permit. Permits of short duration (less than 6 months) as well as students are excluded. Data for 1991 include 108,372 permits delivered following the regularization. The fall in numbers for 1989 results from a review of the foreigners' registers.
[h] Some foreigners with permits of short duration are not counted (mainly citizens of other Nordic countries).
[i] Numbers of foreigners with annual residence permits (including, up to December 31, 1982, holders of permits of durations below 12 months) and holders of settlement permits (permanent permits). Seasonal and frontier workers are excluded.
[j] Numbers estimated from the annual Labour Force Survey.

Source: SOPEMI, Trends in International Migration, Continuous Reporting System on International Migration, OECD, 1993.

decade 1900 to 1910, when the USA was witnessing a very high level of immigration, and fell sharply to less than 10 percent during 1930 to 1950. Legal immigration accounted for a third of population growth in the 1980s and, as a result of the changes in the immigration law, it is expected to represent half of total population growth in the 1990s, or higher if irregular immigration is taken into account. With a lower fertility rate for the US population, even a constant level of immigration would constitute a higher proportion of natural increase.

Although the significance of this way of measuring immigration can be called into question,[14] it can still be meaningful in two ways: first, it can help in maintaining a given rate of total population growth, consistent with the demographic objective of the host society. In other words, the level of immigration could be inversely adjusted to the fall or rise in the fertility rate of the local population in order to reach the demographic target. In the USA, for example, the Federation of American Immigration Reform (FAIR), a pro-limits population organization which aims at a 'zero population growth rate,' estimates that a cap on legal immigration (including refugees and asylees) of 300,000, combined with a total halting of irregular immigration and a three-year moratorium on most immigration, will make it possible to achieve its policy goal.

Second, the immigration-to-total growth measure can be useful in monitoring changes in the ethnic and cultural composition of the national population, when the composition of the new flows differs from that of the national population. As already noted, largely as a result of new legislation in 1965 (abolition of national origins quota) and in 1986 (legalization of irregular alien residents), the ethnic composition of immigrants to the USA has radically changed. The composition of the flows showed some relatively significant changes between 1981 and 1991, but they continued to be dominated by Latin America and Asia throughout the period.

In Canada, European-born immigrants continue to predominate, accounting for nearly half of the immigrant population. However, as concerns the flows, the numbers of immigrants from Asia rose sharply, as did the immigrants from the Caribbean and Latin American countries during 1981 to 1991, while those from the USA have tended to fall. Today more than three-quarters of all Americans are white; by the middle of the next century this may have fallen below one-half. In noting the consequences of this change, *The Economist* quoted an American scholar as saying 'People of 90 [years of age] and older will increasingly have the experience of growing up in one kind of country and growing older in another.'[15]

The significance to be attached to such change depends, however, on the societal model the receiving country sets for itself. The change could be of considerable negative significance if, as in Japan today, the country seeks to maintain racial homogeneity. It would be seen in a completely different neutral or positive light if the country is committed to the model of a multiracial, multicultural society. It would be more positive if the receiving country considers itself to be a racial-cultural melting pot, where national identity, while being anchored in a set of human values, constantly evolves through cultural interactions. It is worth noting in this connection that in Canada a 1986 survey of high school students in British Columbia showed that immigrants and their children knew as much about Canadian values, as defined in the Charter of Rights, as Canadian-born students, and were equally committed to those values. In Western Europe, where membership in society is still tied to ethnicity and nationality, diversity resulting from immigration is less easily accepted than in North America, especially when it is perceived to be a threat to the established cultural pattern.

Broad generalizations could, however, be misleading. Even in North America, there have been, as indicated above, strong exclusionary and assimilationist movements, and the multicultural model, even today, is not above controversy. There are also subtle, but important, differences between Canada and the USA, just as there is diversity within Western Europe. For example, Sweden, long a homogeneous society, has recently been following what would generally be perceived as multicultural policies. The crux of the matter, then, lies in defining the normative societal model.

Related is the fertility rate of immigrant women. The relative fertility rates for the immigrants and the national population could be an important factor influencing the future racial and cultural composition of the receiving society (always assuming that the composition of the flows is different from that of the local population). If white school children now account for fewer than half of California's school children, the explanation probably lies not just in the high concentration of immigrants in the state but also in the higher rate of births for the immigrant population there.

Estimates of foreign births as a proportion of total births over a period of time make it possible to measure the contribution of immigration to the natural increase in the population. As SOPEMI (OECD) puts it, immigrants make a significant contribution to demographic growth in several industrial countries, and help to slow down demographic aging. Compared to Western Europe, both Canada and the USA have higher fertility rates per woman (1.7 and 1.9 respectively, in 1990), and the total fertility rate in the USA may have gone up in recent years. Even so, and despite some controversy on the subject, it is generally accepted that the current rates in North America are below the replacement level. On the other hand, a durable solution to this problem through immigration depends on successive waves of immigrants, since the fertility of immigrant women, as studies in different industrial countries have shown, tends to converge with the overall fertility rate in the host country and to decrease with the length of stay.[16] The role that immigration can play in meeting the imbalances in the age structure of the population and in preventing demographic stagnation or even decline in industrial countries is then linked to the question of fixing the long-term demographic goal. In the USA, as in Canada, the debate on this issue continues. Western Europe is in a similar situation.

Immigrants, labor markets, and the economy

The composition of immigration in terms of age and skill is particularly relevant in the context of labor market needs[17] and the economy of the host country. In the USA, the age distribution of legal immigrants shows a historical concentration in the prime years of labor force participation. This also has distributional significance, given the expected increase in the proportion of older people, who will need to be supported by the working population. For the Asian immigrants who arrived between 1970 and 1980, the proportion aged from 25 to 34 was 31 percent. The proportion was even higher, 43.4 percent for those who were admitted under occupational preference category, reflecting a close correlation between employment-based admission and the younger age structure of immigrants. Although, on average, recent immigrants are found to be younger than the total population only by about three years, irregular immigrant cohorts continue to be much younger than the national population.

In the USA the ratio of immigrant population in the labor force is slightly higher than in the total population (Table 6.5). In Canada, the immigrants' demographic profile is even more conducive to labor force participation, as reflected in the differential in immigrants' shares in total population (15.6 percent) and in total labor force (21.9 percent).

In the earlier phases of immigration in the USA, especially during 1900 to 1920, a very high proportion of immigrants were male, but in more recent years the numbers of male and female immigrants have tended to converge. Research in the 1980s showed that labor force participation for immigrant women was somewhat bimodal: the proportion of immigrant women was higher than US women in highly skilled occupations (28.1 percent), but it also showed more concentration of immigrant women in low-status, white-collar employment (18.0 percent), semi-skilled jobs (17.9 percent), and private household work (13.9 percent).[18]

In Canada, nearly half of immigrants in 1991 were male, although proportions vary considerably between categories: in general males were the principal applicants in the 'selected' categories, while subsequent chain migration (e.g. family class entry) tends to attract more females. Among immigrants who came between 1947 and 1972, higher labor force participation among immigrant women (aged 35 to 44) may have contributed to a higher overall rate of immigrants' participation in the labor force than the rate for the total population, although the difference in age distribution (a higher proportion of immigrants in the labor force age bracket) must have been the main factor.

An important question concerns the educational and occupational characteristics of immigrants. In the USA, data collected for the 1970s (1971 to 1979) shows that a much larger proportion (26 percent) of immigrants than workers in the national population (16.1 percent) were in technical and professional categories. Data for the previous decade (1961 to 1970) confirm a similar difference in favor of the immigrants.

Does the immigration flow raise or lower the education level of the stock of US workers? Limited available data seem to suggest that adult immigrants who arrived between 1965 and 1974 had three-quarters of a year less education on average than the US labor force, and that, prior to 1965, the average was about the same, but there were probably somewhat larger proportions of immigrants in the highest education categories. Data for 1970 to 1980 indicate that, in general, adult immigrants in the USA had a bimodal educational – and to some extent occupational – distribution relative to the national population[19]: there were higher proportions of immigrants in the advanced and middle-level education and at the same time in the lowest education category (Table 6.7).

Data collected for postwar years (1946 to 1961) revealed a similar educational and occupational profile of the immigrants in Canada: the proportions of immigrants in professional and skilled work were higher

Table 6.7 *Percentage of the population with high and low education: US natives, all immigrants, and Asian immigrants, 1980*

Education attainment	Native	Immigrated 1970–80	
		total immigrants	Asian immigrants
Percentage with 4 years' college education (persons 25 years and older)	8.7	9.7	17.6
Percentage with 5 or more years' college education (persons 25 years and older)	7.5	12.5	19.8
Percentage with less than 5 years' elementary school education (persons 25 years and older)	2.9	12.8	7.4

Sources: US Department of Commerce, Bureau of the Census: 1980 Census of Population; Detailed Population Characteristics, March 1984.

than the overall proportion of immigrants in the country's population.[20] Also, the proportions of immigrants from Asia and the United Kingdom who arrived after 1960 with more than secondary education were much larger than the proportion of the Canadian-born stock. But immigrants as of the 1986 census were three times as likely to be functionally illiterate (less than grade five education) as native-born Canadians. A decline was also discernible in the proportions of Asian immigrants with university training in the 1970s, compared to those who came earlier.

The educational and occupational profiles of immigrants are to a large extent correlated with the admission criteria and their channels of entry into the receiving country. In the USA recent increases in immigration entries through legalization, including legalization of resident family members, and refugee and asylum seeking procedures may have contributed to a lowering of the average level of education and skills of immigrants. It was not surprising that only four years of schooling was the average level of education for nearly one million Mexican immigrants who were legalized under the special agricultural worker program. Some analysts have found a strong link between declining education levels and lower earnings for immigrants who came to the USA after 1970, compared to those of the 1950s.[21]

In Canada, the reduced educational attainments of more recent streams of immigrants were perhaps due to enlarged inflows of refugees (e.g. from Vietnam) and to increased entries through family reunification rather than via the point system. Only 17 percent of permanent immigrants to Canada were selected through the point system in 1991 and probably less in 1992, compared with 32 percent in 1971. A study made in 1990 finds that immigrants who arrived after 1978, roughly coinciding with the increase in family class admissions, have not caught up with the native-born people of the same age. The new waves of immigrants were unlikely to equal the income performance of their predecessors.[22]

The changing characteristics of immigrants are also a reflection of the migration dynamics which bind the evolving socio-economic situation in sending and receiving countries. As the pressure of 'survival' migration, as distinct from 'mobility' or opportunity-seeking migration,[23] increases due to poverty and income inequality in sending countries, the composition of the outflow could change, with a shift toward less educated and less equipped migrants. At the receiving end, the change in the composition of migration can be helped by the segmentation of labor market. In the USA, as recent flows have become increasingly diversified in terms of the skills, motivations, and home countries of immigrants, there has also been a 'dramatic diversification of conditions under which newcomers participate in the US labor market.'[24] The situation in the USA and in the sending countries thus tends to create a twofold process, with a mutually reinforcing effect of inflows of less skilled workers. In the USA the creation of a large number of new low-wage and low-skill jobs in the informal or less organized sectors in the past few years may have helped in reducing overall unemployment in the country, but the expansion of these sectors will certainly be a source of additional attraction for low-skilled immigrants.

Two additional points need to be noted. First, immigrants' contribution to improved productivity and economic growth depends not just on their educational and skill levels but also on the innovativeness and drive they bring in with them. Data compiled by the US Census Bureau provide an indication of the impact of immigrant entrepreneurship; between 1982 and 1987 Hispanic firms in the USA showed an increase of 81 percent compared with a 14 percent increase for all US firms; a similar increase was noticeable for firms owned by Asian immigrants. Canada's preference for entrepreneur immigrants has been reflected in a sevenfold increase in their numbers between 1983 and 1989. The benefits of immigrant entrepreneurship need, however, to be weighed against the costs that they often entail in terms of human hardship and social stress resulting from intense competition, long hours of work, and exploitation of family labor.[25]

Although immigrants' prior education and skills may facilitate their further training and vocational readaptation, their relevance needs also to be seen in the context of the profile of skill requirements of the host economy. The provisions of the 1990 US Immigration Act, which aim at increasing the number of skilled immigrants by nearly tripling the number of visas reserved for qualified workers from 54,000 to 140,000, and which set the educational and skill requirements for such immigration at decidedly higher levels, assume special significance in this context.

Similarly, it is envisaged that under the current Canadian policy immigrants selected on the basis of their qualifications will become an increasingly significant component of labor force growth in Canada.[26] But, as in the USA, the segmentation of the labor market would at the same time continue to encourage further inflows of low-skill and less equipped immigrants. Both countries have the opportunity for using labor immigration as an integral part of their human resources development strategy to promote sustainable growth and employment if they choose such courses of action.

Public attitude, policy making, and perception of immigration level

The magnitude or level of immigration could also be analyzed in the context of how it is perceived by the general public. This could be particularly interesting in situations where public feeling about immigration impacts heavily on policy formulation. However, this is not the case in either Canada or the USA.

In both countries government policy toward immigration has, historically, tended to be more positive or liberal than the prevailing (or apparent) public opinion at the time.[27] This is reflected in findings based on a series of public opinion polls (Table 6.8). Despite variations in emphasis, the responses to most public opinion polls in the USA between the 1930s and the 1980s seemed to suggest that Americans were not in favor of immigration. The results of public opinion polls over a period of 45 years (1946 to 1990) showed that only once, in 1953, did more than 10 percent of those surveyed favor increasing the number of immigrants permitted to enter the United States. During this period at least three times as many respondents supported decreasing the number of immigrants admitted (Table 6.9). Yet, as noted above, almost throughout its history the USA has

Table 6.8 *Public opinion concerning the volume of immigration*

Year	Poll	Question	Response			
1953	NORC	In general, do you think the United States is letting too many immigrants come into this country or not enough?	Not enough	About the right number	Too many	Don't know
			13	37	39	11
1965	Gallup	Should immigration be kept at its present level, increased or decreased?	Increased	Present level	Decreased	Don't know
			8	37	33	20
1977	AIPO	Should immigration be kept at its present level, increased or decreased?	Increased	Present level	Decreased	No opinion
			4	37	42	14
1982	Roper	In recent years, there has been a lot of discussion about the number of immigrants allowed to enter our country. On the whole, would you say that you would like to see the number of immigrants allowed to enter our country increased, or would like to see the number decreased, or do you think we are letting in about the right number now?	Increased	Right number now	Decreased	Don't know
			4	23	66	7
1986	NY Times/ CBS News	Exact text not given	Increased	Kept at current level	Decreased	Don't know or no answer
			7	35	49	9

Source: Rita J. Simon, *Public Opinion and the Immigrant* (Lexington, MA: Lexington Books, 1985).

accepted immigrants, though the numbers fluctuated from one period to another. Even more importantly, the country's long experience with immigration has been eminently positive overall.

There may be several possible explanations for this apparent paradox, and one of them may well lie in the complexity and nuance that often characterize people's feeling about immigration or about foreigners. These cannot be easily captured through public opinion polls or easily interpreted. To illustrate, a 1978 poll about Vietnamese immigrants showed that only 32 percent of Americans favored their entry into the USA. Fifty-seven percent opposed, while 11 percent had no opinion. But when asked whether they would like some of the Vietnamese to live *in their own areas,* 48 percent of the same sample group said 'yes,' 40 percent said 'no', and 13 percent had no opinion. This has been interpreted as showing that many Americans, even when opposed to immigration in the abstract may well have positive feelings toward the immigrants they know personally. Or could it be that for many Americans the feeling of human solidarity is stronger when it relates to people as individuals living in the known neighborhood, in contrast with a distant collective group, or a vague entity in the abstract?

Table 6.9   *Distribution of responses about the number of immigrants that should be permitted to enter (percent)*

	1946[a]	1953	1965	1977	1981	1982	1986	1988	1990[b]
More/increase	5	13	8	7	5	4	7	6	9
Same/present level	32	37	39	37	22	23	35	34	29
Fewer/decrease	37 (14)[c]	39	33	42	65	66	49	53	48
No opinion/don't know	12	11	20	14	8	7	9	7	14

[a] In 1946, the question was phrased: 'Should we permit more persons from Europe to come to this country each year than we did before the war, should we keep the number about the same, or should we reduce the number?' In the subsequent polls the question was usually phrased as follows: 'Should immigration be kept at its present level, increased, or decreased?'

[b] In 1990, the question was phrased: 'Is it your impression that the current immigration laws allow too many immigrants, too few immigrants, or about the right number of immigrants into this country each year?'

[c] 'None' was offered as a choice of response only in 1946, and 14 percent selected that choice.

Sources: Roper Center (Storrs: University of Connecticut Press, 1991); Rita J. Simon and Susan H. Alexander, *The Ambivalent Welcome*

In any case, in the USA, as in Canada, the attitudes of the general public have been less influential in shaping immigration policy than those of the organized pressure groups; and within such pressure movements 'a much smaller group consisting of activists has traditionally played a dominant role.'[28]

American values and future immigration trends

Assessing future immigration trends is a perilous task because of the large number of factors involved, several of which are highly unpredictable. An important variable which often does not receive sufficient attention in immigration analysis relates to the nature of the receiving society's involvement in immigration. This point is taken up below.

Immigration brings change. As change affects different individuals and groups and their economic, social, and cultural interests differently, it inevitably creates tension. The USA is in a good position to manage such tension because several of the basic values and principles that underpin the immigration system, such as family reunification and formation, the acceptance of cultural diversity, and protection and assistance to those in danger, are, as Papademetriou puts it, inextricably woven into its own social, cultural, and political ethos.[29] This linkage is eloquently, if somewhat lavishly, elaborated in a recent Ford Foundation report:

America is deeply implicated in the migration flow and its destiny. American employers fuel the immigration, American foreign policy embraces it, and American family values maintain it. As a nation we have been there before. America thrives on its immigrant heritage. Part history, part ideology, immigration embodies the theme of national renewal, rebirth, hope. Uprooted abroad, newcomers have become transplants in a land that promises opportunity.[30]

Canada, like the USA, is an immigration country. Arguments of self-interest, based on economic, demographic, and labor market considerations, may not be embraced by all Canadians with equal conviction, but cancelling the immigration program is inconceivable. This would be, as one Canadian journalist recently put it, like 'cancelling part of what Canada is all about.'[31]

Institutional pluralism and sustainability of the immigration system

The US ability to sustain immigration without causing extreme forms of confrontation also springs from its pluralistic social structure. A variety of socio-political forces and pressure groups – ethnic lobbies, economic and professional associations, organized labor and industry, religious groups, human rights and civil rights movements, and political parties – are all involved in the migration issue. While all or most of them may support certain shared values and principles that underpin immigration, commitments vary, and the perception of immigration, including its benefits and costs, can widely diverge between and within these organizations, especially on specific aspects of immigration.

Not surprisingly, views on the immigration issue cut across all political groupings in the USA. An interesting finding in a poll taken in June 1986 is that the proportions of those favoring decreasing immigration were 48 percent among 'liberals,' 45 percent among 'moderates,' and 57 percent among 'conservatives.'[32] Unlike the European right (who oppose immigration) much of the American New Right tends to support very large or even unlimited immigration admissions.[33] Many nonetheless object to illegal immigrants.

In the USA, even at the governmental level, pluralism asserts itself through the involvement not only of the executive and legislative branches but also of the various departments within the executive branch. Migration policies in the USA are thus shaped by a process of compromise and consensus worked out within broad historical parameters, already recognized and generally accepted by the principal actors. The process leads to a degree of continuity in immigration policies and attenuates extreme positions. The mass expulsion of immigrants and aliens, for example, is hardly conceivable in a pluralistic society with a deep commitment to democratic principles and common humanitarian values. Given the balance of forces in the USA today, and in Canada as well, an abrupt change in the immigration system or in the level of immigration is unlikely – at least to the extent that the public policies of the receiving country determine the immigration level.

But pluralism also brings costs. As societal pluralism impels the USA to accommodate the divergent views and interests of a variety of pressure groups, the policy tends to become diffused and weak in its capacity to address the major immigration issues in a forthright and dynamic manner. The USA may be keen, for example, to encourage a rapid increase in the inflow of skilled immigrants, but it can do so only to the extent that other interests and concerns are also accommodated.

As an aggregation of different components, the immigration system becomes complex to manage, and policy approaches may not always have enough coherence to function as an integrated whole. Strict rules concerning legal immigration, combined with perennially inadequate funding and staffing of border enforcement and the tacit acceptance of large-scale and often irregular crossings of the country's southern borders to meet the labor needs of local US industries, constitutes willy-nilly a policy of meeting several competing demands at the same time. But it certainly cannot claim robust policy coherence.

Implicit in US pluralism there is another constraint. In formulating immigration policies and objectives, the USA cannot avoid being deeply engrossed in analyzing, addressing, and sorting out competing demands and interests of different domestic lobbies or pressure groups. But this compulsive preoccupation with national politics and immediate issues tends to blur the vision of immigration as a global process; it creates a built-in bias for the policy approach to be inward-looking or domestically oriented, at the expense of responsiveness to its global dimension.

Dynamics of immigration and policy coordination

In looking at the situation in the USA, some analysts find, not surprisingly, 'a troubled relation between the objective processes that constitute immigration and the understanding of immigration underlying policy-making. US policies, while carefully devised, have consistently failed to regulate immigration in the intended way.'[34] A central point in this analysis is that the US migration policy fails to achieve its explicit objectives because of its insistence on treating immigration into the USA as an autonomous, separate process from other major international processes. Sassen, for example, questions the viability of an approach which treats immigration as a purely domestic issue and maintains that 'the closer immigration policy comes to recognizing the actual *dynamics* of immigration, the more likely it will be to succeed in its intended aim of effective regulation.'[35]

It would perhaps be misleading to suggest that the external dynamics of immigration have remained totally unnoticed within the US government. A recent report of the Department of Labor, for example, is explicit on the external dimension of labor immigration:

To the extent that US policies and practices contribute to the pace and pattern of regional integration, they help organize the expansion of regional labor flows, international trade, investment, communication and transportation facilitate the narrowing of differences between regions and countries and contribute to the expansion of opportunities and possibilities for international migration. . . . Flows of labor occur within an international division of labor with increasingly integrated production, exchange and consumption processes that extend beyond national boundaries.[36]

However, it is not enough to be aware of the multiple implications of immigration as a global process. The knowledge may be available within US government agencies, but its impact on policy formulation could still be inadequate and uncertain. If the links between the dynamics of migration (including refugee flows) and US concerns in other policy areas, such as trade, foreign investments, aid, foreign relations, and external security, are not duly recognized, divergence in state behavior and contradictions between different national policies may be unavoidable. Official US policies for immigration and international economic relations are now well documented. While seeking to regulate the entry of legal immigrants and reduce irregular flows through its immigration policy, the USA has often followed trade policies which produced just the opposite results.[37] An oft-quoted, typical example concerns US action in the Caribbean area in the 1980s. Introduced in 1983, the Caribbean Basin Initiative was designed to promote economic development and political stability in the region. But around the same time the US imposed a 76 percent reduction in sugar imports from the region. Largely as a result, between 1982 and 1988 the Caribbean countries lost 400,000 jobs. This sharply increased emigration pressures and generated social unrest in sugar-producing countries like the Dominican Republic. More generally, by providing tariff protection to declining, noncompetitive industries, US trade policy often encourages irregular immigration as these protected industries can survive at least partly by using low-cost immigrant labor.

The situation in Canada and Western Europe reveals a similar dichotomy in policy planning affecting immigration and international trade. West Europe's current anxiety over rising pressures for immigration is unmistakable. But this anxiety was hardly reflected in the fourth Lomé Convention which the European Union recently signed with 70 low-income, migrant-sending Asian, Caribbean, and Pacific (ACP) countries. Trade concessions under the convention are hedged with safeguards for EU industries, and market access is circumscribed for several products of the ACP countries' labor-intensive industries through devices such as voluntary export restraints. Since the signing of the first convention in 1975, these countries have lost their market share in the EU, and many of them are poised to become high-pressure points in South–North migration. Even more glaring is the example of the association agreements which the European Union signed with Eastern and Central European countries. In signing these agreements little attention has been given to the migration implications of the European Union's trade policies. Yet, as some recent studies have shown, under a more liberal trade regime a typical Eastern country might be able to export about 20 percent of its GNP to the EU (compared to 3.2 percent in 1988). This would create employment for about 15 million Easterners, thus leading to a fall in the pressure for East–West migration.[38]

Similarly, deficiency in the policy-making pattern affecting migration and external relations and security can lead to unpredictable flows of immigration, making them less manageable. True, the USA has often used migration or migrant groups for foreign policy purposes, and there have also been cases when foreign policy concerns have influenced administrative procedures and practices governing migration matters such as admission of refugees and processing of visa and asylum applications. But, in most cases, this has occurred on an *ad hoc* and *ex post facto* basis. As Zucker and Zucker observe,

When a particular group of refugees serves our foreign policy goals, does not threaten to overwhelm us by its numbers, and can be resettled with little cost or domestic assistance, the members of that group are usually assured of admission. Conversely, members of a group that does not meet any of the criteria may be certain that admission would be denied.[39]

This can hardly be considered as a shining example of policy coordination. At a minimum, it would require that when foreign policy related initiatives or interventions are likely to have major migration (including refugee flow) implications, they should be taken into account well in advance so as to ensure that appropriate responses will be available in time, and not after the event, nor in a haphazard manner depending on the vagaries of public reactions of the particular moment.

It needs to be added that there are now some indications in the USA of an effort to improve the coordination of policies affecting migration and foreign relations, especially in situations where national security is an important consideration.[40] For example, in 1993 the US Department of State announced that international migration considerations will be routinely factored into its long-range policy planning.[41] Recently, President Clinton ordered the Central Intelligence Agency (CIA) to analyze the national security aspects of international migration.[42] Another example was the involvement of the National Security Council in evaluating the initial Mexican proposal for the North American Free Trade Agreement (NAFTA): its positive recommendation was based, *inter alia*, on the consideration that instability in Mexico could adversely affect the United States, through large-scale unwanted migration. Most recent developments in Cuba and Haiti, which threaten to produce large-scale migration to the United States, seem to have heightened incentives for the US administration to take a more coordinated view of migration flows, foreign policy concerns, and security matters. The growing concern over Islamic fundamentalism is likely to further strengthen this trend.

Notwithstanding recent developments, migration issues and their implications have yet to find a systematic recognition in the formulation and implementation of United States national policies. The situation is hardly different in Western Europe. There is, for example, no indication that the European Union's recognition of Croatia and Slovenia as sovereign states in 1990–1 was accompanied by any serious analysis of its implications for the ethno-political situation in former Yugoslavia, and far less of its possible repercussion on cross-border movements of people. Even as late as June 1991, when the ethno-political situation in former Yugoslavia was already heading for a crisis, the issue of migration, not to speak of the specific measures to deal with it, had failed to move up the European Union's political agenda.

A domestic issue and a global process

Increased sensitivity about the external dynamics of migratory movements would enhance the capacity of the migrant-receiving countries to meet the challenge of immigration. This applies to North America as it does to Western Europe. Broader visions and better coordinated approaches are critical elements in evolving a sound framework for regional and international cooperation involving migrant-sending and migrant-receiving countries. Indeed, this may be the only way of making migration more predictable, orderly, and productive in the coming decades. The point bears repetition: immigration is a complex domestic issue, but it is also part of a major global challenge.

Notes

1. It was in 1903, at the height of immigration, that a plaque bearing the poem was affixed to the pedestal as an *ex post facto* inscription.
2. Lydia Potts, *The World Labor Market* (London: Zed Books, 1990), pp. 38–62.
3. Albert Wirz, *Sklaverei und kapitalistisches Weltsystem* (Frankfurt/Main: Suhrkamp, 1984), p. 136.
4. Aldrich cited in R.J. Morrison, 'A wild motley throng: immigration expenditures and American standard of living,' *International Migration Review*, 14, 3 (1980), 342–6. The restrictive measures included categorization of inadmissible aliens, deportation laws, and literacy requirements.
5. OECD, SOPEMI, *Trends in International Migration: Continuous Reporting System on Migration* (Paris: OECD, 1993), p. 21.
6. *Ibid.*
7. OECD, SOPEMI, 1992, *op. cit.*
8. Stephen Castles and Mark Miller, *The Age of Migration* (London: Macmillan, 1993).
9. *Ibid.*
10. The four preferred categories of immigrants were: British subjects with adequate financial means from the United Kingdom, Ireland, and four other domains of the crown; US citizens; dependents of permanent residents of Canada; and agriculturalists.
11. An interesting difference to be noted is that immigrants in Canada show a much higher propensity to emigrate to another country: some 40 per cent of emigrants from Canada move to the USA.
12. International Labor Organization, *International Economic Migration* (Geneva: ILO, 1993).
13. See, in this connection, Julian L. Simon, *The Economic Consequences of Immigration* (Cambridge, MA: Basil Blackwell, 1989).

14. *Ibid.*

15. *The Economist,* March 1991.

16. J.F. Long, 'The relative effects of fertility, mortality on the projected age structure,' paper presented at the Population Association of America, Baltimore, MD, 1989.

17. According to a recent UNDP report, between 1966 and 1986 the proportions of skilled workers among immigrants from developing countries increased from 45 to 75 percent in the USA and from 12.3 to 46 percent in Canada. The report does not indicate the source of the information or the levels and characteristics of the skills. The familiar debate in both North America and Western Europe on projected labor market needs and likely shortfalls (by the year 2000 and beyond) is now well documented. The issues involved are not taken up in this chapter.

18. Marion F. Houstoun, Roger G. Kramer and John Mackin Barret, 'Female predominance in immigration to the United States since 1930: a first look,' *International Migration Review,* 18, 4 (1984), 908–59.

19. Julian Simon, *op. cit.*

20. K.G. Yerma and R. Basavarajappa, 'Asian immigrants in Canada: some findings from the 1981 Census,' *International Migration Review,* 23, 1 (1985), 59–101.

21. George J. Borjas, *Friends or Strangers: the Impacts of Immigrants on the US Economy* (New York: Basic Books, 1990).

22. D. de Vortez, 'Recent evidence on the economic impacts of Canadian immigration circa 1971 to 1986,' paper presented at the House of Commons Standing Committee on Labor, Ottawa, 1990.

23. Bimal Ghosh, 'Migration, trade and international economic cooperation: do the interlinkages work?,' *International Migration,* 30, 3 (1992), 423.

24. US Department of Labor, *The Effects of Immigration on the US Economy* (Washington, DC: US Department of Labor, 1989).

25. I. Light and F. Bonacich, *Immigration Entrepreneurs* (Berkeley, CA: University of California Press, 1988), pp. 425–36.

26. OECD, SOPEMI, 1992, p. 57.

27. Rita J. Simon, *Public Opinion and the Immigrant* (Lexington, MA: Lexington Books, 1985).

28. M.D. Morris, *The Beleaguered Bureaucracy* (Washington, DC: Brookings Institution, 1985), pp. 26–7.

29. Demetrios Papademetriou, 'South–North migration in the Western hemisphere and US responses,' *International Migration,* 29, 2 (1991).

30. R. Bach, *Changing Relations: Newcomers and Established Residents in the US Communities.* A report of the National Board of Changing Relations (1991).

31. Daniel Stoffman, *Towards a More Realistic Immigration Policy for Canada* (Toronto: C.D. Howe Institute, 1993).

32. Julian Simon, *op. cit.*

33. Sharon Stanton Russel and Michael S. Teitelbaum, *International Migration and International Trade* (Washington, DC: The World Bank, 1992).

34. Saskia Sassen, 'Immigration in Japan and the US: the weight of economic internationalization,' in Hedwig Rudolphy and Mirjana Morokvasic (eds), *Bridging States and Markets* (Berlin: Edition Sigma, 1993), pp. 106–9.

35. *Ibid.*

36. US Department of Labor, *op. cit.*, p. 5.
37. Commission for the Study of International Migration and Cooperative Economic Development, *Unauthorized Migration: an Economic Development Response* (Washington, DC: Government Printing Office, 1990).
38. Bimal Ghosh, 'Future of East–West migration,' in Solon Ardittis (ed.), *The Politics of East–West Migration* (New York: St Martin's Press, 1994), pp. 240–1.
39. N.L. Zucker and Naomi F. Zucker, *The Guarded Gate: the Reality of American Refugee Policy* (San Diego, CA: Harcourt Brace Jovanovich, 1987), p. xvii.
40. See Mark Miller's contribution in this volume.
41. *Ibid.*
42. Luis Freedber, 'Immigration now a security concern: smuggling forces White House to bring in intelligence agencies,' *San Francisco Chronicle*, 23 June 1993, p. A1.

7 The political uses of xenophobia in England, France, and Germany

Dietrich Thränhardt

If you talk and behave as though black men were some kind of virus that must be kept out of the body politic, then it is the shabbiest hypocrisy to preach racial harmony at the same time.[1]

Introduction

This chapter examines the relationship between the political process and the origins of extremist political tendencies. Why are racist, xenophobic, and fascist tendencies successful at a given time, and nearly dead at another? Why do some extremist parties which are hardly organized and not very attractive suddenly get so many votes? Why do youth gangs strike out against minorities in the 1990s, and why is it that at other times they suddenly become unimportant?

Scientific explanations of the new racism are highly diverse and often contradictory. *Social deficits* and discrimination are explained by the lack of state intervention on the one hand and by too much state intervention, leading to a *culture of dependency*, on the other. Racism has been explained in the Adorno tradition as part of the *authoritarian character*, particularly under a type of capitalism that contains strong remnants of precapitalist traditions. Contrary to this, however, some recent explanations focusing on the loosening of all societal bonds, rising individualism, and subjectivism have become popular. According to Heitmeyer, 'Processes of disintegration ... form the causes of two interactive developments: on the one hand they are a central cause of xenophobic orientations and ways of behaviour accepting violence, and on the other hand they are the sources of a political paralysis that hinders action against that.'[2]

The frustration–aggression hypothesis, another well known approach, has become so popular in recent years that it has sometimes been used to belittle real crime, depicting gangsters who commit atrocities as poor little victims. Clearly, such thinking is out of proportion, and critics point to the fact that it is not just deprived people who are racist. At some times and in some countries, the best and the brightest have believed in racism, including some noted scientists.[3]

In 1992 and 1993, one discrepancy between England and Germany appeared particularly puzzling: public awareness and the public agenda on the one side, and crime indicators on the other. This discrepancy can serve as a warning against easy explanations. Following the worldwide news coverage of the xenophobic riots in Germany, the *Financial Times* correspondent in Bonn, Quentin Peel, compared the violence in England and Germany and found that in 1991 there were 6559 acts of violence motivated by racism in England and Wales, where the total population numbered 50 million. This was three times more than in Germany, a country of 80 million inhabitants. He also reported that more than 6000 violent racist acts had been reported in England and Wales since.[4] For its part, *The Economist* reported 7780 'racially motivated attacks' in Great Britain in 1991 and noted the Newham Monitoring Project's evaluation that 'the real total is between three and ten times higher.'[5] Racist attitudes by the British police often give reason for complaints.[6] Other reports give examples of grave criminal acts that, unlike the IRA murders, do not feature prominently in the British media.[7] Racist groups in Britain seem to have specialized in using force against minorities, particularly after experiencing defeat at elections.[8]

How far detached such facts are from the public agenda can be shown by pointing to an interpretation offered by the British Home Secretary, Kenneth Baker. Speaking on the BBC in November 1992, he argued for further restrictions in the granting of asylum in Britain. If nothing was done, he said, violence and racism would spread from the continent to Britain.[9] He failed to mention that Britain was no longer a major immigration country in the 1980s, and in some years Britain even had an emigration surplus.

How should we interpret such discrepancies? Is it the famous penchant of the British system to maintain business as usual and good style under any circumstances? Is it hypocrisy?[10] Are there different methods of defining racial or xenophobic crime?[11] Is agenda setting by the media largely incongruent with the facts? Is the world discussing problems of the past instead of the present? Or does the explanation actually lie with the Germans? Is the German left predispositionally masochistic?

This chapter examines the working of one important political institution – the party system. What is the influence of parties, party systems, and particularly party competition on the public awareness of minorities, their definition, their relations with the majority, and their position in politics? Is agenda setting in electoral and other campaigns relatively independent of the situation in a given country? And what about similarities and differences between parties, strategies, and individual leaders?

First phase: conservatives bring down leftist governments

In the three largest European immigration countries, England, France, and Germany, conservative parties have successfully used xenophobic issues against social democratic governments, and in all three countries the xenophobia they stirred up was important in bringing conservative parties to power. In the end, however, this did not result anywhere in radically new immigration policies. Racial political rhetoric had negligible policy consequences. Established economic interests, the legal positions of the immigrants, and the receiving countries' international reputations and obligations did not allow for radical change. On the contrary, conservative governments were responsible for some of the expanded intake of migrants.

In all three countries, there was some intra-party opposition voiced by liberal or Christian elements inside the conservative catch-all parties against demagogic courses, and against making scapegoats of immigrants and minorities. CDU secretary general Heiner Geissler, ousted in 1990 by Chancellor Kohl, and the French UDF politician Bernard Stasi, also no longer a leading figure of his party, were the most prominent examples of internal dissenters. In England, Margaret Thatcher's predecessor Edward Heath cultivated a tolerant line, and in his time the Conservatives tried hard to gain support among minorities.[12]

During elections, the three conservative parties or alliances deliberately created the expectation that decisive changes would take place in policies dealing with racial matters and that the numbers of settled minorities or immigrants would be cut sharply. In all three countries, the climate for adaptation and integration was soured by bitter and emotional campaigns. In the context of public xenophobia, some extremists committed atrocities against minority communities, and this again was used as an argument to show that popular xenophobia had to be appeased, to avoid even greater danger. The media sensationalized the problems and created the images of dangerous *floods* of foreigners rolling against the dams of English, German, or French lands.[13] All of this was relatively independent of the actual numbers.[14] In all three countries, rightist theories by academics or other purported experts could easily be traced to the racist tendencies of the 1930s.

England

The first national opposition leader to introduce the racial issue was Margaret Thatcher in 1978.[15] She deliberately discontinued the tradition of a moderate consensus and, in a speech carefully designed to attract attention to the anti-immigration stand of the Conservative Party, denounced the 'swamping' of Britain by too many immigrants.[16] Before this speech, only a few political entrepreneurs from the party's right wing had gone this far, beginning with Enoch Powell in 1968. Powell's racist approach had built up a large awareness among the electorate, and he successfully made race a factor in British politics.[17] Opinion polls showed that this would appeal to large parts of the public. At the time, more than 80 percent of the electorate thought that too many 'immigrants' (meaning 'non-whites') had come to Britain.[18] The new Conservative strategy proved immediately successful. Whereas they had been neck and neck with Labour immediately before, the Conservatives gained a lead of 9 percent following Thatcher's speech.[19] Thatcher's predecessor Heath attacked her new policy, explaining that 'she was deliberately misleading people.'[20] Nevertheless, in the electoral campaign of 1979, the Conservatives promised to strengthen controls against further immigration and by their tough language they created the expectation of a thoroughgoing anti-immigrant policy. Conservative politicians also pleaded for a voluntary return of the 'immigrants,' even though these held British citizenship and half of them had been born in Britain.[21] The electoral support for the avowedly racist National Front collapsed and was absorbed by the Conservatives. The Conservatives were also able to attract a large working-class vote, and their anti-immigration stand was unquestionably important for their electoral victory.[22] The perception that the Conservatives are tougher on immigration than Labour can be found in British opinion polls to this day.

Germany

In Germany, the immigration/race issue was brought up by the Bavarian CSU and the right wing of the Christian Democrats, who developed a massive campaign, concentrating on Turks and asylum seekers. It was carried forward by different segments of the media, particularly the influential newspaper *Frankfurter Allgemeine*.[23] In some *Land* elections, immigration became a central issue: the Hessian CDU proposed a law to reduce the number of foreigners by one million. In Baden-Württemberg, the CDU campaigned for a 'rotation system' or 'Swiss system' for foreign workers, which would bring 'young, fresh' guestworkers to Germany, and lead to the return of the old ones.[24] Polls revealed that, regarding migration, a majority of Germans ranged 'between tolerance and anxiety.'[25] The Christian Democratic leadership kept a low profile, and limited itself to accusations that the government was not handling these problems well. Chancellor Helmut Schmidt, in the party manifesto of 1980, took great pains to avoid introducing a supportive stand of his social democratic party for local electoral rights for foreigners, because he feared that this would play into the hands of Franz Josef Strauss, his rival in the elections that year.[26] Strauss made some rather demagogic statements on immigration, e.g. on 'Kanacken' ('dagos'), but his campaign focused on the traditional issues of the Cold War and 'freedom versus socialism.' After winning the elections, Schmidt commented that working for the better integration of foreign immigrants went against the 'instincts of our core voters.'[27]

After the 1980 election, the defeated CDU/CSU opposition concentrated on the issue of 'foreigners.' The necessity for a reduction of numbers was brought forward repeatedly, and in the end the SPD government gave in, and announced a law to encourage the return of non-EC workers and their families. A few weeks before the SPD government fell in 1982, CDU leader Helmut Kohl himself demanded a reduction of the number of foreigners in West Germany.[28] In his party's electoral program, Kohl let it be known that *Ausländerpolitik* would be one of four key problems that his government would tackle. This was before the elections. However, during the Christmas break in the 1982–3 campaign the issue suddenly disappeared as a result of a silent consensus between the parties. The electoral program for the second Kohl government in spring 1983 mentioned *Ausländerpolitik* only scarcely. Nothing was announced except a program for 'voluntary return' that in effect changed the date of return for some foreigners rather than the number of those required to leave the country.[29] The issue was successfully exploited until the elections. Then it was dropped and the debate on 'foreigners' died down.

France

In France, the Socialist victories in the elections of 1981 left the right in disarray. The conservative right, which had been in power since 1958, and had relied on the state apparatus and its president's leadership, did not have any popular issues to be used against the triumphant left. Therefore the immigration issue was used as an opportunity to challenge the left. Since the late 1970s, latent misgivings about minorities had sometimes been translated into political action in local politics, especially by some Communist mayors who felt that their working-class towns were particularly exposed to immigration.[30] In 1982, the right took up the issue in great style, concentrating first on the Socialist election promise to introduce local voting rights for foreigners living in the country for five years. They successfully campaigned against this plan.

The first electoral breakthrough for rightists touting anti-immigrant themes occurred in the local election at Dreux, a small city in Northern France, where a large group of *Harkis* had been settled. These were Algerians who had fought on the French side during the Franco-Algerian war. They had been the allies of the French right – the *ultras* – but now they became the first target of its xenophobic campaign. With the help of the extremist *Front National*, the right beat the left in Dreux. Next the Gaullist leader Jacques Chirac became mayor of Paris after a campaign that stressed the rising numbers of immigrants, under the slogan 'ni racism, ni laxisme.'[31] He used his new office to introduce a pattern of bureaucratic harassment of non-European immigrants, who, at every interface with the city services – police, kindergarten, schools, social care – had to prove that they were in the country legally. In 1985–6, immigrants were the main issue in the elections that restored a conservative majority in parliament.[32]

In sum, the three conservative parties or blocs in these different countries were equally successful in their electoral strategies. Focusing on minorities contributed significantly to their regaining power. In the long run, however, politics in the three countries developed quite differently.

Second phase: conservatives govern after xenophobic campaigns

The British Conservatives were able to keep hold of the right wing of the electorate. In the following years, they exploited other confrontational issues like the Falklands War and the crushing of the miners' strike, 'Mr Scargill's insurrection,' as Margaret Thatcher calls it in her memoirs.[33] They were thus able to hide the fact that not much was changing as regards effective policies, at least in the area of dealing with immigrants. Characteristically, the report on the first eight years of Conservative rule contained only a brief passage on 'better race relations.' It was by far the shortest paragraph, saying only that the number of immigrants had declined.

As the immigration was old, and the immigrants were British citizens, it was only at the borders that restrictions could be applied. This, however, symbolically affected the 'immigrants' in the country as well. Even regarding borders, a decision of the Strasbourg European Court of Human Rights forced the British government to abolish British gender discrimination in immigration (e.g. the famous virginity tests). Other ideas which had been put forward in the Conservative manifesto were not practical, as they would also have affected 'white' Britons. The curbing of immigration resulted in a last minute panic, leading to high numbers of applications and implementation problems. Two waves of race riots were symptomatic of the crisis of the inner cities on American patterns. This crisis has not been solved to this day. All these problems, however, were portrayed in the media, which kept the immigration issue alive, ultimately helping the Tories.

By contrast, the issue became disastrous for the French right. After winning the elections of 1986, the rightists proposed a law to discontinue the automatic naturalization of children of foreigners born in France, and carried it through the National Assembly. It was repealed, however, because it was deemed to be unconstitutional by the Conseil Constitutionel, which still had a Socialist majority. Also, students of indigenous and foreign descent (the *beurres*) organized a grand solidarity campaign against the law. They received support from the Socialists who in this way won new credibility among the young generation. The motto was *Ne touche pas mon pôte* (Don't touch my buddy).

The death of one of its followers at the hands of the police at a big demonstration in Paris scandalized the racist overtones of the government's policies. In effect, the issue polarized the public. Liberal humanitarians and some devout Catholics found it difficult to follow such policies, and tended to back the Socialists. They felt especially estranged by the great number of the local alliances between the traditional right and the *Front National* (FN).

On the other hand, xenophobes among the people felt that the government's policies had not brought about any significant change. Consequently, many of them switched to the more vocal and aggressive alternative: the FN, led by the populist Jean-Marie Le Pen. By that time, Le Pen had become a sensation in the French media, which at first ignored him and then suddenly gave him a chance to present his anti-Arab and extremist views in entertaining TV talk shows. Despite some shocking assertions (like calling the extermination of Jews a mere episode of history) and the proof of his participation in torture during the Algerian war, he became increasingly popular, and made large inroads into the conservative and communist electorates. Le Pen won 14.4 per cent as a presidential candidate in 1988, and was the front runner in Marseilles. The FN won 11 percent in the European elections of 1990, more than the Communists, or any other extremist party in Europe at the time.[34] Table 7.1 shows French electoral developments from 1981 to 1993.

West German electoral politics played out somewhere between the British and the French models. The government had been able to drop the xenophobic issues around Christmas 1982 and to switch to other themes, like the missile debate and creating jobs for the young generation. For four years, only the two smaller coalition partners, Free Democrats and Bavarian Christian Social Union (Christlich-Soziale Union or CSU), quarreled about *Ausländerpolitik*, without any result. The suicide of a Kurdish refugee out of fear of being handed over to the Turkish authorities brought an outcry from the liberal public against repression against foreigners.[35]

Table 7.1   *French electoral developments 1981–1993*

1981	Mitterrand, candidate of the united left, elected French president after 23 years of rightist presidents, dissolves parliament.
1982	Obtains a socialist majority, installs a socialist cabinet including four communist ministers.
1983	At the local election at Dreux the conservative–liberal right allies with the newly formed extremist *Front National*, and with their help is able to gain a majority, focusing on an anti-Arab campaign. With 16.7 percent of the local vote, the FN starts its electoral success.
1986	In the regular parliamentary elections, the right regains the majority. Chirac becomes prime minister in a RPR–UDF coalition. *Cohabitation* between him and the socialist president.
1988	Mitterrand reelected president against Chirac, with Le Pen achieving 14.5 percent of the vote in the first ballot. Mitterrand dissolves parliament, and the socialists defeat the right and become the strongest party again.
1989	In the elections to the European Parliament the *Front National* carries 11 percent. In the same year, they make inroads into the electorate of the moderate right and the communists and establish themselves as the country's fourth party instead of the communists. FN is included in many local government coalitions with the rightist parties RPR and UDF.
1993	Large majorities in the parliamentary elections for the conservative coalition, after extremely xenophobic remarks by party leaders Giscard d'Estaing and Chirac. *Front National* consolidated as the third force, ahead of communists and ecologists. Second party in some parts of the country.

It took a second attempt by the conservative media and parties to cause something comparable to the French *Front National*, and it was notable that they did it with the French example explicitly in mind. Before the Bavarian *Landtag* elections, the CSU started a campaign against refugees, particularly from the Third World, which provoked nationwide hysteria during the summer of 1986. The debate centered on the passage of asylum seekers through the Berlin Wall. After some weeks an agreement on closing this back door was reached with the East German authorities.

This episode resulted in further CSU electoral success, which, however, was accompanied by a limited 3 percent success for a new party that had split from the CSU – the *Republikaner*. Since that time, this xenophobic party has been active particularly in Bavaria, largely imitating the *Front National* model. Its slogan *Deutschland zuerst* (Germany first) is a direct translation of the FN's *La France d'abord* (France first). Compared to Le Pen, its populist leader Franz Schönhuber, a long time associate of Franz Josef Strauss, exudes a more moderate tone. The *Republikaner* were not successful in the Bundestag elections of 1987 and 1990, but surpassed the 5 percent hurdle in the 1989 European elections. Their electoral strength has always been heavily concentrated in Bavaria. The *Republikaner* were first founded by two estranged deputies from the CSU. In the words of conservative election researcher Kaltefleiter, the party is 'a legitimate daughter of the CSU and of Franz-Josef Strauss.'[36]

Xenophobia – the third round

In the early 1990s, a third round began in the immigrant politics of xenophobia. The British and the German Conservatives were still in government. Helmut Kohl achieved an outstanding victory in the unification elections of 1990. The Thatcher government, by contrast, was in trouble over economic problems. Margaret Thatcher resigned, only shortly before the Gulf conflict could have given her renewed standing. She was succeeded by John Major, a rather moderate premier in comparison with regard to leadership style.

The Thatcher government had taken the decision to grant proper British citizenship to 50,000 to 80,000 prominent Hong Kong citizens in connection with the handing over of the crown colony to China. This was highly controversial: the right wing of the Conservatives opposed the move as too lenient on immigration, and Labour opposed it as too elitist. Other than the privileges granted to these Hong Kong citizens, however, the government tried to halt immigration completely. This implied passport controls even for EU citizens – in violation of the single market agreements. The British government did not follow the other EU countries in lifting the visa requirements for Poland, Czechoslovakia, and Hungary and benefited from its island position. In the pre-election campaign of 1991, a draft law aimed at further tightening rules regarding asylum was brought before the public. After some weeks, however, the government withdrew the draft, announcing that there would be a new one after the elections. The newspapers commented that all this had been intended to show the public a hardline approach without excessively offending liberals. In the elections of 1992, the Conservatives' anti-asylum stand seemed to have refreshed the public awareness of the party's anti-immigration leanings without, however, alienating more liberal voters or inflaming the public climate.[37] After the elections, the asylum law was reintroduced into parliament and adopted. As a result, almost no asylum seekers entered Britain after this.[38]

Despite the deliberately subdued Conservative presentation, immigration issues were quite influential in the elections, particularly since they occupied a prominent position in the British tabloid press. On the Saturday before the elections, the *Sun* published a large map of the world, with figures and arrows, showing how much immigration a Labour government would tolerate. Because of rather pervasive anxieties about immigrants and foreigners in the British public, the 'tough' stand associated with the Conservatives continues to be appreciated. Critics argue that immigration is largely a symbolic issue in Britain today, since there is none. Still, immigration policies, and public debate about them, are undermining the social position of minorities of non-European origin, who are deemed to be less legitimate than people of European origin. The 'Bolton Speech' by Conservative Member of Parliament Winston Churchill in the summer of 1993 – a sort of 'rivers of blood' approach – was reminiscent of Enoch Powell's stance in 1968. Emphasizing 'repatriation,' it appeared to indicate a hardening at the right fringe of the Conservative Party. Such xenophobic or racist zeal comes as Prime Minister Major is losing authority.[39]

In France, xenophobia continued to be an open and visible issue in party competition. It was Le Pen's number one campaign issue, and other politicians competed with him on it. Although the UNR and UDF ranks still included some liberals, like Simone Veil, there remained not much difference between Le Pen and many conservative politicians. In the local elections of 1991, the *Front National* made important inroads, and some conservative leaders joined its racist, xenophobic, and particularly anti-Arab chorus. Even UDF leader Giscard d'Estaing, who had cultivated a liberal and progressive image during his presidency in 1974 to 1981 jumped on the bandwagon: in some carefully publicized remarks about 'invasions' of immigrants he appeared to be even more radical than Le Pen.[40] Jacques Chirac also made such remarks, and other politicians spoke of the two as an 'infernal couple.'[41]

The socialist government, on the other hand, could not maintain the aura of morality that it had acquired through its anti-racist stance. It tried to calm the xenophobic fears of some of its voters, but lost credibility on both sides. The Socialists lost half of their vote in the elections in March 1993 and were reduced to 17.6 percent, with the conservative right winning a majority, this time by even a larger margin. However, they again had to govern under Mitterrand, who remained the French President. Since then, the *Front National* has not been able to make new inroads, but with 12.4 percent it is now definitely the third force in France. It holds the second place in more than a hundred constituencies. In Dreux, where the FN achieved its first big success with the help of the conservatives, candidate Marie-France Stirbois got 36.84 percent of the votes.[42] It was only the French majority voting system that kept the FN from getting seats in the national parliament.

Following the conservative victory in the 1993 elections, the new majority amended several laws on naturalization, asylum, and security. The minister of the interior, Charles Pasqua, declared that France would no longer be an immigration country. The police were allowed to check people (on any grounds except race) to determine their immigration status. Some saw the new police law as the beginning of a 'hunt' of the second generation *beurs*.[43]

However, it is doubtful that the new laws will reduce the numbers of immigrants decisively, because for the most important group of immigrants, the social and political situation in their country of origin, Algeria, is deteriorating even more than their position in France. Consequently, the situation of the minorities in France might worsen, and inter-community relations as well as minority–police relations could be further strained.

In Germany, rightist extremists lost their appeal during the unification process in 1989–90. At that time, no one was talking about refugees or immigrants. On the contrary, crowds were standing at the borders where young East German couples riding in their *Trabi* cars crossed over. Television coverage encouraged solidarity with young German refugees who were the same age as most of the asylum seekers. As a result, the anti-asylum campaign died down. Right-wing extremists did not do well in the 1990 elections, and riding themes of unification, Chancellor Kohl became widely popular with the German public for the only time in his career. Even in Bavaria the *Republikaner* could not enter the *Land Diet* in 1990. Mikhail Gorbachev's conciliatory overtones and the winding down of the Cold War also diluted German xenophobia, and for more than a year, immigration and asylum became a non-issue in Germany.

However, in the summer of 1991, one year after unification, the flow of asylum seekers dramatically increased, and the anti-asylum seeker campaign was renewed. The sensationalist tabloid, *Bild-Zeitung*, other media, and the 'Christian' parties worked hand in hand in denouncing the asylum seekers. *Bild* produced large posters of asylum seekers in the various regions. The leaders of both 'Christian' parties, CDU and CSU, announced that they would concentrate their public relations activities on 'asylum' problems. As in 1986, a massive campaign was launched during the summer holiday season. It soured the political environment and resulted in violent acts against refugees and in a 6.2 percent electoral result for the extremist *Deutsche Volksunion* (DVU) in the autumn 1991 elections in Bremen. During these elections, asylum was the main issue. The CDU accused the Bremen city government and the Social Democrats in general of being too lenient toward asylum seekers. The SPD mayor responded with some symbolic hardline rhetoric, but his party lost its absolute majority.

Later, during the land elections in Baden-Württemberg and in Schleswig-Holstein in spring 1992, the CDU continued with these immigrant-bashing tactics. Again asylum was the prime issue in the elections, broadly covered again by *Bild* and other media. The CDU did not gain anything out of the dirty campaign. On the contrary, it lost its majority in Baden-Württemberg, whereas the SPD kept its majority in Schleswig-Holstein. The *Republikaner* achieved 10.9 percent in Baden-Württemberg and the DVU 6.3 percent in Schleswig-Holstein. Looking back on the campaign, the leader of the liberals, Walter Döring, commented on the tactics of the CDU prime minister: 'Herr Teufel became the *Republikaner's* megaphone.'[44] The *Süd-*

deutsche Zeitung reported that part of the *Republikaner* campaign had taken the form of simply copying and distributing *Bild* articles.[45] Thus the demagogic campaign had backfired: it aided the extremists, which was contrary to CDU interests and objectives, and also inflicted losses upon the CDU itself. Analysts concluded that the big majority of the rightist parties' voters were protest voters who normally considered themselves as followers of one of the major democratic parties.[46] In parliament, a liberal speaker quoted the Bible: 'They dig a trap for me, and fall in themselves.'[47] Teufel himself commented: 'A shame for the land.'[48] He was not speaking of his own campaign, but rather its results. Some time later, the federal minister of the interior, Seiters, sourly commented: 'The CDU/CSU, too, does not profit from the asylum discussion.'[49]

The majority CDU party found itself caught in its own nets, and it was not easy to get free. In the autumn of 1992, it clung to its strategy, hoping at least to hurt the opposition by denouncing them as soft on asylum issues. The secretary general made an appeal to all party branches to focus on asylum problems, under the motto 'Every additional *Asylant* is an SPD-*Asylant.*'[50] To some extent, they were successful: as in the campaigns of 1982 and 1991, the CDU overtook the SPD in the second half of 1992 in the opinion polls.

In contrast to earlier periods, there was also a definite change in the number of asylum seekers and immigrants. The numbers of asylum applications rose to 250,000 in 1991 and 450,000 in 1992.[51] This was more than for all other countries of Western Europe combined. In earlier years the issue of too many asylum seekers had been played up deliberately and without much foundation. Because Western Germany had more than a million net influx of all kinds every year from 1989 to 1992 (including East Germans, the population had risen from 60 to 65 million between 1988 and 1993), massive housing problems arose. This was compounded by the understaffing of the refugee agencies, and additionally complicated by confused procedures emerging out of various changes in asylum laws. There were many signs that a tactic of letting the problems grow worse in order to increase pressure underlaid government attitudes.

The problems did grow worse. The riots in Rostock in August 1992 resulted from the neglect of the asylum situation by public authorities, complacency on the part of the police and the land government, and sympathy in the population, which all encouraged bands of skinheads in their arson attacks against refugees and immigrant workers. The Rostock riots were the high point of xenophobia in Germany. Even after these attacks, it took a long time until all political authorities in the country became aware of the necessity for a clear stance against xenophobia. This was complicated by the ongoing debate on asylum, which resulted in a compromise between the parties on December 6, 1992. After this compromise, all parties tried to play down the asylum debate, as was the case with the Christmas developments of 1982. Whereas in 1982 it was the

Catholic Church that exerted the pressure, this time it was the Federal President.

Following a further tragic arson attack on a Turkish family in Mölln, in which five Turks died, Federal President Richard von Weizsäcker called for a public rally in Berlin, and invited all important politicians, businessmen, and trade union leaders to participate. Nearly everyone came, except the Bavarian CSU, to join 400,000 Berliners. Despite some ultra left-wing disturbances, the demonstration was considered a success. On December 6, 1992, a few journalists started the *Lichterkette* (chain of lights) in Munich, as a voice for tolerance and an open Germany. They wanted to agitate against a widespread sense of resignation among the liberal public after the party compromise. The *Lichterkette* became the largest demonstration in Munich since 1945, and was followed by many *Lichterketten* in other cities, with millions participating. After its success in several cities, many more politicians and media wanted to be included in this new moral endeavor. Even *Bild* was there. The climate had notably changed.

The sudden changes in the opinion polls during these months in 1992 were impressive. All the polls taken during this time show a similar tendency. Between July 1992 and January 1993, the percentage of recognizable right-wing radicals (*bekennendes Rechtspotential*) in Hamburg changed from 16 to 8 percent. Between October 1992 and January 1993, the percentage of people sympathetic to forceful aggression against asylum seekers in East Germany fell from 17 to 8 percent, and between June and December 1992 sympathy for extreme rightist parties among East German youth decreased by half.[52] Support for the *Republikaner* diminished in the polls from 8 to 4 percent. At the same time, the number of violent actions against foreigners and other minorities also fell dramatically.

Even politicians who had instigated anti-asylum feelings, and had made extreme remarks, now tried to switch to the safe side. The federal minister of the interior and his Bavarian colleague were particularly eager to come down on the *Republikaner* and other rightist organizations. They also tried to convince the public that the falling crime rates against foreigners were their accomplishment.[53] To some degree this is curious, since CSU's political positions had not been far from the *Republikaner* for a long time, and sometimes they had been brought forward even more aggressively. Morally, this sudden change of heart gives grounds for some doubt about CSU sincerity. Nonetheless, it indicates a change in the public climate.

However, after the implementation of the laws restricting asylum by the parliament, a new arson attack occurred in Solingen, followed by a number of similar attacks. This time, the government reacted unambiguously. Contrary to the reaction to the arson attack in Mölln, when government spokesman Vogel had ironically used the term 'condolence tourism,' this time government ministers attended the funeral services in a show of sympathy for victims and disgust over the acts. The Chancellor, however, did not.

These developments show that the public climate and political rhetoric in Germany have had a tremendous influence on voters and particularly volatile youths. For the most part, crime had not been organized; it was rather spontaneous. Violence had been perceived by the public as a necessary reaction to defend Germany against illegitimate intruders. Police statistics show that 70 percent of the criminal actions came from youngsters under 20 years of age; 42 percent were East Germans, and their level of education was rather low. There was not much organization behind it: they were largely driven by the sentiment[54] and came 'from the center of society.'[55]

After these tragic events, racism and xenophobia faded from the public debate. It is not certain, however, that the tolerant atmosphere will last. For example, finance minister Theodor Waigel, chairman of the CSU, has announced that his party will focus on problems of 'national identity and fear of foreigners swamping the country.'[56]

Comparative reflections

In England, France, and Germany, political parties played an important role in activating xenophobia over immigration and putting it on the public agenda. In competitive systems, this seems to be *a reliable weapon of last resort for conservative parties pitted against social democrats*, particularly in relatively quiet times when issues are needed.[57] Evoking xenophobia as a political weapon, however, is not without perils. It can get out of hand, as it did in France early on, or it can explode, as it did in Germany. Knowing that this demogogic weapon is available, it is very tempting to use it in competitive party systems. Politicians need a definite sense of moral responsibility to decide not to use it. In all three countries, there are examples of such politicians, some of them at high levels. One of them is Kurt Biedenkopf, who decided not to use this weapon as the opposition leader in the industrial core land of Nordrhein-Westfalen. However, he lost the elections, and had to step down after intra-party conflicts with Chancellor Kohl.

The special feature of the developments in Germany in 1991–2 in comparison with England and France is that in Germany an incumbent government initiated the aggressive campaign against refugees and the status quo. In the other two countries, and lacking in Germany, the campaigns were initiated by conservatives in opposition and then played down when they took over government. Whatever an opposition aims to do, a government should not campaign against the status quo, or it should do this only with great care and sophistication. To appear to place the legitimacy of the government behind possibly violent behavior, even if this is not intended, is dangerous. In the German system, with its checks and balances, it was tempting to try to pummel the opposition by raising emotional issues with popular appeal, since votes might be attracted while little constitutional damage could occur. The constitution can be changed only with a two-thirds majority, and the opposition is entrenched in some *Länder*. In addition, the main campaigning party was the Bavarian CSU, which has always had a populist style, and wanted to continue with this after the death of its outstanding populist leader Franz Josef Strauss.

But the government campaign soured the German atmosphere much more than an opposition campaign might have. It had greater vigor and power, since the government had much better means of setting the agenda. It left the voters who believed in 'present dangers' no choice but to vote for ultra right-wing parties. It also gave brutal gangs a pretext and legitimation to commit crimes and atrocities, picturing themselves as the heroes of the nation and the administrators of the national will. Crowds felt the same way, particularly in East Germany, when the government sent over asylum seekers, lodged them in some heavily populated city quarters, and at the same time told the people that they were unwelcome in Germany.[58]

Lastly, the phenomenon of a government campaigning in a populist style against minorities also explains the paradox put forth at the beginning of this chapter. There seems to be more racist crime in Britain than in Germany, at least before 1992. However, racist and xenophobic crime was made a central political issue by the German government's campaign. It attracted worldwide attention. Whereas governments usually attempt to play down the negative sides in their countries' image, the German government played them up. Consequently, xenophobic acts were viewed in Germany and abroad in the context of neo-Nazism, which poses a threat to German democracy. Nonetheless, it was a great achievement of the anti-racists to reclaim the streets of the German cities. Unfortunately, their protests could not create as much sensation as the ugly crimes had done.

Notes

1. Bernard Levin, *The Times*, February 14, 1978.
2. Wilhelm Heitmeyer, 'Gesellschaftliche Desintegrationsprozesse als Ursachen von fremdenfeindlicher Gewalt und politischer Paralysierung,' *Aus Politik und Zeitgeschichte*, 2, 3 (1993), 5 (my translation). Heitmeyer's approach is highly popular these days in the concerned German public. See also Wilhelm Heitmeyer, *Bielefelder Rechtextremismus-Studie: Erste Langzeituntersuchung zur politischen Sozialisation mänlicher Jugendlicher* (Weinheim/München: Beltz, 1992).
3. For the American case see Martin Schain, 'Immigration, race and the crisis of citizenship in the United States (1880–1924),' paper presented at the ECPR Workshop, Paris, 1990. For the concept of racialization (and also *deracialization*)

see Robert Miles, 'Racism: the evolution of a debate about a concept in changing times,' in Dietrich Thränhardt (ed.), *Europe – A New Immigration Continent* (Münster/Hamburg: Lit, 1992), pp. 75–104.

4. In *GP-Magazin*, February 1993 (organ of the *Industriegewerkschaft Chemie-Papier-Keramik*). The numbers for Germany are 1483 for 1991, and 2285 for 1992, and the 50 percent rise has been reported as shocking in Germany, see *Süddeutsche Zeitung*, February 8, 1993, p. 31. Most of the English and all of the German violence (here by definition) is violence of the indigenous population against 'immigrants' or 'foreigners.' For the evidence in Britain, see Paul Gordon, *Racial Violence and Harassment* (London: Runnymede Trust, 1986); K. Thompson, *Under Siege: Racial Violence in Britain Today* (Harmondsworth: Penguin, 1988). In contrast to Germany, Britain has experienced racist riots as early as 1958, and there has been a long and intense debate on racialist violence and also police and other official biases. Statistics in Britain show that 'the risk of being a victim of crime still tends to be higher among the ethnic minority groups, with Asians particularly at greater risk of vandalism and robbery/theft from the person. Afro-Caribbeans and Asians see many offences against them as being racially motivated. Being threatened and assaulted because of race is common. For Asians, evidence or suspicion of a racial element in offences against property is relatively frequent.' *Social Trends*, 1992, p. 214, cited in Monica den Boer, 'Moving between bonafide and bogus: the policing of inclusion and exclusion in Europe,' in Robert Miles and Dietrich Thränhardt (eds), *Migration and European Integration: the Dynamics of Inclusion and Exclusion* (London: Pinter, 1995), pp. 92–111.

5. *The Economist*, December 5, 1992, pp. 45–6.

6. Monica den Boer: 'Immigration, internal security and policing in Europe,' working paper, February 1993, University of Edinburgh, p. 31.

7. *Focus*, 7 (1993).

8. Zig Layton-Henry, *The Politics of Immigration: 'Race' and 'Race' Relations in Postwar Britain* (Oxford: Blackwell, 1992), p. 206.

9. Monica den Boer, 'Immigration,' p. 45 (*The Refugee Trail*, BBC Panorama documentary 1992).

10. So says Linda Bellos, 'Racism? We never talk about it,' *Independent*, December 2, 1992.

11. Leading police officers as well as scientists doubt the meaningfulness of police statistics. Even in the intra-German comparison, it is an open secret that the criminal statistics are established in different ways, e.g. showing less crime in Bavaria than in other *Länder*.

12. See Layton-Henry, *The Politics of Immigration*, *op. cit.*, pp. 180 ff. The chapter's title is 'Mrs Thatcher's racecraft.'

13. 'The tabloid press have consistently been willing participants in stereotyping immigrants,' is Layton-Henry's summary for Britain, *ibid.*, p. 205.

14. Germany, where the rising numbers of asylum seekers have been scandalized in 1980–2, in 1986 and 1989, is particularly interesting in this respect, when they amounted to up to 100,000 per year. After the peak of more than 400,000 in 1992 and the related political crisis, however, there is conspicuous silence and a certain acceptance of the fact of more than 200,000 asylum seekers in 1993. In contrast, there is even some discussion of the closing of certain accommodation

facilities and related job losses. Compared to other countries, these numbers are still quite high.

15. There is of course a long history of racism in all three countries. In Britain and France, it is directly related to the colonial past, whereas in Germany it is more difficult to trace the continuity from Wilhelmine imperialism through Nazism to modern xenophobia. In contrast to Britain and France, 'race' is not considered a legitimate term in Germany today, although it is clear that the concept is still in minds of the people. When the Bavarian minister of the interior, the present prime minister Stoiber, tried to introduce the term 'race' into the political discourse (*'durchmischte und durchrasste Gesellschaft'*), he met strong resistance everywhere and had to draw back. In Britain the term 'race' is now omitted in the social sciences, or put in quotation marks. In the public, however, it is still widely used, including the 'race relations' agencies. Routledge's publications' catalogue of spring 1993 speaks of 'race and ethnicity', whereas in some of the books in this section the term is strongly criticized.

16. The statement said 'that people are really rather afraid that this country might be swamped by people with a different culture. And, you know, the British character has done so much for democracy, for law, and done so much throughout the world, that if there is a fear that it might be swamped, people are going to react and be hostile to those coming in.' Martin Barker, 'Racism – the new inheritors,' *Radical Philosophy*, 21 (1984).

17. Shamit Saggar, 'Black participation and the transformation of the 'race issue' in British politics,' *New Community*, 20, 1 (1993), 27. See also Anthony M. Messina, *Race and Party Competition in Britain* (Oxford: Clarendon Press, 1989).

18. Layton-Henry 1985, *op. cit.*, p. 122.

19. Layton-Henry 1992, *op. cit.*, p. 185.

20. *Ibid.*, p. 186.

21. Michaela von Freyhold, 'Rassistische Mobilisierung in England,' in Christoph Butterwege and Siegfried Jäger (eds), *Rassismus in Europa* (Köln: Bund Verlag, 1992), p. 173.

22. Zig Layton-Henry and S. Taylor, 'Immigration and race relations: political aspects,' *New Commonwealth*, 8, 1–2 (1980); Zig Layton-Henry, 'Race, electoral strategy and the major parties,' *Parliamentary Affairs*, 31, 3 (1978), 268–81.

23. A climax in this campaign was the article of the astronomer Schmidt-Kahler on immigration which was openly racist. See *Frankfurter Allgemeine*, September 30, 1980. See also Jürgen Schilling, secretary general of the German Red Cross, on the 'repatriation' of all 'non central Europeans,' *Die Zeit*, December 12, 1980, p. 51. During that time, the new derogatory term *Asylanten* was created, which since has been used for unwanted refugees, particularly from the Third World. See Jürgen Link, 'Medien und "Asylanten": zur Geschichte eines Unworts,' in Dietrich Thränhardt and Simone Wolken (eds), *Flucht und Asyl. Informationen, Analysen, Erfahrungen aus der Schweiz und der Bundesrepublik Deutschland* (Freiburg: Lambertus 1988), pp. 50–61.

24. An idea particularly promoted by the Baden-Württemberg prime minister Hans Filbinger. See Karl-Heinz Meier-Braun, 'Freiwillige Rotation,' *Ausländerpolitik am Beispiel der baden-württembergischen Landesregierung* (München: Minerva, 1979).

25. Institut für Demoskopie Allensbach, *Zwischen Toleranz und Besorgnis. Einstellun-*

gen der deutschen Bevölkerung zu aktuellen Problemen der Ausländerpolitik (Institut für Demskopie: Allensbach, 1985).

26. Vorstand der SPD, 'Unkorrigiertes Protokoll,' Wahlparteitag in Essen, Grugahalle, June 9–10, 1980, pp. 48, 50.

27. *Münstersche Zeitung*, 260, November 8, 1993.

28. *Frankfurter Rundschau*, 203, September 3, 1982.

29. See Dietrich Thränhardt, 'Die Bundesrepublik Deutschland – ein unerklärtes Einwanderungsland,' *Aus Parlament und Zeitgeschichte*, B 24, (June 10, 1988), 3–13. Some years later, the government conceded the return of some of the returnees, particularly those who have grown up in Germany. They are now labelled *Remigranten*. See Gaby Strassburger, *Offene Grenzen für Remigranten. Wiederkehrwünsche türkischer Remigrantinnen und das deutsche Ausländerrecht* (Berlin: VWB, 1992).

30. Gilles Verbunt, 'France,' in Tomas Hammar (ed.), *European Immigration Policy. A Comparative Study* (Cambridge: Cambridge University Press 1985), pp. 127–64. For a detailed analysis see Martin Schain, 'Policy-making and defining ethnic minorities: the case of immigration in France,' *New Community*, 20, 1 (1993), 66.

31. Chirac told the public: 'Le France est bonne mère, mais elle n'a pas de plus les moyens d'entretenir une foule d'étrangers qui abusent son hospitalité. Avec le moyens dont elle dispose, la Ville de Paris a décidé de lutter contre la prolifération des étrangers en situation irrégulière. Sa politique se situera entre deux extrêmes: ni racisme ni laxisme,' *Le Monde*, July 15, 1983. Later, when Chirac had become prime minister, at a visit in Morocco he spoke of '*ni racisme ni xénophobie.*'

32. Dietrich Thränhardt, 'Politische Inversion. Wie und warum Regierungen das Gegenteil dessen erreichen, wofür sie angetreten sind,' *Politische Vierteljahresschrift*, 25 (1984), 440–61. See also the various books by Catherine Wihtol de Wenden; and Rogers Brubaker, *Citizenship and Nationhood in France and Germany* (Cambridge MA: Harvard University Press, 1992), pp. 145–64.

33. Margaret Thatcher, *The Downing Street Years* (London: HarperCollins, 1993).

34. See Martin A. Schain, 'The National Front in France and the construction of political legitimacy,' *West European Politics*, 10 (1987), 234; E. Plenel and A. Rollat, *L'effet Le Pen* (Paris: La Découverte/Le Monde 1984); and James G. Shields, 'Campaigning from the fringe: Jean-Marie Le Pen,' in John Gaffney (ed.), *The French Presidential Elections of 1988*, (Dartmouth: Aldershot, 1990), pp. 140–57.

35. For an evaluation see Simone Wolken, *Das Grundrecht auf Asyl als Gegenstand der Innen- und Rechtspolitik der Bundesrepublik Deutschland* (Berne/Frankfurt: Lang, 1988).

36. Speech at his lecture on German electoral developments at the German–American conference on elections in Cologne, September 28–30, 1989.

37. For developments in Britain, see J. Solomos, *Race and Racism in Contemporary Britain* (London: Macmillan, 1989), and Zig Layton-Henry, *The Politics of Immigration: Race and Race Relations in Postwar Britain* (Oxford: Blackwell, 1992).

38. Monica den Boer, 'Immigration,' *op. cit.*, pp. 32 ff.

39. For Churchill's speech, see *Sunday Times*, June 6, 1993, and his 'Letter to the Editor,' in the *Guardian*, June 12, 1993, p. 19. On Powell, see Gary P. Freeman,

Immigrant Labor and Racial Conflict in Industrial Societies: the French Experience (Princeton, NJ: Princeton University Press, 1979), pp. 606 ff.

40. Christopher T. Husbands, 'The other face of 1992: the extreme-right explosion in Western Europe,' *Parliamentary Affairs*, 45 (1992), 267–84.

41. *Le Figaro*, March 22, 1993, p. 10.

42. *Le Monde*, March 30, 1993, with a detailed overview of the election results.

43. Christian Delorme, 'La chasse au beurs est ouverte,' *Le Monde*, May 15, 1993.

44. *Die Zeit*, 16, April 10, 1992, p. 2.

45. Wulf Reimer, 'Generalstabsmäßig der Toleranz den Boden entziehen,' *Süddeutsche Zeitung*, 89, April 15, 1992.

46. Matthias Jung and Dieter Roth, 'Der Stimmzettel als Denkzettel. Der Rechtsruck muß nicht von Dauer sein,' *Die Zeit*, 16, April 10, 1992, p. 3.

47. *Das Parlament*, 42 (May 8, 1992), p. 6.

48. *Die Zeit*, 16, April 10, 1992, p. 2.

49. *Süddeutsche Zeitung*, 187, August 14, 1992.

50. Letter of CDU secretary general Volker Rühe to all CDU party branches, *Die Zeit*, June 4, 1993.

51. Playing up numbers was an important part of the campaigns. Whereas in former years the monthly unemployment statistics had been at the centre of public attention in the prime news, now the monthly asylum application figures were given this place. Some of the applications are a second, or even a third attempt, sometimes encouraged by local authorities who in this way can receive the financial burden. Another central point in government announcements is the small percentage of accepted applications, which is used to demonstrate to the public the small numbers of 'real' refugees. The additional acceptances by court decisions which effectively double the percentages, are not mentioned at all. There are no official data on *de facto* recognitions on the criteria of the Geneva convention, although this makes up the larger part of the refugees in the country. Further, there are no official data on returnees. As the census of 1987 has shown, the official figures on numbers of foreigners in Germany are likely to be too high.

52. Norbert Kostede, 'Erleuchtung für die Politik,' *Die Zeit*, 5, January 29, 1993, p. 3.

53. 'Seiters verwies auf einen Rückgang der ausländerfeindlichen Straftaten seit vergangenem November. Mit 70 Fällen liege der Januar im Monatsmittel deutlich unter dem Vorjahr. Der Minister führte diese Entwicklung unter anderem auf die von ihm ausgesprochenen Verbote dreier neonazistischer Gruppierungen zurück. Diese hätten einen "starken Verunsicherungs- und Lähmungseffekt im rechtsextremistischen Lager" bewirkt.' *Süddeutsche Zeitung*, 31, February 8, 1993.

54. Data from a forthcoming study by Prof. Eckert and Dr Willems of Trier University.

55. Aus der 'Mitte der Gesellschaft,' according to the president of the state security service in Hamburg, Ernst Uhlau, cited in *Der Spiegel*, 24 (1993), 25.

56. 'Zu den harten Themen, die im Wahlkampf bearbeitet werden sollten, gehöre auch die Frage der nationalen Identität und die "Angst vor Überfremdung",' said Waigel: *Süddeutsche Zeitung*, 281, December 6, 1993. *Überfremdung* (domination by foreign influences) is a Swiss term of the 1960s, used by the anti-foreigner initiatives there.

57. An interesting deviant case is the first oil crisis in Germany, when, despite unforeseen economic problems, trust in the government actually increased under the new Chancellor Schmidt, against the background of the outside danger from 'the oil sheiks.'

58. The former CDU minister of the interior in Mecklenburg-Vorpommern, Kupfer, has explicitly acknowledged the interrelation of government policies and the riots in an interview by the *Westdeutscher Rundfunk*. 'Question: Have you not been successful? The asylum seekers are away and the constitution will be changed. Kupfer: Yes, you could look at it like this. However, we have said before the events in Rostock that solutions must be found to stop the uncontrollable flow of foreigners toward East Germany. Question: Now others have found the solution for you. Kupfer: The rightists have created a sensitivity among politicians to limit the right for asylum, and to put the security needs of the population in the first place – not only in East Germany.' *Westdeutscher Rundfunk*, ZAK, September 25, 1992.

8 Testing tolerance: the impact of non-European migrants on Western European cultures

Beverly Springer

Immigration is the largest and most contentious problem facing the European Union.[1]

The political culture of many European countries is developing a fundamental fissure. Their political leaders and intellectual elites are becoming strongly 'inclusionist' and internationalist. In contrast, the mass public ... is becoming increasingly 'exclusionist.'[2]

Western Europe is located between two of the three major demographic fault lines in the world today. The Oder-Neisse River to the east and the Mediterranean Sea to the south separate Western Europe with its wealth and low population growth from two of the world's regions which are major suppliers of migrants. The large number of migrants already resident in Western Europe tests the limits of tolerance in societies burdened by high unemployment and the rising costs of welfare systems. The threat of further immigration is fueling anxiety and breeding extremist politics. The situation poses a challenge to policy makers throughout Western Europe. It also poses a challenge to European cultures. The ways in which European societies adapt to the presence of ethnically diverse populations and cope with possible new wave of immigrants will determine the very nature of these societies.

The assumption on which this chapter is based is borrowed from a concept in psychology – cognitive dissonance. According to the concept, individuals can hold contradictory cognitions, but they experience tension from the contradiction. When individuals are fully aware of the contradiction, the tension becomes serious and individuals must adjust their thinking in order to lessen the tension. Individuals in societies can also hold contradictory cognitions, but when the contradiction becomes overt, pressure will grow to rationalize or change the 'knowledge' that is in conflict. The resulting tension brings conflict as various groups propose different changes. Social cohesion is strained and fundamental values are questioned.

By and large, individuals in Western Europe believe that a just society is a democracy based on tolerance, individual rights, equality, and equal opportunity. Many also believe that their society is a nation comprising an ethnically cohesive community and one in which the rights of equal treatment are limited to persons who are citizens. Both sets of cognitions have been present in Western Europe since the last century but did not cause serious problems until recently. Countries could both be democratic and follow racist immigration policies. Now, however, the presence of large immigrant groups and the growing number of asylum seekers have made the contradictions obvious. Public debate reaches from local government offices to Brussels and Strasbourg. Dissonance is overt and threatening the stability of the political systems. Some persons demand more inclusionist policies and appeal to traditional democratic values. Others warn that exclusionist policies are a necessity and appeal to traditional nationalist sentiments. The uneasy coexistence of democratic society and exclusionist beliefs creates a dissonance that will be resolved only when one side of the contradiction gains ascendancy at the expense of the other.

The objective of this chapter is to examine the situation in France and Britain, two countries with large and permanent immigration groups, to discern how dissonance is manifested and to assess the impact that the presence of non-Western immigrant groups will have on the cultures of the two countries. How will the contradiction in cognitions be resolved?

Public consideration of cultural norms in France and Britain

Social scientists use three concepts to distinguish different mechanisms that nation states employ in order to cope with the presence of distinctive ethnic minorities. Nation states may be *assimilationist*, blending the ethnic group into the larger society. The physical appearance of the minorities is not a bar to assimilation, but assimilation does involve the loss of at least some of the distinctive cultural attributes of the minorities. Other societies may be *pluralist*, whereby a *modus vivendi* is established between the group and the society, each tolerating the presence of the other and each continuing to maintain its distinctive characteristics. Still others are *exclusionary*. Minorities are neither assimilated nor tolerated. In this case, the presence of ethnic minorities evokes hostile attitudes and threatens social peace. Nation states may exhibit different responses to different ethnic minorities, assimilating some groups and tolerating or excluding others.

The concept 'nation' refers to a population 'sharing a historical territory, common memories, and myths of origin, a mass, standardized public culture, a common economy and territorial mobility, and common legal rights and duties for all members of the collectivity.'[3] The sense of nation or nationalism developed in Europe during the era of imperialism and included a connotation of ethnic distinctiveness, if not superiority. In this same period, racial doctrine 'became part of the common culture of Europe.'[4] The ideas of nation, ethnicity, and racism became intermingled and overlay basic concepts of democracy and the rights of man. The inherent conflict among the concepts did not have to be confronted as long as Europe remained an area of limited migration and the migrants were primarily from other European countries. The challenge for Europe today, when it has become a region of massive and ethnically diverse immigration, is to lessen the hold of nationalism and replace it with a more inclusive European identity. That is an objective of the European Union, but it is an objective which remains remote from realization. Failing the creation of an overarching European identity, European societies must redefine the concept of nation to make it compatible with basic democratic beliefs such as tolerance.

In Western Europe today, about seven million persons who are permanent residents have not obtained citizenship or the right to vote. They are ethnic minorities who are excluded from democratic participation on the basis of the current meaning of nation. The situation is so widespread that social scientists have created a concept to describe the individuals who are tax paying, permanent, but non-voting residents. Such persons are *denizens*. About 60 percent of the foreign citizens residing in Western Europe (excluding the United Kingdom) are persons with permanent work and residence permits, but they do not have the rights of citizens.[5] The existence of the large number of denizens in democratic societies is one of the reasons why cognitive dissonance has become overt. It is increasingly difficult to justify the denial of democratic rights to persons who have acquired the attributes of permanent participants in the society.

The concepts which will be employed in the following discussion need to be defined in the interest of clarity. *Culture* is the basic concept for the study. One formal definition of culture is 'the pattern of meanings embodied in symbolic forms, including actions, utterances and meaningful objects of various kinds, by virtue of which individuals communicate with one another and share their experiences, conceptions and beliefs.'[6] By another definition, 'culture is a classification of the world that allows us to get our bearings in it more easily; it is the memory of the past that belongs to a community, which also implies a code of behavior in the present, and even a set of strategies for the future.'[7] Todorov states that anthropologists consider that culture and ethnic group are synonymous.[8] Furthermore, he distinguishes nation from culture only insofar as nation also includes the idea of a certain geographical place.[9]

Liah Greenfield states that *nation* has come to mean a 'unique sovereign people.'[10] She defines nationalism as a political ideology based on the idea of nation. Nationalism may be distinguished, according to Greenfield, into two types, depending on how membership in the collectivity is determined. Civic nationalism is based on citizenship. It can be acquired. Ethnic nationalism is based on the possession of inherited group characteristics such as language, customs, and physical types.[11] An ethnic group is perceived as one with a sense of a common origin and inherent characteristics and, therefore, cannot be acquired.[12]

The test of democratic peace in Europe today requires the accommodation of the larger society to the permanent presence of ethnic minorities. Public policy is, of course, an important factor in guiding the accommodation, but another crucial factor is the culture of the individual countries. The cultures of Western European countries are not generally regarded as ones that easily accommodate outsiders. The idea of the melting pot has been an American myth, not a European one. Democratic values of equality and tolerance intermingle with traces of ethnic nationalism and memories of religious conflicts. The former must prevail if Western European countries are to accommodate to the presence of ethnic minorities without violence or recourse to extremist politicians. The prolonged economic recession, which strains welfare systems and produces high unemployment, tests the levels of tolerance in Western European societies.

France

The majority of foreign-born people in Europe reside in France and Germany. Those living in France who are foreign-born today constitute approximately 7 percent of the total population. They were 4.5 percent of the population in 1960.[13] Most of the foreign-born belong to distinct ethnic groups. Forty-one percent of them are North African.[14] A much smaller group are from sub-Saharan Africa. A large number of the migrants have been in France for many years and have acquired families and formed communities so that they have become permanent residents. According to Tomas Hammar, 75 percent of the foreign citizens in France are denizens.[15]

The situation regarding ethnic minorities in France has several unique features. Cultural anthropologists and historians agree that French culture is based on diversity. Fernand Braudel wrote: 'from such a heterogeneous collection of peoples and civilizations, France had somehow to be "invented".'[16] The French have prided themselves on their lack of racism. In fact, the country only recently enacted laws barring racial discrimination because most leaders denied that discrimination exists. French scholars claim that the French concept of nation, arising from the French revolution, never had an ethnic connotation. They point to French citizenship policies which historically have been based on *jus soli*, extending citizenship to persons born in France without regard to their ethnic origin. They also note that the French government followed assimilationist policies in its colonies, in contrast to the British, and French policy toward ethnic minorities continues this assimilationist emphasis. As further evidence of the color blindness of the French, scholars point out that intermarriage has long been accepted and, indeed, the number of intermarriages has increased steadily since 1970 and dramatically since 1985.[17] 'Tradition, solidly supported by history, makes France a country of easy assimilation for individuals of different origins.'[18]

French citizenship policy has recently been tightened, but it still remains relatively open and color blind. Persons born with at least one French parent are French. Persons born in France who are children of at least one foreigner who was also born in France are French from birth, referred to as the *double droit du sol*. The same applies to children born in France if a parent was born in Algeria before independence and if the parent resides in France for at least five years. *Double droit du sol* no longer applies to children who are born in France of parents one of whom was born in former French colonies before independence, although Algeria is regarded as having been a department of France and not a colony.[19] This complicated procedure limits access to citizenship, however: the basis for determining citizenship is not blood but place of birth.

The color blind ideal of the French revolutionary tradition is countered by the bitter legacy of recent French history. The Algerian War, which ended officially with Algerian independence in 1962, was an exceedingly bitter affair, with atrocities committed on both sides. The experiences of the war exacerbated the tendency of some French people to be prejudiced against all North Africans. Opinion surveys confirm the existence of this prejudice. In 1990, 76 percent of the French surveyed agreed that France has too many Arabs, in comparison to 46 percent who agreed to a similar statement regarding blacks, and 24 percent who agreed that there were too many Jews.[20] Many observers believe that racism has increased in France since the 1980s and has obtained a degree of public acceptance. Forty percent of the population admit to being racist. Well known intellectuals such as Alain de Benoist give a quasi-respectable façade to racism. The support for the overtly racist *Front National* by influential segments of the French population is a worrisome indicator. According to *Le Monde*, 31 percent of small business owners and 21 percent of professional people supported the *Front National* in the 1988 election.[21] In the 1993 parliamentary elections, the *Front National* increased its vote by 750,000 over the previous election. Although 12 percent of the voters voted for the party, it received no seats.[22] According to a poll conducted for *L'Express*, 53 percent of the French blame immigrants for insecurity.[23] Violence against ethnic minorities has become so widespread that the European Parliament condemned France for its failure to control it.[24]

The French believe that ethnic minorities should be assimilated into their society.[25] Assimilation, not pluralism, is the objective. The belief traces back to French colonial policy which had a 'missionary zeal' to inculcate the French culture into the subject peoples.[26] The French do not believe that foreign workers should live in separate areas or remain outside French culture. The much publicized controversy over the right of Muslim girls to wear veils at school illustrates the point.

The objective of French public policies was, and continues to be, assimilation.[27] The primacy of the French culture is taken as a given. A scholar, writing in the 1970s, contrasted French policy with British primarily on the basis of the greater French emphasis on assimilation.[28] Two decades later, other scholars commented that French social work differed from the British in its emphasis on *insertion and solidarity*.[29] French social workers believe that they should help North Africans and others to blend into the French culture. In contrast, the British approach is more issue-oriented and pragmatic, as will be explained in a moment.

The French have occasionally experimented with education policies that provide for linguistic and cultural diversity, but French education policy is generally directed toward assimilation. Schools have been important in acculturating minority children and have a good record in providing them with education credentials comparable to French children. The children of migrants have educational records that are only slightly lower than those of children of French families from comparable social classes.[30]

Immigrants agree with the French regarding assimilation. Over 90 percent of them believe that immigrants should live where French families live rather than in immigrant communities.[31] A majority of them express an interest in French politics and want the right to vote in municipal elections. A surprising percentage of them indicate that they have good relations with the French. Sixty-eight percent stated that they have rarely or never been a victim of racism from the French.[32]

Religion does not pose a bar to assimilation. Church and state were separated at the time of the French Revolution. Although most French people are classified as Roman Catholic, they are quite secular in their beliefs and oppose state involvement in religious affairs. A major study of values in Western Europe found that the French are less likely to describe themselves as religious than people from the other nine countries that were studied.[33] These characteristics of the French help to explain the relative French tolerance for the practice of the Muslim religion. French racism has not been strongly linked to religious intolerance. According to William Safran, the French have been more receptive to the Muslims than have the Germans, despite the fact that Islam is now the second largest religion in France.[34] Most North Africans residing in France are Muslim, but few of them are fundamentalist, so that religion to date has not posed a bar to assimilation for them.

Although the presence of ethnic minorities in France has led to an increase in racism, it has also evoked a number of positive responses. France has had a large social movement, symbolized by an open hand and the words 'don't touch my buddy,' which has mobilized young people and others against racism. The Socialist and Communist Parties have held demonstrations and conducted campaigns in solidarity with minority groups. Civil rights groups, which have been present in France for decades, continue to educate the public regarding the value of democratic principles. The French Constitutional Council has acted to uphold such principles as well, and has blocked legislation to limit the rights of asylum and the legal protections of migrants.

On the negative side, the Le Pen phenomenon of today echoes the Poujadist movement of the earlier postwar era and traces back to the hate groups mobilized during the Dreyfus Affair in the nineteenth century. This anti-democratic strain in French politics is generally associated with economic dislocations and has had limited legitimacy. The risk has always existed, however, that legitimate political actors will endorse the views of the extremist groups in order to attract their supporters. The risk is heightened today when the country is suffering from high and apparently intractable unemployment and a widening of the already wide income gap.

In conclusion, the presence of non-Western migrants in France brings into the open the contradiction between traditional French beliefs regarding democracy, and intolerance, which also has deep roots in French society. France has both inclusionist and exclusionist tendencies. French nationalism is civic nationalism and ethnic differences are not a bar to participation. Assimilation is a fundamental principle guiding policy as well as a belief among both the French and the new migrant groups. These positive aspects will probably prevail in the test of French tolerance and result in the assimilation of the ethnic minorities. The assimilation will only be partial, however. Assimilation, in French terms, does not require the end of all religious and cultural differences. French assimilation and pluralism are not mutually exclusive. As a result, the impact of the non-Western immigrants will result in a French culture which continues to include a confidence in its own value but which also includes an increased amount of pluralism.

Great Britain

The non-white population of the United Kingdom comprises 4.7 percent of the total, but the foreign born population comprises only 3.1 percent.[35] The British situation is somewhat unique in that most of the non-white population arrived in Britain with the intent to stay. The new arrivals were not regarded by the indigenous population as 'guestworkers.' Britain does have large numbers of Irish workers and temporary workers from the Mediterranean region, but the subject of this discussion is the largest group of immigrants, who are from the Commonwealth and Pakistan. The group includes persons from the Indian subcontinent, the West Indies, Hong Kong, and Africa.[36] Until 1968, people from this group were British subjects who obtained full citizenship rights upon arrival in Britain and even registered as residents. In the years that followed, the British government progressively tightened access to citizenship by persons from the former colonies. In 1988, the British government reported that 40 percent of the persons from ethnic minority groups were born in the United Kingdom and 70 percent of them were British citizens, British Overseas citizens or citizens of British Dependent Territories.[37]

The immigrants arriving in Britain generally settled in communities comprised of relatives and fellow countrymen. Their experience differed in many respects from the guestworkers who were entering countries such as Germany in the same period. The new immigrants usually had a familiarity with the language and with British culture. They were not clustered in the worst jobs: some entered professions and many became shopkeepers or restaurant owners. Increasingly they constitute a force in British politics and, since a majority of them have citizenship, they are more appropriately designated as minorities rather than as immigrants.

The minorities in Britain are more diverse than in France even though they are often referred to indiscriminately as 'black.' Each group has a different status and different experiences as participants in British society. Asians and Sikhs generally have a higher status and Bengalis and West Indians a lower status.[38] Employment patterns vary as well, with the higher-status groups entering the professions and white-collar positions. The different groups have markedly different rates of unemployment. In 1987–8, when the unemployment rate for whites was 9 percent, it was 11 percent for Indians, 16 percent for West Indians, and 25 percent for Pakistani/Bangladeshi workers.[39]

The accommodation of the minorities has not been easy, despite their status as permanent residents and citizens. Race became an issue in British politics before it did on the continent. Britain has had a number of race riots and acts of violence spanning the postwar decades. Relations between the indigenous population and the immigrants spurred a large number of government studies and a literature of scholarly writings on race relations. Racial problems trouble the conscience of Britain.

Two major factors account for the difficulty in British race relations and for the prejudices found in British society. The history of the British colonial empire and postwar economic conditions have both left their marks on British culture. Racial theories, which were so prominent in the nineteenth century, colored British colonial policy. The British followed patterns of indirect rule whenever possible and practiced segregation in the colonies. In contrast to the French, they had no zeal for making black Englishmen, but rather carried the 'white man's burden' as described by Kipling. Assimilation was not a goal of British policy.

In the period following the Second World War, the open British citizenship policy was not motivated by ideals of assimilation but rather by the exigencies of decolonialization. When the British began to dismantle their empire, they offered citizenship to native people from former colonies who feared their new governments. These new citizens arrived in Britain as permanent residents. The economic situation which awaited them was not promising. Postwar Britain did not experience the impressive economic development that occurred in France and led to labor shortages and the need for foreign workers. Between 1948 and 1963, the annual growth rate for GDP in the United Kingdom was only 2.5 percent, compared to 4.7 percent in France.[40] Consequently, the newcomers were not perceived as an asset as they were in France. Racial disturbances occurred in Nottingham and Notting Dale in 1958, and a study found that 36.8 percent of the British were 'prejudiced-inclined.'[41]

Two contradictory perceptions contest as descriptions of British culture. One points to the British as a model of tolerance. The British, in general, regard themselves as tolerant. In contrast, the other perceives Britain as a racist society.[42] Colin Holmes explored the contradiction in a book titled *A Tolerant Country?*[43] He claimed that British politics became more racist between 1950 and 1990 as a result of economic and social change. He noted that the British perceive their country as a crowded island without room for many newcomers. Still, they have welcomed some immigrants while showing hostility to others. Russian and Polish Jews and German gypsies were discriminated against in the era before the First World War at a time when Manchester had a well deserved reputation of tolerance toward most immigrants.[44] In 1919, Liverpool experienced an 'anti-black reign of terror,' providing a precedent for racial violence in recent years. According to Colin Holmes, latent British hostility toward immigrants turns to spontaneous violence when economic conditions deteriorate.[45]

Organizations with an overt racist philosophy have not acquired a popular following in Britain despite the existence of racist feelings. Britain does not have a political counterpart of the French *Front National.* Enoch Powell did not evoke the rapport with people that Le Pen does. Britain has had a

National Front Party, but it does not attract many votes and suffers from factionalism. Britain also has a very small, elite group known as the League of St George, which publishes the *National Review*. Glyn Ford calls the group the most respected of the pure national socialist groups in Western Europe, but also notes that it has only 50 members.[46] Racist acts in Britain seem to be much more spontaneous and random than the work of organized political movements. Many such acts are not even recorded, although the London police did record 7000 racists acts in 1989.[47] Ethnic groups appear to be the scapegoats for the frustrations of British society rather than the basis for the development of fascist political parties.

In 1985, a report commissioned by the Thatcher government on the education of children of minority groups was published.[48] The study found that a national climate of racism affects the schools.[49] Stereotypes formed during the empire linger and shape the behavior of some teachers. The report was damning in its findings regarding the lack of knowledge and understanding of minorities, but it was modest in its recommendations. The authors of the report opposed bilingual education and argued that minorities are best served by conforming to a uniform curriculum from which racist stereotypes have been removed. In the same era, 93 percent of Asians and 67 percent of West Indians believed that their native language should be taught.[50] The report did, however, recommend non-denominational religious education in place of the daily worship and religious education programs mandated by the 1944 Education Act.[51] This recommendation was ignored in later policy making. The Education Reform Act of 1988 requires a Christian content in religious education and school worship. Schools with a predominance of non-Christian ethnic minorities may obtain an exception.[52]

Housing patterns in Britain do not facilitate harmonious relations among ethnic minorities and the white population. Minorities are clustered in London and the West Midlands, but different minorities have different patterns of housing. Asians have the highest rate of home ownership.[53] Blacks have the worst conditions. If they own their homes, they are in poor, inner-city areas. If they are in council housing, they are in the worst ones.[54] During the 1980s, the better parts of the public housing sector were privatized under white ownership. The parts that remained under public ownership had high occupancy rates by blacks and suffered from lack of public spending. Twenty-seven percent of black housing has more than one person per room. Only 2 percent of whites live in such crowded conditions.

The discussion of ethnic minorities in Britain leads to the conclusion that the present situation results from the interplay of three factors: the colonial legacy, democratic values, and economic conditions. The interplay shapes Britain into a multicultural society, but one that is fraught with inherent contradictions. Ethnic minorities are a permanent part of Britain and most of them have the right to full participation. Britain pioneered anti-discrimination legislation in Europe. The British have not been attracted by racist political parties. The existence of the ethnic minorities, however, is a source of tension and minorities have too frequently been subject to random acts of violence. Moreover, government leaders have implied that immigrants pose a threat to racial peace in Britain as a justification for tighter immigration and asylum policies.[55] Numerous authorities call Britain a racist society and many believe that Britain is more racist today than it was four decades ago. John Solomos wrote: 'the visible growth of multi-ethnic communities and attempts to challenge the hegemony of Anglo-Saxon cultural values in such areas as education has resulted in attempts to mobilize political support in defence of conservative and mono-cultural definitions of Englishness.'[56]

The question of why Britain has had an increase of random violence, but not an accompanying growth of racist political movements, leads to one more concluding comment. It may be that Britain is not more racist than it was earlier, but it is more violent. George Orwell wrote many years ago that the British are xenophobic but they have a gentle civilization. By most measures, the British civilization is less gentle today than it was in his time. The 1980s were marked by the violence of the coal strike, increased criticism of the behavior of the British police, and signs of alienation among the long-term unemployed. The values of the Thatcher era were competition, individual initiative, and a denigration of the welfare state. Prosperity came to many but at the cost of widening income differentials and growing unemployment. The fact that people continued to vote for their traditional political parties while some engaged in random violence suggests that the increase in violence does not necessarily indicate an increase in racism.

Conclusion

In both France and Britain, the prevailing national culture has included incompatible values of democracy and of nationalism with a racist element. Both countries have experienced cognitive dissonance arising from a clash of the values of tolerance and of racism due to the presence of ethnic minorities. The British provided better legal protection for the ethnic minorities in the early postwar era, but no major policy has been adopted since the mid-1970s to facilitate the assimilation of minorities. On the other hand, the British system, with its tradition of decentralization, has allowed a degree of multiculturalism to flourish.[57] French culture was more open to the acceptance of ethnic minorities, but the acceptance entails the requirement to assimilate into French culture.

The cultures of France and Britain have both been affected by the presence of non-Western migrants, but each has adapted according its own distinctive set of norms. The tensions which arose have been handled according to norms long present in the countries. In the process, the norms remain but in a revised form. French culture retains its prestige and assimilation remains a necessity, but the culture is more diverse and pluralism is growing under the umbrella of assimilation. The British have had to accept the reality that Britain is a multicultural society because its minority groups are citizens. British law and values have formed a bulwark against racism even though Britain lacked the color blind traditions and the commitment to assimilation that prevailed in France.

A number of variables are important to consider when attempting to assess the impact which the non-Western migrants will have on the cultures in Western Europe. These are:

1   The reasons for the immigration: citizenship, guest workers, asylum, permanent or temporary.
2   The meaning of such concepts as nation or democracy for the society.
3   The society's experience during colonialism.
4   The economic situation, past and present.
5   Demographic factors and how they are perceived.
6   Public policy and political leadership.

The impact of non-Western migrants on the cultures of Western Europe will not be uniform. Each situation has its own profile of variables. However, the study of France and Britain provides grounds for guarded optimism that European cultures, while lacking the pluralist traditions popularly associated with US culture, will evolve as inclusionist societies.

Notes

1. *Independent*, 1994, p. 15.
2. Demetrios Papademetriou, 'At a crossroads: Europe and migration,' in Kimberly Hamilton (ed.), *Migration and the New Europe* (Washington, DC: The Center for Strategic and International Studies, 1994), p. 23.
3. Anthony Smith, 'National identity and the idea of European unity,' *International Affairs*, 68, 1 (1992), 60.
4. Lincoln Allison, 'On European racism,' *World & I*, April 1991, 583.
5. Tomas Hammar, *Democracy and the Nation State* (Avebury, England: Gower Publishing Company, 1990), pp. 12–25.
6. John Thompson, *Ideology and Modern Culture* (Cambridge: Polity Press, 1990), p. 132.
7. Tzvetan Todorov, *On Human Diversity* (Cambridge, MA: Harvard University Press, 1993), p. 251.
8. *Ibid.*, p. 171.

9. *Ibid.*, p. 227.
10. Liah Greenfield, *Nationalism* (Cambridge, MA: Harvard University Press, 1992), p. 8.
11. *Ibid.*, pp. 11–12.
12. *Ibid.*, p. 13.
13. Jacques Voisard and Christiane Ducastelle, *La Question Immigrée* (France: Editions du Seuil, 1990), p. 142.
14. John Salt, 'External international migration,' in Daniel Noin and Robert Woods (eds), *The Changing Population Of Europe* (Oxford: Blackwell, 1993), p. 189.
15. *Ibid.*, p. 22.
16. Fernand Braudel, *The Identity Of France* (New York: Harper & Row, 1990), p. 109.
17. *Ministère des affaires sociales* reprinted in Philippe Bernard, *L'immigration* (Le Monde éditions, 1993), p. 119.
18. *Ibid.*, p. 113, translation by author.
19. *Ibid.*, p. 33.
20. Poll conducted by the French government and reported in Glyn Ford, *Fascist Europe* (London: Pluto Press, 1991), p. xiii.
21. *Ibid.*, p. 20.
22. Howard Machin, 'How the socialists lost the 1993 elections to the French parliament,' *West European Politics*, October (1993), 597–8.
23. 'France: dossier immigration,' *L'Express*, September 16, 1993, p. 31.
24. *Social Europe*, 1992, Supplement 3/93, pp. 105–6.
25. *L'Express, op. cit.*, pp. 30–1.
26. Gary Freeman, *Immigrant Labor and Racial Conflict in Industrial Societies* (Princeton, NJ: Princeton University Press, 1979), p. 32.
27. Sarah Collinson, *Beyond Borders* (London: Chatham House, 1993), pp. 21–2.
28. Freeman, *op. cit.*, p. 40.
29. Crescy Cannan, Lynne Berry and Karen Lyons, *Social Work and Europe* (London: Macmillan, 1992), p. 96.
30. Bernard, *op. cit.*, p. 122.
31. *L'Express, op. cit.*, p. 29.
32. *Ibid.*, p. 29.
33. Stephen Harding, David Phillips and Michael Fogarty, *Contrasting Values in Western Europe* (London: Macmillan, 1986), pp. 68–9.
34. William Safran, 'Islamization in Western Europe: political consequences and historical parallels,' *The Annals*, 485 (1986), 102–3.
35. Daniel Noin and Robert Woods, *The Changing Population of Europe* (Oxford: Blackwell, 1993), p. 211.
36. B. Guy Peters and Patricia Davis, 'Migration to the United Kingdom and the emergence of a new politics,' *The Annals*, 485 (1986), 131.
37. Ian Forbes and Geoffrey Mead, *Measure for Measure* (Equal Opportunities Study Group, University of Southampton, 1992), p. 19.
38. Allison, *op. cit.*, p. 578.
39. Forbes and Mead, p. 20.
40. David Landes, *The Unbound Prometheus* (London: Cambridge University Press, 1969), p. 497.
41. Freeman, *op. cit.*, p. 271.

42. See, for example, *The Empire Strikes Back* (Centre for Contemporary Cultural Studies, University of Birmingham, London: Hutchinson, 1982).
43. Colin Homes, *A Tolerant Country?* (London: Faber and Faber, 1991).
44. *Ibid.*, p. 94.
45. *Ibid.*, p. 100.
46. Ford, *op. cit.*, p. 37.
47. *Ibid.*, p. 78.
48. *Education for All: the Report of the Committee of Inquiry into the Education of Children from Ethnic Minority Groups* (London: Her Majesty's Stationery Office, 1985).
49. *Ibid.*, p. 30.
50. Brown, *op. cit.*, p. 269.
51. *Ibid.*, pp. 771–3.
52. Collinson, *op. cit.*, p. 24.
53. Brown, *op. cit.*, pp. 303–4.
54. *Social Europe, op. cit.*, p. 22.
55. Robert Miles and Diana Kay, 'The politics of immigration to Britain: East–West migration in the twentieth century,' *West European Politics*, April (1994), 28–31.
56. John Solomos, *Race and Racism in Contemporary Britain* (London: Macmillan, 1989), p. 177.
57. John Rex, 'Race and ethnicity in Europe,' in Joe Bailey (ed.), *Social Europe* (London: Longman, 1992), pp. 112–15.

9 Immigration and public finance: the case of the Netherlands

Anton Kuijsten

Introduction

Europe is currently experiencing massive immigration pressures. The Netherlands is no exception to this trend. On the contrary, it looks as though immigration pressures on the Netherlands have increased since Germany changed its constitution in order to be able to better manage ever-increasing numbers of asylum seekers. The net annual immigration flow into the Netherlands is estimated to be about 60,000 persons annually. There is growing public concern about the capability of the country to accommodate these newcomers, provide them with lodging, education, and employment. Except during a few crisis situations, the country has never before experienced such high net immigration over an extended period of time.

In reaction to these developments, immigration matters have become matters of public debate and political discussions. The Netherlands is already one of the most densely populated countries on earth, increasing prosperity and individualized lifestyles have caused an increase in per capita physical space needed, and the amount of space needed far exceeds the requirements of population growth as such. Moreover, the country still has a serious and persistent unemployment problem. Thus, the question policy makers face in the Netherlands is: why allow immigrants to enter the country unless they are genuine refugees who should be accepted for humanitarian reasons?

On the other hand, the Netherlands, like most countries in Europe, faces both incipient population decline and substantive increases in the proportion of its aged to its total population. In fact, these two processes are closely linked, in that both will be the inescapable result of sustained current below-replacement fertility in combination with current mortality levels. Some argue that it is therefore highly probable that in the near- and medium-term future net immigration will have a bigger impact on the size and structure of its population than it used to have. Additionally, there might be a growing need to rethink immigration and immigrant policies in order to allow or even stimulate increasing immigration flows, in an attempt to counter population decline and/or aging, or to recruit labor to compensate for decreasing future numbers of people in economically active age groups.

The question is whether such expectations about the demographic effects of relatively large immigration streams are justified. Mathematical modeling that focuses on long-run equilibrium solutions to the problem of the formal properties of so-called open populations yields conclusions which have been summarized by Espenshade.[1] Ultimately stationary levels of population size, proportion aged and proportion non-natives, to be reached hypothetically only after some centuries, will depend on the levels of fertility and mortality of both the native and the non-native population, as well as on the magnitude of the annual immigrant flows, all assumed to remain constant over a very long period of time. But, as a rule, unless fertility is assumed to return to above-replacement level and/or unless annual net immigration is at a very high relative level, the ultimate stationary population size will be lower than the current one, and the ultimate proportions of the aged and non-natives will be significantly higher than the current ones.

Medium-term projections lead to similar conclusions. Some years ago Lesthaeghe *et al.* tried to answer the question of whether immigrants are substitutes for births. These researchers used different projections for the combined populations of the 12 EC countries in order to demonstrate that the answer to this question should essentially be in the negative.[2] Results of comparable studies for the case of the Netherlands,[3] of Findl *et al.* for the case of Austria,[4] of George *et al.* for the case of Canada,[5] of Steinmann for the case of the Federal Republic of Germany,[6] and of Ahlburg and Vaupel for the case of the United States,[7] all fully support the conclusions of Lesthaeghe *et al.* The basic cause of incipient population decline is below-replacement fertility. In the longer run, it is also the basic cause of high levels of aging. Only a fertility rise to levels approaching replacement can structurally change these perspectives. Relatively small numbers of immigrants will not make much difference, since their net effect will postpone rather than prevent the processes of decline and aging. In order to bring these processes to a halt without the help of a fertility rise among the native population, tremendous numbers of immigrants would be needed. If immigration were used as an instrument to slow down the aging of the population, it would need to be sustained indefinitely because immigrants would eventually assume the fertility and mortality levels of natives.

But if immigration does not seem able to halt the demographic processes of aging and long-term population decline, it might at least solve some current and future labor problems and contribute to the future solvency of the welfare state. European governments, including that of the Netherlands, seem to be even more reluctant on this point. Ethier has offered an interesting analysis of European-style temporary migration which explains the belief that guestworkers are complementary to native workers when they are desired, but are substitutes who can be sent back when they are no longer needed.[8] Indeed, during the 1960s, economic theory emphasized the advantages of using foreign labor in the face of slower population growth and as a 'conjunctural buffer,' and this argument emerged in the late 1960s as the official doctrine of the OECD.[9] A more permissive perception of immigration, similar to that existing in the United States in the nineteenth century and in the last decades of this century, has never existed in twentieth-century Europe (as a matter of fact, it did exist in seventeenth-century Holland). According to Livi Bacci this is perhaps due to the essence and origin of the European nation state, which is built around common concepts such as culture, language, and religion.[10]

It might be for this reason, then, that there is a relatively unfavorable view of the economic impact of immigration behind the current restrictive policies of European countries. However, other reasons may play a role as well. Beyond the current conjuncture, structural changes in the labor market of both Europe and the United States have reduced the kind of demand for massive industrial labor that was hitherto filled by immigrants.[11] If correct, this could be an economic argument against further immigration. Opposition in Europe to labor importation, however, is not founded on economic grounds alone.[12] The European colonial past promoted images of superiority and inferiority, and a similar process of cultural coding has tended to develop with respect to labor imported from the periphery. It is evident that the arrival of large waves of immigrants who speak different languages, practice different religions, or have different habits challenges the cultural status quo of the receiving country and induces some collective stress.[13]

In a highly regulated country like the Netherlands, a social security argument could be added. Immigration and immigrant policies easily suffer from the fact that their failures have a high degree of 'social visibility.' As long as the goal of integration is not fully reached, public sentiments easily become hostile against non-natives living on Dutch social security payments. For many natives who find themselves without jobs, an unemployed guestworker is kind of a *contradictio in terminis*. In such an atmosphere, immigrants become too easily stigmatized as people who only cost the state money, which has to be provided by the native taxpayer.

The economic advantages of immigration, however, could be much greater than those assumed by the 'conjunctural buffer' theory. Simon has advocated a more positive and optimistic view on the economic value of immigration, based mainly on the situation in North America.[14] He argues that the age composition of migrants is the key to their economic contribution to the native community. Immigrants lighten the burden of supporting the aged through contributing to social security payments,[15] since their average educational level is higher than that of the native labor force,[16] and their consumption increases the size of the market.[17] Simon's message is that the presence of immigrants is good for the migrants themselves, good for the community through their large net contribution to the public coffers, and at least not bad for the individual natives.

The problem is whether his analysis is valid for Europe as well as for North America.[18] There may be other factors at stake. According to Livi Bacci, upward mobility in North America, particularly the United States, seems to be closely linked to achievement in working life and professional career.[19] This link seems to be less strong in the older, more structured and stratified European societies, where social status is greatly influenced by birth, family relations, and networks of various types, which are not necessarily always linked to professional achievement. If his hypothesis is true, Livi Bacci writes, then the only asset at the immigrant's disposal – i.e. his or her propensity and ability to work – is comparatively less productive and efficient in the European context than it is in the American one. In the American labor market immigrants do not depress the indigenous workers' wages or displace them from their jobs. Differences in wages between immigrants and indigenous workers of comparable skills are relatively small. Average earnings of immigrants improve sharply with experience in the US labor market. Another interesting structural characteristic of the American case is the existence of a very large (almost 20 million) Hispanic community, which generates 'significant economic opportunities for immigrants, either because many immigrants start businesses in order to cater to members of their national-origin group or because the immigrant entrepreneurs often hire their conationals.'[20] A similar situation does not exist in Europe on the same scale, although there is sufficient evidence that the same principle works in European countries, albeit on a much smaller scale, inside geographically concentrated ethnic communities.

As is often the case in discussions and in research on the economic aspects of aging, and in discussions on the economic consequences of immigration for the public budget, there seems to be a bias toward cost calculations only.[21] However, like native citizens, immigrants do not strain and inflate the costs of public services only. They also pay taxes which may replenish public coffers more than adequately. A balanced assessment of the public finance consequences of immigration, therefore, needs to be based on both sides of the balance sheet. This chapter will approach the problem from an empirical angle by examining the question from a 40-year medium-term perspective, and will determine whether the idea that immigration has higher costs than benefits is justified.

The population projection model used

The demographic model used for my scenario calculations is an extended version of a semi-interacting two-population projection model which was originally set up by Van de Kaa and myself in order to study the impact of immigration on future population size and structure.[22] The model is an extended version of a computer program for making projections of one population only, with variant and time-changing combinations of fertility and mortality.[23]

The baseline population in the present application is that of January 1, 1993, the latest date for which authorized population figures according to sex, age, and nationality were available.[24] At that time, the population of the Netherlands was 15,239,000, where 14,482,000 people (95 per cent) were of Dutch nationality and 757,000 were non-Dutch nationals (with people of Turkish (213,000), Moroccan (165,000), German (49,000) and British (44,000) nationality as the biggest groups).[25] The baseline population has 18.3 percent children (0 to 14), 68.7 percent individuals between 15 and 64 years, and 13.0 percent aged people (65 and over). The subpopulation of Dutch nationals is slightly older (18.0 percent children, and 13.6 percent aged), the non-Dutch subpopulation considerably younger (24.7 percent youngsters, 73.0 percent in working age, and 2.4 percent aged). The present application involves scenario calculations over eight five-year projection intervals until 2033.

The computer program permits a restricted number of options for hypothesizing the future course of both mortality and fertility. For the present application a mortality option was selected which assumes that mortality levels (expressed as a set of five-year survival probabilities for five-year age groups) in the year 2050 will correspond to a life expectancy of 83.4 years for females and 75.1 years for males. Between the first projection interval and the limit year, all age-specific survival probabilities change linearly from their current levels (corresponding to a female life expectancy of 80.1 years and a male life expectancy of 73.9 years), according to the 1988 to 1992 life expectancy tables published in NCBS, to their limit levels around 2050.[26]

The model allows for a much wider range of options for hypothesizing the level of fertility (expressed as the period TFR) around 2050, running from a low of 1.0 to a high of 2.6. Between the initial 1992 level of 1.59 and the selected limit level around the year 2050, the TFR level is assumed to change negative-exponentially, with the biggest changes in the first projection intervals, in order to reach the chosen level asymptotically around 2050. For each projection interval, the age-specific fertility rates are changed *pro rata*, thus keeping the current rather 'old' age schedule of fertility as it was in the early 1990s (Table 9.1).[27] The sex ratio at birth is assumed to remain at its initial level of 488 girls against 512 boys per 1000 live births.

Table 9.1   *Age-specific fertility rates, the Netherlands, 1992 (per 1000 women of each age group)*

Age group	Fertility rate
15–19	7.71
20–24	43.42
25–29	117.40
30–34	110.67
35–39	35.15
40–44	4.44
45–49	0.37

Source: NCBS data.

This program was then extended into a semi-interacting two-population version. First, the initial population is split into two: that of Dutch and that of non-Dutch nationality at January 1, 1993. These populations are then projected side-by-side. Following Espenshade, one may find it useful to imagine that the country is divided into a 'western' half and an 'eastern' half.[28] The western half is reserved for settling the population of Dutch nationality (henceforth 'natives') and their descendants. The eastern half accommodates the population of non-Dutch nationalities and their descendants (henceforth 'non-natives'). Mobility between the two 'regions' is excluded, in the physical sense of geographic moves as well as in the social sense of naturalizations, both for non-natives in the baseline population and their descendants, and for future new immigrants and their descendants.

The mortality and the sex ratio at birth hypotheses mentioned above are assumed to hold equally for both natives and non-natives. The semi-interacting character of the model expresses itself in several ways. Relevant for the present application is that the fertility assumptions for the non-native population are linked to those for the natives. The user can state how much non-native TFR is expected to be above (or below) the hypothesized native TFR in the first projection interval, and how much it is expected to be above (or below) the hypothesized native TFR at the end of the projection period. The program then executes a linear interpolation over all projection intervals of this change in fertility differential, and it applies the resulting interval-specific proportional differences to the series of native age-specific fertility rates assumed to hold for each interval in order to obtain interval-specific series of non-native age-specific fertility rates.

Another aspect of the semi-interacting character is that the program has a built-in evaluation procedure, on the basis of size and/or age structure at the *total* population level; that is, native and non-native population combined at the end of each projection interval. Predefined hypothetical policy targets with respect to future size and/or age structure can be evaluated against the calculated outcomes, for each interval, allowing an extra quantum of new immigrants to be added to the 'eastern' non-native population at the end of that interval, with a fixed sex and age structure. This policy impact variant of the model was used earlier to explore the question of whether immigration might stop aging and/or prevent incipient population decline in the Netherlands.[29] It will not be used in the present calculations. Instead, the scenarios are characterized by time-constant absolute numbers of 'net immigrants' in each projection interval, with a fixed sex and age structure equal to that of immigrants of non-Dutch nationalities in 1992.[30] It is implicitly assumed that the net number of immigrants completely consists of non-nationals. This age and sex structure, shown in Table 9.2, is extremely young: its proportion aged is only 1.1 percent.

The model is of course a highly simplified image of reality. In actuality, mortality and fertility changes never follow smooth (curvi)linear time paths. 'Native' and 'non-native' populations are not separated by bulkheads; naturalizations and intermarriage are firmly grounded in empirical reality. Third-generation descendants of immigrants often can hardly be regarded as non-natives. In fact, a no-migration run, technically easy to do with the model, contains the hidden assumption that both native and non-native populations have zero net migration and zero indirect migration effects. And a quantum-of-immigrants run contains this same hidden assumption with respect to the native population, since all immigrants are added to the 'eastern' non-native population. Finally, the model adds these migrant quantums to the non-native population at the end of a projection interval, regarding them as 'net immigrants surviving until the end of the interval.'

Table 9.2 *Age and sex distribution of immigrants as used in the projections (per 10,000 immigrants)*

Age group	Male	Female	Age group	Male	Female
0–4	320	300	50–54	110	90
5–9	320	300	55–59	60	50
10–14	300	270	60–64	40	40
15–19	380	520	65–69	15	18
20–24	940	860	70–74	10	13
25–29	1210	820	75–79	8	10
30–34	810	560	80–84	6	7
35–39	490	330	85–89	4	5
40–44	280	200	90–94	4	4
45–49	170	120	95–99	3	3
Total	5480 males, 4520 females				

Source: NCBS, 1993, p. 54.

The public finance revenue/expenditure profile

After the demographic scenario projections were made, their results were subjected to profiles containing sex- and age-specific amounts of revenues to and expenditures from public finance.

On the revenue side, figures kindly provided by the Social and Cultural Planning Office of the Netherlands were used. These figures tabulated almost all tax and social premium revenues, from both direct and indirect taxes, that could be allocated to persons in specific sex and age groups in 1991. Two indirect taxes concerning car use only, with a revenue less than 2 percent of the total, are not included. Included in the profile are social security premiums, including premiums for the universal flat-rate state pension scheme, health insurance premiums, income tax, excise tax, sales tax (including import duties), conveyance tax (when selling and/or buying a house), and property tax.

Pension premiums do not include premiums for supplementary pensions (paid by the government) to which civil servants are entitled. The revenue side of the profile is summarized in Table 9.3.

The expenditure side is given in Table 9.4. Here, we have five groups only, not distinguished by sex but by broad age categories. Included in the profile are social security payments, costs of the public educational system, costs of the collective medical care system, costs of in-kind benefits such as old age homes, home help, child protection, public libraries, and public sports accommodations, and a residual category of 'other programs,' annually good for almost 9000 guilders per capita, irrespective of age.

This side of the profile has a higher degree of possible error than the revenue side. The figures for 1981 were taken as the base as used by Vossen in an application regarding the problem of future affordability of pension payments in the aging society of the Netherlands.[31] Since the revenue side

Table 9.3 *Revenue side of public finance profile: mean transfer to public budget, by sex and age, 1991 (in Dutch guilders)*

Males		Females	
Age	Revenue	Age	Revenue
0–17	0	0–17	0
18–24	10,372	18–24	9683
25–34	28,079	25–34	13,458
35–44	35,203	35–44	11,008
45–54	35,264	45–54	9569
55–64	32,680	55–64	7500
65–74	12,416	65–74	5745
75+	9153	75+	6325

Table 9.4   *Expenditure side of public finance profile: estimated mean expenditures from public budget, by age, 1991 (in Dutch guilders)*

Age group	Mean expenditure
0–19	18,500
20–44	14,100
45–64	19,500
65–79	29,400
80+	43,600

has figures for 1991, a crude estimate had to be made in order to raise these 1981-based figures to their 1991 levels. In this ten-year period, the gross amount of social security transfers and so-called personal payments had increased by approximately half. Although the estimate should necessarily remain very crude, a 50 percent increase of every 1981 age-specific per capita expenditure component would be too simple a solution. Increases over the decade were caused by a combination of increases in payment levels and increases (or decreases) in volume exemplified by the proportion of people in a sex/age group eligible for receipt of payment. In those cases where we can assume an almost 100 percent coverage of the policy measure (universal flat-rate state pension, universal child allowance, and the 'other programs'), the demographic projection automatically takes care of the volume component of change. Raising the 1981 per capita expenditure level of these profile components by 50 percent would account twice for this volume component. Instead, for these three profile components their 1981 levels were increased by 25 percent only – that is, the rough amount of increase of old age pensions in those ten years – almost exclusively to keep up with inflation and general rises in wage levels to which the flat-rate old age pensions and child allowance payments are indexed.

These profiles are not complete, neither on the revenue side nor on the expenditure side. Nonetheless, they contain the vast majority of cash flows and in-kind benefits between private households and government influenced by demographic change. But they do not stand for all money the government receives and spends. This drawback could be problematic when one is trying to forecast future revenue/expenditure net balances as such. However, it is not problematic if one only compares the results of the scenario calculations with those of the baseline projection, since the probable errors are equal in all scenarios. What is important for the argument is the pattern of relative differences between the scenario outcomes.

The profile applications are based on *ceteris paribus* reasoning. Since the per capita revenues and expenditures in the profile are tied to specific sex and age groups for the entire population, including current non-natives and future immigrants, the hidden assumption is that age- and sex- specific proportions of persons eligible for various profile elements will not change in the future, neither from the influence of macroeconomic changes nor under the influence of the process of immigration itself. In this way one considers the possibility that demographic change is not even the most important factor. Other factors may be much more amenable to public policy: changes in tax rates, changes in social security eligibility rules, changes in economic policy that affect unemployment levels, even changes in rules that allow access as an immigrant.

The baseline projection

Estimating the possible impact of future migration on the public finance revenue/expenditure balance sheet requires a no-migration baseline projection as a benchmark. Given current below-replacement fertility and the imbalanced age structure of the baseline population because of fertility booms and busts in the past, the results of such a no-migration baseline projection heavily depend on the hypothesized course of future fertility. For that reason, making a few alternative baseline projections with different fertility hypotheses would be a better procedure. Since the objective is to assess impacts of different migration scenarios, however, making more than one baseline projection would unduly complicate scenario comparisons.

Therefore, only one baseline projection was made with the mortality and sex ratio at birth assumptions as mentioned above, with zero net migration for the entire projection period 1993 to 2032, with fertility of native women assumed to fluctuate slightly until 2003 and increase slowly afterwards until the last projection interval 2028 to 2032, when TRF reaches the value of 1.73, and with fertility of non-native women developing from a level 60 percent above that of native women in 1993 to 1997 to 30 per cent above that of native women after 2032. These fertility assumptions and the main results of this baseline projection are summarized in Table 9.5.

According to this baseline projection, the population size of the Netherlands would first gradually increase from its current 15.24 million to around 15.8 million in 2010, and then fall to a little more than 15 million in 2032. Native period TFR gradually climbs to 1.726 around 2030, whereas non-native TFR slowly declines to 2.308 in the same year. The proportion of the aged almost doubles from the current 13 percent to around 25 percent in 2032; since no immigration is assumed, this doubling reflects the impact of the assumed courses of fertility and mortality on the unbalanced age structure of the baseline population. Despite the assumed lack of immigration, the proportion of non-natives (who are in fact all descendants of the non-natives in the baseline population) rises from the current 4.97 to 8.17 percent; this rise reflects the influence of the assumedly higher non-native fertility on the substantially younger age structure of non-natives in the

Table 9.5   *Main results baseline projection*

Period	Population at the end of projection interval	TFR natives	TFR non-natives	Percent non-natives	Percent aged	Public finance revenue/ expenditure balance
1992	15,239	1.596		4.97	13.03	− 4825
1993–97	15,532	1.558	2.493	5.44	13.57	− 4772
1998–2002	15,727	1.587	2.478	5.88	13.98	− 4932
2003–07	15,787	1.615	2.463	6.25	14.74	− 5182
2008–12	15,745	1.642	2.441	6.59	16.72	− 5602
2013–17	15,650	1.664	2.412	6.92	18.78	− 6019
2018–22	15,521	1.687	2.382	7.30	20.67	− 6417
2023–27	15,334	1.707	2.347	7.73	22.75	− 7038
2028–32	15,057	1.726	2.308	8.17	24.72	− 7647

baseline population. The last column of Table 9.5 displays the outcome of an application of the public finance revenue/expenditure profile to the demographic results of the baseline projection.

The profile (Tables 9.3 and 9.4) was applied to the *relative* age and sex structures of the projection population. Therefore, the outcomes of the profile applications came directly on a per capita basis. The results show a public finance balance that is already negative at the moment: a mean per capita deficit of 4825 guilders for the revenues and expenditures included in the profile. At the end of the first projection interval, this deficit diminishes by an insignificant amount. Afterwards, it rises continuously, reaching 7647 guilders in 2032, almost 60 percent more than its level in 1992. Since this increase in the per capita deficit is far from compensated by the post-2010 population decline, the total absolute deficit of the profile will increase by 57 percent, from 73.5 billion guilders in 1992 to 115.2 billion guilders (at constant prices) in 2032.

The immigration scenarios: demographic results

Next, nine immigration scenario projections were made, systematically combining three variants for the assumed amount of future net immigration with three different assumptions for the future non-native/native fertility differential. The future net immigration levels selected were 150,000, 300,000 and 450,000 per five-year interval (that is, half of current net migration, equal to current net migration, and one-and-a-half times current net migration), labeled as low (L), medium (M), and high (H). The selected non-native/native fertility differentials are 1.5 (meaning that non-

Table 9.6 *Total population, according to scenario projections*

	0	1	2	3	4	5	6	7	8
Baseline	15.24	15.53	15.73	15.79	15.75	15.65	15.52	15.33	15.06
L/1.1	15.24	15.68	16.05	16.30	16.47	16.59	16.68	16.71	16.65
L/1.3	15.24	15.68	16.05	16.31	16.48	16.61	16.72	16.77	16.75
L/1.5	15.24	15.68	16.05	16.32	16.50	16.64	16.76	16.84	16.85
M/1.1	15.24	15.83	16.37	16.82	17.20	17.54	17.85	18.11	18.30
M/1.3	15.24	15.83	16.38	16.83	17.22	17.57	17.91	18.21	18.44
M/1.5	15.24	15.83	16.38	16.84	17.24	17.61	17.97	18.31	18.59
H/1.1	15.24	16.00	16.70	17.35	17.93	18.49	19.03	19.52	19.94
H/1.3	15.24	16.00	16.70	17.36	17.96	18.54	19.11	19.65	20.14
H/1.5	15.24	16.00	16.70	17.37	17.98	18.59	19.19	19.78	20.33

native TFR is 50 percent higher than native TFR at the end of the projection period), 1.3, and 1.1, always departing from a common assumed differential of 1.6 in the first projection interval. Assumptions about period TFR of native women, about sex ratio at birth, and about mortality of both natives and non-natives have remained the same as in the baseline projection. This produced nine immigration scenario projections, referred to as L/1.5, L/1.3, L/1.1, M/1.5, etc.

Table 9.6 shows the evolution of the resulting total population size in the nine immigration projections from 1993 to 2032, with the results of the baseline projection in the top row. The differences between the results of the baseline projection and scenarios L/1.3, M/1.3, and H/1.3 exclusively result from the assumed levels of future net immigration and from the implicit assumption that the fertility of immigrant women after 1992 converges towards that of native women as the fertility of non-native women already present in the baseline population is supposed to do, dropping from 60 percent higher at present to 30 percent higher after 2032. Differences in the results of the other scenario calculations from those of the baseline scenario are caused by one additional factor: the assumption that the fertility of non-native women, both currently in the Netherlands and entering after 1992, will converge more (1.1 scenarios) or less (1.5 scenarios) than is supposed in the 1.3 scenarios.

Row comparisons in Table 9.6 clearly show that the assumptions on future net immigration flows have a large influence on the projected population size. The population in 2032 according to the L scenarios (150,000 net immigration per five years) result in a population size that exceeds that according to the baseline projection by 1.6 to 1.8 million (10 to 12 per cent more). The population, according to the M scenarios (300,000 net immigration per five years), exceeds the baseline projection 2032 population size by 3.2 to 3.5 million (21 to 23 per cent), and that according to the H scenarios

(450,000 net immigration per five years) by 4.9 to 5.3 million (32 to 35 per cent).

The fact that the net immigration dimension of the scenarios is of much greater importance than the fertility convergence dimension in determining future population size can easily be seen by comparing columns. According to the supposed degree of native/non-native fertility convergence, after 40 years the difference in population size between the low convergence (1.5) and the higher convergence (1.1) scenario is 0.2 million under the low immigration assumption, 0.29 million under the medium immigration assumption, and 0.39 million under the high immigration assumption. These numbers are dwarfed to insignificance by the impact of the differences caused by the different net immigration assumptions.

Similar conclusions can be drawn with respect to the impact of the scenario assumptions on the future proportions of aged people (65 and over), as can be seen from Table 9.7. As expected, and in line with earlier findings,[32] positive net immigration can indeed slow down the pace of the aging process. The higher the assumed net number of immigrants per five-year period, the lower the proportion aged projection for the year 2032 (and for all years between). However, even a net immigration of 450,000 people per five years (which is an accumulated net immigration of 3.6 million in the entire projection period), plus its second-generation dejuvenating effect, cannot do more than bring the proportion aged of 24.72 percent in the no-immigration baseline projection back to somewhere between 19.5 and 20 percent, still some 50 percent above its current level. This immigration counterbalance to aging is far from negligible, of course, but one should not forget that over a much longer period than 40 years this effect will lose its force because as immigrant fertility and mortality levels converge with those of the native population, the non-native population will 'age on the spot' at the same speed as the native population. Still, the impact

Table 9.7 *Proportions aged (65 and over) according to scenario projections*

	0	1	2	3	4	5	6	7	8
Baseline	13.03	13.57	13.98	14.74	16.72	18.78	20.67	22.75	24.72
L/1.1	13.03	13.45	13.72	14.32	16.06	17.83	19.43	21.20	22.86
L/1.3	13.03	13.45	13.72	14.31	16.05	17.81	19.38	21.12	22.73
L/1.5	13.03	13.45	13.72	14.31	16.03	17.78	19.34	21.04	22.60
M/1.1	13.03	13.34	13.47	13.92	15.45	16.98	18.33	19.84	21.28
M/1.3	13.03	13.34	13.47	13.91	15.43	16.95	18.27	19.74	21.11
M/1.5	13.03	13.34	13.47	13.90	15.41	16.92	18.21	19.63	20.94
H/1.1	13.03	13.22	13.23	13.54	14.88	16.22	17.37	18.68	19.96
H/1.3	13.03	13.22	13.23	13.53	14.86	16.18	17.30	18.56	19.76
H/1.5	13.03	13.22	13.23	13.52	14.84	16.13	17.22	18.44	19.57

Table 9.8 *Proportions non-native population, according to scenario projections*

	Projection intervals								
	0	1	2	3	4	5	6	7	8
Baseline	4.97	5.44	5.88	6.25	6.59	6.92	7.30	7.73	8.17
L/1.1	4.97	6.34	7.77	9.22	10.70	12.19	13.72	15.31	16.97
L/1.3	4.97	6.34	7.78	9.26	10.77	12.31	13.93	15.64	17.45
L/1.5	4.97	6.34	7.79	9.29	10.84	12.44	14.14	15.96	17.93
M/1.1	4.97	7.23	9.60	12.03	14.50	16.95	19.40	21.89	24.43
M/1.3	4.97	7.23	9.61	12.08	14.59	17.12	19.67	22.30	25.03
M/1.5	4.97	7.23	9.62	12.12	14.69	17.29	19.94	22.71	25.62
H/1.1	4.97	8.10	11.35	14.67	17.99	21.22	24.38	27.51	30.66
H/1.3	4.97	8.10	11.37	14.72	18.10	21.42	24.69	27.98	31.33
H/1.5	4.97	8.10	11.38	14.77	18.21	21.62	25.01	28.45	32.00

of the fertility convergence in the scenarios is very modest compared to that of the net immigration size.

As can be expected, the immigration assumptions have a large impact on future proportions of non-native citizens. The numbers arrayed in Table 9.8 show that under the low net immigration assumption the proportion of the population of alien descent will increase more than threefold, from its current 5 percent to a level which is double that of 8.2 percent reached in 2032, according to the no-immigration baseline projection. Under the medium net immigration assumption, this proportion increases fivefold, and under the high net immigration assumption sixfold. The native/non-native fertility convergence hypotheses hardly influence these increases.

The patterns in Tables 9.6 and 9.7 are closely related. Higher net immigration streams lead to a bigger but less aged population, and lower net immigration streams lead to a smaller but more aged population. Convergence of fertility levels of non-native women toward those of native women has a secondary compensating effect on that relationship. This connection implies that substantial immigration does have the expected age structure effects. This makes one curious about the results of an application of the public finance revenue/expenditure profile to them.

The immigration scenarios: changing public finance revenue/expenditure balances

The results of these profile applications have been brought together in Table 9.9. As we can see in the top row, presenting the per capita balances according to the baseline projection (the same figures as in the last column of Table 9.5), there is a small improvement in the negative balance over the

Table 9.9   *Public finance revenue/expenditure balance, according to scenario projections*

	Projection intervals								
	0	1	2	3	4	5	6	7	8
Baseline	− 4825	− 4772	− 4932	− 5182	− 5602	− 6019	− 6417	− 7038	− 7647
L/1.1	− 4825	− 4734	− 4846	− 5035	− 5422	− 5787	− 6131	− 6645	− 7150
L/1.3	− 4825	− 4734	− 4848	− 5038	− 5433	− 5806	− 6154	− 6676	− 7195
L/1.5	− 4825	− 4734	− 4849	− 5047	− 5445	− 5821	− 6180	− 6713	− 7233
M/1.1	− 4825	− 4696	− 4779	− 4921	− 5270	− 5596	− 5889	− 6328	− 6754
M/1.3	− 4825	− 4696	− 4780	− 4928	− 5287	− 5618	− 5926	− 6378	− 6822
M/1.5	− 4825	− 4696	− 4785	− 4937	− 5308	− 5657	− 5958	− 6428	− 6894
H/1.1	− 4825	− 4661	− 4704	− 4809	− 5125	− 5416	− 5666	− 6054	− 6423
H/1.3	− 4825	− 4661	− 4709	− 4817	− 5144	− 5449	− 5720	− 6122	− 6567
H/1.5	− 4825	− 4661	− 4715	− 4832	− 5170	− 5485	− 5770	− 6200	− 6601

first projection interval. Analysis of the profile components shows that in this first projection interval changes in the age structure are favorable, especially through proportional shifts favoring the adult categories that bring in the highest per capita age-specific revenues. The numbers in Table 9.9 reveal that this short-term positive age structure effect will be greater, and persist over a longer period, as net immigration increases. Apparently, the assumed young age structure of immigrants contributes to the persistence of this short-term positive effect: under the low net immigration assumption for one five-year projection interval only, under the medium net immigration assumption for two intervals, and under the high net immigration assumption for three intervals. Until 2010, immigrants might cause a rejuvenation shock. They will have a positive, although modest, influence on the per capita public finance deficit, as based on the components included in the profiles, the higher their numbers get. After this temporary rejuvenation effect has faded away, in all scenario projections the per capita public finance deficit resumes a course of gradual increase, as in the baseline projection. Analysis of the separate profile components shows that, even under the high net immigration assumption, ongoing positive effects on the deficit stemming from continuing young net immigrant streams can no longer compensate for the simultaneous negative effects of ongoing aging, occurring predominantly, but not exclusively, in the sub-population of natives.

However, sustained immigration does have some lasting compensating effects. As the net immigration amount is much more important than the native/non-native fertility convergence, all scenarios lead to mounting but less deep per capita balance deficits than is the case in the baseline projection. The higher the net sustained number of immigrants, the more the per capita baseline projection deficits will be reduced. The more non-native fertility converges toward native fertility, the greater a small extra reduction will occur. This fertility effect runs counter to the net immigration amount effect, since less convergence of fertility in the fast increasing non-native subpopulation means relatively more children and young adults, who in the revenue/expenditure profile 'cost' much more than they 'bring in.'

Discussion

Studies of the possible economic impact of immigration tend to focus on the costs of immigrants that have to be paid from the public coffers. Immigrants, however, also contribute to the public coffer by way of taxes and social security premiums. Since the balance of these revenues and expenditures is very much age- and sex-specific, it is not self-evident that this balance will always be negative, as is often suggested. In this chapter, different demographic scenarios of future immigration have been worked out for the Netherlands. In nine projections, three different assumptions on the future size of net immigration have been systematically crossed against three different assumptions about the degree of convergence in fertility of non-native women and native women. Age- and sex-specific public finance revenue/expenditure profiles were applied to the results of these demographic scenarios in order to assess the possible net impact of immigration on public finance. The results show that immigration can have a positive influence on the per capita balance of public finance revenues and expenditures, by way of making this balance less negative than it would otherwise be according to a no-immigration baseline projection. However, this influence is modest and by far insufficient to compensate for the lasting effects of continuous population aging.

The approach employed here also has its shortcomings. First, the profiles are not complete, either on the revenue side or on the expenditure side. But they do contain the majority of cash flows and in-kind benefits exchanged between households and the government budget, particularly that part of the flows most susceptible to demographic change. Inclusion of the few remaining components will alter the specific deficit amounts as mentioned in Table 9.9, but will not invalidate the general conclusions.

Second, there is the inevitable *ceteris paribus* clause. Such a caveat is inevitable because the data available do not lend themselves to distinguishing between the volume aspect and the level-of-payment aspect in each profile component. If such a distinction could be made, one could run other scenarios on the basis of extra assumptions concerning the future course of unemployment, school enrollment, etc. This study assumes that all these important determinants of the current age- and sex-specific revenue and expenditure levels in the profile will remain constant in the future. Although such an assumption probably makes little difference as far as between-scenario comparisons are concerned, the assumption as such might be essentially unrealistic. For example, it is very important whether future sustained immigration would increase or decrease the employment levels of non-natives. In the current persistent 'mild recession,' several subpopulations of non-Dutch origin show levels of unemployment that are higher, and in some cases much higher, than those of people of Dutch nationality. The rather strict regulations concerning education and work permits for immigrants, particularly for refugees and asylum seekers waiting for a definitive residence permit, cause many immigrants to be at least temporarily heavily dependent on social security, which raises the expenditure side of the profile. For a society that really can benefit from immigration, it looks as though such regulations should be relaxed, if not abolished. If not, continuing immigration might indeed become an economic burden.

On the other hand, such possible negative developments might be (partly) compensated for by other effects that make this *ceteris paribus* approach acceptable. Spencer[33] argues that there are cohort effects which support the hypothesis that future generations of older adults and aged people will be better educated than the current ones, that they will have more qualified and thus better-paying jobs and therefore make higher average tax contributions, benefiting the future revenue side of the profile. This scenario sounds plausible but one should not forget that these same generations will reach old age with fewer children, and more broken marriages and relationships, and therefore with smaller family and kin networks to which they can turn for care. They may therefore need higher public in-kind old age support.

Finally, the results of the analysis were presented in the form of per capita revenue/expenditure deficits. The conclusion that more immigrants lead to lower per capita public finance deficits (Table 9.9) should never divert attention from the fact that more immigrants leads to more inhabitants (Table 9.6). The product of the two is the absolute public finance deficit, and a quick glance at Tables 9.6 and 9.9 is enough to see that the absolute deficit in 2032 according to scenario H/1.5 (134 billion guilders) is much higher than that of 115 billion guilders according to the baseline projection.

Taking these caveats into account, it should also be noted that the findings of this study do not necessarily suggest that immigrants should be allowed to settle in Dutch territory because there are no public costs involved in immigration. It also does not mean that 'costs' or 'benefits,' however measured and irrespective of their balance, are the only criteria by which the desirability of further immigration should be assessed. Rather, the study demonstrates that immigrants do not bring only 'costs,' but also bring 'benefits' to the public coffer, which should increasingly be taken into account when assessing economic consequences of immigration.

Acknowledgment

The author wishes to thank Ms Evelien van der Ploeg for her helpful assistance in running the scenario projections.

Notes

1. 'If a population with an arbitrarily chosen size and age-sex composition is projected assuming fixed below-replacement fertility and a constant annual number of immigrants whose age-sex composition is held constant, the equilibrium-state outcome is a stationary population;' and 'When a population experiences both immigration and low fertility, we have seen that a kind of demographic transfusion occurs as it proceeds to a long-run stationary state. The initial population and its descendants diminish under the pressures of below-replacement fertility, to be replaced by a new population of immigrants and their descendants.' T.J. Espenshade, 'Population dynamics with immigration and low fertility,' in K. Davis, et al., (eds), Below Replacement Fertility in Industrial Societies: Causes, Consequences, Policies (New York: The Population Council, 1986), pp. 254 and 258.
2. 'The answer is that immigration can prevent an overall population decline during the first half of the 21st century, but only if, year after year, record numbers of immigrants are allowed in;' and 'Immigration is even less able to serve as a counterbalance to the effects of very low fertility on the age structure.' See R. Lesthaeghe, H. Page and J. Surkyn, Are Immigrants Substitutes for Births? (Brussels: Free University, 1988), p. 21.
3. A. Kuijsten, 'The impact of migration streams on the size and structure of the Dutch population,' in S. Voets, J. Schoorl and B. de Bruijn (eds), Demographic Consequences of International Migration (The Hague: NIDI Report No. 44, 1995), pp. 283–305.
4. P. Findl, R. Holzmann and R. Münz, Bevölkerung und Sozialstaat: Szenarien bis 2050 (Wien: Manzsche Verlags- und Universitätsbuchhandlung, 1987), pp. 54–5, 57–61 and 63.
5. M.V. George F. Nault and A. Romaniuc, 'Effects of fertility and international migration on the changing age composition of Canada,' in ECE (ed.), Changing Population Age Structures, 1990–2015 (Geneva: United Nations, 1992), pp. 260–71.
6. G. Steinmann, 'Immigration as a remedy for birth dearth: the case of West Germany,' in W. Lutz (ed.), Future Demographic Trends in Europe and North America: What Can We Assume Today (London: Academic Press, 1991), p. 355.
7. D.A. Ahlburg and W.J. Vaupel, 'Immigration and the dependency burden,' in IUSSP (ed.), International Population Conference, Montreal 1993 (Liége: IUSSP, 1993), pp. 61–71.

8. See W.J. Ethier, 'International trade and labor migration,' *American Economic Review*, 74, 4 (1985), 691–707.

9. Aristide R. Zolberg, 'The next waves: migration theory for a changing world,' *International Migration Review*, 23, 3 (1989), 408.

10. M. Livi Bacci, 'South/North migration: a comparative approach to North American and European experiences,' paper presented at the OECD International Conference on Migration, Rome, March 13–15, 1991, pp. 8–9.

11. Aristide Zolberg, *op. cit.*, p. 410.

12. There is also, in the words of Zolberg, 'a desire to minimize the growing social tensions that may arise from the fact that transnational migration brings about the encounter of culturally different groups hitherto separated from each other in space.' Zolberg, *op cit.*, p. 411.

13. *Ibid.*, p. 412.

14. Julian Simon, *The Economic Consequences of Immigration* (Oxford: Basil Blackwell and the Cato Institute, 1989).

15. *Ibid.*, p. 31.

16. *Ibid.*, p. 46.

17. *Ibid.*, p. 168.

18. As stated by Simon, *op cit.*, pp. 9–10: 'Though the discussion is framed to apply to the US, most of the theory and much of the empirical material should apply to other developed countries as well. There are, however, some differences among countries that heavily influence the analysis and conclusions. Two examples should suffice: (1) The relative influence of family assistance for children is much greater in European countries such as West Germany than in the US. This must affect any cost–benefit analysis of additional immigrants. (2) Ethnic variation is now much greater in the US than in most other developed countries. This mostly relates to social rather than economic adjustment, but it can also affect the benefits as well as the costs of an additional person coming from a given area, e.g. the value of having an additional immigrant citizen who is a native speaker of another country's language is less for commercial purposes when there already are many such persons.'

19. See M. Livi Bacci, *op cit.*, 1991, pp. 10–14.

20. George J. Borjas, *Friends or Strangers: the Impacts of Immigrants on the US Economy* (New York: Basic Books, 1990), p. 21.

21. For exceptions, see B.B. Murphy and M.C. Wolfson, 'When the baby boom grows old: impacts on Canada's public sector,' in ECE (ed.), *Changing Population Age Structures, 1990–2015* (Geneva: United Nations, 1992), pp. 133–47; G. Spencer, 'What are the consequences of an aging United States population structure for public revenues and expenditures,' in ECE (ed.), *Changing Population Age Structures, 1990–2015* (Geneva: United Nations, 1992), pp. 186–91.

22. See Kuijsten, *op cit.*, 1995.

23. For a description, see A. Kuijsten, *Demografische Toekomstbeelden van Nederland* (Amsterdam: Planologisch en Demografisch Instituut Universiteit Amsterdam, 1989), pp. 27–33.

24. NCBS (Netherlands Central Bureau of Statistics), 'Bevolking van Nederland naar burgerlijke staat, geslacht, leeftijd en land van nationaliteit,' *NCBS-Maandstatistiek van de Bevolking*, 41, 8 (1993), 33–7.

25. See J. Muus, 'Migration, immigrants and policy in the Netherlands: recent

trends and developments,' report for the Continuous Reporting System on Migration (SOPEMI) of the Organisation for Economic Co-operation and Development (OECD), Amsterdam, 1993.

26   NCBS (Netherlands Central Bureau of Statistics), 'Overlevingstafels, 1992 en 1988–1992,' *NCBS-Maandstatistiek van de Bevolking*, 41, 12 (1993), 67–70.

27   W. Bosveld, C. Wijsen and A. Kuijsten, 'The growing importance of fertility at higher ages in the Netherlands,' paper presented at the European Population Conference 1991, Paris, October 21–25, 1991.

28   Espenshade, *op. cit.*, p. 252.

29   A. Kuijsten, *op. cit.*, 1995.

30   NCBS (Netherlands Central Bureau of Statistics), 'Buitenlandse migratie, 1988–1992,' *NCBS-Maandstatistiek van de Bevolking*, 41, 9 (1993), 49–56.

31   A. Vossen, 'Population aging and increasing public expenditure: is population policy the answer?,' *Zeitschrift für Bevölkerungswissenschaft*, 17, 1 (1991), 49–67.

32   A. Kuijsten, 1995, *op. cit.*

33   G. Spencer, 'What are the consequences of an aging United States population structure for public revenues and expenditures?' in ECE, *Changing Population Age Structures, 1990–2015* (Geneva: United Nations, 1992), pp. 186–91.

10 Ethnic business, ethnic communities, and ethno-politics among Turks in Europe

Nermin Abadan-Unat

Turkey's involvement in large-scale external migration is mainly a post Second World War phenomenon. It started with an experimental project to train 12 craftsmen, sponsored by the Chamber of Artisans of Hamburg in April 1957. In 1960 their number had reached 2700, in 1963 there were 27,500; ten years later 615,827. In 1988 there were 1,521,804 Turkish workers in Germany.[1]

After the oil crisis brought labor recruitment in all European countries to an abrupt stop during the 1970s, family reunification programs spurred the growth of the alien population. Today, there are 2.5 million officially registered Turkish workers in Europe, of which 1.8 million are living in Germany.[2] Although at the beginning of the 1980s receiving countries attempted to encourage repatriation through financial incentives, the results were only partially successful. In Germany these special incentives encouraged in 1983 about 100,388 and in 1984 another 213,469 migrants to move back to Turkey. However, the instability of the Turkish economy, coupled with the authoritarian political climate, quickly caused the return flow to decline. In 1990, only 35,635 persons returned, while 84,346 Turks obtained the permission to settle in Germany as family members. The fact remains that the number of migrants from Turkey in Europe continues to rise through family reunification, asylum applications, illegal migration, and births. This trend is confirmed by statistical data: while there is a gradual decrease in the population of migrant workers coming from Mediterranean countries, the stock of Turks shows the largest increase. Their population showed an increase of 93,500 (19 percent) in Germany in 1990, followed by Italians with 27,200 (13.5 percent).[3]

The stabilization of the Turkish migrant population at high levels has also caused a significant change in the official vocabulary. In the 1950s foreign workers were labeled as 'guestworkers' (*Gastarbeiter*). The word 'guest' emphasized the provisional character of their employment. Gradually, they became 'foreign workers' (*ausländische Arbeitnehmer*); after a substantial increase in recent years, some Germans started to speak about 'foreign population' (*ausländische Wohnbevölkerung*), to be followed in parliamentary debates by the concept of 'foreign co-citizen' (*ausländischer Mitbürger*), which underplayed the fragility of their legal rights. Finally, nowadays the written press often speaks about the 'hyphenated German' (*Bindestrich-Deutsche*), a pejorative term indicating a certain amount of discrimination and unwillingness to incorporate the aliens. Growing racism and xenophobia following the reunification has created a sharper distinction between natives, ethnic Germans, EU members, and the 'rest,' an expression used by the former German Chancellor, Helmut Schmidt.[4] By contrast, international bodies such as the Council of Europe are inclined to recognize the emergence of a multiethnic or multicultural society.[5]

Changing paradigms

These demographic trends also brought relevant changes in the field of academic research. While the 1960s were mainly preoccupied with the evaluation of economic cost–benefit effects, the 1970s focused on modalities of assimilation, adaptation, and integration. From the 1980s onward, more emphasis was placed on the formation of ethnic enclaves, collective organizations, and the interaction of immigrants with the host country. The watershed of 1989 which saw the beginning of the collapse of the communist regimes introduced a number of new paradigms into Western European thinking. The crisis of modernity, articulated in the form of looking for new societal models, the growth of transnational organizations, and the dismantling of nation states, as in the case of former Yugoslavia, Czechoslovakia, and the demise of the Soviet Union, accelerated the debate about communal conflicts. The expansion of markets and improved communication increased contacts and generated competition among communal groups. This competition affected the attitudes of immigrants and resulted in a mobilization of self-initiatives, collective organizations, ideological, ethnic, and religious networks. Such complex processes no doubt found a repercussion in the conceptualization of scientific research. They are reflected in the ongoing debate between two major currents of thought: equilibrium (behavioristic) and historical-structural (conflict) schools.

Analytical frameworks based on macro-level theories have focused on economic forces and shifting market needs.[6] Economists like Piore have substantially dealt with the emergence of 'dual markets.'[7] Social scientists have emphasized global and systematic adjustments such as restructuring stratification in the case of population imbalances.[8] Such systematic analysis embraces both sending and receiving societies and assumes that a two-way adjustment leads to a temporary equilibrium.

Researchers preferring the micro-level approaches take definable groups as a starting point. They attempt to inquire into the modalities which eventually lead to assimilation. In order to explain partial assimilation they use concepts such as 'cultural pluralism.'[9] Others focus on non-integration. According to one interpretation, immigrant groups become an 'underclass,' in Marxian terms.[10] A different interpretation maintains that these groups constitute the basis of a truly multicultural society, where ethnic variation is honored and encouraged.[11] Viewing labor migration as integral to uneven development has a very important secondary implication. It indicates that movements of labor and capital are bound up with class struggles and subject to control mechanisms of the state in the receiving country.[12] This explains why in recent years issues such as the political behavior of immigrants have increasingly attracted the attention of researchers.[13]

Other aspects of migration, such as the impact of ethnic communities and their political or religious organizations on the home country specifically, and on international relations in general, have entered the realm of migration studies. Thus migration suddenly introduces international legal and political considerations into the process, which had until very recently been based on state institutions.[14] In recent years, studies conducted in the discipline of international relations and political science have revealed that the rising demands of ethnic communities and/or acts of violence have deep-seated effects on both the host country and the sending country. As a by-product of migration, racism, xenophobia, and discrimination not only are producing polarization, but are interrelated as well. These studies are closely linked to a reevaluation of the concepts of citizenship and nationality. Finally, the increasing importance of refugee studies and the implementation of international conventions and treaties based on the concept of human rights have provoked a constant articulation of minority rights and demands for recognition of identity rights of migrants, such as in the case of Islamic organizations of Asians in the UK, Maghrebians in France, and Turks in Europe, as well as the nationalist/secessionist demands of Kurdish immigrants and asylum seekers.

Thus one may state, as Abdelmalek Sayad defines it, that with the 'settlement of immigrants into an indefinable provisional,'[15] new phenomena gain weight and deserve to be investigated separately. The three most important new developments, which have been partly created by the segmentation of the labor market,[16] citizenship granting or denying policies of the host country, the spatial concentration or 'ghettoization' of immigrants,[17] and the political demands oriented toward the host and home country are as follows: immigrant enclaves and ethnic business; ethnic communities acting as mini-states; ethnopolitics, meaning radical politization of immigrants' associations, affecting international relations. The purpose of this chapter is to attempt to analyze some of these trends on the basis of the options adopted and initiatives implemented by the Turkish diaspora.

Ethnic business

Utilizing Piore's conceptual framework based on a 'dual labor market,' it is relatively easy to find, in almost all European urban areas with a high density of migrants, ethnic enclaves that tend to foster and encourage an economy of small tradesmen which offers immigrant laborers temporary, unattractive jobs, coupled with menial status and lower wages. Metropolitan cities with pronounced Turkish districts, such as Berlin with Kreuzberg, Wedding, Tiergarten, and Neuköln, Brussels, with S. Josse, and Paris, with Strasbourg-S. Denis, are striking examples of spatial concentration which combines settlement and economic activities. In Paris the centers of '*haute couture*' and 'ready made wear' are benefiting from the cheap and often illegal labor force, working at home or in sweat shops. Such economic activities are producing a large number of ethnic businesses which qualify as 'niches.' These niches defy adaptation. Instead of embarking on a road from initial economic hardship and discrimination to eventual socio-economic mobility, they offer immediate job opportunities based on kinship ties and communal solidarity. Here, a pattern emerges of selective assimilation based on individuals participating partly in the native culture. This pattern permits them to fully practice the customs of their homeland and speak the language of their original culture. The only compulsory requirement is to comply with the rules and regulations of the host country. In other words, 'ethnic enclaves' which enable the flourishing of ethnic business are examples for neither 'melting pot' nor 'salad bowl' models. Ethnic enclaves represent a different mode of adaptation.

Here, first-generation immigrant groups, preserving their culture, identity, and internal solidarity, are able to achieve economic success without any evidence of acculturation. In milieus with a sufficient number of immigrants of a given ethnic group and with sufficient supplies of capital and labor, ethnic business finds an appropriate climate to flourish. In such milieus new immigrants as well as second- or third-generation youth with poor educational records can thrive despite scant knowledge of the host culture and language. The examples given by Portes with regard to Koreatown in Los Angeles and Chinatown in San Francisco can be enlarged by citing 'Little Istanbul' in Berlin, where Turks in possession of a work and residence permit or in collaboration with a 'straw boss' have created a segmented market primarily based on food, vegetables, fruit, and restaurants, which also permits undocumented illegal migrants to find provisional employment opportunities. A study carried out in 1984 by Wilpert and Gitmez revealed that in Kreuzberg, where about a quarter of the Berlin Turks live, 12 percent of the enterprises were in the hands of Turks and as much as 40 percent of the service sector was in Turkish ownership.[18] A more recent study indicates that in Germany about 33,000 self-employed Turks have created about 125,000 job opportunities in 55 subsections. Although these businesses were scattered in various fields, food distribution, food catering, and mending and repair shops were the main focus. Food sales and fast food restaurants accounted for 37.8 and 17.6 percent respectively.[19]

Since the overwhelming majority of Turks are employed in manufacturing industries such as machine tools, motor vehicles, electronics, plastics, and construction services, the relevance of ethnic business is not so much related to job opportunities, but lies in the basis it constitutes for the setting up of collective organizations and eventually 'cultural' associations – which pursue home-oriented political goals. Turkish business in Berlin started with door to door sales of packaged foods, first to workers' dormitories, later in the form of home delivery. The predominant concern was to be able to obtain safe halal meat, which helped Turks enter commerce. This type of trade quickly spread all over Germany, especially to Munich, Stuttgart, and Frankfurt/Main, and concentrated on meat. It was followed by the import of canned foods from Turkey. Subsequently, Turkish music tapes and videocassettes were produced and imported from Turkey. But the real turning point occurred when large-scale chain stores were established. This permitted traditionally oriented entrepreneurs to establish close links with the home country. Between 1978 and 1984, for example, several wholesale Islamic business firms, such as Helal Gıda, Elif Gıda, and Hicret, took root in Germany.[20] These important religious-commercial chains established a variety of activities in addition to the distribution and sale of food items.

The large firms provide community services, such as travel agencies, funeral transportation to the home country, Koran courses, and sport clubs. As Wilpert and Gitmez observed,[21] if one so desired, it would be possible to fulfill most of one's needs for commercial and social relations within the Islamic community, avoiding all contact with non-Muslims.

The business chains also became the arena for the religious and political struggles of various Islamic factions. While Elif and Helal attempted to expand their influence by adopting the 'national outlook' (Millî Görüş), thus becoming a grassroot organization of the National Salvation Party (MSP) in Turkey, a late comer, the Hicret group, stretched its aspirations further. With its more fundamentalist orientation this group approached the Islamic Bank in Saudi Arabia and secured some credit. Although the mismanagement and bankruptcy of the group lead to its dissolution, such economic–ideological connections did not vanish from the scene.

At present, in almost all European countries with a significant spatial concentration of Turks, such as Germany, France, the Netherlands, Belgium, Denmark, and Sweden, there are various types of ethnic business centers. No doubt the emergence and successful implantation of former migrants or small businessmen with limited savings, capital, and know-how in developed economies must be acknowledged as a positive achievement and can serve as a model of high personal motivation or effective interdependence. Nevertheless, ethnic business represents a specific 'niche' and as such can be utilized as a bridge for the propagation of political programs or politicized religious worldviews. As witnessed in a significant number of countries, the growth of political Islam is substantially influenced by the economic infrastructure built up by ethnic business, which enables a close contact with its followers in foreign countries.

A recent hotly debated issue can serve as a good example. Prior to the local elections in Turkey on March 27, 1994, Turkish public opinion was surprised to find out that the chairman of the Welfare Party, Necmettin Erbakan, managed to obtain a special contingent of visas for 5000 pilgrims wishing to go to Mecca. Since Saudi Arabia has adopted a policy according to which each Muslim country is allocated a fixed quota for its potential pilgrims – the ceiling for Turkey being fixed at 60,000 – this exceptional grant created substantial discussion. Erbakan explained that this permission was given 'in order to enable Turkish workers and their families living in Europe to fulfill their religious obligations. This was a pure act of compassion and selfless love for my compatriots.'[22] In reality, travel agencies based in Germany and Turkey, such as the Miraç Co., charged each pilgrim $1700. The real price of such a trip was $1300, and the remaining $400 was split between the travel agencies and the Welfare Party.[23] In order to comply with the official quota, these travel agencies sent their passengers to Baku, Azerbeijan, Tehran, or Moscow and transferred them to a charter flight for Saudi Arabia.[24] This subject was discussed in great length in the Turkish parliament and resulted in the setting up of a special investigating committee.[25]

Profit sharing among firms sympathizing with the Welfare Party constitutes only one aspect of the Islam–business connection. The former Royal Holding, now M-Y GmbH, which distributes food, vegetables, fruits, and cosmetics to the congregation of about 500 mosques in Germany through Selâm GmbH, is owned by close family members of Necmettin Erbakan. The general secretary of the German Islamic Council, Ali Yüksel, who recently declared himself Grand Mufti (Head of all Muslims), assumes the duties of general director.[26] These facts indicate how close the links are between ethnic businesses, political party financing, and party leadership.

Ethnic business will no doubt continue to exist. As Sassen correctly indicates,[27] specialized and expanding service sectors in metropolitan cities held by migrant communities are structures or vehicles that maximize the benefits of individual investment. Thus, home repairs by multiple households become neighborhood upgrading, differences of language and food preferences create a captive market for ethnic shopkeepers. The expansion in the supply of low-wage jobs, particularly in global cities, can be seen as creating objective employment opportunities for immigrants even as middle-income, blue- and white-collar native workers are experiencing high unemployment. However, it should not be overlooked that expanding ethnic businesses constitute at one and the same time an important source of financing and support for political and religious associations whose focus is on the homeland. To assess ethnic business solely as a healthy sign of successful integration in the host society is a serious error. In the case of Turkish ethnic business, there is an undeniable close interdependence between lucrative commercial transactions, indoctrination through religious courses and social control over a major part of the community.

Ethnic communities

In addition to the emergence of visible ethnic enclaves involved in economic activities, ethnic communities of different size, concentration or organization are increasingly playing a determining role in the restructuring of the host society. Their willingness or refusal to integrate, the continuation of discrimination, and heightened tension between the local and foreign population eventually leads to new conflicts. From this point of view two aspects have to be examined: the parameters set by the policies of the receiving country and the composition of the migrant community. In the case of the latter, the nature of migration, spatial concentration, and ethnic and religious differences are playing a determining role. In Europe, the extensive informal networks and social institutions among the migrants, which benefit from existing democratic rights, deserve special attention. They can be partly explained by the conditions which initially triggered migration. In case of the Turkish migration, the model accepted at the beginning was built upon the premise that it would represent a 'temporary exchange of surplus labour,' based on the principle of rotation.[28] The first formal migratory wave was almost exclusively male and came predominantly from Turkey's three largest cities, Istanbul, Ankara, and Izmir, as an outgrowth of internal migration.[29] However, in Germany and other European countries migrants recruited for short stays were able to prolong their residence and were also permitted to ask for nominal recruitment of their kin, relatives, and friends. In addition, preferential treatment was given to applicants from natural disaster areas as well as members of rural development cooperatives. Since all of these factors were related to geographical conditions, it was not long before members of one single village or region were working in the same firm or living in the same city abroad. Such chain migrations, which are particularly noticeable in Scandinavian countries such as Sweden and Denmark, created social networks based on kinship bonds. Wilpert and Gitmez cite some striking cases of such chain migrations: 35 families consisting of 180 people from a few villages of Central East Anatolia (Malatya), 100 families from a single village of Erzincan with about 550 people, and over 250 non-Muslim Kurdish families of about 1850 members from South Eastern Turkey (Siirt).[30]

Similar conditions are cited by Köksal and Alpay in Sweden,[31] where almost half of the Turkish migrants living in Rinkeby, Stockholm, came from Kulu and its adjoining villages, a district of the Turkish province of Konya. Participation in chain migration not only permits the reconstruction of family and village networks abroad, but also permits the distant village community to exercise a certain social control abroad. Informal affiliations and ties are utilized effectively for the survival, socio-economic mobility, and mutual help of all sorts. This close relationship, however, instead of encouraging migrants to widen their horizons and adopt new orientations, leads them to claim identities based on regional, cultural, or religious affiliation. The claim for identity reveals itself mostly at the establishment of a new family. Sharp distinctions are drawn between Turks and Kurds, Alewites and Sunnis. Members of the same ethnic group but from another sect do not marry each other. Even today, prearranged marriages are prevalent. Case studies carried out in France illustrate this tendency. Riva Kastoryanu investigated three different Turkish communities in France: Bellegarde, Metz, and the district of Strasbourg-S. Denis in Paris.[32] Bellegarde is a small town of 11,690 inhabitants in the department of l'Ain. Turks are the fourth largest foreign community. The Turkish population of 554 persons lives in a couple of streets of the old city. They have organized themselves and have succeeded in establishing strong solidarity bonds. According to the social workers, they constitute a 'universe in itself, difficult to penetrate.'

In Metz, a city of medium size with 120,000 inhabitants, there are about 3000 Turks. Here 200 Turkish families live in low-cost housing complexes (HLM) of the district Borny-Metz, near the Citroën factory. Their spatial concentration reflects the profile of a modern ghetto. The visibility of their presence underlines the Turkishness of their lifestyle. The women, knitting in front of their apartment buildings or shredding wool from sheep skin, wear their traditional costumes and diffuse information about their families. The men in their free time visit the coffee house around the corner. The three grocery shops sell halal meat.

Thus, a setting shaped in accordance with the rural milieu from which these migrants come has been faithfully reproduced. The findings of Yıldız Sertel in another Turkish community in France, Chamards in the town of Dreux, confirms this tendency.[33] In both Bellegarde and Borny-Metz the intensity of the social relations among the immigrants prevents a more intensive interaction with the host society and reinforces the isolated lifestyle. However, in this case, due to the diversity of the ethnic origin of the community, there is a polarization between the associations created. For one part of these associations, religious issues carry the greatest importance, for others social and cultural aspects are more relevant. Thus a sharp divergence in the discourse of these associations hints at their different ideological orientations. The leaders of the associations try to enforce claims for a national or religious identity with a special accent on 'Turkishness' or 'Kurdishness.'[34] The question of whether they are part of the working class or only represent a sub-proletariat is a subject specifically studied by Gallissot et al.[35]

In Paris and its Turkish district S. Denis, the prevailing strong social control encountered in Bellegarde and Metz has vanished; instead 'ethnic business' is replacing the close ties of a spatially concentrated ethnic community. In this case, the Turkish labor force is concentrated in the various sweatshops attached to the 'haute couture' and 'ready made wear' sections of the fashion industry. Only half of the Turkish workers (48 percent) actually live and work in the district; others are scattered through the outskirts of Paris. However, the geographic distance among the members of the Turkish community has not affected sociability among the families, though the network of relations here is much more complex. In Bellegarde and Metz, Turkish associations also undertake initiatives which contribute to integration, such as seeking solutions to the educational problems of the second generation, but in Paris the ethnic enclave carries an outspoken economic character. Turks living in the French capital benefit from the anonymity of a metropolitan city and make and secure a sharp distinction between their private and public life. They are eager to retain their culture and identity at home, but are careful not to enter into conflict with their employers. In terms of political activities, instead of trying to influence governmental policies of the receiving country, the existing associations remain cloistered in the ideology they are defending. Their political action is almost exclusively oriented toward the home country or international forums such as the Council of Europe or the UN. In recent years, there has been a revival of ethnic nationalism or politicized ethnicity as well as a search for identity based on religious affiliation.

Social scientists have attempted to analyze bonds within ethnic communities. Clifford Geertz has defined them as 'primordial attachments,' meaning that cognity of blood ties, speech, and custom produces overpowering coerciveness.[36] Other social scientists define these bonds as situational or structural.[37] Either one of these concepts permits us to understand better the conflicts between different ethnic groups within existing or reorganized nation states and also the manifold activities and organizations constructed by migrant communities. In the last case the determining factors are the governmental policies adopted by the host countries, such as exclusion or inclusion of foreigners, the formal recognition or denial of ethnic minorities, the support furnished by local/national governmental organizations, the interdependence with political formations of the home country, the moral support furnished by the international community, and the dynamics of the ethnic groups. Considering that migrant communities are bound to remain in an asymmetric relationship toward the host country, it seems appropriate to investigate first the possibilities available for Turkish migrants through collective organization and associational activities.

Different patterns of collective organization among Turkish migrants

In Western societies organizing politically is a part of pluralist democracy. Immigrant groups are in fact organizing politically in order to make demands upon host countries. However, the outlook of the respective host societies toward migrant communities determines the impact of such organizational activities. In this respect the following typology can be made:

1   State-sponsored activities at national and local levels based on the recognition of 'ethnic minorities,' such as those applied in Sweden and the Netherlands.
2   State-sponsored activities, particularly at a local level, without recognition of minority status, such as those implemented in France.
3   Differential treatment of migrant associations without formal recognition, such as in Germany.
4   Migrants' associations as mouthpieces for individual demands and grievances, such as applied in Switzerland.

It is obvious that the impact of migrant communities on the shaping of public policy in the host country as well as upon the fostering of 'islands of isolation' depends largely on the types of policies adopted by the host states. Furthermore, even in the case of state-sponsored networks of support, the strong bonds of solidarity among a given group, particularly in chain migration, might not suffice to weaken such a network.

Sweden

In Sweden immigration is organized around the concept of 'ethnic minority communities.' Migrant associations are looked upon as acting as a liaison between the institutions of Swedish society and the migrant communities.[38]

Migrant associations are funded by the national government and provide formal channels of participation at the national level through consultative bodies and advisory councils. Because each nationality group is expected to be represented by a national federation, the emergence of one umbrella federation is imperative.

The Turkish Federation (TF), founded in 1977, has thirty member associations nation wide with a membership of about nine thousand. In 1988, the TF had a budget of 2 million Swedish Kronor (SK) or US$344,448. In addition, government subsidies are given for special projects, such as aiding migrant women and youth. The religious associations of migrants follow the same organizational model. The Swedish Muslim Association (SMA) works closely with the TF. Furthermore, Swedish immigration authorities sponsor for all new immigrants language programs, covering 240 hours, dispensed during working hours. Illiterate Turkish women are also offered literacy courses. Although the overwhelming majority of Turkish migrants attend these courses, open and disguised segregation processes in the labor market and the allocation of housing in communities with a large concentration of Turks have produced 'Ghettos in a welfare society,' such as Rinkeby in Stockholm, analyzed in detail by Sema Köksal.[39] Paradoxically, a sheltered and protected lifestyle in a well organized society, while facilitating adjustment into a new culture, actually hinders integration. The cultivation of traditional values continues, particularly in migrant centers of the lower-income class.

The Netherlands

The Dutch political system, known as the *Verzuiling* system, is based on a vertical structuring of interest groups in all spheres of public life and requires cooperation among different confessional/secular groups. In 1980, this tradition inspired the Dutch government to officially adopt a new policy, labelled as 'multiethnic.' It comprised three major goals: to promote the development and the emancipation of ethnic communities, to promote equality in the legal field, and to improve the economic and social position of ethnic communities.[40]

The first goal emphasized the group rather than the individual. In this sense the teaching of the mother tongue in public and private schools was encouraged. In addition, it enabled the creation of private schools of whatever religious denomination, these schools being totally subsidized by the state. Thus in recent years about twenty Islamic and a few Hindu schools have been established. At present there are two Islamic Turkish primary schools in Rotterdam. Furthermore, parallel to the Swedish model, consultative assemblies for the majority groups were established on both local and national levels. The creation of immigrant associations was also sponsored by the state.

The second goal being equality before the law, members of ethnic minorities with a residence of over five years in the Netherlands were given the right to vote at local elections. As a result of the enlargement of political rights at the local election of 1990, 36 Turks were elected to municipal assemblies.[41] The third goal of the multiethnic policy was the insertion of ethnic minorities into the economic and social mainstream society. This goal was not achieved, particularly with regard to unemployment: Turks at 21 percent and Moroccans at 36 percent unemployed were strongly excluded from the labor market. Due to the restructuring of the national economy, employment opportunities for minorities have diminished.

After ten years of practice, it became evident that a paternalistic attitude toward ethnic minorities, based more on social aid than economic participation, results in the marginalization of some migrant groups. This induced the Scientific Council to adopt a new plan in 1989. Based on economic and social integration, the new plan abandons the cultivation of minority languages and cultures and leaves these to the initiative of the members of the respective ethnic group.[42]

At present the Turkish Advisory Council, consisting of about ten federations and associations, participates in the work of the National Advisory Council. The existing framework obliges a collaboration between the Turkish Islamic associations and the various political and civic Turkish associations. However, cooperation between migration issue oriented associations and others is mainly limited to the leadership, and there is not much interaction among the members of these associations. Nevertheless, all these associations are invited to present advisory reports on major governmental legislative proposals. In 1986 to 1987, six out of 14 were taken into account.[43]

France

The French political system, built upon the concept of the unitary nation state, represented a 'refugee and immigration friendly' country with a 'neutral' policy approach until recently. However, the rapid rise of the rightist, anti-immigration *Front National* party of Jean Marie Le Pen, which obtained over 11 percent of the votes in 1983, caused an important change in the French nationality law. While previously citizenship, based on *jus soli* (place of birth), was automatically granted to the second generation, at present it only constitutes an optional right once the age of 18 has been reached. The official immigration policy has not changed since the beginning of the twentieth century. It is based on a categorical refusal to recognize 'ethnic communities.' Instead, it facilitates the social integration of migrants by creating diverse social service networks at the local level and encouraging associational activities. However, the rapid arrival of large numbers of Muslim migrants – at present there are about three million in France – led to the emergence of organized Islamic communities using their religious affiliation as a bargaining power. This led, as Leveau succinctly remarks, 'to a collapse of the French system.' The immigrants' felt need to mobilize their communities and to accentuate their pressure on the central government increases their tendency to resort to the expression of cultural and religious identities. That strategy comes into conflict with the constitutional principle of state secularism.[44]

Migrant initiatives proved to be very effective. First in 1973, on the occasion of a protest against rent increases at publically funded low-cost housing sites, workers from Turkey and the Maghreb started to negotiate with the managing company, Sunacotra. As a result, the company endorsed the workers' demands and converted TV and game rooms of these buildings into praying rooms, first in Bobigny-Paris, and later in other places with heavy Muslim worker concentrations. As Keppel notes, 'housing authorities tried to make amends for economic deprivation with spiritual compensation!'[45] The next step was taken in 1976, when the Maoist faction of the CGT (federation of French trade unions), in order to widen its membership, secured the installation of prayer rooms in the factory of Renault at Billancourt during Ramadan. This time, Islamic demands were granted at the workplace in order to assure social peace. Finally, in the mid-1980s, due to the mobilizing efforts of the *Harkis* – young Algerians born in France, who are thus French citizens – municipal authorities were compelled to permit the construction of mosques. Backed by the financial aid of the Islamic international missionary organization Jama'at al Tabligh and some French church organizations, they were able to implant 'one thousand and one mosques in France and emerge as a social partner!'

There is no doubt that these developments affected the Turkish migrants greatly. In 1966, Turkey signed a bilateral agreement with France. Prior to the agreement in 1962 there were only 111 Turkish workers registered. Their number rose to 50,860 by 1975. At the last census in 1991 they had reached 240,000.[46] The fast growth of Islam in France exercised its impact on the associational activities of the Turkish community. Similarly, in Germany, while the ideologically oriented political associations enjoyed the support of individual contributions and private international organizations, and are still exclusively oriented toward Turkey, a semi-official French institution, the *Fonds d'Action Sociales* (FAS), anxious to create a counterbalance against the proliferation of Turkish Islamic associations, decided to subsidize leftist, secular, and socio-cultural associations. This induced some of these associations to take a more active part in discussing governmental policies and open the way to integration.[47] But in other cases, ethnic, religious, rightist organizations transformed themselves into 'cultural' associations in order to qualify for financial help. At present there are 76 in Paris, 51 in Strasbourg, 17 in Marseille, 59 in Lyon, and in all France a total of 203 associations.[48] These associations are constantly in the process of formation, dissolution, and remaking. While political/religious affinities draw them to the Welfare Party in Turkey, ethnic affinities cause them to break away. Kurds claim a separate ethno-national identity. Anxious to underline the 'Turkishness' or 'Kurdishness' of their members, they call themselves either 'Association des travailleurs turcs' (Association of Turkish Workers) or 'Association des travailleurs de Turquie' (Association of workers from Turkey). Thus associative activities are reconstructing political identities, developed and redefined in exile. At present, the most powerful associations in France are the Kurdish ones and the Islamic Union, which is an unofficial branch of the Welfare Party in Turkey. Both are oriented toward Turkey. The other local associations are rather instrumental; their function consists of creating a framework for rapid entry to French society.

Germany

More than thirty years have elapsed since Turkey signed its first bilateral agreement for the 'export of surplus workforce' with Germany on October 10, 1961.[49] While in 1961 their number was barely 7000, they reached 1,854,945 by 1992 and, at 28.5 percent, became the largest group of foreigners in Germany.[50] Although the number of foreigners in Germany has continued to rise over the years – 22.7 percent in 1980, 28.2 percent in 1990 – the Federal Republic adamantly refuses to be qualified as an 'immigration' country. This explains its refusal to grant foreigners the right to vote at local elections. Naturalization procedures are also slow: in 1992 only 1184 Turks were naturalized in Germany, while in France 14,773 Turks became French citizens.[51] These figures underline the major goals of German immigration policy: to give priority for German citizenship to ethnic Germans from East Europe, to acknowledge free movement and settlement only to citizens of the EU, and to admit asylum seekers in conformity with the amended article 16 of the German Constitution.

Although there are advisory councils and aliens' assemblies, in essence these are not officially considered as bargaining partners. These characteristics explain why associative activities in Germany have developed very differently from in Sweden and the Netherlands. Turkish associations in Germany, at present numbering 1341, are fragmented and highly politicized. A breakdown indicates Münster (203), Stuttgart (179), Berlin (159), and Munich (131) as cities with a high concentration of associational life.[52] It also has to be added that while there are federal funds for the integration of migrants, they are not allocated to umbrella organizations. Funding can only be obtained at the local level. Thus collective initiatives depend to a large extent on individual contributions and financial support from other Islamic countries.

Turkish associations are pursuing two divergent paths. A significant group of migrants with a prolonged residence in Germany[53] continuously fight for political rights and dual citizenship. These efforts are backed by the integration-friendly 'Euro Turks.' However, the majority of Turkish associations represent nationalist, cultural enclaves with a minimal interest in German society. In particular, radical organizations with religious, ethnic, and radical right or leftist outlooks cast a different profile. The aggressive tone of the leadership indicates their unwillingness to establish a peaceful dialogue with the host society. This segment of the Turkish diaspora looks exclusively toward Turkey. It rallies around organizations with extreme rightist, nationalist, or leftist orientation, Islamic organizations devoted to a change of power in Turkey, or ethnic organizations such as the Kurdish association, which collaborates with terrorist organizations and harbors secessionist objectives. The growth of such associations that refuse integration has been partly influenced by the rise of racism and xenophobia after German reunification and the growth of asylum seekers. A brief look at the various Turkish associations gives the following picture.

Para-political associations

Extreme right-nationalist organizations

The Federation for the Turkish Idealist Associations of Europe (ATÜDF). This federation takes its roots from the neo-Fascist National Worker's Party (MÇP) of the 1970s, which established a number of local chapters in 1973 in Kempten. Following the violent, aggressive acts of its youth branch, the 'Grey Wolves,' these chapters were dissolved following a ban on the establishment of branches of foreign political parties in Germany. However, this ban was overcome by the establishment of a variety of associations such as the Greater Ideal Association (Büyük Ülkü Derneği), the Turkish Community (Türk Cemaati), and Turkish students and youth associations (Türk-Genç). All these associations became united under one umbrella to constitute the Federation of Turkish Idealist Associations in Europe (Avrupa Türk Ülkücü Dernekleri Federasyonu, ATÜDF). With its center in Frankfurt, it boasts 170 member associations in Germany. The federation cooperates closely with the renamed rightist party of Alparslan Türkeş, the National Action Party. The ideology of this federation is based on extreme nationalism which rejects integration in order to prevent Turks becoming a 'secondary race.'[54]

Leftist organizations

The largest of these is the Federation of Migrants' Associations (Göçmen Dernekleri Federasyonu, or GDF). This federation incorporates the membership of the dissolved Federation of Workers Associations (Isçi Dernekleri Federasyonu, or FIDF), which was cooperating closely with the Turkish Labor Party in Turkey. The GDF has about 60 local chapters and some 15,000 members. This federation has an orthodox Marxist orientation. Since 1988 its influence has diminished.[55]

Ethnic organizations: Komkar and Birkom

The large number of Turkish workers of Kurdish origin – an estimated 450,000 out of 1.8 million – in Germany produced a significant growth of ethnic associations. While a large number of splinter groups dominated by radical Alewites and Kurds, anxious to dissociate themselves from the 'schematic' leftists, have created independent associations such as the Federation of Democratic Workers Association (DIDF), the largest Kurdish organization in Germany is the Association of Kurdish Workers for Kurdistan, Komkar. This separatist federation has a large network in Europe, aims to develop collective consciousness, and wants to see an independent Kurdish state in southeast Turkey. Another Kurdish separatist and militant association is Birkom. Established by those who left Turkey in 1980 and who were close supporters of Abdullah Öcalan, Apo, leader of the secessionist guerilla group PKK, it is also not interested in integration. It is solely an organization for fomenting future rebellion and claiming to be a legitimate nationalist organization. Recently, the decision of some European governments to declare this group's efforts as 'terrorist action' caused serious clashes in Germany.[56] Following the lifting of the parliamentary immunity of pro-Kurdish deputies and their incarceration in Turkey, PKK supporters in Europe, particularly in Germany, blocked highways, set themselves on fire, and caused public unrest, urging the German government to suspend all military assistance to Turkey.

Religious and religious–political associations

Islamic Cultural Centers (Islam Kültür Merkezleri, or IKMB)

At the end of the 1970s and early 1980s, this organization represented the largest religious movement in Germany. Backed by the followers of the Süleymanlı sect, whose founder Süleyman Hilmi Tunahan (1888 to 1959) fought in the 1920s and 1930s against Atatürk's secular reforms, this umbrella organization has its center in Cologne. In the 1980s, the organization controlled about 210 mosques, each with a congregation of approximately 300 members. At present the IKMB claims to have 20,000 registered members and 60,000 sympathizers. The most important characteristic of this organization is its negative attitude toward integration. It evaluates school subjects such as music, art and sport as 'un-Islamic' and prohibits all contact with 'infidel' foreigners.[57]

The National Vision Organization of Europe (AMGT)

Established in 1976 as a branch of the National Salvation Party of Turkey – which dissolved in 1980, and then reemerged as the present Welfare Party – this organization is also headquartered in Cologne. With 30,000 registered and about 85,000 sympathizers, the organization currently represents the most powerful Turkish religious organization in Europe. The political agenda of this federation is to fight all modernization and westernization. All attempts at integration are defined as treason toward Islam. Any interaction with non-Muslims is discouraged; an intensive missionary activity focuses on the establishment of Koran courses. The federation vigorously supports the Turkish newspaper *Millî Gazete*, the leading news outlet for the Welfare Party in Turkey, also published in Germany. The AGMT implements elite training and offers generous scholarships for eligible Turkish students studying in Germany. The chairman of the Welfare Party, Erbakan, who is a professor of engineering who studied at German universities, utilizes the federation for his political agenda during his frequent visits to Europe.[58] The findings of a special investigating committee of the Turkish parliament indicate that 5.9 million Deutschmarks which had originally been collected as a special fund for the Bosnia-Hercegovina relief work went to the private account of Mr Mercümek, a member of the Welfare Party headed by Erbakan.[59]

The Union of Islamic Associations and Communities (ICCB)

This association, established in 1984 by Cemalettin Kaplan, represents a dissenting wing of the National Vision Association. Until 1980, Kaplan was a civil servant at the Turkish Directorate of Religious Affairs in Adana. After his move to Germany, he was suspended from his official duties because of his anti-secular and fundamentalist views. After losing his Turkish nationality, he became 'homeless,' settled down in Cologne and started to build up his own organization. Strongly influenced by the Iranian model and Ayatollah Khomeini's teachings, Kaplan's association advocates the creation of an Islamic Turkish Republic. In a self-drafted constitution, he pleads for the reintroduction of the *Sharia* and the replacement of the Turkish script by the Arabic alphabet. For blasphemy, he demands the death penalty. Recently Kaplan declared himself the Caliph of the Islamic World Community. The ICCB has about 3000 members and 5000 sympathizers. It has established a boarding school for youngsters aged 16 to 18, operates a food import firm and a publishing house, and produces VCR tapes and a journal called *Tebliğ*. All members are obliged to contribute 2.5 percent of their yearly income and acquire bonds at a value of 1000 Deutschmarks.

The Union of Turkish-Islamic Cultural Associations (TIKDB)

This association represents the dissenting wing of the previously discussed rightist nationalist ADÜTDF. It focuses on the preservation of the national and cultural values of the Islamic faith. Politically, it supports the Motherland Party in Turkey, a right of center party founded by Turgut Özal in 1983 and currently the ruling party in the parliament.

The Turkish Islamic Union for Religious Affairs

While the above cited Islamic organizations try to establish contacts with Turkish political parties, Türkiye Diyanet İşleri Birliği (DITIB) represents a governmental organization, created partly to counterbalance the spread of fundamentalist Islam in Germany. Linked directly to the Turkish ministry of the interior, this union is an umbrella organization embracing 700 associations with a membership of 90,000. The union functions with the support of 215 civil servants who are graduates of divinity schools.

While the influence of para-political and ethnic associations remains limited in terms of radiation, the organizational strategy extends to a much higher number of Turkish migrant families. These religious associations – which function in both Europe and Turkey – focus their activities not only on religious matters. There are activity fields for each cohort. The first generation is organized within the congregation of mosques, the second and third in sport associations, boarding schools, and Koran courses.

These associations – with the exception of the DITIB – have the same goals: to increase the political power of Islam in Turkey, to change the political system there, and to reorganize private and public life according the rules of Islam. The Koran courses have been widely discussed in Germany. When the curriculum was made public, it showed militant, nontolerant Islam. This creates more problems with regard to coeducation. The wearing of scarves – in France and also in Belgium – transforms itself into a debate about the freedom of worshipping versus the freedom to develop one's personality. Parents refuse to allow their daughters to participate in swimming lessons and class tours. Gender segregation in all walks of life is increasingly being advocated by these associations, thus contributing to a further self-imposed 'island-like' lifestyle.

Conclusion

Detailed research clearly indicates that Europe's largest non-EU immigrant population, the Turks, have passed through three new developmental phases: the expansion of ethnic business, the growing importance of collective organization forms of the ethnic community, and the fast growth of ethno-politics.

Reluctant to return to their home country, increasingly more Turks opt for self-employment. These initiatives have produced prosperous ethnic business enclaves. No doubt the presence of well organized enterprises securing new jobs for European or Turkish citizens constitutes evidence of a successful entry into the mainstream economy. Nevertheless, ethnic business mostly serves the consumers of the ethnic community. For migrants, operating within the realm of such enclaves helps to overcome social isolation. It helps to solve personal and financial problems and facilitates communication within the migrant community. In other words, ethnic business reinforces the structure of spatial or mental ghettoization. By presenting a potential labor market, such niches indirectly induce young immigrants to discontinue their vocational training. Furthermore, by being closely interlocked with religious associations, ethnic business prepares the ground to defend group interests based on religious identity. Thus, one may state that ethnic business becomes a pillar for the diffusion of political religious-tinted ideology by enabling the establishment of institutions such as Koran courses, boarding schools, and private radio and TV stations. Furthermore, ethnic business represents the cornerstone of an ethnic subculture. As a major element of religious associative organizations, it also contributes to the accentuation of polarization.

Similarly, ethnic communities living in spatially concentrated conditions, particularly in the case of chain migration embracing a large number of persons with similar origin, produce unwillingness to integrate. Varying according to the immigration policies of the host countries, the coopera-tion of immigrants with local authorities in order to obtain additional rights for the safeguarding of cultural values leads toward instrumental multi-culturalism. Such a trend might under certain circumstances reinforce a kind of *de facto* apartheid.

Finally, extreme ethno-politics based on ethnic or religious identity, particularly in the case of complex networks, prepares the ground for revolutionary actions, such as movement toward establishing a Federal Islamic Republic in Turkey or the realization of Kurdish separatist demands. In both cases, associative initiatives may end in subversive actions, violence, and armed conflicts. In such cases, immigration as a process leads to the emergence of new actors in the field of international relations.

Have these recent developments attracted sufficient attention among the academic community dealing with immigration studies? As Heisler correctly points out, new forms of migration, unusual foreign policy steps to deal with them, and fundamental shifts in global and regional international relations have converged. Considering these changes Heisler suggests an 'institutional political sociology.' Ethnic pluralism – multiculturalism, pluriculturalism, multiethnicity – have become core concepts in the current discourse on immigrant incorporation. Here, the following question arises: how far can one go in protecting particular cultural values without destroying the political community at both ends?

Another issue which deserves particular attention is the concept of social movements developed by Touraine. He argues that social change results from groups organized to promote conflict and develop alternative institutions. Following this perspective, immigrants must find their place in society as groups by organizing themselves. Here, again, the question arises: does the use of democratic rights include the right to ask for legal segregation on one side – the racist, xenophobic argument – and for changes in the borders and the political system of the home country on the other? These questions are vitally important given the fact that interdependence is constantly growing, that the claim for a more equitable citizenship will not diminish, and that the state of the law will not permit the denial to fundamental rights.

Notes

1. For 1960, 1963, and 1973 see Nermin Abadan-Unat, *Turkish Workers in Europe, 1960–1975: A Balance Sheet of Achievement and Failures* (Leiden: E.J. Brill, 1976), p. 13; for 1988 see United Nations, *International Migration: Regional Processes and Responses* (New York: United Nations, 1994), p. 23, table 1.2.
2. The breakdown of Turkish citizens working or living in Europe is as follows: 1,854,945 in Germany, 248,656 in the Netherlands, 240,000 in France, 150,000 in Austria, 84,935 in Belgium, 37,000 in Denmark, 65,000 in the UK, 10,000 in Norway, 50,000 in Sweden, 73,024 in Switzerland. Ministry of Labor (*Çalisma Bakanlığı ve Sosyal Güvenlik Bakanlığı*), 1992 Yearly Report (*1992 Yılı Raporu*), Ankara, 1993, p. 3.
3. Bundesanstalt für Arbeit, *Ausländerbeschäftigung 1980 bis 1990*, 1991, no. 10, p. 1471.
4. Helmut Schmidt, *Handeln für Deutschland* (Berlin: Rowohlt, 1993), pp. 160–2.
5. *Community and Ethnic Relations in Europe*, Council of Europe, 1991, MG-CR (91) Final, p. 9, paragraph 33.
6. See Alejandro Portes, 'Modes of incorporation and theories of labor immigration,' in Mary M. Kritz *et al.* (eds), *Global Trends in Migration: Theory and Research*

in International Population Movements (New York: Center for Migration Studies, 1981), pp. 279–97 and Saskia Sassen, *The Mobility of Labor and Capital: a Study in International Investment and Labor Flow* (London: Cambridge University Press, 1988).

7. Michael J. Piore, *Birds of Passage: Migrant Labor and Industrial Societies* (New York: Cambridge University Press, 1979).

8. See Hans-Joachim Hoffman-Nowotny, 'A sociological approach toward a general theory of migration,' in Mary M. Kritz *et al.* (eds), *Global Trends in Migration: Theory and Research in International Population Research* (New York: Center for Migration Studies, 1981), pp.121–43; and Aristide R. Zolberg, 'International migration in perspective,' in Mary M. Kritz *et al.* (eds), *Global Trends in Migration: Theory and Research in International Population Research* (New York: Center for Migration Studies, 1981), pp. 3–27.

9. See Frieda Hawkins, *Canada and Immigration: Public Policy and Public Concern* (Kingston, Ontario: McGill-Queen's University Press, 1988); and Nathan Glazer and Daniel P. Moynihan, *Beyond the Melting Pot: the Negroes, Puerto Ricans, Jews, Italians, and Irish of New York* (Cambridge, MA: MIT Press, 1971).

10. See Stephen Castles and Godula Kosack, *Immigrant Workers and Class Structure in Western Europe* (London: Oxford University Press, 1973); Jonathan Power, *Migrant Workers in Western Europe and the US* (Berkeley: University of California Press, 1985) and Michael J. Piore, *Birds of Passage, op. cit.*

11. See Hawkins, *op. cit.*; and A.H. Richmond, *Immigration and Ethnic Conflict* (London: Macmillan, 1988).

12. Ayşe Öncü, 'International labour migration and class relations,' *Current Sociology*, 38, 2 (1990), 177.

13. See Mark Miller, *Foreign Workers in Western Europe* (New York: Praeger, 1981); William Rogers Brubaker (ed.), *Immigration and Politics of Citizenship in Europe and North America* (Washington DC: University Press of America, 1989); Marilyn Hoskin, *New Immigrants and Democratic Society, Minority Integration in Western Democracies* (New York: Praeger, 1991).

14. Martin O. Heisler, 'Transnational migration as a small window on the diminished autonomy of the modern democratic state,' *Annals of the American Academy of Political and Social Science*, 485 (1986), 164.

15. Abdelmalek Sayad, 'Les trois âges de l'immigration algérienne en France,' *Actes de la Recherche en Sciences Sociales*, 15 (1977).

16. Piore, *op. cit.*

17. Alejandro Portes, 'Towards a structural analysis of illegal immigration,' *International Migration Review*, 12, 4 (1978), 469–84.

18. Ali Gitmez and Czarina Wilpert, 'A micro-society or an ethnic community? Social organizations and ethnicity amongst Turkish migrants in Berlin,' in John Rex, Daniele Joy and Czarina Wilpert (eds), *Immigrant Associations in Europe* (Aldershot: Gower, 1987), p. 99.

19. Ismail Duymaz, 'Selbstständige Erwerbstätigkeit von Ausländern als Integrationsindikator,' *Zeitschrift für Ausländerrecht und Ausländerpolitik*, 2 (1988), 27–8; Zentrum für Türkeistudien, *Türkei-Sozialkunde* (Opladen: Leske+Budrich, 1994).

20. Gitmez and Wilpert, *op. cit.*, pp. 105–6.

21. *Ibid.*, p. 104.

22. Necmettin Erbakan, 'Hac kontenjanini hayir için istedim,' *Cumhuriyet*, February 14, 1994, pp. 1 and 15.
23. Mustafa Balbay, 'RP'nin gerçek yüzü ve Hac ticareti,' *Cumhuriyet*, February 10, 1994, pp. 1 and 17.
24. Kemal Yurteri, 'Dinci şirketlerden sinir ötesi çalim,' *Cumhuriyet*, February 10, 1994.
25. The Saudi government is allocating each year to all Muslim countries a quota for the admission of their citizens wishing to fulfill their obligations of pilgrimage. The representative of the Van der Zee Company, Besir Darcin, a close friend of Erbakan, succeeded in overcoming these restrictive clauses by enabling in 1993 about 10,000 Turkish citizens living in Europe to obtain the required visa by sending them via third countries. Seen as a violation of the Saudi–Turkish intergovernmental agreement, this company was excluded in 1994 from benefiting from the allocation of quotas.
26. Necmettin Erbakan, 'Milli görüs ticaret hatti,' *Cumhuriyet*, March 23, 1994, p. 19.
27. Saskia Sassen, *The Global City* (New York: Princeton University Press, 1991), p. 315.
28. Nermin Abadan-Unat, *Turkish Migration to Europe, op. cit.*, p. 17; R. Weber, 'Rotationsprinzip bei der Beschäftigung von Ausländern,' *Auslandskurier*, October 5, 1970, 10.
29. Nermin Abadan-Unat, 'External migration and social mobility,' in P. Benedict, E. Tümertekin and F. Mansur (eds), *Turkey: Geographic and Social Perspectives* (Leiden: E.J. Brill, 1974), pp. 371 ff., table 4.
30. Gitmez and Wilpert, *op. cit.*, p. 95.
31. Sema Köksal, *Refah Toplumunda 'Getto' ve Türkler* (Istanbul: Kökaal, 1986), p. 126, table 22; Şahin Alpay and Halil Sarıaslan, *Effects of Immigration: the Effects on the Town Kulu in Central Turkey of Emigration to Sweden* (Stockholm: EIFO, 1984).
32. Riva Kastoryano, 'La présence turque en France,' *Hommes & Migrations*, 1172–3 (1994), 72–8; Hamit Bozarslan, 'Une communauté et ses institutions: le cas des Turcs en RFA,' *Revue Européenne des Migrations Internationales*, 6, 3 (1990), 63–81.
33. Yıldı Sertel, *Nord–Sud: crise et immigration – le cas Turc* (Paris: Ed. Publisud, 1987), pp. 134–5.
34. Riva Kastoryano, *Etre Turc en France: réflexions sur familles et communauté* (Paris: L'Harmattan, 1986).
35. This question is largely discussed in R. Lissot, N. Boumaza and G. Clement, *Ces migrants qui font le prolétariat* (Paris: Ed. Méridiens, 1994), pp. 93–104.
36. Clifford Geertz, *The Interpretation of Cultures* (New York: Basic Books, 1973), p. 259.
37. Pierre Bourdieu, *Outline of a Theory of Practice* (Cambridge: Cambridge University Press, 1977); J.D. Eller and R.M. Coughlan, 'The poverty of primordialism: the demystification of ethnic attachments,' *Ethnic and Racial Studies*, 16, 2 (1993), 183–202.
38. E.L. Lithman, *Immigration and Immigrant Policy in Sweden* (Stockholm: The Swedish Institute, 1987), pp. 29–31.
39. Köksal, *op. cit.*

40. J. Rath, 'Political action of immigrants in the Netherlands: class or ethnicity?' *European Journal of Political Research*, 16 (1988), 623–44.
41. Cities with Turks on the municipal assemblies: Almelo (1), Amesfoot (1), Amsterdam (17), Arnhem (3), Bergen ov Zoom (1), Devenba (1), and Dordrecht (1).
42. Han Entzinger, 'L'Immigration aux Pays-Pas du pluri-culturalisme a l'intégration,' in K.A. Wierow (ed.), *Racisme et modernité* (Paris: Editions la Decouverte, 1993), pp. 409–10.
43. Yasemin Soysal, 'Workers in Europe: interactions with the host society,' in Metin Heper, Ayşe Öncü and Heinz Kramer (eds), *Turkey and the West – Changing Political and Cultural Identities* (London: I.B. Tauris, 1993), p. 230.
44. Rémy Leveau, 'Maghrebi immigration to Europe: double insertion or double exclusion,' *The Annals of the American Academy of Political and Social Science*, 524 (1992), 176.
45. Gilles Keppel, *Les banlieues de l'Islam* (Paris: Seuil, 1987), p. 136.
46. Ministry of Labor, *op. cit.*, p. 66.
47. Riva Kastoryano, 'Etre Turc en France et en Allemagne,' *op. cit.*
48. Ministry of Labor, *op. cit.*, p. 76.
49. Nermin Abadan-Unat, *Turkish Workers in Europe, op. cit.*, p. 6.
50. Ministry of Labor, *op. cit.*, pp. 16, 68.
51. *Ibid.*, p. 15.
52. *Ibid.*, p. 12.
53. Out of 1.7 million Turks, 1.2 million have lived for over ten years in Germany, *ibid.*, pp. 13–14.
54. Nermin Abadan-Unat, 'Die politischen Auswirkungen der türkischen Migration im In-und Ausland,' *Orient*, 1 (1979), 2; A. Sezer and Dietrich Thränhardt, 'Türkische Organisationen in der BRD,' in Karl-Heinz Meier-Braun and Yüksel Pazarkaya (eds), *Die Türken* (Frankfurt/Main: Ullstein, 1983), pp. 119–51.
55. Dietrich Thränhardt, 'Patterns of organization among different ethnic minorities,' *The New German Critique*, 46, Winter (1989), pp. 16–19.
56. *Verfassungsschutzbericht 1987* (Bonn: Bundesministerium des Innern, 1988), p. 148.
57. Kurt Biswanger, *Türkisch-islamische Vereine als Faktor deutsch-türkischer Koexistenz* (Munich, 1988).
58. I. Halil Özak, 'Verflechtungen: Radikal-islamische Gruppen in der BDR,' *Entwicklungspolitische Korrespondenz*, 5/6 (1988), 32–6; *Hintergründe türkischer extremistischer islamischer Aktivitäten in Deutschland*, Deutscher Gewerkschaftsbund, 1988, no. 15.
59. The mismanagement of voluntary donations for relief work in Bosnia-Hersegovinia and its transfer to the personal account of an influential member of the Welfare Party became the subject of a parliamentary investigative committee. According the findings of this multiparty committee, a total of DM 5.9 million has been transferred to the Düsseldorf branch of the Yapì Kredi Bank in the name of Süleyman Mercümek. The inquiry was carried out with the cooperation of the German judiciary, who charged that 'money laundering' with the purpose of political propaganda was carried out on German soil.

PART III

THE CHALLENGE OF IMMIGRATION: SOME POLICY RESPONSES

11 International migration and security: towards transatlantic convergence?

Mark J. Miller

Concern over the security implications of international immigration is not unique to the post-Cold War period. Students of Roman history may recall how migration of several ancient tribes down the Rhone Valley was viewed with alarm in late Republican Rome. It threatened the Greek colony at the present-day site of Marseilles, which was linked by treaty to Rome. Marius was dispatched with his legions and defeated the invading tribes at the battle of Aquae Sextie. This helped to set in motion events which led to the supplanting of the Roman Republic by the Empire. A short while later, when the ancient Helvetians began to emigrate and similarly were viewed as threatening Rome and its allies, Julius Caesar was sent to meet them and thus began the Gallic Wars.

World history is replete with such events. To paraphrase the Ottoman historian Kemal Karpat, rare is the historical epoch not marked in important ways by immigration.[1] The contemporary migratory epoch, defined by the preeminence of international migration for employment, dates back to the second half of the nineteenth century. In several states, conservative and/or reactionary political movements had defined immigration as a national security threat by the time of the First World War. Charles Maurras, the theoretician of the monarchist Action Française party in France, for instance, viewed international migration with alarm and as detrimental not only to France's economy and society, but to its national security as well. Conservatives on both sides of the Atlantic feared that immigration brought with it labor militancy, radical political ideas, and the specter of revolution. To a degree, they were right. Generally, however, their fears were exaggerated.

With a few exceptions, most notably France, the interwar period witnessed declining international migration. In the United States, the Red

Scare resulted in deportations of left-wing aliens. In France, as recounted by Gary Cross, right-wing fears of subversive aliens were paralleled by republican concerns over Italian fascist encaderment of Italian migrants and the role played by the Polish government and Roman Catholic clergy among Polish immigrants.[2]

The Nazi seizure of power in Germany resulted in a large outflow of Jews, left-wing Germans, and trade unionists, particularly to France. The defeat of Republican forces in Spain resulted in another huge influx. During the Second World War in Europe, refugee and immigrant populations suffered horribly and were decimated. Few recall today their role in anti-fascist resistance. Defeat of the Axis powers and revelation of the scope of crimes committed during the war discredited the extreme right. One legacy of the Second World War was the association of national security concern over international migration with discredited right-wing extremism. Still today, there are those who regard the post-Cold War concern with the international migration and national security nexus as an aspect of the reemergence of the extreme right as a political force across Europe since the early 1980s.

Prior to 1983, when the *Front National* in France scored its breakthrough in the municipal elections of Dreux, the extreme right was an insignificant force in the politics of virtually all Western European countries. Nonetheless, post-1945 migrations were seen as connected to national security on both sides of the Atlantic in a number of ways, although national security concerns generally were neither paramount nor decisive factors in policies, save perhaps in refugee admissions. It would seem, for instance, that the Federal Republic of Germany's decision to recruit foreign workers from Turkey was influenced by Turkey's membership in NATO, but the many bilateral treaties of the sort were preponderantly viewed as labor market rather than strategic policies.

National security dimensions of international migration prior to 1989

Western democracies have generally reserved a right to revoke alien residency if aliens engage in activities threatening to national security. Governments have considerable latitude in defining what constitutes unacceptable behavior by aliens on their soil, but, on the whole, there has been relatively infrequent recourse to deportation to remove aliens who threaten national interests. At the same time, the contingent nature of alien political activity in Western democracies has constrained immigrant involvement in politics and has contributed to its specific and characteristic nature, particularly in Western Europe.

Western European guestworker recruitment in the 1950s and 1960s, of course, differed in important ways from the situations in North America, although there were more transatlantic commonalities than sometimes thought. Admissions of foreign workers were usually viewed through a labor market optic, and there was a presumption of eventual return home. The general assumption was that labor migration could benefit all involved – sending and receiving states and the immigrants themselves. There was not much debate over the wisdom of foreign worker admissions, and the policies were not seen as particularly significant, although most Western European recruitment was organized on a bilateral basis and was seen as contributing to good bilateral relations. Foreign workers simply were not viewed as political actors. They were presumed to be passive and politically inconsequential for the most part.

Yet even back in the halcyon period of guestworker recruitment, there were connections between international migration and national security. Homelands, in particular, fretted about the political activities of their citizens or subjects abroad. It was not unusual for aliens in Western democracies to be more free to participate politically abroad than in their homelands. Cherifien's Morocco, Salazar's Portugal, Franco's Spain, and the Colonels' Greece all had reason to fear immigrant and refugee political organizations abroad, and they not infrequently sought cooperation from Western European governments in muzzling them. Sometimes, they succeeded. But for all the contingency of alien political activity, aliens generally had, and have, the ability to organize politically even if this is done secretively or under the cover of cultural or trade union organizations.

Immigrant involvement in political violence appears to have been rare in the 1950s and 1960s. Immigrants also were not targets of widespread violence. The Algerian war constitutes a special case, but FLN fundraising activities in metropolitan France, and the eventual decision to strike at targets in France, the horrendous toll of internecine Algerian revolutionary violence in metropolitan France, and horrific governmental repression of the FLN and its presumed supporters, particularly in 1961, in some ways presaged later developments throughout Western democracies.[3] The specter of political terrorism has much to do with the relatively new prominence of international migration in national security thinking, particularly in the United States.

Only a small fraction of immigrants in Western democracies have become involved in violent activities, and fewer still in political terrorism. One way in which the Algerian conflict foreshadowed future events was the bloody struggle between Messalists and the FLN in metropolitan France. By the late 1960s and early 1970s, a number of conflict-filled situations in states sending significant numbers of migrants to Western Europe had spilled over, as it were, to migrant communities. Croatian Ustachis and Yugoslav governmental agents clashed on German soil. Turkish extremists fought one another across Western Europe, but particularly in Germany. Such incidents necessarily affected perceptions of national security. By the mid-1970s, German statistics on left- and right-wing extremists on German soil included significant numbers of aliens.[4]

Alien involvement in political violence seemed to increase in the late 1960s in Western Europe. Alien students and activists played a role in the May/June events of 1968 in France, and hundreds were deported. Violent clashes erupted in France over immigration between extreme right and left (mainly student) groups. Later, some of the right-wing campus activists would help to form the *Front National.* This violence, however, was overshadowed by growing violence against Arab immigrants in France. A wave of killings in 1973 led Algeria to suspend further worker emigration to France. Franco-Algerian relations were adversely affected by the violence.[5]

Palestinian terrorism and Israeli counterterrorism on Western European soil constituted a more widely publicized dimension of violence by aliens. The Munich Olympics massacre in 1972 sparked a wave of deportations. The 1970 Murer strike in Geneva involving Spanish workers in a protest over their housing, the 1973 strike by Turkish workers at Ford-Cologne, and a wave of strikes and protests by mainly North African workers in France served to publicize immigrant grievances and to underscore their growing presence. Events like these contributed to Western European decisions to curb further recruitment of foreign labor in the 1970s.

Characteristically, decisions to reduce or halt further foreign worker recruitment were linked to or soon followed by steps to better integrate foreign communities. Since the mid-1970s, the legal status and rights of most legally admitted alien residents of Western Europe have improved. By the mid-1970s, warnings of an 'immigration timebomb,' or eventual immigration-related social explosions, were not uncommon. Thoughtful Europeans had good reason to worry that foreign worker settlement and family reunification might eventuate in American-style minority problems. The hope was to forestall such outcomes through integration policy, curbs on further foreign worker recruitment, and crack downs on illegal immigration.

From roughly 1975 to 1985, Western European efforts to stabilize international migration on the whole appeared to be successful. More secure employment and residency rights enabled many resident aliens to participate more fully in their countries of immigration. The embryonic alien participation and representation of the 1970s blossomed in the 1980s. Still, despite the fuller measure of democracy available to aliens in Western Europe in the 1980s, national security concerns occasionally slipped into debates over international immigration.

The auto strikes in France in 1982 and 1983, largely perpetrated by foreign workers, constitute a case in point. The government of Pierre Mauroy eventually suggested that Muslim strikers were being manipulated by the revolutionary Islamic government in Teheran. There is little reason to grant credence to the allegation, but the charge was emblematic of growing fear of Islamic fundamentalist contagion to Western Europe. In both Western Europe and North America, the new significance attached to the national security implications of international migration has much to do with fear of Islamic fundamentalist activity, as both areas have witnessed a massive arrival of Muslim immigrants since 1945.

Middle Eastern terrorism also afflicted Western Europe in the 1980s. The most significant episode actually involved an extremist Lebanese faction largely comprised of Lebanese Christians who slipped in and out of France during a sustained bombing campaign. While it bears repeating that only a handful of determined and resourceful individuals can wreak havoc in an industrial democracy, the correlation of immigration and political terrorism is unjustified. What is most striking is how few Islamic immigrants join violence-prone groups.[6] Organizations like the outlawed Mouvement des Travailleurs Arabes in France appeared to have meager success recruiting members in the 1970s, just as radical Islamic groups did in the 1980s. Moreover, the multiplicity of rival Islamic fundamentalist factions, many of which are not revolutionary and violence-prone, tends to lessen the threat posed by Muslim immigrants.

The North American situations differed appreciably from the Western European cases, primarily due to the lesser role played by temporary foreign workers and policies applicable to them in the United States and Canada. Most resident aliens admitted to the United States and most landings in Canada were expected to eventuate in permanent stays and the eventual acquisition of citizenship. In both North American democracies, resident aliens enjoyed a quite liberal legal status, although they faced restrictions in voting and running for public office. The ease of access to citizenship made their lack of voting rights less problematical, and, due in part to the emphasis upon family reunification in North American immigration policies, legally admitted immigrants in North America faced less daunting integration problems.

Nonetheless, national security concerns were not absent from post-Second World War immigration policies in the United States and Canada. Refugee admissions were strongly influenced by foreign policy considerations. As in Western Europe, immigrant communities participated from abroad in the politics of their homelands. The most extreme example of this pattern involved the Cuban exiles, who, aided by the US government, launched the ill-fated Bay of Pigs invasion in 1961.

Immigrant and ethnic groups can be powerful, even decisive, factors in the formulation of US foreign policy. A number of students of US policy toward the Arab–Israeli conflict have identified pro-Israeli lobbying and other activities as the principal determinant of US foreign policy toward that long conflict.[7] Most immigrant and ethnic groups do not, however, possess the political resources of pro-Israeli US Jews. It appears exaggerated to maintain that immigrant and ethnic groups are singularly important in the formulation of US foreign policy.[8]

Immigrant political activities in North America, are nonetheless quite extensive and sometimes have had national security implications. The demonstrations by Iranian students in the late 1970s and early 1980s were viewed with alarm by the US government and prompted countermeasures. Palestinians, who arrived in large numbers in the United States and Canada after the 1967 war, are known to be highly mobilized and politically active. Israeli officials have complained about Palestinian fundraising and political activities. The Palestinian Islamic fundamentalist organization Hamas is said to be based in the United States and to use it as a 'safe haven' for its frequently violent operations in Israel.[9] From time to time, alleged terrorist activities or membership in terrorist groups are invoked by the US government to detain and deport Palestinian immigrants. Eight members of the Popular Front for the Liberation of Palestine were detained on the grounds of membership in a terrorist organization. Their detention became a *cause célèbre* of a sort in the early 1990s, as such heavy-handed and questionable actions by the US government are rare.

Aliens in the United States and Canada generally enjoy a wide latitude of freedom of expression and participation. Consular voting by aliens is tolerated on US soil, and various manifestations of homeland-directed political activity are not uncommon. Ecuadorean and Mexican candidates, for instance, regularly take to the hustings on US soil. The relative ease of access to US and Canadian citizenship as compared to many European states appears to have made the political status of alien residents in North America less problematic than in European democracies. However, most interestingly, millions of alien residents in North American democracies opt not to naturalize or are discouraged from doing so by various barriers of an administrative nature.[10] Hence, there is mounting concern in the United States over the effective disenfranchisement of large parts of communities in major urban areas where there are many illegal immigrants and long-term resident aliens. Indeed, proposals have been made to accord municipal voting rights to aliens in the Washington, DC area. These initiatives call to mind the campaigns for alien parliaments and municipal voting rights in Western Europe in the 1970s and 1980s. One of the first acts by the Clinton administration's new Commissioner of the Immigration and Naturalization Service, Doris Meissner, was to announce a campaign to facilitate naturalization. The issue of alien participation in local and regional government in Western Europe, of course, remains divisive two decades later.

While alien participation and representation in North American democracies has not been extensively or systematically scrutinized, it is largely unproblematic. The rights and possibilities for alien participation and representation vary by state and province. Even illegal immigrants have succeeded in unionizing in Arizona.[11] Relatively few aliens are involved in political violence. There would appear to have been less spillover of home-land political violence in North America than in Western Europe, although the potential for that to occur is certainly evident. The Haitian community has witnessed politically motivated killings, as have the Vietnamese and Filipino. A number of Palestinians have been killed. The murder of the anti-Arab extremist Meir Kahane, the World Trade Center bombing by anti-Israeli Arab Muslim fundamentalists, and a subsequent attack by a Lebanese Druze immigrant on a bus full of Orthodox Jewish students constitute alarming, but quite exceptional, events.

There have been episodes of urban unrest in the United States and Canada involving significant numbers of aliens and immigrants. The Washington, DC area experienced several days of unrest in largely Hispanic neighborhoods prior to the South Central explosion in Los Angeles in the spring of 1992. Korean immigrant shopkeepers were targeted during the South Central violence of 1992, and a number of Central American and Mexican immigrants appear to have been involved in the disorders. Caribbean-origin communities appear to have been principally involved in the unrest that affected Toronto soon after the Los Angeles explosion. These incidents resemble the urban unrest that has principally involved immigrant-origin communities in Western European countries such as the United Kingdom, France, and Belgium since the early 1980s. The unrest suggests that immigrant integration is far from solely a European pre-occupation. Mounting concern over the capacity of the United States to integrate immigrants as successfully as in the past has resulted in an additional dimension of transatlantic convergence in immigration policy. That parallel was not there in the 1960s or the 1970s. It is only quite recently that the rough political consensus in support of legal immigration policy has crumbled and immigration-related issues have figured prominently in US politics.

The high politics and politicization of immigration in the 1990s

Elsewhere, I have argued that the confluence of five principal factors contributed to the largely novel saliency of immigration-related concerns in the foreign and domestic politics of Western European states after 1989.[12] The collapse of communism raised the specter of *Völkerwanderung*, of uncontrollable mass migration of peoples from the East. The enormous increase in asylum applications undercut the creditability of governmental migration control policies. The progress toward European socio-economic and political union involved the prospect of elimination of internal frontiers and gave rise to exaggerated fears of, for example, unemployed Turkish residents of Germany moving to France. The growth of anti-immigrant politics, the affirmation of Islamic presence in the 1970s and 1980s, and the persistence of serious integration problems two decades after the advent of integration policies also played roles, as did continuing illegal immigration.

A marked increase in bilateral and multilateral diplomatic activity on international migration bears witness to the new high politics of international migration in Europe. There can similarly be little doubt about the growing tendency to view international migration-related questions through a national security optic. Sharon Russell and Charles Keely reported that asylum policy is viewed in this way in Western Europe.[13] The growing concern over forced migration, particularly in the former Yugoslav area, has heightened awareness of the migratory consequences of the use or threat of force in European history.[14] The violent impasse in Algeria has stoked fears of massive emigration. Austria, Italy, and Spain have involved their armed forces in efforts to prevent unwanted migration.

It is true that all of this has coincided with the reemergence of anti-immigrant politics on the extreme right, but what is cause and what is effect? National security concerns, we have seen, were present before the reemergence of the extreme right. In Europe as in North America, the end of the Cold War has ushered in a long overdue reexamination of national security. Given the immensity of the migratory challenge facing Western democracies in coming decades, it is scarcely surprising that international migration would be viewed as pertinent to national security. Indeed, in many respects this new saliency attached to international migration appears salutary. Immigration policy for too many decades was typically assigned to the back burner, way down the list of governmental priorities.

If one can assume that there has been a qualitative change in immigration policy since the late 1980s, as the flurry of diplomatic activity appears to suggest, a number of intriguing research questions arise. Has the high politics of international migration in Europe changed in any manner the ways in which immigration policies are formulated? For instance, are foreign ministries and defense agencies playing a greater role in such policy making in the 1990s than they were in the 1960s? Have ministries of labor and social affairs become less influential? Are there ways to measure such transformations?

One suspects that longitudinal institutional research would reveal more continuity than change. Legitimate national security concerns, for example about extremist violence against alien residents and immigrant-origin populations, unfortunately have a long history in countries like France. Anti-immigrant violence in Germany and elsewhere has prompted unwarranted concerns about the stability of democratic institutions in Germany and elsewhere in Europe. In this respect, national security linkages to international migration appear exaggerated. Many Europeans who vote for anti-immigrant extreme right parties are not anti-immigrant ideologues but rather protest voters. There are some indications that anti-immigrant electoral appeal has crested in France. One ought to worry about immigrants and their status in Europe and about the growth of anti-immigrant politics; but now, as in the past, there is a need for balance and perspective. Regulation of international migration and integration of immigrants represent an enormous challenge for the future of Europe, but many of the essential elements for coping with the challenge are in place. The new saliency attached to international migration issues by Europeans may portend that further constructive steps will be taken, especially in the realm of international cooperation. The new high politics of international migration in Europe, of course, will not quickly abate international migration pressures from the South in particular.

In North America, immigration has quite suddenly figured more prominently in discussions of national security and vice versa. The Department of State announced in 1993 that, henceforth, international migration considerations would be routinely factored into long-range planning. President Clinton ordered the CIA to prepare a national security estimate concerning international migration. US policy toward Haitian migrants has had a national security component since the early 1980s. Indeed, the so-called 'Mariel boatlift' of Cuban migrants was in many respects a turning point. When the Mexican government proposed NAFTA, the initiative was referred to the National Security Council, which eventually recommended US support for the initiative. This was significant in several respects, perhaps most because the US Congress jealously guards its traditional prerogatives in immigration policy making.

The growing Islamic presence in the United States and the aforementioned terrorist incidents have also contributed to the shift. There is a worrisome anti-Islamic, anti-Arab, and anti-Palestinian overtone to the new saliency of immigration in national security thinking. A number of American scholars have concluded that the wars of the future will result from 'the clash of the civilizations.'[15] There is an unwarranted tendency to regard the growing Islamic presence in the United States as an inevitable source of conflict and instability. Some US foreign policy analysts have identified Islamic fundamentalism as a key strategic threat to US interests in the post-Cold War period. This assessment appears to have contributed to the new saliency of the immigration–national security nexus.

Immigrant integration problems and issues are substantial in the states most heavily affected by the massive legal and illegal migrations to the United States in recent decades. These tensions have magnified the impact of the relatively rare incidents of political violence involving aliens. Non-political criminal activity by aliens has also contributed to a palpable political backlash.[16] On the whole, though, it would be inaccurate to equate the relatively novel national security prominence of international migration to xenophobia. Rather, it occupies a prominent place on the agenda because of growing awareness that socio-economic and demographic disparities, combined with the transportation and communications revolutions, render democratic societies permeable to unlawful or unwanted entry. In many respects, the national security linkage to international immigration simply involves long overdue recognition of the importance of international migration in global affairs. Increasingly, policy makers are aware of the implications of transnational politics and the globalization of the economy. The NAFTA recommendation, for instance, was based on the realization that instability in Mexico would inevitably adversely affect the United States, among other ways through unwanted migration.

The vital national security interest in immigrant rights

National security policy is unavoidable in a world organized into state structures. It serves no good purpose for scholars to ignore the real world or wish it were different. The national security implications of international migration are a legitimate area of research and an increasingly salient one on both sides of the Atlantic. Much of the public discussion of the national security–immigration nexus in Europe and North America has had anti-immigrant overtones. Perhaps there is an inevitably restrictionist impulse in the emerging debate. Immigration scholarship can make a significant contribution to the debate.

This analysis has suggested that there is little reason to fear alien political activities as a disruptive or destabilizing force in Western democracies. There are grounds for concern and vigilance. On the whole, the great mass of post-Second World War immigrants have been sufficiently integrated into Western democracies. The key to this has been the extension of many rights and relatively liberal legal status to most legally admitted aliens. The improved legal status of most legal alien residents of Western Europe since the recruitment curbs transformed this area into at least a *de facto* area of limited legal immigration, in many respects similar to Canada and the United States, although with generally less generous admissions policies.

We would do well to take note of the democratic interest in safeguarding migrant rights in the current climate of mounting concern over international migration and its national security implications. The generally liberal status accorded to legally admitted aliens in Western democracies has helped to forestall the development of political extremism and alien violence. The empirical record over the past 50 years on both sides of the Atlantic is unambiguous in this respect. Europeans and Americans should worry more about violence perpetrated against alien residents and immigrant-origin populations. It is high time that the concept of security be inclusive of our growing immigrant populations. There is an urgent need for measured and informed assessments, for instance, of Islamic immigrant politics. One suspects that Muslim immigrants, in their immense majority, long for integration and acceptance in the host democracies. We would do well to recall that adaptation and integration take time – sometimes generations.

Notes

1. Kemal Karpat, 'Ottoman population records and the census of 1881–1893,' *International Journal of Middle East Studies*, 9, 237 (1978), 237–74.
2. Cross, *Immigrant Workers in Industrial France* (Philadelphia: Temple University Press, 1983).
3. See J.L. Einaudi, *La Bataille de Paris* (Paris: Editions du Seuil, 1991).
4. See Mark J. Miller, *Foreign Workers in Western Europe: an Emerging Political Force* (New York: Praeger, 1981).
5. See Mark J. Miller, 'Reluctant partnership: foreign workers in Franco-Algerian relations, 1962–1979,' *Journal of International Affairs*, 32, 2 (1979), 219–37.
6. See, for example G. Kepel, *Les Banlieux d'Islam* (Paris: Editions du Seuil, 1987); and R. Leveau and G. Kepel, *Les Musulmans dans la societè française* (Paris: Presses de la FNSP, 1988).
7. R. Ovendale, *Origins of the Arab–Israeli Wars* (New York: Longman, 1984).
8. Y. Shain, 'Democrats and seccesionists: US diasporas as regime stabilizers,' in Myron Weiner (ed.), *International Migration and Security* (Boulder, CO: Westview Press, 1993), pp. 287–322.
9. E. Yaari, 'A safe haven for Hamas in America,' *New York Times*, January 27, 1993, p. 23.
10. D.S. North, *The Long Gray Welcome* (Washington, DC: NALEO Education Fund, 1985).
11. H. Delgado, *New Immigrants, Old Unions* (Philadelphia: Temple University Press, 1993).
12. See IMR's special issue, IMR, 'Internal migration and the new Europe,' *International Migration Review* 26, Summer (1992); and Mark J. Miller, *The Future of International Migration to Europe* (European University Institute, working paper no. 92).
13. Remarks by Charles B. Keely at the panel on International Migration and Security, Center for Migration Studies National Conference on Immigration and Refugee Policy, Washington, DC, March 1994.
14. IMR, 1992, *op. cit.*
15. Samuel Huntington, 'The clash of civilizations,' *Foreign Affairs* 72, 3 (Summer 1993), 22–49.
16. United States Senate Subcommittee on Investigations, *Criminal Aliens in the United States* (Washington, DC: US Government Printing Office, 1994).

12

The European Union and the immigration problem: small steps and possible solutions

Chris Bourdouvalis

Introduction

Although the European Union institutions have taken a number of initiatives to harmonize immigration policies among member states, harmonization is far from complete. During the past six years the immigration issue has received more attention within the EU than ever before. The urgency in dealing with immigration matters stems partly from the fact that with the completion of the 1992 project and the implementation of the Maastricht Treaty, the free movement of labor within the EU is allowed and accepted. It is therefore imperative that citizens of the EU countries be distinguished from non-citizens, and that non-citizens be treated similarly at all EU borders. The harmonization of immigration policies has been a part of the Social Chapter of the Treaty of Rome for a long time. With EU internal borders actually open now, the Treaty of Rome needs to be taken seriously.

But perhaps the greatest challenge for EU action regarding immigration is posed by outside factors. The lifting of travel restrictions by governments in Eastern Europe and the Soviet Union/Russia, from the late 1980s onward, has rendered East–West travel unimpeded and migration readily possible. The demand for traveling to the West had become so great that some experts describe the prospect of an influx of migrants from the East as one of the most urgent issues that the EU faces. 'The specter that haunts Western Europe is no longer communism, as Karl Marx asserted in the *Communist Manifesto*, but immigration from North Africa and the collapsed Eastern Europe and the Soviet Union.'[1]

The Western press has been sensationalizing the immigration issue.

Business Week underlined the urgency of immigration pressures by asserting that 'the floodgates are bursting' and that 'a tidal wave of immigrants could spoil the EC's vision of the future.' There are 'barbarians at the gate of an economic boom,' said *The Financial Times*, and *The New York Times* reported 'an urgent need for one policy' to 'stem the refugee tide,' as 'west Europe braces for the migrant wave from the East.'[2]

The countries targeted by most immigrants are the largest and the wealthiest in continental Europe – Germany, France, and, to a lesser extent, Italy – although nearly every EU country is today a receiving state. Influx into Germany is mostly from the East, whereas immigrants to France and Italy come predominantly from the South. The smaller and the least economically developed EU countries are also susceptible to immigration pressures. Greece, one of the poorest EU members, has recently been receiving immigrants from Albania, Iraq, and the Eastern European countries. The poorer countries in the EU, such as Spain, Portugal, Greece, and Italy earlier on, had been accustomed to exporting labor. But during the past few years this trend has been substantially altered. These traditional sending countries that have recently become countries of destination do not have experience with immigration and therefore are not well equipped to cope with this new phenomenon. This adds to problems involved in defining common immigration policies for the European Union.[3]

In Germany and France immigration has caused social and political upheavals. Anti-immigrant outbursts in Germany have led to violence resulting in the deaths of foreign nationals. Political parties promoting xenophobia have gained ground. The avowedly anti-immigrant *Republikaner* party in Germany, for example, registered notable success in the Berlin area in 1989.[4] In France, the *Front National* has been even more successful, where in the 1988 first round of the French presidential election, Le Pen, the *Front National*'s candidate, received 14.4 percent of the vote.[5] Since 1988, the *Front National*'s public support has remained high.[6] Anti-immigrant feelings in the major receiving countries rose constantly during the 1980s, and this trend is apparently continuing as human insecurities – economic, political, and military – all along the southern and eastern frontiers of the European Union escalate. Further deepening Western European consternation about immigrants has been a long economic recession in most of the Common Market countries that has rendered difficult the absorption of the new-comers.

Almost all of the continental countries of the EU have been willing at least in principle to extend the harmonization of EU policies into the sphere of immigration. Denmark is an outlier among this continental group. For their part, the UK and Ireland have been the most reluctant to accept common immigration policies, though there is some evidence from Britain at least that the new urgencies are forcing a closer look at the situation. As the *Financial Times* observed:

When British Prime Minister John Major warned European heads of state that Europe faced a right wing backlash unless the European Community took immediate action to stem the tide of immigration, he touched a raw nerve. Immigration – both legal and illegal – has moved to the top of the political agenda all across the Community. Many politicians are starting to think, and a few to say, that Europe is already full, with an estimated 10 million immigrants, and that the need to harmonize immigration policies is now urgent.[7]

Most of the EU leaders have recognized that independent national policies will be insufficient to confront an immigration crisis that continues to deepen. For this reason, a search for common EU policies regarding the admission and handling of immigrants has begun. Immigration matters have been discussed on several occasions at the highest inter-governmental levels within the EU, as, for example, during the meeting of interior ministers convened at Thessaloniki, Greece, in May 1994.[8] The European Commission has also studied the immigration situation and on several occasions reported on it to the Council of Ministers, urging action.[9] The Commission's prerogatives were somewhat enhanced by the Maastricht Treaty, which made immigration matters so-called Pillar Three issues in the realm of justice and home affairs, where according to Cornelis de Jong 'the Commission is now fully associated with the work in this area and has obtained a shared right of initiatives with the member states themselves.'[10]

Events in Western Europe and trends in the EU indicate that there are pressures that may lead to an eventual common EU immigration policy. The rest of this chapter focuses on the specific problems surrounding immigration policy and specific initiatives that have been taken by the EU. Later, some suggestions are offered that might contribute to policy harmonization.

Foreign population in the European Union

The foreign population in the EU accounts for more than 4 percent of its total population. In 1993 the foreign population in the EU countries was approximately 16 million. Thirty-six percent are EU citizens and 64 percent are non-EU immigrants (see Table 12.1). The largest single sending country to the Union is Turkey, with 14.1 percent of the total non-EU immigration. There is a particularly large Turkish presence in Germany, and high concentrations of Turkish guestworkers there have generated anti-immigrant attitudes.[11] Morocco, Algeria, and Tunisia account for another 12.4 percent of the migration flow, and the majority of these North Africans are taken in by France, where there are also social and political tensions, as other chapters in this book show.

Countries of the EU host a large number of immigrants who came during earlier periods of rapid economic growth. These immigrants, who by many accounts contributed importantly to Europe's economic flourishing up to the early 1970s, were invited by the host governments. However, there is another group of immigrants, the political asylum seekers, who were not specifically invited, but who came because doors were in fact open to them. But for the unbearable conditions in their homelands, these people would not have migrated. Before the collapse of communism, the number of political asylees was much smaller than it is now because the communist governments were able to control outflows of people rather rigorously. But after the fall of the communist regimes and with the turmoil in many regions of the former communist world as well as continuing human insecurity in some North African, Middle Eastern, and Sub-Saharan African countries, the number of asylum seekers exploded.[12] Applications for

Table 12.1 *Foreign residents in EU countries (by citizenship, thousands, on January 1, 1991)*

	Number	Percentage
Total non-nationals	15,906	100
EU nationals	5756	36
Non-EU nationals	10,150	64
Turkey	2247.8	14.1
Morocco	1053.4	6.6
Algeria	640.8	4.0
Tunisia	283.7	1.8
Yugoslavia	785.3	4.9
Poland	368.4	2.3
Romania	78.5	
ex-USSR	52.5	
India	195.2	1.2
Iran	170.0	1.1
Pakistan	140.8	
Vietnam	98.5	
Philippines	94.5	
Lebanon	87.8	
United States	357.0	2.2
Japan	81.6	
Canada	59.9	
Austria	212.4	1.3
Switzerland	98.7	
Sweden	60.2	
Stateless and unknown	911.7	5.7

Source: Adapted from Meisner *et al.*, *International Immigration in a New Era* (The Trilateral Commission, 1993), Table 6.

asylum increased dramatically through the late 1980s, continuing into the 1990s. 'In 1980, Europe's annual caseload was under 20,000. By 1992, it had reached 560,000, more than doubling since 1988.'[13]

As Table 12.2 shows, 78 percent of the asylum applications are received by Germany. This can be explained by three important factors. First, Germany is considered by asylum seekers to be the most liberal country in Western Europe in terms of reviewing applications.[14] Second, Germany is the largest and richest country of the EU. Third, Germany is closer to the countries from which people are fleeing than are most of its EU partners.

Also interesting in Table 12.2 is the fact that Italy receives a very small number of applications from asylum seekers even though it is one of the largest and most prosperous countries in the EU. But Italy is also the country with the largest number of illegal immigrants, which some attribute to the lax security that exists along the borders of the country. This has created concerns among other members of the EU in connection with implementing the Schengen Agreement, which all but eliminates monitoring along member countries' internal borders. France, one of the strongest supporters of the Schengen Agreement, has become very reluctant to implement it out of concern that under the full implementation of Schengen illegal immigrants to Italy could readily cross into France.

Other Southern European countries, such as Greece, Spain, and Portugal, are also blamed for inadequate border security. Of all the Southern European countries, Greece is perhaps the most vulnerable. It borders upon some of the poorest countries in Europe: Albania, the Former

Table 12.2   *Asylum applications in EU countries in 1992*

	Number	Percentage
Germany	438,200	78
France	26,800	5
United Kingdom	24,800	4
Belgium	17,650	3
Netherlands	17,450	3
Denmark	13,900	2
Spain	12,650	2
Luxembourg	3,429	
Italy	2,500	
Greece	1,950	
Portugal	700	
Ireland	n.a.	
Total	559,829	

Source: UNHCR Regional Office for the European Institutions, Brussels, May 1993. Adapted from *International Immigration in a New Era* (The Trilateral Commission, 1993), Table 7.

Yugoslav Republic of Macedonia (FYROM), and Bulgaria. Furthermore, there are two conflicts ongoing around Greece. The Bosnian conflict, presently under ceasefire but still tenuous, and Kurdish wars in Iraq and Turkey have become the largest sources of refugees in Greece. Complicating the situation for the Greek government is the mountainous terrain of the border with Albania, which abets the flow of illegal immigrants.

There is also the problem of smuggling illegal immigrants into the countries of the European Union. Such trafficking in human cargoes is well known along the border between Mexico and the United States. It was not a problem in Europe until a few years ago, though it seems to be becoming acute. Organized criminal gangs, labor contractors, and other unscrupulous facilitators extort large sums from immigrants or their relatives in Europe in payment for illicit conduct across EU borders. Penetrating the EU has therefore become a lucrative business in itself.

Greece, particularly exposed because of its geography, has been especially burdened by the smuggling of people. Activity increased rather markedly after the 1991 Gulf War. The Greek government frequently brings the issue to EU forums, where it is seeking financial assistance to increase the capabilities of its coast guard. The Greek appeal to the EU follows from the fact that immigrants smuggled into Greece are *de facto* smuggled into the EU and they may ultimately end up anywhere in Western Europe. Though inadequate border controls are usually blamed for the increase of immigrants into the Southern European member states of the EU, an additional factor may be the attractiveness of the cheap labor force that comes from Asia, Africa, and the ex-Soviet bloc countries. Employing moderately and even highly skilled immigrant laborers at abnormally low wages renders Southern European countries' businesses more competitive and furthers their efforts to catch up with their counterparts in the North. Illegal immigration is therefore not entirely unwelcome. Businessmen in the South argue that cheap labor is crucial to them in order to compete in a single market created by the 1992 project. This approach, reminiscent of arguments offered by business leaders in the mid-1960s who spoke out for importing labor and against the rotation principle, has created a number of disagreements among the EU governments and complicated efforts toward a common immigration policy.

Problems caused by immigration into the European Union

The problems caused by immigration into the EU range from racial discrimination to political violence and everything in between. Daily news and the mass media make these problems visible to publics and usually arouse anti-immigrant sentiments. As mentioned, the conflicts with and over immigrants have been most visible in Germany and France, but anti-immigrant attitudes are in evidence elsewhere, and anti-immigrant incidents have also been reported in the Netherlands, Austria, Italy and Denmark. There has been unrest in the United Kingdom too involving immigrant issues, but this has been more complicated in social origin and dynamics. Bitterness almost everywhere has been exacerbated by very slow economic growth.

Right-wing political factions in some countries openly spread anti-immigrant venom. But a common, and recurrent, observation is that while uninvolved citizens condemn acts of violence against the immigrants, they nevertheless often report they understand the right wing's frustrations and grievances. This rather pervasive, permissive attitude must be a serious concern for many governments in Western Europe, for it signals that if the current situation continues frustration will expand. In such an environment, right-wing violence against immigrants could escalate and popular acquiescence in it, or even overt support for it, may grow. With regard to Germany in the early 1990s,

Acts of violence committed by rightist groups against foreigners numbered 2285 in 1992, according to the federal police, a sharp increase over the previous year. The first four months of 1993 saw 670 attacks compared with 420 for the period of 1992. Seventeen deaths occurred in 1992; by May 1993, nine had been killed. The perpetrators have been angry young people who are without political ideology, except for a minority of Neo-Nazis.[15]

Much of the violent behavior in Germany has targeted asylum applicants. The large number of applications that pile up every day in the offices of the German immigration authorities make their expeditious handling impossible. Meanwhile, the applicants remain in Germany and are at least minimally accommodated. In addition, applicants whose requests for asylum have been rejected are usually permitted to stay in Germany on humanitarian grounds, and they too are accommodated by public authorities. With the daily arrival of new asylees, numbers awaiting decisions or slipping quietly into German society increase. The inability of the German and other EU governments to expel rejected applicants for asylum creates the impression that public authorities are unable to cope with the immigration problem. Regarding the handling of asylum seekers at least, this is not an entirely erroneous impression. But it does raise the question of governability, while it leads to skepticism about the meaning of national sovereignty and governments' ability to enforce and protect it.[16]

The apparent inability of governments to deal with the immigration influx invites criticism and gives ammunition to rightist political groups and parties. While the *Republikaner* party in Germany and the *Front National* in France are the best examples, more recently there has been the rise of the Northern League in Italy, whose platform outspokenly emphasized anti-immigrant attitudes, and the People's Party in Austria, whose political program relies heavily on anti-immigration rhetoric.

Significantly, it appears that the political right's attempts to capitalize upon anti-immigrant sentiments, and the political successes reaped accordingly, have pushed some of the more moderate European parties and politicians toward immigrant-bashing. In fact, in times of high unemployment and economic recession political parties of all ideological persuasions have found electoral pay-offs in taking tough stands against immigrants. Mainstream political parties such as the Christian Democrats, Social Democrats, and Socialists in many countries, including Germany, have been aping the extremists' anti-immigrant rhetoric not because they fundamentally believe in discrimination, but because they do not want to lose electoral support. A good example is the former French prime minister, Edith Cresson, who announced a massive deportation of Arab immigrants during her premiership.

The EU's response to immigration

EU institutions have taken a number of steps to harmonize national immigration policies, though there are disagreements about how these policies should be implemented. Important results of the intra-EU policy dialogue have been achieved under four agreements: the Schengen Agreements, the TREVI Group, the Convention on Asylum, known as the Dublin Convention, and the External Borders Convention.

The Schengen Agreements deal with external immigration and were primarily inspired by the 1992 project. Not all Union members are parties to these agreements, which initially sought to remove border controls by January 1993. The United Kingdom, Ireland, and Denmark are not yet signatories, and because not all EU members are participating in the agreements, Schengen is not actually an EU program and its institutions are not involved. The accords are, however, widely 'viewed as a blueprint for the coming regulations in Europe ... as is foreseen by the Single European Act.'[17] The Agreements provide for a common information system, and a set of rules and regulations imposing carrier (i.e. owners or operators of ships and aircraft) liability for inspecting entry documents before taking passengers abroad.[18] The most relevant items of the agreements deal with border controls after the program is in full implementation: the accords institute a three-month visa for the territory of the signatory countries, a first entry visa of a limited character charging the receiving country with the responsibility for legal stays and possible extradition, and a transit visa that allows individuals a period of no more than five days en route within the Schengen countries to a third country; entry permits for longer than three months are considered to be national visas, giving only transit rights to the person concerned.[19] In addition to these specifics, the Schengen countries have a common list of about 115 countries whose nationals will require visas to enter Schengen territory.[20] The Schengen regime took effect on March 26, 1995 after being postponed several times due to a number of technical difficulties, including inadequate policing systems in a number of the Schengen countries.

Given the complexity of the Schengen accords, and the number of countries that managed to bring their visa regimes and border control policies into line, one has to conclude that Schengen constitutes an indispensable step toward the realization of the 1992 project, and certainly a positive step toward a harmonized immigration policy among members of the EU. Commenting on the Schengen Agreements, Tony Bonyan affirms that: 'The measures included in the Schengen are significant, not least because the European Commission has acknowledged that they constitute a laboratory of what the Twelve [EC Countries] will have to implement ... since the Schengen countries are confronted with the same problems facing the Community.'[21]

The other significant development at EU level deals with the refugee policies. In order to effectively confront the waves of immigrants flowing into the countries of the EU, the Council of Ministers, acting collectively on behalf of Europe, produced two international conventions: the Dublin Convention and the External Borders Convention. The first provides that asylum seekers will be allowed to file their application in one EU member state only. The second provides for continuous cooperation among member states in imposing visa requirements on nationals of the same countries, and similar cooperation in sanctioning those people who do not possess the required visas or travel documents. One key to the harmonization of policies Europe-wide is the standardization of national procedures for dealing with similar kinds of problems. The two conventions are steps toward such standardization, though, of course, they have to be implemented by the signatories.

A fourth major step that the EU countries have taken on the immigration issue comes under the heading of the TREVI Group. The history of TREVI goes back to 1976, when, at the request of the British government, the group was formed to combat terrorism. It sought to help combat violent activities in the EC by facilitating the coordination of the policies of EC interior ministers. By 1987, when the Single European Act was put into effect, the TREVI Group 'had expanded its remit from the initial focus on terrorism to embrace all the "policing and security aspects of free movement" including immigration, visas, asylum seekers and border controls.'[22] The TREVI Group is constituted in four different working groups. One deals with terrorism, both inside and outside the EU, a second is concerned with police cooperation, the third was established in 1985 and deals with serious crimes and drug trafficking, and the fourth was established in 1989 specifically to consider the policing and security implications of the creation of the Single European Market.[23] The TREVI Group is not an institution created by the Treaty of Rome, but is rather an entity created by the Council of Ministers. It is supervised by the ministers of the interior.

Along similar lines, a provision in the Maastricht Treaty of 1993 established a European police agency known as Europol. The newly formed agency was given a home in the Dutch city of The Hague. Though still under development, the agency will eventually command an advanced computer system where all criminal records will be stored, and through which these can be speedily retrieved all over the EU. Combating illegal immigration is among the responsibilities given to Europol.

Between 1974 and 1987, few initiatives were taken by the Community institutions to insure or extend the benefits of the EU's immigrant workers. But the Single European Act of 1986 in its Social Dimension gave new impetus to dealing with workers' social protection. It should be kept in mind that the aspects of the Single European Act dealing with the Social Dimension represent only 'a non-binding statement of intent.' Still, the significance is that there is a recognition on the part of EU leaders that workers have to be protected by the EU's institutions. Nationals are, of course, protected by their governments through a variety of social insurance and other schemes that have been in existence for some time. The Social Charter, therefore, is mostly designed to give protection to immigrant workers, though admittedly the immigrants in specific question are workers moving from country to country within the EU, and not people entering the EU from the outside. Nonetheless, the Social Charter leaves ample room for generalizing.

The leaning of the EU institutions, somewhat in contrast to the recent mood and manner of many of the member governments, has been supportive of immigrants, at least to the extent that there are recognized obligations to see to immigrants' well being within their new countries. The European Parliament (EP), for example, has taken a variety of actions to promote social benefits in the EU, including, notably, dealing with the plight of immigrants. EP deputies have repeatedly expressed their dismay over the anti-foreign sentiments and demonstrations appearing in EU member countries. The EP has also expressed its favorable support for non-Union immigrants. At the 49th anniversary of the Auschwitz liberation, a group of EP members, which included Egon Klesp, its president, expressed their great concerns for racist attitudes that have been openly reappearing in Western Europe. They also emphasized the necessity for accommodation and assistance to the immigrants. The EP has been very instrumental in promoting the notion of European citizenship, which, for immigrants might possibly be a pathway around some of the member countries' restrictive naturalization laws.

The European Commission has taken supportive stances regarding immigrants. For one thing, the Commission has been determined to take advantage of the Social Chapter written into the Maastricht Treaty. With the ratification of the Maastricht Treaty, the Commission, in cooperation with the EP, launched an aggressive campaign initiating new policies with regard to immigration. One new, large educational program of the European Communities called 'Socrates' aims to better educate immigrant workers, and it commits substantial resources to the task.

The Maastricht Treaty does not clearly delegate powers to the Commission in immigration matters, though the Commission has nonetheless already taken the initiative in formulating proposals for programs to help solve immigrants' problems. This has prompted a great deal of reaction on the part of some national governments – Britain, Denmark, and France in particular – who insist that the Commission is interpreting the Maastricht Treaty too broadly and that Brussels has been overstepping its authority with regard to immigration, which, they say, must remain a matter to be dealt with among sovereign states. Still, with the assistance of the EP, the European Commission has issued a 35-point program which speaks to a range of immigration issues, both internal and external.[24]

An important proposal on immigrants' rights came from Social Affairs Commissioner Padraig Flynn, who called for a number of new pieces of EU legislation that would include, among other things, greater expenditures on education and training programs for immigrants. The Flynn program, which focuses mainly on non-European immigrants, has two main concerns. One is how to restrict the influx of illegal immigration to the Union and the other is how to create reasonable living conditions for those who are already within its borders. For the first objective the Commission advocates laws similar to those in the United States. The second objective is harder and more complicated to accomplish for two reasons – people's attitudes and existing national legislation. To combat anti-foreign prejudices, the Commission proposes strict measures against those who discriminate against immigrant workers. As for the complications involved in dealing with diverse national laws, the Commission proposes that all immigrants who legally reside in the EU should become citizens of the Union automatically, regardless of country of origin or country of residence. By becoming residents of the Union and citizens of the Union, immigrants would have the right to travel unrestrictedly within the Union and to seek employment in all member states.

In pursuing its objectives, the Commission is likely to meet stiff resistance from the several national governments, who rightly view the Brussels initiatives as circumventions of national sovereignty. But the Commission can likely count on the support of the EP and the European Court of Justice, which normally side together on social issues.

The Maastricht Treaty contains the concept of 'Citizenship of the Union,' a most innovative, albeit controversial, departure that may well affect immigrants quite directly. Perhaps the most interesting article concerning citizenship of the union is the Maastricht Treaty's article 8b, which deals directly with the civil rights of immigrants:

Every citizen in the Union residing in the member state of which he is not a national shall have the right to vote and to stand as a candidate at municipal elections in the Member State in which he resides, under the same conditions as nationals of that State. This right shall be exercised subject to detailed arrangements to be adopted before 31 December 1994 by the Council, acting unanimously on a proposal from the Commission and after consulting European Parliament, these arrangements may provide for derogations where warranted by problems specific to a Member State.[25]

Initiatives in the immigration field suggest that the European institutions have become more assertive in taking bold decisions on issues that were considered strictly national. Even though common policy in the field of immigration has not yet been achieved the EU appears to be moving toward that end. The process, interestingly, has been rather piecemeal and haphazard, as it has been combining and interweaving national initiatives, like TREVI, with intergovernmental ones, like Schengen and the drafting of conventions, with community undertakings like Socrates and the 35-point program. Whether this process is up to actually dealing with the immigration crisis in Europe remains to be seen.

Going beyond what has been done

Neither the coordinated immigration policies that the EU has made to this point nor the immigrant-supportive actions of its institutions have been sufficient to solve the problem of managing immigration of considerable magnitude flowing in from outside. If the member states of the EU want to ameliorate the effects of the uncontrolled immigration of the 1960s and 1970s and to reduce the disruption and anxiety stemming from the streams of people crossing into Europe today, a combination of policies have to be initiated. These also have to be responsibly executed by all governments concerned. The Schengen Agreements are positive steps toward controlling who enters the Union. Immigrants with criminal backgrounds should rightly be kept out. But the Union has also to develop an effective common policy that will reduce violence against immigrants and eliminate the political pandering that is inflaming public opinion.

The EU cannot, of course, legally prohibit political parties from behaving the way they do on immigration issues. However, the European Parliament has at its disposal the budget of the European Communities that provides funding for social projects. The Parliament has always been one the most liberal institutions in the Union and the one most committed to extending social policies. The Parliament has debated immigration issues several times, and deputies have frequently expressed their positive support for immigrants who have been abused by political extremists. In October 1990, the Parliament was gathered to discuss a report prepared by its Committee on Inquiry into Racism and Xenophobia.[26] Since then, the Parliament has repeatedly condemned action against immigrants. Through its budgetary powers, it should be able to allocate more funds for projects that assist immigrants' causes, and at the same time it can bring pressure to bear on political groups *within itself* whose national colleagues and counterparts pursue anti-immigrant policies. By doing so, it will indirectly involve the Union in the common immigration policy, at least as regards the treatment of immigrants. As a moral actor, it may register some positive influence in the direction of sanity and civility.

A second course of action that the EU may consider has to do with squelching incentives to hire low-wage labor and to thereby discourage illegal immigration via smuggling or otherwise. Not only should the EU assist vulnerable countries to control immigration at their borders, but it also needs to assist poorer member countries in ways that will heighten their competitiveness on the Single Market. The Union has to convince governments and businesses alike that it is committed to economic development by providing financial and technical assistance in order to develop their economies. They will then not have excuses for hiring illegal immigrants, or for turning blind eyes to trafficking in human beings. Programs might even be conceived that link distribution of development funds to evidence that illegal immigration has been brought under control.

Third, there is the avenue of dealing with the root causes of migration. Brochmann, for example, proposes to identify all countries that send large numbers of immigrants to EU countries and to develop long-term policies with them. Economic assistance to those countries that are considered sources of immigration will keep potential immigrants at home. Workers go where there are jobs, and when there are jobs at home they do not seek to move.[27] Southern European countries are good examples of these strategies. During the 1950s and 1960s, Greece, Spain, Portugal, and Italy were the major senders of immigrants to the industrialized countries to the north of them. Assistance from the European Community and the modernization of economies created better economic conditions in the traditional sending countries, and the flow of labor has been reversed.

Fourth, Germany is very generous to immigrants because of its constitution. It also permits all individuals to reside legally in Germany providing that they prove they are of German blood. Nevertheless, many newcomers who are not officially immigrants, because of their German blood, tend to provoke discomfort and resentment among their neighbors because of their heterogeneous characteristics and their needs for housing and other governmental assistance. More serious, however, is the fact that the German constitution is very rigid in matters of granting German citizenship to individuals who are not of German blood, even when such people are actually born in Germany. There are already proposals to amend the constitution in order to reflect the changes in immigration policies. The first proposed change is to put limitations on the flow of immigrants to Germany. This change will provide a legal foundation for imposing immigration quotas similar to those imposed by the government of the United States. The second proposed change will make it easier for immigrants who are not of German blood to become German citizens. Obtaining German citizenship will be tantamount to gaining citizenship in the EU, and under the Maastricht Treaty any EU citizen can work in any country of the Union. Internal migration will then become an option for the second generation non-Germans and this should begin to alleviate the concentration of ethnic groups in Germany.

Fifth, there needs to be an open debate about immigration in Europe, and an effort needs to made to better educate public opinion about immigration's impacts. An open debate will serve two purposes: one is that it will engage the public in a process where useful ideas can be generated; the second is that the public will be informed and will understand that the presence of immigrants is not necessarily detrimental to European societies or economies. Quite to the contrary: immigrants contributed and continue to contribute to the expansion of the European economies. This point needs to be understood by the many, average EU citizens whose perception is that immigrants enter Europe only to take from it without giving anything in return. Immigrant-bashing is not the answer to Europe's economic and social woes, and this message needs to be delivered more clearly and forcefully than it has been thus far.

Notes

1. Gary S. Becker, 'Barbarians at the gate – or boon?,' *Business Week*, October 7, 1991, 20(A).
2. John Rossant, Igor Reichlin and Blanca Riemer, 'The floodgates are bursting: a tidal wave of immigrants could spoil the EC's vision of the future,' *Business Week*, September 9, 1991, 52(A); Becker, *op. cit.*; Robert Rice, 'Trying to stem the refugee tide,' *World Press Review*, November 1991, 13; Alan Riding, 'West Europe braces for migrant wave from East,' *New York Times*, December 14, 1990, 10(A).
3. Gary P. Freeman, 'Modes of immigration politics in the receiving states,' paper presented as part of the conference, Immigration into Western Societies: Implications and Policy Choices, at the Biennial Workshop of the European Communities Studies Association, Charleston, SC, May 13–14, 1994.

4. Thomas Faist, 'Immigration, integration and the ethnicization of politics,' *European Journal of Political Research*, 25 (1994), 439–59.

5. Anthony A. Messina, 'Political impediments to the resumption of labor migration to Western Europe,' *West European Politics*, 13 (1990), 31–46.

6. Ronald Triesky, *France in the New Europe: Changing yet Steadfast* (Belmont, CA: Wadsworth Publishing Company, 1994), p. 112.

7. *The World Press Review*, November 1991, p. 13.

8. *Makedonia*, May 6, 1994, 2(A). Note: *Makedonia* is a daily Greek newspaper published in Thessaloniki, Greece.

9. For this essay, I extensively cited documents on the immigration that were produced by the Commission of the European Union. To anyone who is interested in the issue I suggest that they may consult these documents.

10. C.D. de Jong, 'European immigration policies in the 21st century?,' paper presented as part of the conference, Immigration into Western Societies: Implications and Policy Choices, at the Biennial Workshop of the European Communities Studies Association, Charleston, SC, May 13–14, 1994, pp. 5–6.

11. Meisner *et al.*, 1993.

12. C.D. de Jong reports in his chapter in this volume that although Western European governments were very concerned about mass exodus from the Eastern European countries, the mass exodus occurred only from Yugoslavia.

13. Doris Meisner *et al.*, *International Migration Challenges in a New Era* (New York: The Trilateral Commission, 1993), p. 49.

14. Thomas Faist claims that because the German laws on asylum are so liberal, a number of analysts argue that this has led to very restrictive administrative rules and a comparatively low recognition rate.

15. Doris Meisner *et al.*, *op. cit.*, p. 51.

16. *Ibid.*

17. Philip Muus, 'International migration to Western Europe: South–North and East–West dynamics,' in Lydio Tomasi (ed.), *In Defense of the Alien* (New York: Center for Migration Studies, 1992).

18. Martin Baldwin-Edwards, 'Immigration after 1992,' *Policy and Politics*, 19 (1991), 199–211.

19. Philip Muus, *op. cit.*, p. 95.

20. Julian J.E. Schutte, 'Schengen: its meaning for the free movement of persons in Europe,' *Common Market Law Review*, 28 (1991), 549–70.

21. Tony Bonyan, 'Towards an authoritarian European state,' *Race and Class*, 32 (1991), 24.

22. *Ibid.*

23. *Ibid.*

24. *The European*, February 4–10, 1994, 1(A).

25. Council of the European Communities and Commission of the European Communities, *Treaty on European Union* (Luxembourg: Office for Official Publications of the European Communities, 1992), pp. 15–16.

26. Patrick L. Ireland, 'Facing the true "fortress Europe". Immigrants and politics in the EC,' *Journal of Common Market Studies*, 29 (1991), 470–80.

27. Brochmann, *op. cit.*

13 Europe's search for policy: the harmonization of asylum policy and European integration

Emek M. Uçarer

Introduction

In 1995, the office of the United Nations High Commissioner for Refugees announced that there were approximately 18.2 to 20 million international refugees under its mandate, and another 24 million are estimated to be displaced within the borders of their own countries.[1] Such people, forced to leave their countries of origin as a result of fear of persecution or generalized violence, make up a growing portion of contemporary migration movements. They also happen to be the group that is most vulnerable and in most pressing need of protection against human rights violations which force them to seek shelter elsewhere. Though the bulk of these refugees remain within Third World countries, changes in the international system at the end of the 1980s have raised concerns that developed countries might soon be swamped with asylum applications. Nowhere were these concerns more pronounced than in Europe, where the applications for asylum have increased by 800 percent in the course of a few years.[2] This increase was met with alarm, which reflected itself in increasingly negative public opinion and a sense of urgency among public policy makers.

The phenomena of forced migration[3] and asylum as an institution of humanitarian protection offer an opportunity to examine the extent to which theories of international relations help to explain the efforts being made to deal with a global crisis. This chapter will consider the attempts to deal with asylum issues in Europe during the past decade. As such, it will focus on the outcome of such efforts among the members of the European Union, where there seems to be growing consensus that asylum-related issues need to be addressed in multilateral forums with the aim of creating an international regime which establishes standard procedures for handling asylum applications. Coming to agreement about such arrangements, however, is no easy undertaking. Regional cooperation that would generate collective measures regarding asylum run into the very difficulties that have generally challenged the integration process in Europe; seeking consensus runs the risk of being entangled in questions of sovereignty, and sovereignty is at the heart of many migration-related issues. But as the success in fulfilling the requirements of the Single European Act with respect to the free movement of persons within the Union territory has become yet another litmus test for the depth of the European integration process, establishing an EU immigration and asylum regime begins to have symbolic as well as practical significance.

Theories of integration, regimes, and the European Union

In the aftermath of the Single European Act and the negotiation of the Treaty on European Union (Maastricht), there is renewed academic interest in European processes.[4] Early integration theorists envisioned European integration happening in different ways. For federalists, European integration meant creating the United States of Europe – a constitution, a central government, and a subdivision of authority between the federation and its constituent units. Transactionalists, building upon the work of Karl Deutsch, understood integration to be a process of community formation fostered by communication and assimilation among peoples to produce a 'supranationality' which would lend legitimacy to supranational institutions.[5] Functionalists, after David Mitrany, saw international integration as a process of cooperative problem solving that would create an interconnected web of functionally specific international organizations and progressively delegate more and more policy making to the supranational domain.[6] Furthermore, the integration process would move forward as such functionally specific cooperation in one field would create pressures to set up similar arrangements in related fields, thereby widening the scope of cooperation.

Neo-functionalists, following Ernst Haas, saw international integration as essentially a political process that would progressively focus parties' and pressure groups' attentions on policy making at the supranational level and thereby shift political activity and authority from national governments to international institutions.[7] The upshot of several decades of 'integration theorizing' directed toward trying to understand happenings in Western Europe was that European integration was 'all of the above' inasmuch as authoritative federal-like institutions were emerging, transnational assimilation was taking place, particularly at elite levels, policy making was gravitating toward the Brussels center, policy domains were slipping from national control, and politics were relocating to the supranational arena. Unexpectedly, for the theorists at least, while all of this was happening and while national autonomy became increasingly constrained, states' sovereignty nonetheless remained very much intact.[8]

More recent, and perhaps somewhat more useful, theorizing with respect to European integration has shifted attention from what the members of the European Community/Union were constructing politically and institutionally, to what they have been responding to in their environment and how they have been responding. In effect, they have been responding to their increasing *interdependence*, and what they have been doing is trying to manage this interdependence in ways that maximize its potential benefits and minimize its costs. Managing interdependence takes the forms of setting objectives, making rules, and agreeing upon procedures for collective action. In the theoretical literature of international relations, this has come to be called establishing *regimes*.

According to the generally accepted definition of Stephen Krasner, regimes are 'principles, norms, rules and decision-making procedures around which actor expectations converge in a given issue-area' in international relations.[9] Implicit in the definition is a notion of order, a desire to institute established patterns which render situations manageable. In Oran Young's thinking, regimes deal with 'coordination problems or situations in which the pursuit of interest defined in narrow individual terms characteristically leads to socially undesirable outcomes.'[10] Particularly interesting are the processes through which such arrangements are concocted, and research has thus attempted to isolate processes of regime formation and the social forces that drive these.[11]

How a regime is formed is affected by the international context as well as by domestic factors. How and why different actors, be they states, NGOs, or individuals, converge around governing principles, norms, and standard operating procedures is essential to understand why regimes form around certain issue areas and not others.[12] And, once a regime is in operation, it is equally important to understand how it is upheld and how it shapes the continuing behavior of all involved.

The regime literature offers three explanations of how regimes form: self-generation, negotiation, and imposition.[13] Issues that are dealt with in the EU typically meet the definition of a negotiated regime 'that arises from a process of bargaining in which the parties engage in conscious efforts to hammer out *mutually agreeable provisions* to be incorporated into an *explicit agreement*.'[14] Once a regime is put in place, however, it may be maintained, or it may be altered or allowed to fall into disuse.[15] When and why these results occur are also interesting questions.

Conceptualizations of the EU see it as weaker than a federation and stronger than a regime. Keohane posits that 'The European Community can best be viewed as a set of complex overlapping networks, in which a supranational style of decision-making, characterized by compromises upgrading common interests, can under favorable conditions lead to the *pooling of sovereignty*.'[16] Similarly, Puchala envisions the EU as a concordance system, which is 'an international system wherein actors find it possible consistently to harmonize their interests, compromise their differences and reap mutual rewards from their interactions.'[17] Thus the EU is an inter-related patchwork of different governing arrangements where parties come to consensus as a result of negotiations usually catalyzed by international institutions.

The nature of these negotiations has been the subject of debate. Contention between different academic approaches to the EU is over the question of whether it is exemplary of a special type of negotiation that is unique to the EU organization, or whether members engage in conventional inter-governmental power politics that are not much affected by the EU context or tradition.[18] One influential study argues that EU states engage in rational choice calculations in an essentially competitive decision-making structure where the powerful prevail and set the outcomes.[19] This argument rejects the notion that a special *communautaire* dynamic has been fostered by the EU apparatus and its history – i.e., that European politics are driven by more than a simple intergovernmental calculus, and that they involve a particular 'European' mindset which invariably produces mutually acceptable outcomes for most of the actors. Examination of EU progress made in addressing asylum-related challenges multilaterally further points to the 'stop-and-go' nature of European negotiations. Periods of progress are followed by periods of stagnation. But progress registered usually creates a ratchet effect which provides a partial shield against spillback during periods of stagnation.[20]

Asylum as a domestic, European, and global issue

The current global refugee regime

Regional arrangements in Europe for handling asylum seekers are grounded, at least in theory, in the dicta of the global refugee regime. The *principles* that underpin the global regime and its conception of migration flow from the general principle of the sanctity of human life and from a liberal understanding of the freedom of individuals to move freely.[21] These principles are set forth in documents such as the Universal Declaration of Human Rights in articles 13 and 14.[22] But another main principle of the global refugee regime is the principle of state sovereignty, i.e., states ultimately decide who may cross their borders.

Skran identifies the *norms* of the global refugee regime as asylum, assistance, and burden sharing.[23] The two periods in the formation of the refugee regime, namely the interwar and the postwar periods, demonstrate considerable continuity with respect to the norms and principles under-pinning the regime, though there are clear changes with respect to the scale, scope, and decision rules of the current institutional framework.[24] The development of a global refugee regime dates back to the end of the Second World War, which displaced thousands of people, although ini-tiatives taken as early as the 1920s, which sought to create a framework to assist, regulate, and monitor refugee flows, should also be acknowledged.[25] Interwar attempts at a refugee regime were launched under the auspices of the League of Nations and initially prompted by the exodus from Russia in the years immediately after the Bolshevik Revolution. The interwar regime was organized around a central institution – a High Commissioner in the person of Fridtjof Nansen. The major actors defining and implementing the interwar regime were of course the governments of the major powers, but even then interested and committed NGOs helped to keep refugee issues on the global agenda.[26] Refugee affairs under the League of Nations set precedents that carried forward into the post-Second World War period. The post-Second World War refugee regime based its legitimacy on the newly founded United Nations, successor to the League, and its institution-alized activities centered on the United Nations High Commissioner for Refugees (UNHCR) located in Geneva.[27] The principles and norms of the earlier regime also carried forward: respect for human life, the right to move freely, asylum, assistance, and burden sharing.

Major steps forward in defining norms and rules relating to the recogni-tion, settlement, and monitoring of refugees, as well as in elaborating an institutional framework, came about in 1951 with the drafting of the Convention Relating to the Status of Refugees. The Convention emphasizes asylum. Authority to assist individuals seeking asylum is given to the newly established UNHCR, which, through states' contributions to its operating budget, distributes the cost of refugee assistance across the world commu-nity.[28] The 1951 Convention was also instrumental in enumerating the *rules* of the refugee regime. 'Refugee' is defined in article 1A(2) of the Conven-tion as someone who finds himself outside his own country of nationality unprotected by his own government, and who has a well founded fear of persecution on political, religious, or racial grounds should he return. While this definition has been criticized by scholars because of its ambiguity and limited scope, it persists as the authoritative demarcation of refugee status, it establishes the grounds on which individuals are granted or denied such status, and it sets the guidelines for global refugee statistics.

An asylum seeker is an individual who is seeking recognition as a refugee in another country. Whether or not refugee status is granted ultimately rests with the government of the receiving country, though summary expulsion is contrary to the global regime. The granting of asylum is connected to the *non-refoulement* principle, which stipulates that states must refrain from 'summary reconduction to the frontier of those discovered to have entered illegally and summary refusal of admission of those without valid papers.' As outlined in article 33 of the Convention, the *non-refoulement* principle also stipulates that states cannot return or expel refugees to a state where the person's life and freedom would be threatened.[29]

Europe's regional refugee regime

The global refugee regime has provided the backdrop against which the EU states have sought to deal with the asylum crisis that exploded at the end of the 1980s. In 1994, UN High Commissioner Sadako Ogata observed that 'It was in Europe that the institution of refugee protection was born, it is in Europe today that the adequacy of the system is being tested.'[30] Immigration in general and asylum in particular have the tendency to become issues at times when increased influx is compounded by economic troubles in receiving countries. Receiving countries typically first attempt to deal with the problem by way of domestic policy making to formulate new rules about immigration or to change existing ones. Unilateral policy making and problem solving are almost always national governments' first preferences: they create the illusion of lower transaction costs as they are comparatively easier to negotiate, implement, and monitor than are multilateral arrangements.

European governments' initial responses to increased asylum applications were no exception to this 'try to do it yourself first' rule of thumb. Starting in the mid-1980s and reaching a climax in 1992, members of what was then called the European Community faced almost geometric annual increases in applications for asylum. Table 13.1 shows that the magnitude of this increased influx varied for different members states, but the percentage increase was consistently massive for all of them. Asylum seeking had evolved from a manageable situation into a major problem.

There were a number of strategies available to deal with the problem. States could:

1   Act unilaterally by enacting domestic legislation, or bilaterally by nego-
    tiating executive agreements between receiving and sending, or
    receiving and transit countries.
2   Act multilaterally by engaging in intergovernmental negotiation in a
    broad arena containing receiving and sending countries outside as well
    as inside the EU.
3   Act multilaterally within the EU but not via the institutions of the EU
    Union, where the confines of the EU, would delimit who was in and who
    was out of the negotiations, but nothing more.

Table 13.1 Asylum applications in the current member states of the European Union: 1983–1995

Country	1983	1984	1985	1986	1987	1988	1989	1990	1991	1992	1993	1994	1995	Total
Austria	5900	7200	6700	8700	11,400	15,800	21,900	22,800	27,300	16,200	4356	–	–	148,256
	10.03	7.89	4.33	4.73	7.42	7.98	7.69	5.78	5.31	2.42	0.85			4.10
Belgium	2900	3700	5300	7700	6000	5100	8100	13,000	15,200	17,754	26,883	14,340	3106[a]	129,083
	4.93	4.05	3.43	4.18	3.90	2.58	2.83	3.30	2.96	2.65	5.25	4.78	3.31	3.58
Denmark	800	4300	8700	9300	2800	4700	4600	5300	4600	13884	14,351	6651	1351[a]	81,337
	1.36	4.72	5.63	5.05	1.82	2.37	1.61	1.34	0.90	2.07	2.80	2.22	1.44	2.25
Finland	–	–	–	–	50	50	200	2500	2100	3634	2023	849	215[a]	11,621
					0.03	0.03	0.07	0.63	0.40	0.54	0.40	0.28	0.23	0.32
France	14,300	15,900	25,800	23,400	24,800	31,600	60,000	56,000	46,500	28,872	26,662	26,044	8086[b]	387,964
	24.32	17.43	16.69	12.71	16.14	15.96	21.06	14.20	9.05	4.31	5.21	8.70	8.61	10.75
Germany	19,700	35,300	73,900	99,700	57,400	103,100	121,000	193,000	256,000	438,191	322,599	127,210	50,238[a]	1,897,338
	33.50	38.71	47.80	54.16	37.36	52.06	42.47	48.93	49.82	65.45	63.03	42.49	53.48	52.59
Italy	3000	4500	5,400	6,500	11,000	1300	2200	2200	31,700	2589	1323	1834	833[b]	76,879
	5.10	4.93	3.49	3.53	7.16	0.66	0.77	1.19	6.17	0.39	0.26	0.61	0.89	2.13
Netherlands	2000	2600	5700	5900	13,500	7500	14,000	21,200	21,600	20,346	35,399	52,576	11,985[c]	214,306
	3.40	2.85	3.69	3.20	8.79	3.79	4.91	5.38	4.20	3.03	6.91	17.56	12.76	5.94
Portugal[d]	1500	400	100	300	200	300	100	100						3000
	2.55	0.44	0.06	0.16	0.13	0.15	0.04	0.03						0.08
Spain	1400	1100	2300	2300	2500	3300	4000	8600	8100	11,700	12,615	10,230	1886[a]	70,031
	2.38	1.21	1.49	1.25	1.63	1.67	1.40	2.18	1.58	1.75	2.46	3.42	2.01	1.94
Sweden	3000	12,000	14,500	14,600	18,100	19,600	32,000	29,000	27,300	84,018	37,581	18,640	3523[b]	313,862
	5.10	13.16	9.38	7.93	11.78	9.90	11.23	7.35	5.31	12.55	7.34	6.22	3.75	8.70
UK	4300	4200	6200	5700	5900	5700	16,800	38,200	73,400	32,300	2800	41,000	12,720[b]	274,420
	7.31	4.61	4.01	3.10	3.84	2.88	5.90	9.69	14.29	4.82	5.47	13.69	13.54	7.60
Total	58,800	91,200	154,600	184,100	153,650	198,050	284,900	394,400	513,800	669,488	511,792	299,374	93,943	3,608,097

Source: Adapted and calculated from the *Migration News Sheet*, July 1995, and *Migration and Population Change in Europe*, (New York: UNIDIR, 1993).
The percentages indicate each country's intake of each year's total asylum applications. Total percentages apply to the entire period between 1983 and 1995.
[a] As of 3/95; [b] as of 4/95; [c] as of 5/95; [d] UNIDIR.

4   Act multilaterally by using the community apparatus and charging the European Commission to take the lead in developing community legislation that would harmonize the plethora of national regulations pertaining to border crossing, asylum, and the like.

Strategy 3 was, in effect, a compromise option which represented a hybrid between options 2 and 4. It steered around supranationalizing immigration policy, which challenged states' sovereign prerogatives. But it defined the domain within which a multilateral immigration regime would apply, and it limited participants in negotiations to a group among whom consensus might be reached. As it turned out, the first three strategies were all attempted – and found wanting – so in the post-Maastricht environment there are mounting pressures to push toward the fourth strategy and to effectively supranationalize immigration policy throughout the EU. But let us not get ahead of the analysis.

Coping strategies: 1985–1995

Strategy 1: unilateral and bilateral attempts

As expected, European receiving states initially attempted to remedy what they perceived to be an asylum onslaught by altering their national policies. This was nothing new in Europe. Recipients of guestworkers in the 1960s had resorted to the same tactic in the 1970s when Europe was caught up in the global recession and faced growing unemployment. To wit, they changed their guestworker policies and banned additional foreign workers from countries with which they had once signed special labor agreements.[31] Such tactics seemed to work reasonably well at the time. Nonetheless, migration scholars question whether the restrictionist moves did effectively curb the increase in the foreign population or even greatly affect the entry of prospective workers. Despite the bans, there was a steady increase in the percentage of the foreign population in the receiving countries as a result of programs such as those that allowed family unification for foreign residents. A similar dynamic was evident in the treatment of asylum seekers from the late 1980s onward, where countries attempted to deal with the issue nationally by making more rigorous policies regarding the review of applications, by shortening the review process, and by expelling more expeditiously those who were not granted refugee status. Germany went so far as to amend its Basic Law in an effort to bring its liberal asylum laws into line with the more restrictive practices in neighboring countries. Similar to the changes in procedure that were taking place elsewhere, such as in the Netherlands, Germany changed policy in order to make itself a less attractive country of destination for potential asylum seekers.[32] At the height of the debate over the amendment of the Basic Law, the Kohl government's attitude was underlined by Antonius Halbe, a senior political adviser, who argued that 'The numbers are more than we could cope with ... Most of the people were coming for economic reasons, not because of political persecution ... It is not the job of the German political system to absorb all the migrants of the world and assure them a better life.'[33]

Following the overhaul of the German asylum law, which took effect in July 1993, the number of asylum seekers plummeted from an average of 37,000 a month to about 10,000. Two provisions of the new German law have been particularly effective in thwarting would-be asylum seekers. One holds that any refugee arriving overland in Germany via a 'safe third country' – i.e. a democracy where human rights are observed – is ineligible for asylum. All nine of Germany's contiguous neighbors have been declared safe third countries by Bonn, providing Germany with a *cordon sanitaire*. The other key provision involves assessing whether the home country of a refugee is one where political persecution by the state is evident. Critics contend that Bonn's list of persecuting nations is too limited and that it excludes cases such as Somalia or Liberia where there is no state. Germany has also cracked down on airlines that bring in aliens without proper passports or visas. Only about 1 percent of asylum seekers now come by air, and to prevent them from taking refuge in the German legal system, they are shuttled into special transit areas considered to be outside German territory. Bonn has also sharply curbed welfare payments to asylum seekers.[34] National efforts to contain asylum seeking are perceived to be initial steps toward a more comprehensive regional regime. Helmut Kohl put the matter succinctly: 'The new regulation of the right to asylum ... was an important precondition for the fact that Germany can fully participate in a common European and asylum policy.'[35] On the bilateral front, the German government beefed up border patrols and signed treaties with Poland and the Czech Republic to make it more difficult for refugees to use those countries as transit points for entry into the German eastern *Länder*. Bonn is also paying these countries to ensure a more meticulous border patrolling on their part. Germany is not alone: at the time of this writing, there were approximately 38 readmission agreements in operation between the members of the EU and sending and transit countries located predominantly in Eastern and Central Europe and the successor states to the USSR.[36]

Though there is numerical evidence of radically declining asylum applications in Germany, which comes from a combination of strict enforcement of the constitutional changes and an increasingly deteriorated perception on the part of prospective applicants of Germany as a welcoming state, it is questionable what the new German policy change did for the overall situation. In fact, there is increasing evidence that prospective asylum seekers have been diverted to other EU member countries, such as the Netherlands, which have experienced, as an unexpected consequence of unilateral German action, an increase in asylum applications. This further calls into question the overall efficacy of such unilateral action, which inevitably becomes the target of complaint by another EU member, whose complaint must be dealt with at the regional level. This explains why, even in the face of the relative success that resulted from unilateral and bilateral policy making, efforts were reoriented toward multilateral attempts within the European arena.

Multilateral attempts: Europe-wide endeavors

Daniele Joly characterizes the 1970s and early 1980s as a period of 'uncoordinated liberalism' regarding immigration and asylum issues. The 1990s, by contrast, have been years of 'harmonized restrictionism,' at least as far as EU member states have been concerned.[37] How Europe managed to wend its way from disparate, often conflicting, national policies toward an effort to create and implement a regional regime to deal with immigration and asylum questions is instructive.

Until making efforts to harmonize European asylum policies, the European states were operating under the global refugee regime institutionalized by the 1951 Convention Relating to the Status of Refugees, and a 1967 Protocol that elaborated commitments under the Convention. The international legal framework for harmonizing European asylum policies therefore was, at least in part, guided by the 1951 Convention, though regional public customary law and the European Human Rights Convention also provided elements of backdrop. The Council of Europe was an initial debating forum concerning asylum and ways to harmonize national policies. As early as the 1970s it produced documents encouraging the harmonization of procedures with respect to the processing of asylum applications in the context of the existing global framework. But it failed to establish exactly how this harmonization was to be brought about.[38] The tremendous increase in asylum applications beginning in the late 1980s instigated a series of multilateral negotiations in Europe aimed at bringing about a coordinated and centralized response to what many European countries came to regard as a national security issue.[39]

Strategy 2: the Schengen Agreements

In the 1980s, Western European countries that were net recipients of migratory laborers faced a dilemma. The development of a single European market, the abolition of internal borders and the implementation of joint external borders, complicated at the end of the decade by burgeoning numbers of asylum seekers, necessitated cooperation between the Common

Market countries. On the one hand, asylum as an institution of humanitarian aid needed to be safeguarded in keeping with the 1951 Convention.
But, on the other hand, the financial burdens of this institution forced
recipient countries to cap the inflow to stabilize the growth of public
expenditures and to control the threat of xenophobia.[40] As the internal
economic borders of the European Communities were technically open,
and quite porous in any event, there was increasing concern about sharing
the burdens associated with migration, added concern about 'beggar-thy-
neighbor' attitudes exhibited by some recipient states, and a realization that
issues with such transnational and complex consequences could hardly be
coped with by national legislation alone. All of these concerns cumulatively
led to efforts to seek solutions at the regional level.

This frenzied pace of intergovernmental and multilateral activity, and the
magnitude of time, effort, and resources poured into the clarification of the
regional immigration/asylum regime reflected perceived salience of the
issue for the parties involved. In 1991 alone, there were 100 official meetings
among European Community members and eight ministerial conferences
focused on immigration questions. This drive toward regionalization was a
marked departure from most European countries' earlier positions, which
held migration and the treatment of asylum applications to be matters of
specific concern to sovereign states.[41]

The first catalyst for increased diplomatic attention to the asylum issue in
particular and migration issues in general was the integration agenda set
forth in the Maastricht Treaty which entered into force on November 1,
1993.[42] The ultimate objective of doing away with border controls within the
European Union, an explicit commitment at Maastricht, complicates the
movement of third country nationals within the Union, asylum seekers
being one of these groups. Many recognized that the abolishing of internal
borders within the Union would invariably necessitate enforcing tougher
controls on the Union's external borders. If, once inside the Union, a
migrant could move about relatively unimpeded by national borders, the
external borders of the Union consequently became crucial. Which, how,
how many, and when third country nationals, among them the asylum
seekers, could or would be accepted into the common territory therefore
also became an EU question of some urgency.

Increased intergovernmental activity to deal with asylum issues began in
the period immediately preceding the finalization of the Single European
Act. In 1984, there were only two major intergovernmental forums in
Europe dealing with asylum issues, both of them within the Council of
Europe. These were respectively the Sub-Committee on Protection of
UNHCR's Executive Committee and CAHAR, the Ad Hoc Committee on
the Legal Aspects of Territorial Asylum, Refugees, and Stateless Persons.[43]
These two forums were expected to deal with an almost 50 percent increase
in applications within a year. The result was the beginning of a proliferation

of various groups which engaged in negotiations to find ways of dealing with the emergent pressures.

The first such forum to emerge was the Schengen group. It was initially comprised of the cluster of EC countries that signed the Schengen Agreement after January 1984, and agreed, in accord with it, to remove controls at their common borders. The initial aim of the Schengen Agreement was to unblock truck traffic normally backed up at national borders, and to thereby expedite the flow of international commerce. The Schengen Group consisted initially of Germany and France, but the agreement was quickly extended to include seven adjacent countries.

Schengen was the first intergovernmental agreement that concretely addressed the elimination of border controls inside the European Common Market. The signatories wished to abolish completely 'if possible, by 1 January 1990' all checks on both goods and individuals at national borders.[44] EC citizens would eventually travel freely across these borders, though the Agreement provided for a gradual transition to fully open borders that took account of security needs in the borderless area.

Schengen's provisions were in line with the program advocated in a European Commission White Paper which spelled out the measures that had to be taken with regard to immigration controls, visa and asylum policies, as well as cooperation between police forces and vigilance concerning drug trafficking and other such menaces. The Schengen program turned out to be quite complex; opening borders turned out to have all manner of implications, political as well as legal, and these resulted in very lengthy negotiations and a missed deadline regarding implementation. Other regional matters, such as the German unification, further delayed the original deadline set in the agreement. Nonetheless, the negotiations ultimately resulted in 1990 in the signing of the Convention on the Application of the Schengen Agreement, which established the transnational institutional framework for dealing with asylum issues that will be discussed in a moment.

In the meantime, other regional forums were created to exchange views and seek common responses to refugee problems. The most important among these were the Inter-governmental Consultations on Asylum, Refugee and Migration Policies in Europe, North America, and Australia, the Ad Hoc Immigration Group of Senior Officials, the Nordic Joint Advisory Group, the Central European Initiative Group (formerly called the Hexagonale), and the Group of National Coordinators on the Freedom of Movement of Persons, otherwise known as the Rhodes Group.[45] Of these, the first was initiated by Sweden, the second was an EU group composed of ministers of the interior and justice, the third was a Nordic coordination group, the fourth included both Western and East-Central European government officials, and the fifth was affiliated with the Council of EC Ministers.

The Rhodes Group took an important step by circulating a document entitled 'Free movement of persons: report to the European Council by the Co-ordinators' Group,' drawn up at its meeting of 5–6 June 1989 held in Palma de Mallorca, generally known as the 'Palma Document.' This report criticized the proliferation of forums which were dealing with migration and refugee matters. It emphasized the need for cooperation among the various groups and it recommended that the discussion of immigration and asylum issues be concentrated in the Ad Hoc Working Group on Immigration, the Council of Europe and the UNHCR.[46] Emphasizing the need to establish a 'responsible state' for the processing of asylum applications, it paved the way for the Dublin Convention.

As foundations for a regional asylum regime, three important documents emerged from the multilateral European diplomacy of the 1980s. Each represents an element of principled consensus or commonly agreed practice, and all commit EU member states to cooperate on matters of asylum. The first is 'The Convention Applying the Schengen Agreement of 14 June 1985 Between the Governments of the Benelux Economic Union, the Federal Republic of Germany and the French Republic on the Gradual Abolition of Checks at Their Common Borders,' signed in Schengen, Luxembourg, on June 19, 1990.[47] The second is the Dublin Convention, the implementation of which is pending ratification. Third, there is a draft of 'The Convention between Member States of the European Communities on the Crossing of Their External Frontiers,' completed in 1991, in response to increasing East–West migration pressures, but not yet signed because of outstanding disagreements between the UK and Spain about the status of Gibraltar.

Of the three multilateral arrangements, Schengen goes the furthest in terms of establishing institutional capacity and making way for implementation. While confirming the principle of the abolition of checks on individuals at internal borders, The Schengen Implementation Convention also deals with matters such as the surveillance of external borders, the harmonization of visa policies, the freedom of movement of third country aliens, criteria for designating the country responsible for processing particular asylum applications, cooperation between police forces, extradition, narcotics, and the Schengen Information System (SIS). Once the Agreement is fully implemented, the common external border of the Schengen group will be similarly monitored regardless of which Schengen country monitors it. The Schengen Agreement was negotiated and signed outside the EU, even though all signatories are EU members. However, it anticipates an all-EU immigration and asylum regime in the future, and Schengen group members intend to accede to EU arrangements when these materialize. Under Schengen, for example, third country nationals are those individuals who are not EU citizens, while the convention also stipulates that as soon as an EU-wide policy is put in place EU regulations will prevail.

Since the signing of the Schengen Convention, work has been concentrated in two areas: preparing for implementing the Convention and enlarging the Schengen group. Interestingly, though the Convention itself is not an EU arrangement, accession to the group has been reserved for EU members *only*. Italy, Spain, and Greece joined the group in 1990, 1991, and 1992 respectively, leaving only Denmark, Ireland, and the United Kingdom from the original EC 12 and the new members Finland, Sweden, and Austria outside the accord.[48]

In December 1994, the Schengen Executive Committee, the governing body established in the accord, decided to implement the Schengen Convention as of March 26, 1995, since all the preconditions, including an operational Schengen Information System, had been met. The Convention is not in force in all of the signatory countries, but implementation is taking place at a reasonable pace. The integrated 'territory without internal borders' of the Schengen group been nicknamed Schengenland.[49] Though many observers expressed pessimism about the actual implementation of the Schengen agreements, those more confident in the arrangement agree with Callovi that 'The practical results achieved by the Schengen Group show that, once agreement is reached on the objectives, the goal of abolishing border checks on individuals is politically feasible and the technical problems which have to be solved for that purpose in order to maintain the current level of internal security are not insurmountable.'[50] Though there is stiff resistance from the non-signatories, most notably from the UK, which derisively refers to the Schengen signatories as 'Schengenites,' there is reason to believe that Schengen could be the foundation for an EU immigration and asylum regime and the prototype for future integration projects.[51]

Strategy 3: The Dublin Convention

The second document that came out of the European intergovernmental negotiations of the late 1980s is the 'Convention Determining the State Responsible for Examining Applications for Asylum Lodged in One of the Member States of the European Communities.' This is the Dublin Convention, signed on June 15, 1990.[52] Unlike the Schengen accords, the Dublin Convention establishes an explicitly EU-wide arrangement to deal with the complications of mounting, and often multiple, asylum applications lodged in member states. As noted, desperate asylum seekers have not hesitated to look for sanctuary in several countries simultaneously, a phenomenon that has come to be known as 'refugees in orbit.' Even though the Dublin Convention was negotiated before the official separation of the community architecture in the Maastricht Treaty (to be discussed below), it is an example of the kind of experience that strategy 3 would generate, i.e.

cooperation among EU member countries that is not really EU cooperation because the community apparatus is not used so as not to dilute sovereign prerogatives or symbolism.

The Schengen Agreement and the Dublin Convention are strikingly similar in that they attempt to designate which state shall be responsible for the handling of the application of each particular asylum seeker.[53] Articles 28 through 38 of the Schengen Agreement say that one state shall be responsible for processing each application regardless of where the application is actually filed.[54] In the event of multiple applications, states receiving them have the right to send the applicant to the state identified as responsible, which in turn must accept the applicant and process the application.[55]

In essence, the Schengen Group and its initiatives have been welcomed as the testing ground for the larger EU community as regards abolishing internal border controls. A healthy symbiosis has thus existed between the Schengen countries and the EU, in that, as noted above, the Schengen countries drafted their agreements with a view toward expanding their applicability to the EU. In turn, the Union has taken the Schengen arrangements as guiding principles around which to fashion EU-based agreements.

While not exactly a duplicate of the Schengen Agreement, the Dublin Convention bears a strong resemblance to the Schengen regulations. By participating as an observer in the Schengen negotiations, the European Commission tried to ensure that the Schengen Group did not move in directions that would conflict with EU rules and objectives. It further appears that the successful negotiations within the Schengen Group provided momentum for the Union itself to conduct similar negotiations that could eventually lead to the absorption of the Schengen architecture into the Union. There seems to be a growing inclination on the part of the EU to somehow fold the Schengen arrangements into a larger unitary EU institutional setting and decision-making arena.

There are, however, serious concerns on the part of some international lawyers that, with regard to their prescriptions for the handling of asylum applications, both the Schengen Agreement and the Dublin Convention represent an infringement of the 1951 UN Convention on refugees. Given that any regional arrangement must function in at least expressed compliance with the general global refugee regime, Meijers points to two essential matters, 'both of which flow from the two objectives contained in the [Schengen] draft: 1. the abandonment of the duty of each Schengen State to offer every refugee a certain measure of protection; 2. restrictions on the carriage of refugees not in possession of the documents demanded by the five [sic] States.'[56]

It has been argued that the 1951 Convention obligates its signatories to extend protection to all refugees who apply, and the signatory state may not refuse to deal with any person who falls under the jurisdiction of the Convention. It therefore binds its signatories to review all applications to determine refugee status, by which token every refugee stands the chance of asylum being granted in every state that is party to the 1951 Convention. Thus, 'When a group of States agrees that only one of that group is obliged to determine the existence of the status of refugee, thereby diminishing the refugee's chance of asylum, those States appear to act in contravention of the Convention. Such unlawful action deprives a refugee of the freedom to choose the State to which he or she wishes to flee ... The Schengen draft would deprive the refugee of both of these advantages, namely the multiple chance and the free choice.'[57]

This legal argument, which has credible following among experts on international refugee law, hints at the divergence of the emergent asylum regime in Europe from the overarching global regime. While the European documents profess correspondence to the global refugee regime, they also include a set of restrictive measures which would be in contradiction of the underlying principles of the global regime. Implementing these would constitute a violation of the intent of the 1951 Convention. Arguments such as these point to the complexities of formulating a regional regime by adding the complicating effects of the global level, which regional decision makers often overlook. Interpretations of the 1951 Convention naturally vary, and many EU members are today conveniently settling for the more restrictive readings of the law which legitimize the growing restrictionism that is slowly being codified into practice in the industrialized world.

The Treaty on European Union

During the very period when immigration and asylum issues were being urgently projected into multilateral forums in Europe, Europe itself was preparing for its biggest institutional shuffle since the founding of the EC. The Maastricht Treaty in 1993 transformed the European Community into the European Union, and in so doing institutionalized an EU decision-making structure to deal with asylum and related issues. Gathering steam from 1991 onward, negotiations about the structure of the emergent European Union resulted at Maastricht in a 'three pillared' edifice (that some enthusiasts imagined to be a new European temple). The symbolic 'pillars' supporting European unity were in effect realms of public policy that would be closely coordinated at the Union level. Pillar I was the Treaty of Rome, amended and expanded, and matters economic that it addressed. Pillar II was foreign and security policy or 'CFSP,' still more a vision than a reality, but a Maastricht commitment nonetheless. Pillar III symbolized European policy coordination in justice and home affairs and henceforth would be the arena within which the Union's common immigration and asylum policies would be hammered out.

Technically speaking, issues relating to asylum were put under Title VI of the Maastricht Treaty, which institutionalized what was described above as strategy 3; that is, a procedural and political halfway house between inter-governmentalism and supranationalism. Title VI of the Maastricht Treaty sets up an institutional arrangement that allows intergovernmental negotia-tions to take place within the newly engineered 'European temple,' though the influence of the temple's custodians in the European Commission is considerably constrained. During the pre-Maastricht preparatory negotia-tions, the Commission adopted a pragmatic stance sensitive to the fundamental issues of national sovereignty inherent in questions of immi-gration and asylum. Measures associated with any program for a frontier-free EU would have to be drawn up by intergovernmental bodies, so that, in the short run, the Union's institutions would be marginalized in policy making. Still, the Commission aspired to eventually get the Union's institutions into the policy-making and review processes that would be involved in later stages of the harmonization. Therefore, contentious issues like border controls and the standardizing of the review of asylum applica-tions would be discussed mainly among national governments, who would be subject to only limited EU oversight.[58]

Asylum issues have risen to the top of Pillar III's agenda. In the Declara-tion on Asylum contained in the Maastricht Treaty, member governments set down their objectives by agreeing to engage in 'common action to harmonize aspects of asylum policies by the beginning of 1993.'[59] Even though this deadline was not met (as is often the case with EU projects) there has been steady progress toward the realization of these goals. Title VI also created a new Coordinating Committee of senior officials (the K.4 Committee) who 'give opinions for the attention of the Council, either at the Council's request or on its own initiative; [and] contribute to the preparation of the Council's discussions.'[60] This body oversees the various intergovernmental forums at work on asylum questions, such as the Ad Hoc Group on Immigration, and it works as a specialized COREPER specific to this issue.

While possibly expediting intergovernmental cooperation on asylum questions in the context of Pillar III, the creation of this group of 'coor-dinators' inserts a new level of policy consultation and debate, and unfortunately also adds to the institutional confusion that Maastricht's Title VI created regarding jurisdiction. The net effect of this proliferation of the levels of preparations has been an unwillingness to assume responsibility at any level. Furthermore, while the Council and the European Court of Justice have some limited capacity to be involved in the formulation and the review of European level asylum policies, it is unclear what the role of the Commission would be, if any. The confusion is augmented by reservations about the democratic deficit that this setup creates, be it by the secretive nature of the negotiations, the marginalization of the European Parliament, or the lack of full jurisdiction for the European Court of Justice.[61]

Confounding matters still further is the Maastricht provision that would allow the decision-making arena to be shifted from Pillar III to Pillar I as specified in article K.9 of Title VI. This article erects a bridge between the Union proper and the intergovernmental setup within it. It stipulates that 'The Council, acting unanimously on the initiative of the Commission or a Member State, may decide to apply Article 100c of the Treaty Establishing the European Community to action in areas referred to in Article K.1(1) to (6), and at the same time determine the relevant voting conditions relating to it. It shall recommend the Member States to adopt that decision with their respective constitutional requirements.' Article 100c, which was added to the Rome Treaty in the course of preparations for Maastricht, stipulates that 'The Council, acting unanimously on a proposal from the Commission and after consulting the European Parliament, shall determine the third countries whose nationals must be in possession of a visa when crossing the external borders of the Member States,' which would also 'apply to other areas if so decided pursuant to Article K.9.'[62] Decisions on these matters are to be made by unanimity until January 1, 1996 and by a qualified majority after that, which requires 54 votes in favor cast by at least eight members. The voting procedure pursuant to the implementation of article K.9 is to be determined at the time decisions are taken, which may mean that it be done by unanimity initially, and then later become subject to a qualified majority. Exactly who is to have the final say about what regarding the emergent EU asylum regime therefore remains murky, though such opaqueness may prove functional in this politically sensitive policy domain.

The current agenda under Title VI

In work actually in progress under Title VI, the emphasis is on arriving at 'soft law' set forth in resolutions, conclusions, and recommendations rather than mandatory measures. The process is not fashioning legally binding instruments, but it is clarifying the rules and decision-making procedures of the emergent regime. Procedures are being harmonized; acceptable standard operating procedures are being defined, especially as these relate to the establishing of minimum guarantees for the protection of refugees. The concept of safe third country is being clarified, the interpretation of the 1951 Convention's definition of a refugee is being standardized, criteria for the treatment of manifestly unfounded claims are being established, and a mechanism for burden sharing among the members states is being worked out. Notably, transnational uniformity has apparently been rejected as a founding principle for the EU regime. What are being more reasonably called for are arrangements that amount to 'equivalent procedures in all Member States.'[63]

In 1992 resolutions on 'manifestly unfounded claims' and 'host third countries' were adopted. During the same year, EU member states agreed upon the contents of a conclusion on 'safe third countries,' the provisions of which were subsequently incorporated into national legislation of the member states.[64] The Resolution on Minimum Guarantees for Asylum Procedures, finally adopted at the Judicial and Home Affairs Council on June 21, 1995, spells out guarantees concerning the examination of asylum applications, stipulates the rights of asylum seekers during such examinations, establishes appeal and review procedures, defines procedures to be followed for manifestly unfounded asylum applications, outlines procedures for making asylum applications at national borders, and lists additional safeguards that apply to unaccompanied minors and women. EU member states are currently working on a common interpretation of the definition of a refugee in line with the 1951 Convention.

All of these efforts have been fraught with difficulty, and consensus has invariably come only after considerable dilution of the measures adopted. The EU process has also displayed the tensions that are slowly being created between regional efforts to deal with specific, urgent, and highly politicized problems, and the liberalities and assumed universalities of the global refugee regime. These tensions show in the concern with which UNHCR, the legal guarantor of the 1951 Convention, Amnesty International, and other refugee rights advocates have been following the developments in the European Union.[65]

Despite the substantive progress which intergovernmental activities have recorded on asylum questions, there are already signs of discontent with Title VI and Pillar III of the Treaty of European Union. Part of the discontent on the part of the member states comes from difficulties in trying to oversee the implementation of the agreement reached in the context of Pillar III of the intergovernmental treaties. The Dublin Convention, for example, has not been fully ratified yet, and such ratification headaches are endemic to the implementation of international legal instruments produced in the way that Pillar III processes produced them. This makes it difficult to deal with urgent issues in a timely fashion, and the asylum issues being debated under Pillar III are urgent. The Commission, in a 1994 report to the Council and the Parliament, pointed to the shortcomings of the institutional arrangements under Title VI.

However, the Maastricht Treaty in general and Title VI in particular are subject to review and revision during the European Union's Intergovernmental Conference (IGC) which began in Turin in March 1996, and member states appear inclined to wait until the IGC to reconsider decision-making procedures under Title IV. If, regarding Title IV, the Commission prevails in its opinion that 'neither the legal instruments provided nor the administrative structures set up appear to be capable of satisfying the need for coordination in this area,' immigration and asylum matters may be ultimately dealt with in the EU in ways similar to external agricultural issues, or commercial policies more generally.[66] Though many interested non-governmental organizations and some organs of the EU have prepared documents suggesting the amendment of Title VI, it seems that this particular issue has not been on the EU agenda long enough for Union processes to have taken root.[67]

A possible model for the harmonization of asylum policies: do all roads lead to Brussels?

This chapter charted multilateral cooperative efforts on asylum-related issues in Europe after the mid-1980s. There is clear evidence that liberal policies and incoherent frameworks are no longer the norm, although there is equally convincing evidence that the harmonization efforts have come about in a relatively haphazard and *ad hoc* manner. The record suggests that receiving states initially seek to deal with the asylum/migration influx by way of unilateral policies or bilateral deals, and only after the inadequacy of these policies is established do they turn to multilateral arenas, seeking cooperation with their neighbors. This they do very cautiously and incrementally, typically negotiating intergovernmentally, protecting sovereign prerogatives and limiting influence from international organizations or other authorities.

European experience, however, begins to suggest that such intergovernmentalism may also prove inadequate for establishing and implementing multilaterally inclusive regimes. As one an observer noted, 'intergovernmental co-operation may be the member states' chosen method for policy development, but it has shown itself already to be slow, messy, halting and untransparent in its progress.'[68]

To go back to Krasner and the theory of regimes, one might argue that under current arrangements in Europe, EU member states are in the process of affirming the principles and norms and determining the rules of an integrated asylum policy that would amount to a regional regime in the issue area. The principles and norms of the European regime should complement those of the global refugee regime – and whether they do is of principle concern – but with the important distinction that the emergent European regime is much more restrictive in its aspirations with regard to the actual handling of the cases. What is not at all clear at this point, and what this chapter has principally shown, is that the decision-making procedures of the European asylum regime are neither clearly established nor universally accepted. Table 13.2 compares the existing arrangements.

Table 13.2 *Properties of refugee regimes*

	Global	Unilateral/ bilateral	Multilateral Schengen	Title VI	Communitarian
Principles	*Pacta sunt servanda,* sovereignty, humani-tarianism	Sovereignty	Sovereignty	Sovereignty	Pooled sovereignty
Norms	Asylum, assistance, burden sharing	Repatriation	Responsible state	Responsible state, manifestly unfounded claims, minimum guarantees, safe third country	*Acquis communautaire*
Rules	Refugee definition, *non-refoulement*	As specified in executive agreements	As specified in Schengen I and II	As specified in Title VI, article K	As specified in regulations, directives, decisions, and recommendations
Decision-making procedures	As laid down in the Convention	Domestic politics Bureaucratic politics	Unanimity	Unanimity, Title VI, article K	Qualified majority
Institutional framework	UNHCR	None	Schengen Executive Committee	Pillar III	Pillar I
Type	Diffuse, formal	Specific, formal	Specific, formal	Specific, formal	Semi-specific, semi-formal

Recent efforts to harmonize procedural aspects of asylum regulations across the EU demonstrate a mixture of the first three of the strategies laid out earlier in this chapter. Though the evidence presented here does not altogether confirm a clear evolution through time, whereby solutions are sought at ever higher levels of multilateral cooperation, there is a correlation between the increase in the number of asylum seekers and the political agendas set by the Single European Act and Maastricht. Urgency and politicization obviously put border control issues on the European agenda and raised them to high priority. Governments then had to come upon ways to handle the pressing issues, and the dynamics of trial and error – or half-hearted initiatives and unsatisfactory results – apparently led them from unilateralism to multilateralism, and from intergovernmentalism at least to a consideration of increased supranationalism.

Table 13.3 outlines some important results of multilateral efforts to produce a European asylum regime. It juxtaposes developments in the Schengen framework with the activities under Title VI. Progress is apparent, but the fact remains that cooperation has remained intergovernmental.

Table 13.3   *Major developments in asylum and immigration: 1985–1995*

	European Union	Schengen Countries
1985	**Jun** White Paper to establish the internal market without frontiers	**Jun** Schengen Agreement for the gradual abolition of internal borders, signed by France, Germany, and the Benelux countries
1986	**Dec** Establishment of the Ad-Hoc Group of Immigration Ministers in London to work out compensatory measures	Negotiation of the Implementation Agreement
1987	**Feb** Single European Act amends the EC Treaty art. 8A	Negotiation of the Implementation Agreement
1988	**Dec** Establishment of the Group of Coordinators Free Circulation (Rhodes Group)	Negotiation of the Implementation Agreement
1989	**Jun** The Palma document is issued on measures to establish free circulation of persons	**Dec** Signing of the Implementation Agreement postponed upon a request from Germany after the opening of the German borders
1990	**Jun** Dublin Convention signed by 11 members, to be followed by Denmark one year later	**Jun** Schengen Implementation Agreement is signed **Dec** Italy accedes to the agreements
1991	**Jul** Draft External Borders Convention **Dec** Working Program WGI 930, 'Maastricht Program' **Dec** Treaty on European Union establishing the three pillars	**Mar** Agreement between the Schengen countries and Poland **Jun** Spain and Portugal accede to the agreements
1992	**Jun** Adoption of decision on an Information Clearing House by ministers responsible for immigration **Dec** London resolutions on manifestly unfounded claims, safe third countries, safe countries of origin, CIREA, and refugees from Yugoslavia	**Sep** Decision of Central Group that harmonization of asylum be undertaken by the EU members and not at the Schengen level **Nov** Greece accedes to the agreements

Table 13.3 *continued*

1993	**Jun** Resolutions on Yugoslavia and family reunion **Nov** Entry into force of the TEU. Establishment of the K.4 Committee and three steering groups (Immigration/Asylum, Police Cooperation, Judicial Cooperation) **Nov** Commission issues its report on the possibility of applying Article K.9 of the TEU to asylum policy **Nov** First Council of Justice and Home Affairs (JHA) in Brussels	**Sep** Implementation of the Accords to enter into force after ratification by the five founding states **Oct** First Schengen Executive Committee Meeting **Nov** Second Schengen Executive Committee Meeting **Dec** Third Schengen Executive Committee Meeting
1994	**Jan** Commission proposal for the External Borders Convention Commission proposal for a regulation determining the third countries whose national must be in possession of a visa when crossing the external borders of the member states **Feb** Commission Communication to the Council and Parliament on Immigration and Asylum **Jun** Second JHA Council, Luxembourg	**Feb** Entry into force of the Accords postponed *sine die* because of the non-operational SIS **Apr** Fourth Schengen Executive Committee Meeting; all conditions satisfied, except the operational SIS **Jun** Fifth Schengen Executive Committee Meeting **Oct** Application of the Accords postponed again
1995	**Mar** JHA Council fails to agree on uniform visa formats **Jun** Minimum Guarantees resolution is adopted by the JHA Council **Jun** Commission issues its report on the functioning of the TEU, strongly criticizing the Third Pillar	**Mar** Schengen Convention is applied, 10 years after the signing **May** France is accused of having violated the Convention; France requests a six month trial period

Source: Adapted from UNHCR, *UNHCR and Its Partners in Europe* (Geneva: UNHCR, 1995) and *Migration News Sheet*, various issues

The hasty deal that was struck to simultaneously appease the federalists and the anti-federalists by creating the pillar structure, and especially Title VI, at Maastricht may have been an appropriate move at the time. And the episode may have given member states time to observe, and learn from, the kinds of problems Title VI procedures engender. This learning process in progress could conceivably ease opposition to asylum and immigration matters being handled by the Union proper.

Developments in the context of the EU suggest that the regional refugee regime has not yet completed its gestation period. As students of European integration well know, such governing arrangements can take a long time to consolidate. The answer to the question of whether all roads lead to Brussels in the formation of a regional asylum regime is therefore indeterminate, though it appears to be a (very) qualified yes. Whether this involves a complete shift of asylum issues to Union competence, or whether Title VI will be substantially remodeled to allow for qualified majority voting with increased powers for the European Parliament and the European Court of Justice, remains to be seen.

Analysis here has also revealed significant tensions between the similar, yet divergent, regimes that govern responses to asylum seekers. This divergence is most obvious between the global refugee regime and the regional arrangements still under construction in Europe. Current efforts undertaken under Title VI seek to address some of the issues not dealt with in the 1951 UN Convention by introducing the concepts of 'responsible state,' 'manifestly unfounded claims,' and 'safe third country' as pragmatic innovations to deal with what the member states overwhelmingly perceive as an unwieldy situation. Whether the creation of such new norms is in keeping with the spirit of the global refugee regime lies at the heart of the criticism of the EU being voiced by human and refugee rights activists who have long been promoting tenets of the UN Convention. If the norms and the principles of the global refugee regime are indeed being challenged by 'counter-regime norms' in Europe, this may indicate a serious challenge to the global refugee regime. What this would mean for the future protection of potential refugees whose access to countries of asylum seems to be adversely affected by the rules that Europeans are currently making remains to be seen.

Notes

1. See Roland S. Schilling, 'Refugees and immigration in Europe and the Third World,' in Friedrich Heckmann and Wolfgang Bosswick, *Migration Policies: a Comparative Perspective* (Bamberg: European Forum for Migration Studies, 1995).
2. Intergovernmental Consultations, *Full Round of Consultations: Statistical Tables* (Geneva, 1992).
3. Admittedly, international refugees are not the only kind of forced migrants. Rosemarie Rogers distinguishes between recognized refugees, externally displaced, and internally displaced as different types of forced migrants. She argues that 'whether a person ends up in one or the other category is often accidental.' Nonetheless, while there is a compelling argument that any asylum regime must

indeed take into account the status of all three types of forced migrants, the fact remains that the current asylum regime deals with forced migrants to the extent that they fall under the legal definition of a refugee specified in legal instruments governing the regime. Rosemarie Rogers, 'The future of refugee flows and policies,' *International Migration Review*, 26, 4 (1992), 1112–43.

4. See Michael G. Huelshoff, 'Europe and the Federal Republic of Germany: 1992 and the revitalization of integration theory,' *German Studies Review*, 125 (1990), 125–39 for an evaluation of progress to date and a discussion on a new research agenda in integration theory.

5. Karl Deutsch, *France, Germany and the Western Alliance: a Study of Elite Attitudes on European Integration and World Politics* (New York: Scribner's Sons, 1967); Karl Deutsch *et al.*, *Political Community in the North Atlantic Area* (Princeton, NJ: Princeton University Press, 1957).

6. Huelshoff, *op. cit.*

7. See J.S. Nye, *Peace in Parts: Integration and Conflict in Regional Organization* (Boston: Little, Brown and Company, 1971); and Leon Lindberg and Stuart Scheingold, *Europe's Would-be Polity* (Englewood Cliffs, NJ: Prentice Hall, 1970).

8. Paul Taylor, *The Limits of European Integration* (New York: Columbia University Press, 1983).

9. Principles are 'beliefs of fact, causation or rectitude,' norms are 'standards of behavior defined in terms of rights and obligations,' rules are 'specific prescriptions or proscriptions for action,' and decision-making procedures are 'prevailing practices for making and implementing collective choice.' Stephen D. Krasner, 'Structural causes and regime consequences: regimes as intervening variables,' in Stephen D. Krasner (ed.), *International Regimes* (Ithaca, NY: Cornell University Press, 1983), p. 2. Another commonly cited definition of regimes is set forth by Keohane and Nye, who conceptualize regimes as 'sets of governing arrangements' which include 'networks of rules, norms and procedures that regularize behavior and control its effects.' This definition is essentially the same put forth by Krasner.

10. Oran Young, 'Regime dynamics: the rise and fall of regimes,' in Stephen D. Krasner (ed.), *International Regimes* (Ithaca, NY: Cornell University Press, 1983), p. 97.

11. Oran Young, 'International regime initiation,' *International Studies Notes*, 19, 3 (1994), 44.

12. Young classifies regimes on how they form, arguing that there are three types of orders: spontaneous, negotiated, and imposed. See Oran Young, 'Regime dynamics,' *op. cit.*, pp. 99–101 for the properties of these regimes.

13. Oran Young, 'Regime dynamics,' *op. cit.*

14. Young, 'International regime initiation,' *op. cit.*, p. 44, emphasis added.

15. Krasner, *op. cit.*

16. Robert O. Keohane and Stanley Hoffmann, 'Conclusions: community politics and institutional change,' in William Wallace (ed.), *The Dynamics of European Integration* (London: Pinter Publishers, 1990), p. 277, emphasis added.

17. Donald J. Puchala, 'Of blind men, elephants and international integration,' *Journal of Common Market Studies*, 10, 3, (1972), p. 277.

18. The first position would be favored by Helen Wallace in 'Making multilateral negotiations work,' in William Wallace (ed.), *The Dynamics of European Integration*

(London: Pinter Publishers, 1990). The second is implied in Andrew Moravscik, 'Negotiating the Single European Act: national interest and conventional state-craft in the European Community,' *International Organization*, 45, 1 (1991), 19–56; and Andrew Moravscik, 'Preferences and power in the European Community: a liberal intergovernmentalist approach,' *Journal of Common Market Studies*, 31, 4 (1993), 473–524.

19. Moravscik, 1991, 1993, *op. cit.*

20. See Dorette Corbey, 'Dialectical functionalism: stagnation as a booster for European integration,' *International Organization*, 49, 2 (1995), 253–84.

21. Undoubtedly, some of these 'rights' clash with the sovereignty principle, which is the dominating principle in international relations as well as international law today. Disputes between the rights of an individual and the rights of the state provide the basis of the conflict that guide the study of migration.

22. Article 13 of the Universal Declaration of Human Rights states that '(1) Everyone has the right to freedom of movement and residence within the border of each state; and (2) Everyone has the right to leave any country, including his own, and return to his country.' Article 14 (1) stipulates that 'Everyone has the right to seek and enjoy in other countries asylum from persecution.'

23. Claudena Skran, *Refugees in Inter-war Europe: the Emergence of a Regime* (Oxford: Clarendon Press, 1995).

24. See Claudena Skran, 'The international refugee regime: the historical and contemporary context of international responses to asylum problems,' *Journal of Policy History*, 4, 1 (1992), 8–35.

25. *Ibid.*, p. 14.

26. For a lengthier discussion on the role of NGOs and INGOs in the refugee regime, see Skran, pp. 18–19.

27. See Louise Holborn, 'The League of Nations and the refugee problem,' *Annals of the American Academy of Political and Social Science*, 203 (1939), 124–35.

28. Skran, *Refugees in Inter-war Europe, op. cit.*

29. *Ibid.*, p. 69.

30. Sadako Ogata, 'Refugees: a comprehensive European strategy,' speech given to the German UN Association and the German Association for Foreign Policy, Bonn, June 21, 1994, p. 1.

31. Germany in November 1973, The United Kingdom in January 1973, France in July 1974, Belgium in August 1974, the Netherlands in December 1974, Switzerland in January 1975, Austria in 1975, and Luxembourg in March 1982.

32. The Associated Press News Service reports on April 14, 1994 that 'the government has announced a strategy to bar asylum hoppers, those economic refugees who trawl Europe for the best deal.' This involved sending teams to borders to grab entering asylum seekers, deciding within 24 hours if individuals can even apply for asylum, returning back anyone arriving from a country considered safe, and furthermore pledging Dutch support to Belgium, Germany, and Luxembourg to bar each other's asylum rejects.

33. Quoted in Frank Wright, 'Nation seeks asylum from wave of refugees: open door policy got out of control,' *Star Tribune: Newspaper of the Twin Cities*, December 13, 1993, p. 11A.

34. The payments were drastically cut, reducing the amount of benefits from $1000 in cash per month to $52 per adult per month and additional in-kind assistance

such as groceries. See 'German law discourages asylum-seeking migrants: explosive political issue largely defused,' *Washington Post*, November 15, 1994, p. A1.

35. Quoted in 'Kohl views 1993 achievements, 1994 tasks,' *International Intelligence Report*, January 3, 1994.

36. Belgium has such agreements with the Czech Republic, Poland, Romania, and Slovenia; Denmark with the Czech Republic, Estonia, Lithuania, and Latvia; France with Poland and Romania; Italy with Poland; Luxembourg with the Czech Republic, Poland, Romania, and Slovenia; the Netherlands with the Czech Republic, Poland, Romania, and Slovenia; Austria with the Czech Republic, Hungary, Poland, Romania, Slovakia, and Slovenia; Greece with the Czech Republic, Poland, Romania, and Slovenia; Germany with Bulgaria, the Czech Republic, Croatia, Poland, and Romania; Spain with Romania; and Sweden with the Czech Republic, Poland, and Romania. Furthermore, Poland has a readmission agreement signed with the Schengen group. For more precise information with regard to the nature of these agreements, as well as their status of implementation, see *Migration News Sheet*, 148, July 1995.

37. Daniele Joly, 'The porous dam: European harmonization on asylum in the nineties,' *International Journal of Refugee Law*, 6, 2 (1994), 159. See also Daniele Joly, *Refugees: Asylum in Europe?* (San Francisco: Westview Press, 1992).

38. Some of these documents are 'Social situation and social measures concerning people seeking political asylum or having refugee status in the member states of the Council of Europe,' 'The harmonisation of national procedures relating to asylum,' and 'Problems raised by certain aspects of the present situation of refugees from the standpoint of the European Convention on Human Rights.'

39. While migration, of which refugees is but a subset, was initially regarded as low politics, in the post-Cold War era it is increasingly being treated as a high politics issue. For further clarification on this debate see Doris Meissner *et al.*, *International Migration Challenges in a New Era: Policy Perspectives and Priorities for Europe, Japan, North America and the International Community. A Report to the Trilateral Commission* (New York: Trilateral Commission, 1993); and Ole Waever, Barry Buzan, Morten Kelstrup and Pierre Lemaitre, *Identity, Migration and the New Security Agenda in Europe* (New York: St Martin's Press, 1993). This debate can be seen as a result of growing concern with the role of state sovereignty in an era where mass movements of peoples have become more visible as a result of destabilizing events, such as the fall of communism, civil wars, increasing poverty, and resurgent nationalism, to name a few.

40. Increased assaults on asylum houses in Germany and the extreme right-wing electoral rallies in France and Germany, among others, which focused on playing the asylum card, are recent issues which caught the European eye. See Emek M. Uçarer, 'The challenge of migration: the German case,' *Mediterranean Quarterly*, 5, 3 (1994), 95–122, on xenophobia and assaults on asylum seekers.

41. Doris Meissner, *op. cit.*, p. 55.

42. The Maastricht Treaty adds a third pillar to European integration under which migration-related issues fall. Title VI of the treaty deals with cooperation in the fields of justice and home affairs. The Council of Justice and Home Affairs Ministers oversees issues concerning practical or harmonization related measures. Its work is couched solely in terms of intergovernmental negotiations.

43. Jonas Widgren, *The Informal Consultations 1985–1992* (Geneva: Inter-

governmental Consultations on Asylum, Refugee and Migration Policies in Europe, North America and Australia, 1993).

44. Article 30, Schengen Agreement.
45. For an excellent overview of the creation, scope and membership of these groups, see Sharon Stanton Russell and Charles B. Keely, 'Multilateral efforts to harmonize asylum policy along regional lines in industrial countries,' forthcoming; and Charles B. Keely and Sharon Stanton Russell, 'Responses of industrial countries to asylum seekers,' *Journal of International Affairs*, 47, 2 (1994), 398–417.
46. Stanton Russell, *op. cit.*, p. 10.
47. *Convention Applying the Schengen Agreement of 14 June 1985 between the Governments of the Benelux Economic Union, the Federal Republic of Germany and the French Republic on the Gradual Abolition of Checks at Their Common Borders*, June 19, 1990, 30 ILM 84.
48. Austria was granted observer status on June 27, 1995 and was expected to sign the agreement in April 1996.
49. Bolten, *op. cit.*
50. Giuseppe Callovi, 'Regulation of immigration in 1993: pieces of the European community jig-saw puzzle,' *International Migration Review*, 26, 2 (1992), 353–72.
51. The term Schengenite came up on various occasions during an interview at the Permanent Representation of the United Kingdom to the European Union. During this interview, which was conducted in Summer 1995 in Brussels, the First Secretary in charge of JHA noted that though crossing the border between France and the UK has become appreciably more of a hassle after the implementation of the accords, the UK was nonetheless happy not to be part of it.
52. *The Convention Determining the State Responsible for Examining Applications for Asylum Lodged in One of the Member States of the European Communities*, June 15, 1990, 30 ILM 427.
53. See Kay Hailbronner, 'The right to asylum and the future of asylum procedures in the European community,' *International Journal of Refugee Law*, 2, 3 (1990), 341–60.
54. Schengen, art. 29(3); Dublin, art. 3(2).
55. Schengen, art. 33; Dublin, arts 10–11.
56. H. Meijers, 'Refugees in Western Europe: 'Schengen' affects the entire refugee law,' *International Journal of Refugee Law*, 2, 3 (1990), 433.
57. *Ibid.*
58. Treaty on the European Union, Title VI.
59. Treaty on the European Union, Addendum.
60. Article K.4, Title VI of the TEU.
61. See Alan Butt Philip, 'European Union immigration policy: phantom, fantasy or fact?' *West European Politics*, 17, 2 (1994), 168–91; Daniele Joly, 1994, *op. cit.*; and C.A. Groenendijk, 'The competence of the EC Court of Justice with respect to inter-governmental treaties on immigration and asylum,' *International Journal of Refugee Law*, 4, 4 (1994), 531.
62. The other stipulations of interest of article 100c are as follows. (1) The Council, acting unanimously on a proposal from the Commission and after consulting the European Parliament, shall determine the third countries whose nationals must be in possession of a visa when crossing the external borders of the member

states. (3) From 1 January 1996, the Council shall adopt the decisions referred to in paragraph 1 by a qualified majority. (6) This Article shall apply to other areas if so decided pursuant to Article K.9 of the provisions of the Treaty on European Union which relate to cooperation in the fields of justice and home affairs, subject to the voting conditions determined at the same time. (7) The provisions of the conventions in force between the member states governing areas covered by this Article shall remain in force until their content has been replaced by directives or measures adopted pursuant to this Article.

63. Preamble to the Minimum Guarantees resolution.
64. Amnesty International, 'Europe: harmonization of asylum policy. Accelerated procedures for "manifestly unfounded" asylum claims and the "safe country" concept,' Amnesty International EC Project, 1992; Sarah Collinson, 'Towards further harmonisation? Migration policy in the European Union,' *Studi Emigrazione/Etudes Migrations*, 31, 114 (1994), 225.
65. See Johannes van der Klaauw, 'The challenges of the European harmonization process,' paper given at the Cost A2 Refugees in Europe Meeting, Amsterdam, May 25–28 May, 1995; 'UNHCR concerned by EU agreement on asylum procedures,' press release, March 10, 1995, Geneva; 'Information note on Article 1 of the 1951 Convention,' information paper, March 1995, Geneva; European Council on Refugees and Exiles (ECRE), 'EU policy on minimum guarantees for asylum procedures: NGO's shared concerns,' press release, January 1995, Brussels; Amnesty International, 'Europe: human rights and the need for a fair asylum policy,' EUR, March 1, 1991; Amnesty International, 'International protection of refugees threatened by powerful governments,' press release, Amnesty International Secretariat, October 1, 1993, London; Amnesty International, 'Europe: harmonization of asylum policy; Amnesty International's concerns,' EUR, January 1, November 1990.
66. In contrast, the Council in its report on the functioning of the TEU levels similar criticisms in a much milder tone. 'Commission strongly criticizes functioning of third pillar,' *Migration News Sheet*, 147/95–06, June 1995, 1.
67. See *Proposals for the Amendment of the Treaty on European Union at the IGC in 1996*, Standing Committee of Experts on International Immigration, Refugee and Criminal Law, March 1995; The Starting Line, 'Proposals for amendments to the Treaty on European Union,' in Simon Hix, *The 1996 Intergovernmental Conference and the Future of the Third Pillar*, CCME Briefing Paper, no. 20, May 1995; ECRE, 'Position on the functioning of the Treaty on European Union in relation to asylum policy,' Brussels, June 1995; Jean Louis Bourlanges and David Martin, *Report on the Functioning of the Treaty on European Union with a View to the 1996 Intergovernmental Conference – Implementation and Development of the Union: Explanatory Statement*, European Parliament Committee on Institutional Affairs, May 12, 1995, no. PE 212.450/fin./Part I.B.2; Jean Louis Bourlanges and David Martin, *Report on the Functioning of the Treaty on European Union with a View to the 1996 Intergovernmental Conference – Implementation and Development of the Union: Co-Draftsmen's Working Documents*, European Parliament Committee on Institutional Affairs, May 4, 1995, no. PE 212.450/fin./Part III.
68. Alan Butt Philip, *op. cit.*, p. 188.

14 Immigration in the twentieth century: which framework for policy response?

Reinhard Lohrmann

Introduction

Immigration is an issue in which state authorities intervene through the adoption of legal provisions and policy decisions. This intervention arises from the very notion of state sovereignty. In conformity with this sovereignty, state authorities decide on the question of who belongs to the community of citizens and who does not, what the rights of citizens and noncitizens are, which aliens will be authorized as residents of a state and which will not, who will be entitled to work, and what the criteria for admission of aliens are.

In past decades migrants were admitted to Western industrial states in conformity with policies related to labor market needs, to demographic goals, and to humanitarian and family issues. Some countries recognized immigration as a contribution to nation building. Pull factors dominated policy decisions which set the framework for migrants' admission and integration. However, during the past two decades a significant shift has taken place from a predominantly demand-induced migration toward migration in which push factors have exercised increasing influence. This has resulted in new migration situations in many Western industrial countries, and profound changes in the formulation of policies, of responses to them, and in their effectiveness.

One less acknowledged aspect is that, as a result of this shift and of the effects of a lasting migration tradition, the role of governments has become less proactive and policy and administrative measures have become less effective. Previously, when pull factors exercised the dominant force, governments set the policy framework in advance of the occurrence of labor movements and intervened actively in the migration processes. A typical example is the Federal Republic of Germany, where, in the early 1960s, rapid economic development led to growing labor shortages and difficulties in filling vacancies. Rising requests for the recruitment of foreign labor were discussed among government authorities, political parties, representatives of industry, and trade unions. A clearly framed policy concept resulted from these discussions, in which the actual recruitment of migrant workers by the Federal Employment Office, the payment of equal salaries and social benefits, and the migrants' enrollment in the nationwide social security system were the basic elements. State authorities played a proactive role in setting the system in place. Similar processes took place in several other West European states.

However, after a number of years, during which the migration processes had matured and developed their own dynamics, and push factors came to the forefront, new issues arose requiring policy responses. These included the housing needs of families of migrants, requests for family reunion and settlement, the schooling of migrant children, minority situations, the expression of different cultural values, the practice of foreign languages and resulting communication difficulties, and the prevention of and coping with rising irregular migration and asylum requests. State authorities dealt with these in a more reactive manner in response to developments which were neither anticipated nor planned. Measures were taken in reaction to processes which had developed autonomously. Not surprisingly, they usually failed to produce quick results. For instance, the handling of asylum claims could take several years until a final decision was made. The adoption and implementation of legislative changes could take months and some-times years until they entered into force to produce effects. However, new legislative and administrative measures could be circumvented or neu-tralized, such as when migrants choose a clandestine status instead of running the risk that their asylum claim would be rejected and that they would ultimately be expelled.

Thus, in matured migration processes, not only do migration policies tend over time to become increasingly reactive, but their success and effectiveness also tend to diminish. Policy responses move away from a proactive role to one of attempting to contain further migration and to cure anticipated problems by providing legal and administrative regimes for resident groups of immigrant origin in order to integrate them into the host societies under favorable conditions and thereby reduce tensions of an ethnic nature. But the effectiveness of managing and directing migration movements and influencing their consequences has had a way of declining over time.

The factors determining migration to Western societies

In contemplating policy responses to migration issues, due attention needs to be given to its determinants. Among the factors which have exercised a strong influence on recent migrations, and are likely to continue to do so in the future, are those of a demographic, social, economic, ecological, political, religious, and ethnic nature. First, the demographic developments of the past decades will determine the number of persons entering the labor force in the coming years. Insofar as the number of children born in earlier years is known, the number of persons who will enter the labor force each year can be determined. According to the International Labor Organization, an estimated 43 million people are being added annually to the global labor force, the majority in developing countries.[1] This figure needs to be seen in relation to the 820 million persons who are unemployed or underemployed throughout the world, which is approximately 30 percent of the world's active population. Given the modest overall growth of the world economy, unemployment and underemployment are still on the rise and it is doubtful whether an adequate or greater number of jobs can be realistically created in the coming years.

In Western industrial states, the aging of the population will lead, in some countries, to a reduction in their labor forces in the early twenty-first century. Given these developments, it is likely that the currently rather high unemployment rates will have started to decline by that time and some labor shortages can then be expected to appear in both skilled and unskilled categories. If this trend is confirmed, it is likely that it will exercise an increased pull effect on young nationals in low-income countries to seek immigration opportunities in Western industrial states.

Second, given the wide income and wage differentials between developed and developing countries – which are further increasing due to the large disparities in GNP per capita between Western consumer societies and developing countries – both opportunity-seeking and poverty-driven migration can be expected to continue and develop strong dynamics in the future. The rise in illicit trafficking in migrants by powerful international crime organizations operating worldwide, which has been observed for the past few years, gives an indication of additional forces behind those migration dynamics.

Third, the growing internationalization of the economy is at the roots of an increasing volume of international labor mobility, economic migration of a temporary nature, part of which is directed toward Western industrial countries. This concerns mainly skilled migrants. The determinants of this new type of temporary migration are related to international business, technical cooperation, trade in services, the provision of vocational training, and international scientific cooperation. It is expected that this form of migration will markedly increase in the coming years, among other things as a result of further international economic liberalization.

Fourth, well established personal networks of connections between immigrant communities in Western industrial states and families and friends in developing countries of origin contribute to feed immigration flows, both legal and illegal.

Fifth, accelerating ecological deterioration, due in particular to deforestation and desertification, has forced, up to the early 1990s, an estimated 25 million migrants to leave their homelands, some as international migrants. Over 135 million people may be at risk of displacement as a consequence of severe desertification.[2] They represent a potential of displacement which is higher than the current total number of migrants and refugees in the world. Searching for new living opportunities, some of the ecologically displaced persons will try to emigrate to Western industrial countries. Desertification, one of the primary factors of ecological degradation, is still not yet well recognized as a major push factor behind future mass migrations. Halting and reversing desertification through land rehabilitation programs and the appropriate use of scarce natural resources in dry lands is a preventive policy response. However, such measures are insufficient in number. The definitive loss of dry lands, which can no longer be rehabilitated, is progressing and forcing out inhabitants. Areas for human settlement continue to be lost forever.

Finally, political crises and ethnic and religious conflicts are strong determinants of migration. Some areas of risk are known, but the actual outbreaks of crises are hard to forecast. Recent developments in the former Yugoslavia, the Caucasus area, the Horn of Africa, Eastern and Southern Africa, and Central America are cases in point. Some such crises develop suddenly and unexpectedly and are difficult to prevent at short notice. Political crises and ethnic conflicts are likely to continue to provoke major internal and international population displacements. Economic deterioration, with ensuing weakening of national political and social structures, tends to reinforce these processes.

Policy response in the national context

The consequences faced by receiving societies as a result of the above determinants consist of the following: an increased potential for economic and personal network migration, often in the form of illegal migration, a likely rise in refugee migration, and the possibility of substantial ecologically induced migration. These challenges are not exclusive to Western societies; many developing countries are likewise exposed, and they too face difficulties in initiating effective policy response.

Until the 1980s, most Western industrial states designed their migration policies in a strict national context, taking into consideration the prospects for the development of their national economies, labor markets and demographic situations, and their humanitarian commitments. This holds true for the three traditional immigration countries – Australia, Canada, and the USA – as well as for various Western European states. Ethnic, cultural, and geo-political considerations interfered in many instances with respect to the dominant ethnic composition, cultural affinity, and historic links with countries of origin. Thus, France recruited foreign labor primarily from Latin culture countries, predominantly Catholic European countries, as well as nationals from its former colonies. Germany signed bilateral recruitment agreements in the 1960s, first with European countries such as Italy, Spain, Greece, Portugal, Yugoslavia, and Turkey, with which economic and political ties already existed. Later, Germany also signed recruitment agreements with non-European countries such as Tunisia and Morocco and, regarding nurses, South Korea and the Philippines. These latter agreements responded to specific foreign policy considerations. Switzerland and Luxembourg chose only European countries, such as Italy, Spain, and Portugal, as recruitment countries. Concern about the possible social repercussions of admitting foreign workers was not dominant in Europe in the initial phase of recruitment in the 1960s. These considerations emerged only later, when the migration processes had matured and difficulties in the social integration of migrants appeared.

Unlike the Western European receiving countries, the traditional immigration countries had already, as of the 1960s, proceeded to a shifting of their immigration policies from favoring predominantly Anglo-Saxon and European origins to worldwide admission ceilings. They thus, deliberately or inadvertently, moved toward the adoption of the concept of a multicultural society instead of monoculturalism. Understandably, this concept, closely related to policy options for permanent immigration, was not shared at the same time in Western Europe, where migration was still conceived as a temporary phenomenon.

An important turning point in the migration policy of Western European states was the sharp increase in the price of oil in late 1973, which resulted in a slowing down in economic activity and reduced employment opportunities. Receiving countries decided to halt the recruitment of migrant workers. However, family reunion and, since the end of the 1970s, increased asylum seeking ensured that there was no decline in the number of migrants in Western European countries. The underlying principle behind the admission of family members and asylum seekers is rooted in Western European liberal political culture and constitutional and legal systems committed to the protection of the family and to sheltering persons persecuted for reasons of race, religion, ethnic origin, and political opinion.

Thanks to this commitment to the protection of the family and related humanitarian principles, all Western industrial states maintained their basic policies but realized that, in the course of the 1980s, their admission ceilings were repeatedly and increasingly 'boosted' beyond desired levels because of sustained family reunion and increasing refugee admissions and asylum requests. Programs designed to encourage economic migrants to return to their countries of origin met with modest success in France. In Germany, higher numbers of returnees were registered for a few years in the 1980s. But these returns were quickly outpaced by new arrivals of the family members of resident aliens and asylum seekers.

Thus, global immigration figures increased during the 1980s in many European countries. As this increase contradicted the declared policy priorities of these countries, they were often interpreted as failures at meeting national policy objectives. An aggravating factor was the arrival and presence of an increasing number of irregular migrants, who are not reflected in migration statistics. This phenomenon concerns in particular the South European countries, which shifted in a rather short time span during the 1980s from former emigration to immigration countries and received a high inflow of irregular migrants. But Northern European countries too were increasingly receiving higher numbers of irregular migrants.

Policy consultation at multilateral level

The relative failure of the migration policies of European receiving countries in meeting their admission objectives and managing mounting migration dynamics led in the 1980s to an increasing concern about the choice of policies. A growing need was felt for consultation on migration issues among receiving countries facing similar immigration problems. Policy consultation, which had taken place in previous decades within the OECD, the United Nations, and the International Organization for Migration, shifted in emphasis from the exchange of experiences in migrant recruitment and admission and integration to immigration containment. Intergovernmental consultations intensified markedly. By the mid-1980s the number of intergovernmental meetings on migration issues reached unprecedented levels.[3] Policy discussions on migration also intensified in other international organizations, in particular the EU, and later played a role in the negotiations of the NAFTA. As regards the OECD, the non-European member states – Australia, Canada, the USA, and Japan – joined the Working Party on Migration in the course of the 1980s. Until then, the OECD was a forum for the discussion of migration issues only among the European countries.

Earlier, a multilateral policy dialogue about immigration took place in the Council of Europe and the International Labor Organization (ILO).

The former, taking place in a regional context, emphasized admission criteria, legal status, and cultural issues such as the integration of migrant children into the school system of receiving countries and the recognition of the cultural values of countries of origin. The latter focused on recruitment conditions and the protection of the rights of migrant workers arising from actual employment. The ILO also tried to bring together sending and receiving countries to sign agreements on the conditions of organized recruitment and employment. In both organizations policy dialogues led to the elaboration and adoption of multilateral regional or global conventions benefiting the migrants. However, the actual implementation of some of these conventions by national governments took place on a modest scale only.

More advanced intergovernmental policy dialogues, with real decision making and policy coordination, developed only within the EU. During the 1960s, the EU progressively introduced the principle of free movement of workers, allowing nationals of member states to seek and take up gainful employment in other member states. The possibility of free movement was later also extended to various independent professions, thanks to the mutual recognition of diplomas and professional qualifications.

The introduction of the principle of the free movement of workers was accompanied by the enrollment of intra-EU migrants in the national social security systems of the states of employment and the transferability of acquired social security rights from one member state to another. The whole system was set in place as a result of intra-EU negotiations among member states, in accordance with the provisions of the Treaty of Rome of 1958, according to which the European Commission assumed the role of proposing policy and legislative decisions. Commission proposals are discussed and negotiated among member states, and, once decided, directives and other legal provisions are enacted and become binding for all member states.

In the course of the 1980s, and in view of growing concern about mounting asylum requests and irregular migration from third countries, the intergovernmental policy dialogue among EU member states moved beyond the issue of freedom of movement of workers and dealt also with the handling of asylum procedures. In the Dublin Convention, the principle was agreed upon, *inter alia*, that in order to simplify asylum procedures an asylum seeker can lodge a request in one member state only.

The Maastricht Treaty of February 7, 1992 deals with some external aspects of immigration policy that were agreed upon among the 12 member states after intensive political negotiations. The treaty sets the framework for future dialogues and policy discussions on asylum, refugee, and immigration issues at both Union and intergovernmental level. It also holds potential for the adoption in a later phase of a single EU policy on these issues applicable on a par in all member states.

At the United Nations, discussions and negotiations of policy responses to migration issues took place in several of its bodies during the 1970s. An open-ended working group of the General Assembly worked throughout the 1980s to draft a convention on the protection of the human rights of migrant workers and members of their families. Regarding brain drain migration from the developing countries – which represents a loss of skilled human resources and, in many instances, handicaps the development of the countries hit by the outflow – several proposals were made in the mid-1970s to set in place a compensation system. The aim of the system was to assist developing countries that are suffering from the outflow of skilled and highly skilled workers who were nonetheless brought up and educated in these countries before they were attracted to industrial countries which offered better professional remuneration and working conditions. Proposals included the establishment of an International Compensatory Facility, suggested by His Highness Crown Prince Hassan ibn Talal of Jordan at the International Labor Conference in 1977.[4] This facility would draw its resources from labor-importing countries and the resources would be diverted to poorer labor-exporting countries in proportions relative to the estimated cost incurred due to the loss of labor.

Intensive negotiations took place on the issue, in particular in the UNCTAD Committee on Transfer of Technology, where several expert groups met to deal with the issue under the heading of 'reverse transfer of technology.' However, developing and developed countries maintained diverging views, concerning in particular the measurement of human resource flows and the calculation of the level of compensation. There were also differences about the feasibility of implementing a scheme, and rather fundamental disagreements about the principle of compensation itself and its justification. Negotiations came to a halt by the mid-1980s and have not been resumed since.

New potential for global intergovernmental negotiations on international migration has more recently arisen during the discussions on trade liberalization, in particular trade in services, during the Uruguay Round and with the creation of the World Trade Organization (WTO). The GATT Conference held in Marrakech, Morocco, in April 1994 was significant in this respect. The setting in place of liberalized trade in services under the GATT agreement will lead to an increase in personnel providing services in states other than their own. The modalities of the organization of those movements and of the return of personnel have been the subject of negotiations in a subcommittee on trade in services and movement of natural persons established in 1994.

In this connection, a proposal was made to conclude an international agreement on economic migration between source and receiving countries.[5] This agreement should encourage labor-surplus countries to adopt broad-based development strategies, placing emphasis on job creation, demographic planning, and human resource development. In turn, migrant-receiving industrial countries should modify their trade, aid, debt relief, and investment policies and proceed to planned assistance for restructuring wasteful, non-competitive industries that depend on irregular immigrant labor. The agreement should further provide guidelines for industrial countries to create specific outlets for legal and orderly migration and cover demographic and labor-market needs, including short-term movements of personnel for trade in services.

The negotiation of this agreement will certainly not be easy, as painful decisions will have to be taken by industrial states to restructure non-competitive industries. These will have severe social repercussions. The expected beneficial effects of such an agreement on migration movements will also require time. However, the long-term beneficial effects could be substantial, as they would facilitate the containment of migration dynamics in the future.

Which policy response to mounting migration dynamics?

Which policies will Western industrial countries choose to provide for the better management of migration and to improve predictions about flows so as to reduce the fear that movements of people will get out of control? A basic consideration in this respect is the feeling in Western industrial states that there is a growing number of potential migrants – residing in developing countries and other countries facing severe economic deprivation, low income levels, high un- or underemployment or persecution for political, religious, and ethnic reasons – who will seek at all costs to enter a Western state and make a living there.

An analysis of immigration statistics confirms that, in many countries, the number of persons admitted as immigrants or non-immigrants has grown markedly and does not really tend to diminish. It is true that in some countries, such as Austria, Germany, Greece, and the USA, that were affected by exceptional circumstances in 1989 to 1991, new policy measures have contributed to reducing the number of certain arrivals, but this probably cannot be considered as a real reversal of the trend. Public opinion in many receiving countries is concerned about the level of immigration and calls for policy measures to reduce it. Given that Western states are committed by law to offer refuge to persons persecuted in their home countries and allow family reunion to legal foreign residents requesting it, and given that ongoing migration processes pursue their own dynamics, there is only a limited margin for policy response designed to reduce migration in significant proportions. Still, there is urgent need for improved intercommunity relations, which have deteriorated in various Western countries, as problems of a serious nature originating in social, cultural, and religious differences have surfaced among migrants, ethnic minorities of foreign origin, and local populations.

A credible policy response will have to take the following factors into account: the commitment to family reunion and the protection of refugees, the need for harmonious community relations, and the need for a balanced age structure of the resident population. This implies, on the one hand, that all Western industrial countries recognize that a certain amount of permanent and temporary immigration is unavoidable in view of binding legal and humanitarian commitments, and due to increased interrelationships among countries, the liberalization of the economies, expanded trade in goods and services, and expanding trans-national cultural communication. On the other hand, the goal of harmonious intercommunity relations must be achieved. Each society will have to adopt a minimum immigration scheme for legal permanent and temporary migration, as well as take measures to facilitate the integration of migrants in the host society and promote understanding and tolerance of and among different ethnic groups. At the same time, each state will have to establish criteria for containing immigration to manageable proportions.

However, this latter goal cannot be achieved in isolation from neighboring countries and countries of origin. International cooperation will in many instances be required for the success of efforts to achieve orderly migration. There are encouraging examples of the negotiation and conclusion of bilateral and subregional agreements on temporary migration, on the readmission of temporary migrants, and on rejected asylum seekers and irregular migrants among Western and Eastern European states, and cooperation between police authorities to combat trafficking in migrants. However, negotiations on ways and means to reduce disruptive migration are not really being undertaken.

The need for consultation and cooperation with all actors concerned is recognized in the above-mentioned concept of a global economic migration agreement. Its success will depend on the preparedness of the states concerned to consider the interests of both groups of countries, i.e. sending and receiving. The desire for orderly migration into industrial countries is matched by developing countries' needs to reduce poverty and to initiate sustainable development. Industrial states cannot expect cooperation in combating irregular migration from developing countries when these countries do not have the opportunity to improve their economic and social situation. To this effect, they must receive full access for their products to the markets of Western industrial states. The latter must make trade concessions, increase foreign direct investment, and strengthen economic and technical international cooperation. In some international forums it has been said that the migration impacts are too often absent from national and international economic policy and trade negotiations and a change in the approach has been advocated. This statement is still valid today.

Western industrial states must develop an understanding of the linkage among outlets for legal immigration, assisted return migration, enlarged trade possibilities for source countries, increased direct investment, debt relief and development cooperation, and the volume of disruptive international migration mobility. The risks of widespread uncontrolled mass migration, the destabilization of flourishing societies, and ethnic and inter-community conflicts are likely to increase, and the outbreak of violence and hopelessness may generalize, if cooperation between source and receiving countries is unsuccessful. The challenge to Western industrial states in the twenty-first century will be to display the capacity to choose policies which favor harmonious economic development in developing countries and cooperation between source and host countries in seeking a common approach to manage international migration.

Although the need for negotiations toward the solution of international migration issues is emphasized, it must be kept in perspective that such negotiations and their possible conceivable results will have their limitations. It is unrealistic to think that the modest programs for legal immigration into industrial states advocated here can provide a significant outlet for offering employment to the several hundred millions of un- and underemployed people in the developing countries.[6] But global negotiations on economic and related issues, which take into account likely migration implications, can set in place activities which contribute to increased economic activities in source countries, which over time will lead to employment and development there and thus reduce emigration dynamics. Furthermore, negotiations focusing on economic migration cannot be expected to also offer a strategy to contain migrations resulting from political crises and ethnic and religious conflict. These require foreign policies and conflict prevention strategies in which economic and social development is one factor only.

The need for subregional, regional, interregional, and global negotiations

What will be an appropriate framework for policies aimed at attaining the goal of better managing international migration in the future? Bilateral negotiations and agreements are useful and necessary, but if isolated may turn out to be too narrow because of the internationalization of the economy and the multiple interrelationships among states. It is therefore desirable that agreements be concluded in a larger coordinated framework. It will also be necessary for migration policy issues to be negotiated at subregional, regional, and interregional levels. These are appropriate frameworks for discussions among states that form part of the same geographical area or integrated economic zone. NAFTA and the EU are examples of groups which should embark on negotiations with other states and groups of states with which close relations are established, such as Central European, Southern Mediterranean, Central American, and Caribbean states. Beyond that, global negotiations, such as on trade in services in the WTO, will be indispensable, particularly for those regions and countries which are not covered by regional agreements. The progressing internationalization of the economy calls for global negotiations on a variety of issues, including international migration.

The need for intensified multilateral policy dialogue, consultation, and cooperation also exists concerning a number of related technical issues, such as combating internationally organized crime trafficking migrants, readmission agreements on illegal migrants transiting through third countries, clarifying the legal and social status of the increasing number of temporary migrants residing in other countries for the purpose of training, technical cooperation, the provision of services under liberalizing trade in services, and initiating action for the prevention of ecologically induced migration. States will increasingly have to be prepared to determine their position on such issues, with due regard for the situation of other states. The multiple intergovernmental activities on migration issues currently taking place need to intensify in the future. Solutions have to be sought at various levels and in an increasing number of interrelated subject areas. The framework for policy dialogues and responses on migration issues will be multifaceted and increasingly diversified.

Conclusions

Because international migration is a global phenomenon which is largely determined by factors and processes in play beyond individual countries and regions, and because migration has linkages with economic, social, and political developments in developed and developing countries, the policies of Western states can no longer be based on national labor market and demographic considerations alone. Due regard needs to be given to the social and economic situation in countries of origin.

Policies in Western industrial states during the 1980s and early 1990s have become increasingly reactive to emerging migration processes originating in low-income countries, which have developed their own dynamics. A more proactive policy approach is needed to confront these processes and contain uncontrolled disruptive migration. This implies that responses be sought at the international level, among receiving countries as well as in discussions with countries of origin.

But this is not sufficient. Migration needs to be dealt with at the global level as well, in discussions and negotiations with developing countries and other source countries, through foreign policy dialogues aimed at the conclusion of global migration agreements covering economic cooperation, technical cooperation, trade policy, foreign direct investment, and debt relief policies. Legal immigration programs need to be elaborated in all Western receiving states.

When all is said, there are no readily available answers to the global challenge of mounting migration. This is all the more reason for continuing policy discussions at all levels with renewed urgency.

Notes

1. International Labor Organization, *World Labor Report 1994* (Geneva: ILO, 1994).
2. 'The Almeira Statement on Desertification and Migration,' in Juan Puigdefábregas and Teresa Mendizábal (eds), *Desertification and Migrations* (Logrono, Spain: Geoforma Ediciones, 1995), pp. 319–22. See also Norman Myers and Jennifer Kent, *Environmental Exodus. An Emerging Crisis in the Global Arena* (Washington, DC: Climate Institute, 1995).
3. Sharon Stanton Russell and Charles B. Keely, 'Multilateral efforts to harmonize asylum policy along regional lines in industrial countries,' paper contributed to the European Community Studies Association Workshop on Immigration to Western Societies: Implications and Policy Choices, Charleston, South Carolina, May 13–14, 1994.
4. J. d'Oliveira e Sousa, 'The brain drain issue in international negotiations,' in Reginald Appleyard (ed.), *The Impact of International Migration on Developing Countries* (OECD Development Centre, 1989), pp. 197–209.
5. Bimal Ghosh, 'For an international agreement to tame economic "international migration",' *International Herald Tribune*, April 11, 1994.
6. According to estimates of the International Labor Organization (ILO) there were in 1994 some 820 million persons un- and underemployed the world over, approximately 30 percent of the world active population. Close to 700 million of them are in developing countries.

15 European immigration policies in the twenty-first century?

Cornelis D. de Jong

Introduction

The question mark at the end of the title of this chapter is just as important as the title itself: it is not self-evident that there will be anything like 'European immigration policies in the twenty-first century.' This chapter elaborates on the plausibility of the forging of a European immigration policy on the basis of the following specific questions. What immigration challenges is Europe facing today? How is Europe responding? What form will future immigration challenges take? How should Europe prepare itself to meet such challenges?

Before I address each of these questions it seems proper to define what is meant by 'Europe.' The main emphasis in this chapter is on the European Union. It would, however, be wrong not to make reference to the many countries that are part of the Union's pre-accession strategy: the analysis shows that in seeking a proper answer to immigration challenges the Union should take an active interest in close cooperation with its neighboring countries.

Actual immigration challenges

In its 1994 Communication on Immigration and Asylum Policies (hereafter referred to as the Communication), the European Commission distinguishes three regions from which the Union faces considerable immigration challenges: Central and Eastern Europe, Northern Africa and Turkey, and other parts of the world.[1]

The main thesis of the substantive part of the Communication is that the Union should be particularly attentive with regard to immigration challenges from neighboring countries. Since it is much less costly for potential immigrants from neighboring countries than from other parts of the world to reach the Union's territory, major migratory movements are far more likely to come from the former countries than from the latter.

This seemingly innocent statement provides the basis for a major shift in emphasis that prevails throughout the Communication: instead of focusing primarily on politically explosive immediate issues related to the number of asylum applicants – many of them coming from non-neighboring countries – the Commission prefers to take a longer-term perspective that concentrates on immigration pressure as a whole, i.e. on both present and potential migratory movements, irrespective of the forms they take.

Immigration pressures from Central and Eastern Europe are different from those originating in Northern Africa and Turkey. For many years, member states have been extremely concerned about the possibility that the fall of the iron curtain would eventually lead toward massive East–West migratory movements. These concerns were the reasons behind summoning the ministerial meetings in Vienna, Berlin, and Budapest, where all member states and many other European governments were represented. As it turned out, however, the only mass influxes came from former Yugoslavia. To date, population movements of similar magnitude have not taken place, neither from Central Europe nor from Eastern Europe including the former Soviet Union. It is now believed that only in extreme situations, such as widespread famines or major outbursts of violence, will the Union have to face mass migratory movements coming from the East.

Developments in Northern Africa, on the other hand, are far more worrisome. High population growth rates combined with high rates of unemployment create an environment for increasing migration from most Northern African states. An increasing number of illegal immigrants have already arrived, especially in the Southern European states. This, however, is only the tip of the iceberg. The number of Algerians arriving in France, for example, indicates that the Union will be faced with an even more difficult to handle situation, once poor economic performance feeds fundamentalist movements and heightens tensions between various groups in the country. Already, member states are facing an increasing number of Algerian asylum applicants. Under present conditions, the majority of these applications cannot be considered to be manifestly unfounded. In practice some member states have found it difficult to repatriate Algerians whose asylum applications have been rejected. Taking into account the rather unstable situation in other Northern African states, similar developments could conceivably occur with respect to yet other nationalities from this region.

Migratory flows from other parts of the world are partly related to traditional and colonial ties or the pursuit of asylum, or a combination of both. Major refugee producing countries are, for example, Iraq, Iran, and Somalia. In these instances, migratory flows can be explained by deficient human rights situations. This is less obvious an explanation for countries such as Ghana, India, and Pakistan, which also figure in the list of major countries of origin with regard to asylum applicants. In these cases, the traditional ties with one or more member states would be a better explanatory factor for the migratory movements concerned.

It is almost impossible to make precise predictions about future developments concerning migratory movements from other parts of the world. The Union will undoubtedly be faced with refugees from any part of the world where there are gross violations of human rights and the means exist to physically escape the country in order to seek refuge in Europe. In addition, it is a well known fact that the existence of significant numbers of compatriots invites the arrival of more immigrants of the same nationality. There is not yet a reliable method of predicting the numbers involved.

While a more in-depth presentation would require specific analyses by country of origin, the main trends of the actual immigration pressure should be clear: there is actual and increasing immigration pressure from Europe's southern neighboring countries; a more stable pattern concerning East–West migration, but with the potential for mass influxes, especially in case of major outbursts of violence due to ethnic or other tensions; and a rather unpredictable and not yet immediately worrisome picture concerning immigration pressure from other parts of the world.

Europe's response to existing immigration pressures

Within the European Union, immigration policies were traditionally regarded as being of extreme importance to the national security of each member state. It was not until the mid 1980s that member states considered it useful to exchange information on their immigration policies and not until 1991 that they agreed on the need to harmonize them. Until the entry into force of the Treaty on European Union – the Maastricht Treaty or TEU – on November 1, 1993, immigration policies were discussed in the context of purely intergovernmental cooperation.[2] The TEU mentions immigration policies in its Title VI on cooperation in the fields of justice and home affairs. Although the procedures governing this title are not of a traditional, communitarian nature, the Commission is now fully associated with the work in this area and has obtained a shared right of initiative, together with member states themselves. A non-binding information and consultation procedure has been foreseen with regard to the European Parliament, and member states may include immigration provisions in conventions, thus rendering the European Court of Justice competent to deal with their interpretation.[3]

However, it is still difficult to discover a unique European response to immigration challenges. Even today immigration policies are almost fully within the ambit of national policy making. The common principles agreed to until now are very general and typically not binding. Perhaps even more important is the fact that until the beginning of 1994, there had hardly ever been a general debate among the member states on how to deal with immigration pressures. Immigration ministers, and since the entry into force of the TEU the Council of Justice and Home Affairs Ministers, have been focusing on specific issues concerning practical or harmonization related measures. But they have not yet found the opportunity to discuss the more general questions concerning a long-term strategy to meet immigration challenges.

When the Commission submitted its Communication, it had the creation of a proper basis for a more general debate in mind. A crucial concept in this respect is the need for a comprehensive approach. Harmonization of immigration policies is an important element of such an approach, but at the same time taking action in response to migration pressure requires a wide variety of policies, and this calls for integrating immigration-related policies into the external relations of the Union.

There seems to be a general willingness among member states to broaden the scope of their discussions. In May 1994, the justice and home affairs ministers devoted one of their informal meetings to a discussion of, *inter alia*, the furtherance of a 'root causes' approach which would seek to deal with potentially unmanageable immigration flows by ameliorating conditions that drive people to move. At the same time, the Development Council expressed an interest in 'immigration and development' and requested the Commission to prepare an informal discussion paper on this subject.

These are encouraging signs and the Commission will continue to emphasize the need to make the comprehensive approach to immigration operational. The Commission uses a wide variety of instruments in this regard. It responded favorably to a request by the Greek Presidency to finance a conference held in Athens from June 27 to 29, 1994 on the Communication, and in particular on the setting up of a root causes policy.[4] The conference became a public event, involving representatives of member states, but also of the Union institutions, international and non-governmental organizations, and academia. Such a conference was not expected to take any concrete decisions. However, it helped to create the right atmosphere for consensus-building on the need for a truly comprehensive approach.

Other initiatives taken by the Commission concern the carrying out of specific studies. For years, the Commission has financed studies on the Maghreb countries and Turkey: these studies indicate that immigrants from these countries tend to originate from specific areas and are members of specific layers of society. Hence, the studies create the basis for well targeted root causes policies. EUROSTAT has recently started a new project which should further develop better statistical insight into root causes of immigration pressure. Finally, specific projects have been commissioned with regard to the relationship between ecological developments and immigration pressures and with regard to the movements of people in need of international protection.

Apart from these studies, there is increasing awareness among the Commission services that they should cooperate in order to incorporate immigration policies into the external relations of the Union. An inter-service group has been assigned to monitor the implementation of the suggestions contained in the Communication. Practical results of this form of cooperation have already become visible in the numerous references to cooperation in the field of immigration which figure in the recent external agreements of the Union. In the most recent agreements, efforts to reduce migratory pressures have become the subject of a separate chapter. Similarly, the preparation of the United Nations International Conference on Population and Development, held in Cairo in September 1994, the Conference on Security and Cooperation in Europe (CSCE) Review Meeting in Budapest, and the Euro-Mediterranean Conference in Barcelona, in November 1995, have also duly taken into account the immigration aspect.

There are, however, limits to what the Commission can do. In particular, with regard to the management of migration, the Council itself will have to take the necessary decisions. In order to establish a European policy in this regard, it seems inevitable that the Council needs to decide to speed up the harmonization process. Equally importantly, measures should be identified to solve short-term absorption problems which confront the individual member states. Instead of the natural tendency to take restrictive measures which would divert immigration pressures to countries with more liberal policies, member states should get used to the idea that the only solutions of a longer-term nature are European solutions, where a sense of regional solidarity supersedes short-term national considerations.

Future immigration challenges

One of the problems identified by the Commission in its Communication is the lack of specific information on potential migratory movements.[5] Some migratory movements are by definition impossible to predict: a sudden change of political climate, unexpected ecological or manmade disasters and many other factors may lead to mass migratory movements which would be hard to predict. Other developments are easier to identify: the analysis concerning Northern Africa, as outlined above, is an obvious case, as it would be difficult not to predict increasing migration pressures from that region of the world. Similarly, refugees will continue to come from non-neighboring countries as long as the human rights situation does not improve.

Migration theory is often not specific enough to render reliable predictions. It may offer good explanations for actual migratory movements, but in order to make specific forecasts about migratory movements, explanatory factors should be related to information that is specific to the country of origin. This, however, is only seldom done.

Presently, there is no reason why migration pressures should subside. As long as the Union has not yet developed effective policies to take action on immigration pressures, the underlying causes are unlikely to be addressed. Migration management has never been an effective instrument to deal with immigration pressures, since all that control policies can hope to achieve is the diversion of migratory flows, from legal into illegal forms of migration and from countries with the most restrictive toward countries with more liberal policies. In the past decade, despite increasingly restrictive measures that were taken, the total number of both legal and illegal immigrants has continued to rise in all member states.

Europe's responses in the twenty-first century

The appropriate European response to the challenges of immigration is one that is multidimensional. Such a multidimensional approach should strengthen cooperation within an enlarged Union with an extensive dialogue with the major countries of origin.

Cooperation within the Union

The European integration process has never been smooth: after periods of stagnation, sudden decisions bring about major changes that advance the process. Developments in the field of justice and home affairs are no exception to this general pattern. The major breakthrough in 1991 was followed by a period of consolidation and even a slowing down of cooperation.

The Union finds itself at a crucial stage: immigration challenges resonate with the specific political circumstances in many member states. Despite individual short-term success, no government has been able to address these challenges authoritatively. All governments now agree that immigration has become a European issue. But does the Union provide the necessary arrangements to meet such high expectations?

Title VI of the TEU should not be underestimated: it creates a number of instruments for deepening cooperation in the fields of justice and home affairs. Article K.9 even opens the door for a transfer of asylum and immigration policies to the Union institutions within the framework of the Treaty. Such a major step would, however, require a unanimous decision of the Council.[6]

The new Intergovernmental Conference (IGC) that opened in 1996 will examine the TEU arrangements with a view to proposing modifications, where necessary. Some fear that an enlarged Union is not likely to adopt a more communitarian approach. Others see the TEU as a transitory instrument which was always intended to be replaced by a more communitarian instrument after 1996. It is certain, however, that the possible communitarization of asylum policies will be seriously discussed by the IGC.

The personal stance of the author is not that of a traditional European integrationist. In the field of immigration and asylum policies there are certain limits to what is provided for under Title VI. Whenever these limits frustrate the application of practical solutions, an argument in favor of a modification of Title VI is in order. But very often, the present arrangements do in fact provide the right framework for the solutions that are needed in the immigration area.

Most succinctly put, a long-term strategy in the field of immigration and asylum should contain harmonization of policies, solidarity and an operational root causes approach.

Harmonization of policies

In the context of European integration, the 'harmonization of policies' sounds like a familiar and clear concept. But what does it mean in practice? Some member states are of the opinion that the adoption of resolutions and other politically committing instruments are sufficient steps toward providing the desired level of harmonization. It is not self-evident that this is true. Due to their non-binding character, resolutions will not provide any common jurisprudence. Furthermore, there is no procedure to monitor their implementation. That is, regardless of the rhetoric of harmonization, governments tend to follow their own interests and to bow to political forces at home. These are not just theoretical problems. Even a quick glance at recent legislative changes in a number of member states can raise doubts as to whether these are still fully in line with the resolutions adopted by immigration ministers in 1992 and 1993 on asylum and family reunification. The UNHCR, for example, is of the opinion that the German legislative changes concerning manifestly unfounded asylum applications fall short of the guarantees required by the 1992 resolutions. Similarly, it can be argued that the legislative changes in the Netherlands concerning family reunification may be contrary to some of the provisions of the 1993 resolution on this subject.[7]

Would it be possible under the institutional framework of Title VI to ensure proper implementation debates of legally non-binding instruments? Though the answer to this question is in the positive, whether this is politically feasible leaves doubts. One thing is certain: neither national judges nor the European Court of Justice can play a role in this regard. The nature of a legally non-binding instrument makes it impossible for national judges to use them as a basis for their jurisprudence. The European Court of Justice, in turn, can only be empowered on the basis of a Convention, and its mandate will be limited to the subjects dealt with in that Convention. Since the role of the European Parliament is also extremely limited in the context of Title VI matters, it will be up to member states themselves and the Commission to provide the necessary guidance on the implementation of legally non-binding instruments. This is a tall order.

It is unlikely that member states will raise implementation issues unless they are of the opinion that differences in implementation have a direct bearing on their national condition. In point of fact, even in those cases where formal interstate complaint mechanisms have been established, they are hardly ever used. This is even more true of cooperation in the fields of justice and home affairs. There is still a wide gap between the general political stance that only a European answer will meet the immigration and asylum challenges and the traditional attitudes of the national ministries concerned with the protection of national sovereignty. Many of the representatives of these ministries would prefer not to criticize their colleagues to avoid being exposed to criticisms themselves. Live and let live is still a very topical adage in this context.

The Commission seems to be the more innate player in this field. It has gained a formal role in taking action in those cases where the implementation of Union legislation is lacking. However, no such formal role was attributed to the Commission by the provisions of Title VI of the TEU. Nonetheless, members states are not prevented from asking the Commission to prepare reports on the implementation of the resolutions adopted thus far. Member states are already required to send their legislative changes to the Commission based on a mechanism set up by the Commission in conformity with article 118 of the EC Treaty. The Commission should therefore have a good deal of information at its disposal and can request additional information when necessary. Such a new role for the Commission would undoubtedly be a valuable step forward, but it is by no means an easy or rewarding task with which the Commission would be entrusted. No matter how diplomatically worded, the Commission's reports are likely to stir up emotions when they contain criticisms concerning member states' implementation of common policies. Still, the Commission has to be critical in order to ensure a common interpretation of the instruments concerned.

Apart from the difficulties mentioned above, the adoption of legally non-binding instruments is especially deficient in the fields of immigration and asylum policies for yet another reason: by definition, immigration and asylum policies are designed to offer the right framework for decision making in individual cases. Essentially, the decisions are quite simple yet extremely important for the individuals concerned, because they determine whether the individuals are 'in' or 'out.' The applicant may either remain in a country or be compelled to leave it. Particularly because the decisions are so clear-cut and important, the principle of equality before the law should be fully respected. Within each member state, respect for this principle is ensured by review and appeal procedures, as well as through proper training of the officials who take the first decision in each case. But how is the principle ensured within the Union as a whole? The potential role of the Commission in monitoring member states' implementation of legally non-binding instruments will undoubtedly be limited to the monitoring of policies and legislative measures. It would be impractical and indeed impossible to monitor the implementation at the level of decisions in individual cases, where in fact the monitoring actually needs to be done.

By way of conclusion, the adoption of legally non-binding instruments may be a very useful exercise in that it allows member states to get acquainted with each others' policies and it may even provide for some general guidelines, but it is clearly insufficient to ensure respect at European level for the principle of equality before the law. Therefore, taking into account the overriding importance of this principle in the area of immigration and asylum policies, further steps should be taken.

As a first step, conventions could be elaborated, still in conformity with Title VI of the TEU. Conventions are binding under international law. The Commission has, for example, suggested in its Communication the elaboration of conventions on manifestly unfounded asylum applications, on the application of the third host country principle, and on family reunification. In all of these areas member states have already adopted resolutions. The elaboration of conventions would at least make it possible to introduce the competence of the European Court of Justice to deal with matters of interpretation. This would be a significant step forward in providing for equality before the law at European level.

Title VI makes it possible to depart from traditional procedures concerning the Court of Justice. Member states have often expressed the concern that procedures would be prolonged by the introduction of the court's competence. This might have been the case if Title VI had foreseen Union arrangements in this field. Since this is not the case, procedures could be introduced, through which the court's decision will generally not have suspensive effect, i.e. the expulsion measures will be carried out without awaiting the outcome of the procedure. This may come across as unfair and to some extent it may indeed be. However, compared with the present situation, where no access to the court is available, it is a step forward. Of course, it would be preferable to go further and, for instance, make provisions for a procedure whereby the court would initially be enabled to decide on a provisional measure ensuring suspensive effect in urgent cases. This would be comparable to the existing practices of the European Commission for Human Rights, where most states have voluntarily agreed to generally honor any request the Commission makes for the postponement of the proposed repatriation of the person concerned.

The ratification procedure with regard to formal conventions takes considerable time. The Dublin Convention, signed in 1990, still awaits ratification by two member states. Here we have one of the flaws of the present arrangements: progress will necessarily be slow, if one has to rely on conventions as the only effective legally binding instrument.[8] Another disadvantage of conventions is that at least traditionally national parliaments can only vote yes or no regarding ratification and have no right of amendment. The role of the European Parliament is also extremely weak under the Title VI arrangements. It may be consulted on draft conventions, but this is not automatic as it is under Union procedures. Traditional Union procedures with regard to instruments such as directives and regulations would not have the disadvantages mentioned here, and this would therefore be an important argument in favor of applying article K.9, providing for a transfer to the domain of Union law.

Full harmonization not only requires the existence of legally binding instruments upon which national courts as well as the European Court of Justice can build their jurisprudence; it is equally important that the authorities dealing with individual applications receive similar instructions. Within the framework of practical cooperation these training-related aspects can in principle be discussed. Recently, the Commission has come up with some practical suggestions, such as common training programs and the exchange of personnel. In the long run, some form of joint inspection could be set up. This is not uncommon in the field of external border controls, as demonstrated by the Benelux countries and the efforts to set up the Schengen area and the Schengen Information System.

Solidarity

Solidarity is another indispensable aspect of a long-term strategy. The 1994 Commission Communication sets out a prudent line of action in this regard by suggesting that, as a first step, the Council could take stock of the existing absorption capacities of member states. So far, no discussion has taken place on how member states have organized their staffing arrangements. This may partly explain why the issue of 'burden sharing' is still so controversial. As long as member states are not convinced of the fact that the state or states asking for some form of burden sharing have done their utmost to run their organization as efficiently as possible, they may retain their reservations about granting it.

Other steps which deserve consideration are the common funding of projects in member states with relatively little traditional experience with asylum or in those states which face sudden and substantial increases of the number of applications for asylum. Similarly, projects could be financed to ensure fair and efficient asylum procedures in neighboring third countries, if these are transit countries and the member states regularly apply the third host country principle with respect to them.

A particularly interesting step would be to agree on common funding of assistance to those member states who are prepared to consider asylum applications for which they would not be responsible under the Dublin Convention. Such a step would make it possible for some member states to assist others that are legally responsible for the asylum applications concerned, but are already overloaded. As long as asylum policies are not fully harmonized, member states could also be rewarded for dealing with asylum applications for which they are not responsible, if they consider that their own policies would lead to a different, more positive outcome than would have been the case in the responsible member state. In this way, the objections of those arguing that Dublin-type arrangements are only justified in case of fully harmonized policies could be overcome. Although theoretically valid, these ideas may be difficult to put into practice, since the Dublin Convention contains a number of rather complicated criteria for determining responsibility. In many cases, the identification of the state responsible is not therefore a straightforward matter and the application of this criterion may well lead to a high level of bureaucratization.

Hence, other forms of direct burden sharing should also be considered. A traditional method of burden sharing is the admission of people upon request by the UNHCR. In this scenario, we are not dealing with spontaneous arrivals, but rather with vulnerable groups which come under the mandate of UNHCR and are eligible for resettlement. This system could be broadened. It has been suggested, for example, that European reception centers be set up in regions of origin. Spontaneous asylum applicants could then be required to go to these reception centers, even if they had entered the territory of the Union. Then, only if it were established that the applicants were refugees in conformity with the Geneva Convention would they be admitted to one of the member states. Finally, and most dramatically, a quota system could be considered. According to such a system, responsibility for asylum applications could be transferred to other member states once the quota had been filled in the first responsible member state.

More realistic than these rather ambitious proposals would be action to stimulate cooperation among the various services competent to deal with asylum applications. Secondment of staff in order to increase the absorption capacity in member states facing overloaded asylum procedures might prove useful. At the same time, practitioners would become familiar with one another's implementation procedures, which is highly important for the harmonization process.

All of the measures outlined above would help to create the sense of solidarity needed in the Union. Not all of them are easy to implement. The most straightforward and effective way to promote solidarity would be to create a European Immigration Service under the auspices of the Commission. The transfer of responsibility for asylum applications would then no longer be a matter for interstate negotiations. Allocation would be mandated by the service. Under the present circumstances, such a step is hard to conceive of. It would, however, be the best way to achieve full harmonization of asylum policies and create the best framework for a just and fair distribution of the caseload. The Commission has never advocated this idea and it is doubtful whether it would be interested in taking on the task of managing such an important service. Moreover, whereas the Commission is at present in the privileged position of being able to concentrate on long-term solutions, its major preoccupation might very well become immediate and short term if it had to carry the responsibility for asylum procedures in practice as well.

An integrated approach

The main argument put forward in the 1994 Commission Communication on Immigration and Asylum Policies is that a comprehensive approach is the only long-term answer to the challenges posed in immigration-related areas. Control policies are necessary, but by themselves they are unlikely to be effective. They need to be matched by efforts to counteract the mounting migration pressure.

Does the TEU make the development of such a comprehensive approach possible? The answer is yes, although there are clear limitations. The introduction of common foreign and security policies on the one hand, and justice and home affairs cooperation on the other, into the realm of the Union are important steps forward in this regard. All EU Councils are prepared by COREPER, the Committee of Permanent Representatives. COREPER should therefore be held responsible for ensuring the necessary coordination between the various projects. With the institution of the TEU, the role of the Commission has also been somewhat strengthened, as it now enjoys a shared right of initiative in all areas concerned.

However, in practice, the situation is not yet perfect. The General Affairs Council (GAC) has so far paid only limited attention to the broader immigration related issues. The agenda of this Council tends to be rather heavy and immigration has not yet been identified as a major issue for foreign policy. It remains to be seen whether the GAC will one day effectively take up its responsibility with regard to the Communication. If it does not, this would signify a major setback for the development of a comprehensive approach. It is important to note, however, that the TEU arrangements *per se* cannot be blamed for any lack of progress in the GAC; if the political will exists to discuss actions to deal with migration pressures, the present institutional arrangements provide every opportunity for such discussions.

One of the major limitations of the TEU concerns the fact that different budgetary provisions apply in the cases of Title V (Common Foreign Policy and Security Cooperation) and Title VI (Justice and Home Affairs Cooperation) than in the case of traditional Union cooperation. Decisions on expenditure require unanimity of the Council and are therefore difficult. Member states are free to decide whether they will use the Union budget for Title V or VI actions or whether they will opt for *ad hoc* arrangements. The Commission therefore has no direct control over daily expenditures, as it has with regard to Union policies. This would mean that even for the most minuscule expenditure it will have to secure a unanimous Council decision. These are arrangements that are not likely to contribute to rapid progress in these areas, as taking action in response to migration pressure requires money. If the money is not readily available, these policies will be toothless.

Similarly, the TEU arrangements complicate the dialogue with third countries. In the framework of the external agreements of the Union, the Commission plays a crucial role. It submits draft negotiating directives to the Council. Upon Council approval, it can then carry out negotiations on the basis of its mandate. Once agreement with external interlocutors has been concluded, the Commission becomes responsible for the preparation of the meetings of the cooperation or association council which is normally created in the context of the agreement. With regard to justice and home affairs cooperation, member states are reluctant to allot a similar authority to the Commission. Although the Commission may include Title VI aspects in general draft negotiating directives, member states tend to insist that this does not affect the respective competencies of Commission and themselves. It remains to be seen how much leeway the Commission will obtain with regard to the preparation of association and cooperation councils. A revision of the TEU might strengthen the Commission's position in this regard, which would undoubtedly reinforce the Union's flexibility and effectiveness in its external relations.

Dialogue with third countries

If the Union is serious about taking action in response to migration pressure, it will have to look into the situation in major countries of origin. The existing data on root causes are still rather fragmentary and the Commission is actively seeking ways to improve the quality and quantity of available information in this respect. However, a full and reliable picture will never be obtained if the Union were to be looking only inward, for the best sources of information are the countries of origin themselves. Similarly, exchanges of information with other transit or receiving countries could prove to be extremely useful.

Apart from this limited form of cooperation regarding information, a dialogue with countries of origin will have to provide the necessary basis for further action. The furtherance of the socio-economic development of the Union's neighboring states is the only effective answer to counter illegal movements in the long term. Much of the existing migration pressure can probably be explained by a lack of socio-economic opportunities in the countries of origin, combined with eased communication and improved infrastructure which make it easier to move from one country to another. Perceived this way, migration pressure is the automatic consequence of the lack of success of development and economic cooperation.

Illegal immigration tends to undermine the social fabric of the society as labor conditions for those employed illegally are far inferior to what is required by law. Tolerating illegal employment thus results in tolerating the exploitation of people. The dilemma is clear. If the Union does not drastically change its attitude *vis-à-vis* its neighboring countries and open up its markets while promoting investment opportunities in these countries, it risks putting its internal social policies at stake. Illegal immigrants will continue to enter, as no control policy can be fully effective in this regard. Increasingly, official social standards will be undermined by illegal employment. Public life too may be affected: housing facilities for illegal immigrants tend to be minimal; if they are not engaged in illegal employment, they may have to resort to criminality or begging, thus further undermining stability.

Taking action on migration pressure can in the end have far-reaching consequences. A renaissance of human rights and development policies and a further push toward free trade and international investment are among the likely results. Instead of taking a hostile or indifferent attitude, policy makers in the field of development cooperation should start taking immigration policies seriously. A dialogue with countries of origin cannot be one-sided. If the Union asks, for example, that the countries of origin improve their human rights record or step up efforts to reduce population growth rates, it cannot remain aloof to the requests of these countries if they point out that they need the Union's support for their socio-economic development. Micro-projects in the field of traditional development coop-eration should be matched by major shifts in approach in the field of trade and investment policies.

The Commission stands ready to give a proper follow-up to its 1994 Communication, even in the context of the current institutional arrange-ments, which can, at times, be a hindrance. One hopes that in the course of policy formulation, all of the policy areas will be addressed as a whole, not only within the Commission, but also at the national and Council levels. Only then can a real response to immigration challenges be brought about. Immigration policy should not only be defined in terms of control, for it is just as much a foreign policy and a development and economic cooperation issue.

Notes

1. Commission of the European Communities, *Communication from the Commission to the Council and the European Parliament on Immigration and Asylum Policies*, EC Commission, February 23, 1994, COM (94) 23, Final.
2. *Treaty on European Union*, CONF-UP-UEM 2002/1/92 REV 1, Brussels, February 12, 1992.
3. See the Treaty on European Union, article K.3(2)(c) and article K.16.
4. For the necessity to deal with root causes of migration pressure, see the Commission Communication, *op. cit.*, pp. 13–18.
5. Commission Communication, *op. cit.*, pp. 12–13.
6. Commission of the European Communities, *Reports to the Council and the European Parliament on the Possibility of Applying Article K.9 of the Treaty on European Union to Asylum Policy*, EC Commission, November 4, 1993, COM (93) 1687 Final and November 20, 1995, COM (95) 566 Final.
7. See, for a comparison between the Netherlands policies on family reunification and the 1993 Resolution, C.D. de Jong, 'Het recht van vreemdelingen op eerbiediging van het gezinsleven: rechtsvergelijking,' *Nederlands Tijdschrift voor de Mensenrechten*, 19, 1 (January–February 1994), 48–56.
8. Although joint actions (mentioned in article K.3 of the TEU) may also be legally binding, there is no consensus on this among member states.

Conclusions
Immigration into Western societies: implications and policy choices
Donald J. Puchala

Can general conclusions be drawn from this volume's collection of writings by experts on immigration? The answer must certainly be yes, because, interestingly, the anthology as a whole is something greater than the sum of its parts.

The magnitude of immigration into Western societies is not ascertainable with very much precision, a point repeatedly made by the contributors to this volume. A composite estimate suggests that in recent years flows into industrialized countries have been in the neighborhood of two million people per year, and that over the past decade some 16 million people have legally crossed into Western societies to settle, work, or escape. But such estimates are very rough for a host of technical reasons, such as how immigrants are defined and counted, who does the counting and when, or how many people cross the same borders several times. Estimates of the magnitudes of illegal immigration are even less reliable, but the flows have been sizable, particularly South-to-North flows.

Quantitative assessments of the immigration phenomenon can be improved, and likely will be, but in this instance seeing the trees should not be allowed to obscure the forest: immigration flows into Western societies are very substantial, and because they have been high for several decades they have altered the labor forces, the societies, the politics, and the cultures of receiving countries in notable ways. Immigration is altering Western European and North American ways of life, and questions about the continuing acceptability of immigration's impacts have risen everywhere to become major issues of public policy. On all of these points the authors contributing to this volume substantially agreed.

No general conclusions were reached in this volume concerning the economic consequences of immigration. This is because economic impacts vary greatly with circumstances, and any sweeping generalizations about the costs or benefits of taking in newcomers must therefore be treated cautiously. Economic impacts have depended upon the kinds of immigrants entering – the costs of accommodating asylum seekers, for example, are greater than the costs of integrating guestworkers (as long as these workers remain employed). Different concentrations of immigrants, as among countries and locations in Europe, states in the USA, and regions in Canada, skew the burdens of providing social services for them. Countries may benefit generally from the efforts of new workers, citizens and taxpayers, but localities where large numbers of immigrants settle may bear the brunt of servicing the new arrivals. Costs to receiving countries also vary depending upon whether immigrants come with or without families (or bring their families later), whether immigrants bring skills in demand in the receiving society or have skills that are redundant, and whether immigrants settle permanently or eventually return to their homelands. The cost–benefit calculus also has to do with more fundamental demographics, such as age structures and fertility rates, of both immigrant groups and the communities into which they enter.

Costs also change with economic conditions in receiving countries. Southern Europeans, North Africans, and Turks who entered Western Europe as guestworkers in response to labor market demand in the 1960s brought little cost and considerable benefit to the receiving countries. Their labor figured positively in the 'economic miracles' that several of the European Common Market countries experienced. However, assumptions that immigrants would return home, or could be sent home, during economic downturns in the receiving countries proved erroneous. Most stayed, and when recessions occurred many became unemployed and sought protection in European welfare state safety nets. At the moment, improving economic conditions within the European Union may ameliorate some of the abrasiveness in political debates about immigrants. This may be true with regard to North America as well. But improving conditions will also attract more immigrants!

For the past several years Germany has borne an inordinate proportion of the cost of both South-to-North and East-to-West immigration into Europe, although the East-to-West flow has not turned out to be the deluge that many expected when Eastern borders were opened in the late 1980s. Still, dangers of upheaval in Russia and neighboring countries emerged from the former Soviet Union have not disappeared and the potential for a human outpouring continues to exit.

France is also a major country of immigration, increasingly too a country of ethnic ghettos and otherwise segmented communities, the receiving country for countless thousands of Algerians and other North Africans moving in search of employment and increased incomes. Many North African migrants who encounter difficulties entering France legally apparently manage to find their way into Italy or Spain illegally. The borders of the United Kingdom have been traditionally open to peoples from Britain's former colonial empire, and in recent decades these have come in large numbers. The United States and Canada are traditional immigration countries whose present-day cultures reflect their cosmopolitan heritages, and whose accomplishments as societies owe a great deal to immigrants' contributions. Their borders remain open – though some today would wish to fence them – and the influx of peoples continues.

The common thread running through this volume's discussions of all of these receiving societies, as well as others like the Scandinavian countries and the low countries, is that the inflows of migrants are becoming increasingly difficult to accept for a host of economic, political, and cultural reasons. Or at least this is how the immigration situation is widely perceived in the receiving countries. Almost every country, moreover, has attempted to adjust public policies in efforts to deal with the perceived immigration problem, usually by restricting entrance. Yet for many and complex reasons closely examined in this volume, none of these national efforts has been wholly successful. There is therefore today an atmosphere of uncertainty and frustration surrounding the discussion of immigration issues in many industrial countries, and this setting is rather unhealthy socially and politically.

The politics generated by the immigration flow into Western societies over the past several decades have been impassioned and volatile, to say nothing of increasingly complex. Over time in both Western Europe and North America the immigrants themselves have become increasingly organized, sophisticated, and successful in the democratic arenas of their new countries. Their efforts have been directed by and large to gaining recognition of their presence and affirming and protecting their rights in society and in workplaces. One unfortunate indicator of immigrants' success in furthering themselves has been the mounting resentment of them displayed by extremists on the political right in almost all Western countries. There has also been some willingness even on the part of the moderate politicians to make issues out of immigrants and immigration for electoral purposes. The success of politicians at scapegoating immigrants has varied from country to country, with time and with other issues that are linked to immigration questions. Some evidence suggests that the current vehemence of anti-immigrant politics in Europe may be dissipating somewhat, particularly in Germany and the United Kingdom, though it seems to be escalating in the United States, where it is linked to more general anti-foreign resentment and isolationist impulses.

Troublesome too have been extremist political activities targeted at sending countries and perpetrated by immigrant groups operating from receiving countries. Amid the protection and toleration of liberal societies in the West, radicals in immigrant communities have been playing at politics in their homelands, often in opposition to governments in the home countries, and frequently by subversive means. There is something ironic, though historically not uncommon, about exploiting the safeguards of democracy in one country in order to subvert democracy in another.

Immigration is altering the cultures of Western receiving countries. In most dramatic fashion with regard to Europe, the boundaries of cultural communities are becoming incongruent with the boundaries of states, or even with the perimeter of the European Union. There is a Mediterranean cultural community – Muslim, Arabic, Turkic, Persian, Greek, Greek Ortho- dox – whose social, economic, and political networks extend through North Africa, the Eastern Mediterranean, Anatolia, the Balkans, and now well up into Italy, France, and Germany. An important portion of this Medi- terranean cultural community resides nowadays within Europe, but it is not strictly speaking a part of European civilization. Its transactions and commu- nications are 'trans-national' with respect to established political boundaries throughout Europe and the Mediterranean littoral, though it is more accurate to describe them as oblivious to these boundaries. The significance of *Méditerreanée* as an emergent second civilization within European geographic space must not be exaggerated, but neither can it be discounted.

With regard to immigrants from non-Western cultures, assimilation into Western receiving societies has been halting, even within second and succeeding generations. The 'melting pot' metaphor is therefore not appropriate, but neither is the ghetto image altogether apt. Rather, what is happening is cultural pluralism, i.e. emergent diversity rather than homoge- neity, with social order cemented (when it is) by toleration rather than identity. Culturally pluralistic societies are much more difficult to govern than national ones. The authors contributing to this volume reached no firm conclusions concerning the likely success of adjustments to cultural pluralism in Western societies, though it would appear that 'culture wars' that strain civility and challenge democratic institutions are going to affect Western societies for the foreseeable future.

With regard to public policies, most contributors to this volume found it useful to distinguish between immigration policies, having to do with admission into receiving countries, and *immigrant* policies, having to do with the treatment of residing aliens once admitted. Generally speaking, neither kind of policy seems to be particularly well conceived or administered in most Western countries, and the European Union is still a long way from even having policies regarding immigration matters. However, running through several of this volume's chapters was the prevailing presumption that ultimately there would be immigration policy making at the level of the European Union, that the Union's borders were most properly Europe's borders and therefore the places where monitoring ought to occur, and that supranationally coordinated regimes would be preferable to nationally haphazard ones.

Yet there is little prospect that any Western country separately, or the European Union or some transatlantic cluster of countries collectively, is going to be able to stop immigrants from entering. Emigration flows are the results of countless individual or family decisions made by people in search of enhanced human security. Only by making people more secure – economically, politically, culturally – in their homelands might they be dissuaded from moving when opportunities to move present themselves. From Western perspectives, and to the extent that constraining immigration is deemed desirable, there is much to be said for policies aimed at ameliorating the 'root causes' of emigration, and in this volume much was said on the subject of root causes. This means directing foreign policies toward changing conditions in sending countries, namely poverty and oppression, that account for emigration or at the very least anticipating that most Western foreign economic, political, and security policies will invariably affect emigration decisions and immigration flows. Planning to deal with these effects should be accordingly engaged.

Of course, significantly changing adverse conditions in many of the primary sending countries is fanciful, at least in the short run, and even if it were possible to rapidly enhance human security in sending countries, immigration flows into Western societies will not slow appreciably for some time. This is because there are follow-on phenomena associated with immigration, such as bringing wives and families later, that multiply initial inflows. As a result, Western countries all face the problem of establishing policies for admission or rejection, inclusion, or exclusion, consonant with clearly defined national interests. As a first step these national interests need to be clearly defined. The European Union faces the rather daunting task of either defining common denominators among the immigration regimes of member states or defining a European Union interest, establishing an immigration policy in accord with it, and gaining its adoption by EU member governments.

Among matters that need to be considered in rationalizing immigration policies is first that there is a trade-off between legal exclusion and illegal immigration. To restrict legal entrance is to encourage illegal entrance. As illegal immigration condemns individuals to exploitation and insecurity while it economically and morally corrodes receiving societies, it should be discouraged. Still, unrestricted immigration into Western societies is out of the question. How, then, is the balance between legal exclusion and illegal immigration to be struck?

There is also a trade-off between pluralism and community. Since cultural assimilation is not accompanying late twentieth-century immigration to anywhere near the extent that it accompanied immigration earlier in this century, receiving societies are becoming culturally pluralistic. At some degree of diversity societies lose their communal underpinnings and become a congeries of differently identifying groups. Historically, such multicultural societies were common, but they were most successfully ordered by imperial governments. Governing multicultural societies *democratically* is problematic because full representation combined with incompatible values among represented groups could lead to political immobilism. Under such conditions governing majorities seldom emerge. On the other hand, if governing majorities are constructed, majority tyranny could stifle multicultural representation, leading to unrest. Worse still, to deny political access to immigrants, and even to their children, as happens in countries where citizenship is based on the principle of *jus sanguinis*, is to distort and ultimately jeopardize democracy itself. What, then, are the limits of multicultural diversity, how can such limits be reasoned in the context of preserving democracy, and how can such limits be incorporated into immigration and immigrant policies?

One of the most interesting, and not altogether anticipated, results of inviting experts to apply themselves to immigration problems among industrialized countries was that their compiled efforts contained in this volume speak a good deal about their normative concerns as culturally formed Westerners about the objective situations that were the foci of analysis. As immigration experts, the writers were concerned, as they were instructed to be by the editors, with identifying practical problems posed by flows of people into industrial countries. They were similarly concerned with matters of immigration policy, and their efforts brought forth a wealth of reasonable recommendations. Yet the analyses were overlaid almost throughout by moral and philosophical questions. Responding to greatly increased immigration into industrial societies turns out to be as much a challenge to Western values, and the institutions that embody these, as it is a test of absorptive capacities.

Among the matters that perplexed some of the analysts was the question of whether liberal societies could justifiably close their borders to persons fleeing from tyrannical conditions elsewhere. Should there be limits on the granting of asylum, and upon what ethical principles or by what moral justifications can such limits be defended? In fidelity to their liberal traditions, Westerners must welcome immigrants and asylum seekers. Yet at what point does preserving liberal values in openness conflict with preserving liberal values in democracy? Can granting physical and residential access to societies be separated from granting access to political participation and institutions? There is also the issue of liberal economy: if free flowing goods, services, and capital stimulate flows of labor, as they must under open market conditions, what justification is there for closing labor markets while other markets are left open? At what point, on the other hand, does keeping societies open to immigrants interfere with maintaining them as modern welfare societies? Should granting physical and residential access be separated from granting access to welfare benefits? And what about the more perplexing cases where access is not actually granted, but newcomers appear nonetheless? At what point does keeping societies open to immigrants interfere with keeping them either culturally homogeneous or manageably pluralistic? What ought Europeans and North Americans to do when any of these crucial points are reached?

These larger normative questions were directly broached in some of the chapters, though they latently influenced almost all of the writing. Because they bothered the authors with moral choices – among the right, the good, the expedient, the practical, and the politic – they injected a certain amount of tension into the volume. The main thrust of expert analyses was that immigration into Western societies needs to be much more strictly managed than it has been to date. Indeed, much of the analysis concerned forms, ways, and means of societal closure. It was widely acknowledged among the authors that immigration can be more strictly managed. But *management* invariably implies manners and means of excluding immigrants and the rationales for doing this. Such rationales remained problematic. Agreement about the fact that it is necessary, expedient, or practical to restrict immigration was therefore tinged with a certain reluctance to acknowledge that it is morally acceptable to do this. It has to be morally problematic to talk about closing societies, excluding groups of people, or segregating communities when all of this flies in the face of a cosmopolitan tradition that extends at least from the eighteenth century and a humanist tradition that is the core of Westernism.

Migration is a global phenomenon. Extraordinary waves of migration have recurred throughout history, and the world of the late twentieth century appears again to be entering into an era of *Völkerwanderung*. The primary demographic movements today are among non-Western countries, figuratively from South to South, and their greatest impacts will not be registered in Europe or North America. However, to the extent that some of the demographic movements today are from South to North, they are transcultural, trans-racial, trans-civilizational, and therefore extraordinarily consequential for receiving societies. The overriding conclusion of this volume is that such movements can be, and undoubtedly will be, disruptive; Western societies will change because the demographic composition of their populations will change. Some of the prototypical *nation* states of Western Europe could well become multinational states. On the other hand, changes invoked by South to North immigration will also be creative as new perspectives and energetic people cross-fertilize the traditional West. For the past five centuries new perspectives and energetic people have been moving from Europe outward, and the world dramatically changed as a result. The late twentieth-century *Völkerwanderung* may be the beginning of a reverse flow that could equally dramatically change the world.

Index